Altered Perceptions

An 18 Month Diary, One Day at a Time, In the Life of a Mental Health Service User

I0127186

Yvonne Stewart Williams

chipmunkapublishing
the mental health publisher

Published by
Chipmunkapublishing
PO Box 6872
Brentwood
Essex CM13 1ZT
United Kingdom

http://www.chipmunkapublishing.com

Edited by Aleks Lech

Chipmunkapublishing gratefully acknowledge the support of Arts Council England.

Monday 28th November 2005

Dear Yvonne,

This morning, I did not text C the love of my life or my sponsor although I read my 'Just for today' text and my 'basic book' and prayed before setting off to see my son's social worker (CQSW) with some toy's, footware and clothing for him, stopping off briefly on the way to speak to my Community Psychiatric Nurse (C.P.N). The meeting with my son's CQSW was an important meeting. It was to arrange a contract between me and the local authority which, once was agreed to by me, was typed and signed by me to indicate my agreement with the CQSW as to the mutual code of conduct for my behaviour with my son when I next see him. Which is to be the day after tomorrow, at lunchtime, when his school day ends. I last saw the same CQSW in June 2005, just some nearly six months previously when I was telling her that I had accepted an invitation from the cabinet minister, the Rt Hon Tessa Jowell, minister for Culture, Sport, Media and Women's issues to attend a celebratory function at the House of Commons on the 30th June 2005. I had told her that I was going to take my son with me, and I did. After leaving the meeting I got on two buses to make my way from Streatham Hill to Denmark Hill to attend an hour weekly group psychotherapy session.

The traffic was slow and I was late getting to the session which had started some fifteen minutes prior to when I got there. By the time I arrived I was feeling emotionally down, doubting my competence as a mother, struggling to think of what positive contributions I could enhance my six year old son's life with. After getting feedback from the group I decided that I would write. A member of the group mentioned that Cooltan Arts, ran a writing workshop, for mental health service users, but when I went there I found out that it was poetry so if there is a fusion of poetry you will know why. After returning home from Cooltan I set to work on writing my first step. I started it yesterday the day after my sponsor gave me the task of answering six questions. But me being me managed to confuse the issue and amalgamated four of the questions into two. Before I knew where I was with question one it was time for me to grab a bite to eat and set off to a twelve step meeting, where I met my sponsor outside. I knew he would be there and I wanted to be near him because I felt a bit vulnerable and I hadn't made contact with him all day. It was the first time that this had happened since he became my sponsor ten days ago. I cried in the meeting and received a lot of warmth from the other people that were around. My sponsor texted me tonight and after I responded I sent a text to C to tell her I love her.

Tuesday 29th November 2005

Dear Yvonne,

As I recall 7.30am this morning and my sluggish start to the day, even though I had eight and an half hours of peaceful sleep last night in my bed on my own as usual. I am listening to the 'Simplified' Simply Red CD on volume three of my music system, as it is the one CD that reminds me of Pandora Wrightman, my son's parent and toddler teacher. Pandora was the first teacher at my son's school that I came out to as a lesbian. Later, when my son entered the kindergarten and I was inappropriate with one of the parent's I wrote letters to the schools management committee and other parties clarifying the kindergarten's position on homophobia, the school's college of teachers of which Pandora was a member, responded to my letter. The letter stated that over the years, they have had several same sex parents and that a parent's sexuality had never been an issue and they would certainly never stigmatise a child because of either parent's sexuality. I came to believe them due to the way teachers such as Pandora worked with me and my son. C on the other hand distanced herself.

I recall reading my 'Just for today' this morning and not being able to register a word that I read and looking at my basic text and after reading a dozen lines without it penetrating my comprehension abandoning my attempt and finding that the only thing that I could utter to my omnipotent Higher Power was "please keep me clean, sane and sober today, allow me to utilise the growth opportunity that you place my way and let me do your will." I just felt muddled and insulated in my head and simply could not think straight. But with that I leapt out of my warm bed getting warmly dressed comsuming a cup of Marks & Spencers non concentrated orange juice and a few mouthfuls of the same brand breakfast cereal, and headed off out of my flat to get the bus to Brixton underground station, so that I would not be late for my 10am horse riding lesson in Enfield at the Trent Park Equestrian Centre. At the tube station I instinctively collected the 'Nine to Five & Midweek magazine' and on the Piccadilly line a 'Metro,' both were free and today they had Sir Elton John and his partner David Furnish in common and the topic was 21st December onward's Civil Partnership.

Anyway I got to the stables fifteen minutes early and so I was able to watch another rider taking a jumping lesson which helped to elevate my mood and watching the rider reminded me to purchase some riding gloves for the 1hr lesson. Today was my third lesson. I have one lesson each week at the same time so far with a horse named Bilbo and my instructor who's name is Ben, is the same instructor that gave my son his first riding lesson 16 months ago on a pony named Furby. Today I had a good lesson I could at least get on Bilbo and do a rising trot on my own, when I could get Bilbo started. Today I understood why it is that my son dislikes trotting, chosing instead to have the pony walk whilst he surveys the sky commenting on the passing aircrafts. For a start my legs don't seem strong enough to entice Bilbo to trot and when he walks Ben complains that I am going so slow that I almost appear to be reversing. True I am 44 years of age having just had my 44th birthday last month and I suffer with oesteo-arthritis of the left hip and not only am I unfit, having not partaken in any active exercise in years, but I am also quite rotund in stature. Anyway, whatever the reason, it is hell for me to get off Bilbo's back at the end of each lesson and when I eventually manage I do a good John Wayne impersonation.

Today Ben told me to ask for Hughie next week instead of Bilbo so I gave Bilbo some carrots in his stall at the end of my lesson today, maybe for the first and last time. On the way back from the stables today, whilst heading to a 12 step self help meeting, I decided to get some books that I ordered from Waterstone's bookshop 'An Unquiet mind' by Kay Redfield Jamison and 'Depression and How to Survive it' by Spike Milligan and Anthony Clare and whilst there I decided to also purchase 'Touched with Fire' also by Kay Redfield Jamison before stopping off at Foyles bookshop and purchasing an audio book of 'The Picture of Dorian Gray' by Oscar Wilde and read by John Moffat. I was hoping to purchase another play by Oscar

Wilde to go with 'Lady Windermere's Fan' which I enjoyed listening to last Friday afternoon, but I was unsuccessful. As it was, I only got to the meeting five minutes or so before it commenced but luckily for me someonce who was not staying for the meeting gave me a 'It Works How and Why' book. I was pleased and sent a text to my sponsor whilst I was on the bus to tell him about my fortune before I started to read step one. I stopped off for a Mcdonald's meal for lunch before going home to telephone my mum. She had called me on my mobile whilst I was out yesterday and I'd said that I would return her call, but I forgot. When I ultimately did call her she was not in and she ended up ringing me again on my mobile, but this time spoke to me for a while. I love my mum and know that she loves me unconditionally and these days she is the only person who says she loves me each time she speaks with me. I used to have a female friend, one of my son's godmothers who used to cuddle me tight, look me straight in the eyes and say "I love you Yve" but she hung herself from the rafters of her roof two years ago. She had been fighting with bi-polar affected disorder ie manic depression for about fourteen years, two years longer than me and didnt get into recovery for her drug addiction. I met her when I had my first hospital admission in York Clinic, Guys Hospital, London. She looked out for me, held my hand and gave me cigarettes, ran my baths in the morning, made me cups of tea, talked to me because I wasn't talking, or wasn't eating much and she shared her visitors with me and tucked me into the hospital bed at nights. She slept in the very next bed to me separated by a thin curtain. When she went off the ward, she would assign a babysitter to me to do all the jobs that she did. I loved her unconditionally. It was platonic, she unlike me was no lesbian, though she knew I was because I came out to her right from the start.

Wednesday 30th November 2005

Dear Yvonne,

This morning I was awake at 5.30am listening to the World Service change over to radio 4, all the time thinking of my son and how he loved to hum along to the "What should we do with the drunken sailor" part of the medley. I soon went back to sleep and at 9.30am was successful in receiving the message in the 'Just for today' and 'basic book'. Actually whilst on the subject of my daily ritual yesterday, I went to bed laughing as I now believe I had a spiritual awakening from Monday 28th Nov (Being ourselves) '.True humility is, simply, acceptence of who we are...' to Tuesday 29th (Our higher power's care) 'if we ask, our higher power will care for us...' If you read the texts that I said I couldn't understand, and compare them with the events of my life in those two days, it will be clear where I get my reasoning from. Anyway, today was a very special day and I woke up feeling good. I saw my son for just over an hour today. It was a supervised visit with his CQSW in the room with us. It was the first time that I had seen him or heard his voice since September 16th 2005, the day before both he and I were to listen to, the Rt Hon M.P Ann Widdecome at the Shaw theatre. (I ended up going on my own, and asking her for an autograph for him, in his absence). On that day the CQSW's with the police removed him from my care. I dialled 999 to see if I could prevent them from taking him, but I couldn't. Today my son was telling me that he kept thinking about me and that he had forgotten what the sound of my voice was like. He is four weeks away from being six and a half years of age and I love every hair on his head. He is my miracle because not only did I have him via artificial self insemination, I had him six years into the start of my mental heath history with the support of my family and friends who were not in the dark about the facts.

My general practitioner Dr Melanie Houghton, who put me on folic acid, then arranged the maternity hospital and provided a lesbian friendly nurse to visit me at home and chart my son's developement as I live in a flat within the lesbian and gay section of a housing co-op in Brixton. My son was the first child born into the lesbian and gay community housing that would be actively living there. The psychiatrists who reduced my medication to a fetus friendly dose, made it possible for me to breastfeed my son for the first two years of his life. The professors of psychiatry arranged for me to stay in a mother and baby unit for women with a history of mental illness and reassured me that a woman would be able to sleep there overnight in the same room as me and my son as I was an open lesbian. The CQSW's, both my mental health team and the children's and families team worked collaboratively and did the assessments and reports.

My individual one to one psychotherapist who was also a trained psychiatrist gave me a one hour session once a week until one or two weeks before my son was born. A solicitor advocated on behalf of my unborn child and myself and a mental health advocate who made that possible was from 'Communicate' the hospital user group. When my son was born, I had a caesarian section surrounded by a room full of female doctors and nurses with only one male attendant (a lesbian heaven) I was in the maternity ward for five days as I had to be induced as my son was overdue. After that, I was taken from the maternity ward to the mother and baby unit of the Bethlam Royal psychiatric hospital, where I remained under two professors of psychiatry for almost three months. I breastfeed my son from birth, whilst being on a small dose of Stelazine oral anti-psychotic medication before resuming life in the wider community. I did not relapse for just over three years and that was even though prior to my son's conception, I was a revolving door case, being sectioned on average twice each year. By the time my son was conceived I had just been released from hospital some three or four months previous.

For the last two and a half years, my son has been removed by the local authorities, approximately four times including this occasion. The last time before this, when my son was placed in foster care, I had to fight for him in the Royal Courts of Justice and he was still on a supervision order when the local authorities took him from me in September of this year. I am just grateful that my son is getting a Waldorf/Rudolf Steiner education and has been attending kindergarten regardless of my relapses and that most of his school friends have known each other since the school's parents and toddler group for the nought to three and a half years.

Thursday 1st December 2005

Dear Yvonne,

It is half past midnight and I have read my 'basic book' and said my prayers to my higher power and been in bed for the last few hours and still can't seem to get to sleep and I am hoping that I won't feel too tired to attend my poetry class at 11am today. It is going to last until two and then I have an appointment with my C.P.N which includes him giving me my fortnightly suppy of medication. Perhaps I am still wide awake because I had a cup of normal tea at yesterday's evening meeting. I had been on decaffeinated tea and coffee because I am sensitive to caffine, but the addict in me thought just one cup of weak tea wouldn't make a difference especially as I was thirsty. I would have been better off having plain water but there you go that is one of the reasons why I am attending ninety meetings in ninety days, after reaching an all time low,(just seven days after obtaining the Rt Revd Gene Robinson, the openly homosexual Bishop of New Hampshire's) autograph in my personal copy of 'Who's Who in Gay & Lesbian History' edited by Robert Aldrich and Garry Wotherspoon.

This book not only has James the first and Henry Stuart listed but Jesus too! I had enjoyed participating in the service of the Changing Attitude's 10th Anniversary weekend, which Gene Robinson was in London, England to support at St Martin-in-the-Fields on Saturday 5th November 2005, which was incidently also the 400th year Anniversary of the Guy Fawkes Gunpowder Plot. Because of the time of night that it is I have now decided to read 'Amazon Spirit meditations for lesbians in recovery' by Eleanor Nealy and it has drawn my attention to the fact that today is World's A.I.D.S Day. So I have decided to play my Queen + Paul Rodgers 'Return of the Champions' CD on volume just below one, so that I do not disturb the neighbours. I am playing this live album because it reminds me in part of Wednesday 27th July 2005 when my son and myself went to the Dominion theatre to see Ben Elton's 'We Will Rock You.' I then returned with my son four days later on Sunday 31st July to enjoy the Soho Pride Party. This cd allows me to remember Freddie Mercury's contribution to the world. After I have listened to both discs I will try listening to an audio book of Virginia Woolf's 'To the Lighthouse' read by Juliet Stevenson or perhaps Orlando read by Laura Paton, if I am still awake. I have the DVD of the film by Sally Potter, I got it free with the Sunday Telegraph, which made a change from 'Little Britain' that was free with the News of the World or even 'The Madness of King George' which was free with the Guardian.

Anyway since it is World's A.I.D.S Day, I can reminise on life before my Schizo - affective disorder, mental health diagnosis, when I worked for the C.L.A.S.H Project (Central London Action on Street Health) in the nineteen eighties, which gave me a good working knowledge of HIV/AIDS preventative issues. I did pre-test counselling with female clients about HIV/AIDS, I did outreach HIV/AIDS training with female clients in Holloway Women's Prison, Middlesex Lodge, Kelly Bail Hostel as well as homeless persons projects such as Bina Gardens, Rufford Street, Haberdashers House and Stonewall Housing Association. I gained extensive experience of offering, organising and implementing services to drug users throughout my employment at C.L.A.S.H, mainly whilst working detatched in Kings Cross, making contact with drug users on the street, issuing clean works and information regarding health problems, such as ones that was dealt with by the HIT Team, Angel Drug Project, Hungerford Drug Project, City Roads and Cleveland Street Needle Exchange. I also gave out information regarding, rights on arrest, such as the information given by RELEASE in addition to this, I offered services to women working in the sex industry as prostitutes in Kings Cross, Stanford Hill, Soho flats during detatched sessions and drop-in service. As well as that, I also financed out of my own pocket but received a lot of voluntary support for a project by the name of ABANTU a dance for all lesbians & gay men of African descent and their friends. The aim of the project was HIV/AIDS awareness and related problems. The benefit's aim was to create activities, events and health seminars for black lesbians and gay men, The first dance was held on Saturday 25th April 1992 it was followed a few months later by a women's only ABANTU function which was held at Wesley House Women's Centre. I couldn't fund it longer because of my house. I was in mortgage arrears with negative equity and was eventually repossessed. During this time there was a group of approximately seven lesbians including me, who were in full time employment in differing fields.

We came together to volunteer to produce and run HIV/AIDS preventative workshops for lesbians, ie older lesbians, deaf lesbians, young lesbians and black lesbians. Allison Culverwell, who was my boss at C.L.A.S.H and had a strong friendship with the late Sheila Henderson of 'Positively Women' plus Hope Massiah, who wrote 'African Women's Health Issues' were two others. I also remember another of my son's godmothers L, a French white heterosexual, married biological mother of three HIV negative mixed raced children, (her husband is also HIV negative) who is living with the virus one day at a time. L, has been so supportive to me around my mental health issues, my sexual orientation and my son and she and her children were present at my son's blessing and his Church of England christening.

Thursday 1st December 2005

Dear Yvonne,

I have woken up bright and perky at 7.30am today, after finally going back to bed this morning at 3.15am and having had just over four hours of peaceful sleep. I dreamt of someone wearing a dress suspiciously similar to the one Quentin Crisp wore in the film Orlando. I have no idea why but, King James, has now come to my mind. Maybe since reading in the 'Who's Who of Gay & Lesbian History' edited by Robert Aldrich and Garry Wotherspoon that King James had homosexual tendencies, being suprised by it, but then having that knowledge confirmed by also reading 'Queer Facts the greatest Gay & Lesbian trivia book ever' by Michelle Baker & Stephen Tropiano foreword by Graham Norton. I verbalised this fact to Lady Antonia Fraser writer of 'The Gunpowder Plot terror and Faith in 1605' in the auditorium during the question and answer section of her talk on that book at the British Library on October 31st of this year, that perhaps the reason that Guy Fawkes wanted to rid James the first was due to his homosexual tendencies being too pronounced.

I was thinking of and painting a mental image to myself of the distress still said to have been endured by the likes of Quentin Crisp in his autobiography 'The Naked Civil Servant' as late as the 1900's, (I later viewed the film with John Hurt playing the part of Quentin Crisp at the National Film Theatre on November 24th of this year). But whilst Lady Antonia Fraser did not deny that King James' sexual orientation was non too conservative, she stated that the real reason may have been because he was a Scot in England and favoured other Scots. You may wonder why I am interested in King James' sexuality, well you see aside from the fact that we, he and I share that (homosexuality) in common we also share a namesake. When I met my mother's father, Mr David Stewart in 1988, he was blind with cataracts and on feeling my short cropped hair he kept calling me grandson even though he knew I was a woman of 27 years of age with a mortgage, something he had never had, as he had always been a landowner who built, and lived in his own houses. I had also travelled out to Jamaica. David Stewart, unlike his Scottish father before him, had never left his country of birth.

Friday 2nd December 2005

Dear Yvonne,

Today I am playing Will Young's 'From Now On' CD on volume three as today I have decided to mention some of my favourite things and with this CD I think only of C when the track 'Evergreen' is resonating in the airwaves. I have just returned from changing $20.00 at the post office. I have had the U.S dollars since my son's last birthday, when he received it in the post from my Aunt Catherine, my mother's sister who resides in Florida very close to my mother's eldest brother Leslie. Aunt Catherine and uncle Leslie have entertained my son and myself in their homes twice. On the second visit, my mother also accompanied my son and myself and since then, my Aunt sends my son a birthday card each year. My son was made to get the travel bug early thanks to my mother who first financed both my own and his first trip and accompanied my son and myself to Toronto Canada before his first birthday, In fact he celebrated his first birthday whilst still in Canada visiting my mother's sisters Aunt Madge Stewart and Mary Stewart, plus countless of my mother's mother's only surviving brother and his children, grand and great grand children.

Plus, cousins of my mother's from other brothers of my grand mother, Louise Stewart nee Williams. Since going to Canada my son has been not only to the U.S.A before and after the September 11 tragedy but he had also been to Jamaica twice. The trips were tacked onto the U.S holidays and financed by my mother from her pension. Last year, when my son was placed in foster care and I was in court and didn't know if I would get him back, my Aunt Catherine flew over to London England to support me and my mother by appearing with us at the Royal Courts of Justice for the hearing. While she was here, she and my mum also accompanied me to see my son on my supervised visits with the local authority on occasions and she cheered me up by spending her 74th birthday partying at Southopia a private members women only bar where men are allowed only as guest's, We invited her son Eric and he was outnumbered at the private function of about seventy women to each man present. Both, Aunt Catherine and my mother, also had lunch with me at the First Out Cafe Bar, a cafe that has been frequented for at least eighteen years by a large volume of the gay and lesbian population and is situated nearest Tottenham Court Road underground. Aunt Catherine even visited the Glass Bar, a strictly women's only private members bar near Euston Station Underground with me and selected and read a Whoopi Goldberg book from the bar's library. Anyway about the twenty dollars, well once it was exchanged I purchased some perishables from Marks & Spencers in Brixton.

I have a Sunday morning tea commitment I made sure I also purchased the milk for it today. Now the reason that I have chosen to have a favourite things day is because yesterday at my first poetry class I experienced metaphorically speaking what I can only describe as a baptism of fire and after being stripped of everything I, my family, friends and colleagues stood for all I had left was my recovery and I made a conscious decision to hand it over to the higher power and cement the foundation of my recovery with a meeting, contacting my sponsor, reading some literature and talking to my C.P.N with whom I had a pre arranged meeting after the poetry session. What was it you may well be saying ? But like I said today is about a few of my favourite things. Cooltan rang me this morning to invite me to go to a gallery next Wednesday in the women's only session and I accepted as I had nothing yet booked in my diary, but for the life of me I cannot remember the name of the artist that is exhibiting and I was just told who it was minutes ago. I will discuss the poetry event, but not just for today. http://www.mooncycles.co.uk is a website that I adore. I find that I can really appreciate the work that has gone into the bodypainting and the photography and because it incorporates yoga and pregnant women I find it deeply visually artistic and interesting.

Karin Kallmaker and Ann Bannon are writers who's work I admire, as not only do they give me a sense of the life of lesbians and women loving women relationship but, in the case of Karin Kallmaker, the texts are racey enough to remind me that I do love women even though I am not actively engaged in a non platonic relationship at this present moment. And maybe it is the fact that Karin Kallmaker is a lesbian and has a to die for relationship with her first love and has children makes her a type of role model for me. Whereas Ann Bannon's much cherished Bebo Brinker series is a history of the lifestyle of women loving women before there was such a thing as gay and lesbian rights, and leaves me feeling grateful for the life I live today as a result of their struggles. 'Mulholland Drive' a film by David Lynch, an artistic surreal same sex feature which I first watched at the cinema with a heterosexual good friend of mine before getting myself a copy of it for my birthday when it became available. It makes me mindful of unrequited love and I can still remember to this day the foreign language song sung in the film and how there was a still in the cinema when it was performed. I also have a soft spot for the film 'Some Like it Hot' and not just because C likes it as well, but I always laugh when I watch it. 'Kissing Jessica Stein' is a film that I am also fond of, because it discards the stereotypes.

I enjoyed watching 'Kinsey' the film, as from it I was able to feel grateful for the work that people like Kinsey have done to dispel the homophobic stigma and what it cost them. Lisa Gormack's debut as a film director with 'Do I Love You?' the first UK lesbian feature in 10 years, was enjoyed by me in person in April 2004 at the Prince Charles cinema, when I attended the questions and answer session and obtained an autographed 'Pink Paper' for Doctor Ros Ramsey, my at the time consultant psychiatrist, (I had a crush on her) before returning the following viewing and obtaining permission from Lisa Gormack to be able to write a proposal for the film to be secured for sexuality educational purposes at the library of the institute of psychiatry (I.O.P) which I submitted whilst also giving a verbal presentation in a ward round lead by Dr Ros Ramsey.

I have been subscribing to the Pink Paper since my last birthday and latest inpatient psychiatric admission, when I was detained on a section three ie six months and could not access a copy on the locked women only ward as I had no pass and I wasn't allowed out of the ward even with an escort. Just over seven years ago, I was personally instrumental in ensuring that the 'Pink Paper' was distributed throughout the trust, including the Women's Royal Voluntary Service (W.R.V.S) hospital shop of which I am a member, each week up until one month before my son was born in 1999. The 'Pink Paper' is a free fortnightly lesbian and gay newspaper. Another of my favourite films is the first UK lesbian feature 'Thin Ice' which is listed in the book 'Lesbian Film Guide' by

Alison Darren and is to my knowledge only obtainable via the www.wolfvideo.com website and not just because I am credited on the film as being a runner in my Muslim Ex Husband's surname. He divorced me and in the divorce proceedings document amongst other things he mentioned that I said he was GAY. I don't know about him but, the bride's family was not confused by her sexual orientation record of being a lesbian since the age of 18, and so sexual diversity WAS reflected at the wedding, on my side at least. At the time of my wedding, I was still under contract as a full time lesbian housing manager with special responsibilities for rehousing and resettlement at GAP (Girls Alone Project) house while still on sabbatical from 59 Greek Street Women's Hostel as a full time lesbian admin hostel worker, making up the collective quota in representation of equality. Both employment posts were advertised in the Guardian newspaper. Anyway once again back to favourite things, I love 'Lesbian Lists' a Dell Richards book, because it tells me things that I did not know and reminds me about things I knew. I am also fond of quotes books and 'The New Penquin Dictionary of Modern Quotations' by Robert Andrews, plus 'The wit and Humour of Oscar Wilde' edited by Alvin Redman (as Oscar is not in the aforementioned quote book) keeps me interested as does 'The Quoteable Churchill' a prime collection of wit & wisdom' and not only do I enjoy watching documentaries including 'The Greatest Briton of all time Churchill' exclusive extended edition of the major ITV1 series narrated by Sir Ian Mckellen, but it reminds me of the joy my son found in the Winston Churchill museum in Whitehall when I took him there this summer. He just loved it.

Saturday 3rd December 2005

Dear Yvonne,

It is now 4.15am and I have been tossing and turning in my bed with no sign of sleep for the last two hours. So, I have sort out this autobiographical prose that I wrote on the 3rd October 2001 about the insight that I had on a acute bi-polar related incident at my abode. So whilst I am listening to the World Service on the radio, I will copy it.

Way Back When

The handcuffs were too tight. I could feel them cutting into the fleshy parts of my thin wrists, which were held together forcibly behind my back.

I groaned with the ensuing pain, whilst my left cheek was still throbbing. Its untimely collision with the hard, cold wall, was caused by what I would now describe as an over zealous woman police constable, who had satisfied herself, that she was just doing her job. As my pulse raced wildly, my bottom lip quivered simultaneously. I felt tense, indignant, while she slowly frisked my scantily clad body from head to toe. Perspiration oozed from my pores and had streaked my face. I was afraid, but felt defiant. I spoke, but was told to "be quiet" and remain facing the wall with my legs apart.

I could see, from the corner of my eye police officers in droves, donned in bullet proof vests. On the sight of their intense volume I became increasingly agitated and instantly filled with anger, which overflowed with hostility. I reacted to this alien situation by becoming surly. A combination of fear and hatred permeated my persona and caused me acute mental anguish. I felt psychologically tortured which consequently left me feeling physically drained.

A wave of helplessness swept over me. I was deeply unhappy inside, I wanted to cry, but my tears were stubborn and would not surface. My emotional insubordination had resulted in further inner turmoil which I, under the then circumstances, was unable to give vent to. Hence I remained vexed in spirit.

I could hear sirens permeating the air from deep within the premises. Coupled with these sounds were those of tyres which seemed to screech to an abrupt halt, after suddenly altering speed within the vicinity of the building. The drivers, perhaps maddened by the unscheduled alteration to their travel plans, persistently beeped their car horns, a wide assortment of which could be heard from where I stood, while the drivers waited impatiently for their journey to be resumed.

My inner thoughts were being drowned out by the seemingly never ending overwhelming din. Walkie-talkies crackling, mobile phones ringing, doors creaking open and banging shut, dog barks mingled with raised voices, heavy footsteps ascending and descending the stairway. Everything resonating and finally culminating in the then, fast filling stairwell.

I was there a lone black lesbian in the midst of chaos. In my own small way trying to stand up, for my civil rights and seeking to be treated with dignity and respect. I didn't accept any stereotypical presumptions which were made by the system about me, I obstinately held on to my principles, to the best of my ability.

Life had changed from its usual quiet and peaceful, if slightly mundane routine. It had almost become predictable, monotonous and dull. I found it difficult to reconcile this old reality with my then, new found predicament complete with unpredictable events and stresses. The juxtaposition of the two realities produced in me feelings of disbelief. It seemed at the time that, if I were to pinch myself, I would have awakened from the nightmare I found myself in, only moments earlier. This didn't happen. Instead I was sandwiched between two burly, though stoic policemen and frog marched from the building and into the night air.

Although I believe that I am a stronger, deeper person as a direct result of this trauma, memories of this unsavoury chapter in my life are, nevertheless occasionally provoked whenever I hear the song 'Way Back When' sung by Brenda Russell.

Saturday 3rd December 2005

Dear Yvonne,

I am back again and it is 8am and I went to bed at five thirty this morning. I am playing MaryMary's Incredible CD on volume 2. I love the whole CD but I am currently listening to track 2 'God Bless' as I write. I also have a soft spot for track 8 'This Love'. I have booked myself in two meetings for both today and tomorrow as I need them. I received my first Christmas card yesterday. Actually the card was addressed to both me and my son and it is from E my ex girlfriend who is also another of my son's godmothers. E and I ceased to have a physical relationship ten years or so ago. We met in the summer of 1993, a couple of months after the onset of my bi-polar affected disorder and a few weeks before my husband served his divorce papers on me, when I had just had my first inpatient admission and was medicated with Stelazine, stiff limbed, teeth grinding with locked jaws due to the high dose that I was on, the patients on the ward used to call me Pinocchio.

I was thin and wouldn't eat much because I was vegan before the onset of my mental illness and had been for years following being only slightly vegetarian as a child as I disliked meat and dairy products from a young age. But because of my budget changing from full time employment to six months without finances as I had resigned from my last employment in December 1992 before gaining government finances as well as my dietary tolerance change due to the intake of medication and especially since being pregnant with my son I am no longer vegan. Well now about the Christmas card from E, she sent me a 'Woodland Trust for all' card, the back of it says "Give every child the chance to plant trees..." Well I don't know as yet what to do as she does not know that my son has been taken into care, although my mother told me that she rang E to find out if she knew where I was (they call each other from time to time as my mother, E and myself went to France for the day whilst E and me were still in a non platonic relationship) and they know each other. Plus E met my mother again at my son's blessing at the Seventh Day Adventist and E travelled up from Westerham Kent for the weekend just to attend. Leaving Kent is something E seldom does.

Anyway E is difficult for me to respond to as it is only last year after my son was taken into foster care and the court case was in process that she scolded me and I promised that I would ensure that it didn't happen again! But I am powerless over mental illness and much like, sadly, the alcoholic footballer, the late George Best, who is going to be buried in Northern Ireland this morning. The only thing that sets me and the late George Best apart is he died battling his disease and I am still alive battling my disease one day at a time. Last year I bought the Bill Wilson-His life and the Creation of Alcoholics Anonymous 'My Name Is Bill' by Susan Cheever and ironically both 'Cheers the complete first season on DVD and Frasier the first season on DVD and just for today, I am trying to do something about my powerlessness, even though at times like this it doesn't make it any easier to live with the disease. On Monday 3rd May 2004 after feeling like Uma Thurman's character in Quentin

Tarantino's film 'Kill Bill' and being prescribed Sodium Valporate anti depressant to take with my Stelazine by Dr Ros Ramsey I wrote the following:

WHEN A WOMAN IS THE BEST MAN FOR THE JOB

When a woman is the best man for the job Dr Ros Ramsey, I think of you quietly seated near to me having introduced me to the audience, cast and production crew. Just where your eyes are focused I don't know, and what your think of I just can't say, but when my verbal spiel ends the lines of one of the scenes in my live autobiographical theatre performance, you begin your on stage cameo appearance from the professionalism of the production crew without missing your cue. I hear your words flow from your mouth, with the right tone and unlike film production where there can be many takes to achieve the desired end result. Theatre like my life does not have that luxury, once the initial rehearsal is over and the paying audience is in attendance each performance is fresh. And with each varied audience is the idiosyncratic ambience. Although I am in this setting, the main member of the cast, I also have the duel role of audience. Watching my life unfold before me whilst participating in it powerless to curtail the never ending drama. Like watching a type of ongoing work of art. a 'celebrity' in my own right, though ill equip to prevent desfunctionalism. And you, my dear Ros Ramsey, a pivotal part of the stage crew of performer functional lifestyle, in the ongoing art of the celebrity, when entering the theatre for yet another performance.

I can honestly say, that had you not been a woman, and one only needs to view my past behaviour, though that is not always an indication of future development, I may not have been moved to almost speechlessness to find myself in the midst of an all women professionals in a ward round during the 2004 'National Women's Health Week'. And when I look into your eyes, I see that ultimate cure to what ails me. And I dare look so infrequently, as only a woman could checkmate my personal desire, for emotional detachment and inevitable self-destructiveness, when I find myself yet again performing on stage, I find myself totally exposed when I look at you. And when I am uncompromisingly honest with myself, I recognise in myself a lifetime of hard work, dedication and tenacity. And listening to your compassionate tone. and careful word selection, my vulnerability seems not only pronounced and indefensible but, I feel exposed to my very core. Because, as time went by, I became more selfish in my perfectionist attitude. Not wanting to suffer fools gladly, until. I worked with you and discovered the replenishing attributes of working in contrast to that philosophy and becoming a kind of work in progress.

Ros Ramsey, you and I share so little stage time, but you are personally in my thoughts several times each day. And not least at night, when I self administer my prescribed medication and find myself pleased to do so. I am not embarrassed about remembering you so often and not wanting it to stop, just about the fact that I don't know when it began. Added to that is the fact that I only know two personal things about you, namely that your name is Ros and that you are a mother. I don't know the colour of your eyes. And lately I have startled myself by realising that, because of our seating arrangement when we are in close proximity of one another, I may not be able to recognise you in person, when out in public. The fact that I would want to is a deviation from my past intentions. Having worked with doctors, nurses, social workers and the like, throughout my paid professional employment beginning as a trained general nurse specialising in male surgery in my early twenties, and going on to work in the community including mental health and now personally being on the receiving end of patient centred care and never once loved one, until now.

Sunday 4th December 2005

Dear Yvonne,

Yesterday my sponsor and I met to do step one and last night I had ten hours of peaceful restful sleep and started my period today. My short term memory loss is not as pronounced as it has been for the last few days. As it is Sunday my ritual is to play gospel in the R'n'B, Hip Hop, Funky, Classic House and Party tune genre so I put on 'God's Property' a CD by Kirk Franklin's Nu Nation and played it through whilst I got ready to go to a morning meeting which was to be followed by a lunchtime meeting. Whilst eating my breakfast track 6 'Love' came on and I was moved. The books 'Church boy' an autobiography by Kirk Franklin, 'Eternal Victim / Eternal Victor' by Donnie McClurkin and 'A Minority of One' by Harvey Gillman are three books that I cherish. I am currently listening to the 'I can see clearly now' CD by Gospel Ganstaz track 12 'Let us pray' which is a favourite of mine and so I have started the CD from that point so that I get to hear it play twice. I have been an attender of the Religious Society of Friends ie the Quakers since the early part of 1993 before my first hospital admission. I used to attend the Westminster meeting house regularly before my son was born but since my son was seven weeks old I have attended Streatham meeting house with him and they send him birthday cards, but I have taken him to Westminster meeting house and Friends house even though dear old Friends such as Audrey Woods and Margorie Whiteman never met my son and I have so much to be grateful to them for, especially around the issue of my sexuality and my Schizo-affective disorder.

Monday 5th December 2005

Dear Yvonne,

Today it has become law that same sex couples can register their union and from December 21st will have the same rights as heterosexuals in the eyes of the law except that it will be called a civil partnership. George Micheal is on the front page of today's Evening Standard giving his opinion as it relates to him and his partner but no hope for me at this time as the love of my life is married to a man she has children with. She loves her children, She loves her husband and is not a lesbian. How inappropriate! My son's social worker rang me just after I got in from my group psychotherapy and has arranged another supervised contact appointment for me to spend time with my son. It will be on Wednesday 7th December 2005 at 1pm and finishing at 2.20pm but this time she will not supervise it. The contact is going to be supervised by my son's court guardian. Needless to say I cancelled my arrangement to go to the gallery to see Monks painting exhibition with Cooltan. I sent a text to my dear friend B and asked her to contact me. I haven't been in touch with her since at least June of this year and so she does not know that I had a warrant out for me to be obtained and detained 3th October 2005 and that I spent almost six weeks in a locked ward on a section three (six months) and that my son is in foster care again as I have a pattern of distancing and isolating myself from my family and friends each time I experience an acute phase of my illness.

Tuesday 6th December 2005

Dear Yvonne,

I was a lot clearer in my mind when I woke this morning and got off to a good start and obtained the 'Metro' on the Victoria line. On its front page was the headline "Suicide bid costs the NHS £2.8m" apparently someone suffering post natal depression with her second child took an overdose... fortunately for me when I had my son I was being supervised twenty four hours a day in a mother and baby unit in a psychiatric hospital. I did not suffer from post natal depression and though my son had gripe each evening and woke for feeding almost each hour twenty four hours each day my mental illness was not activated, The unit and staff were pleasant and while my son and I were there we had the total eclipse of the sun when it became night in the day and there was baby massage and lots of activities for us mums and babies and lots of support and guidance both for me as a new mum and as someone with an ongoing mental health condition and I really am grateful because of it. Now then, about my third horse riding lesson. The name of the horse was Bill and my instructor was Ben. I got on Bill well enough, the best mount yet and spent at least half of the lesson doing rising trot with crop in hand and I actually used the crop, I felt a bit more confident on Bill's back and he seems to be easier to ride than Bilbo was and at the end of the lesson I was still unsure of how to get off him but managed to dismount the best yet. After my John Wayne walk eased off I realised that even though it is one hour each week it is really therapeutic and I am learning something that I can measure. This lesson Ben held Bill twice, once so that I could get on and to allow me to get off. Sent a text message to E thanking her for the Christmas card and she has replied with a text hoping that I am well and asking me where I have been? Well that's done it. I am going to have to tell her on her landline.

Wednesday 7th December 2005

Dear Yvonne,

Last night I rang E and told her everything and she was so

compassionate and really supportive. I told her that I was going to send her a copy of 'An Unquiet Mind' by Kay Redfield Jamison (which I did today) so that she would gain an insight into my disease and she said that she is going to phone me at the weekend. Later tonight I have to tell B what I told E and ask her to co write with me. Earlier today, I had another supervised contact with my son at the local authorities building. This time the supervision was with my son's social worker and his court guardian. I think it went well but at the end when it was time for my son to leave, he started to hold on to me and cry. I decided to tell him that I have a mind problem and that it takes a long time to heal and even though it seems as if it has, it hasn't, and that he is not able to come home with me as I am not able to look after him at the moment. I love my son and truly believe that he was the best thing that I did but his well being must come first as I don't want to ruin his development. I saw my son for an hour and a half today and it only seemed like a few minutes because time really flew. He asked me what I was going to do this evening and I told him that I was going to a meeting. He was a bit disappointed that I couldn't find his little bus, but I told him that I would keep looking for it. This morning on radio 4 there was an item about people of colour being three times more likely to end up in a psychiatric hospital than anyone else. But I was half asleep and didn't hear the reason why. My sponsor told me that he and I will be meeting up soon to start on step two. I am going to have Christmas dinner with the fellowship this year. I received a letter from the co-op to let me know that there is going to be a rent increase. So tomorrow I am going to submit my request for it at Olive Morris House ie the housing benefit office. Spoke to B and told her all she was very compassionate and has arranged to see me sometime after 7pm on 14th December 2005 at the Lambeth LGBT forum party.

Thursday 8th December 2005

Dear Yvonne,

Today before I went to my poetry class, I did my washing at the local launderette and got to the class about a quarter of an hour late. But it was a good lesson centering on Oscar Wilde and the poets of that genre. We had lunch together today and I enjoyed it choosing by fluke the same lunch as the tutor selected before she had voiced her choice. Afterward I had an appointment with my C.P.N and the psychiatrist. We discussed my medication as I explained that I had noticed some facial twitching and mentioned that I didn't want to look 'odd' even if I do have Schizo- affective disorder. We agreed that we could start reducing the meds a mil or two at a time starting in February when my healthcare team settles as I won't be having that psychiatrist and may not be having my current C.P.N as there are going to be changes. But in the meantime the psychiatrist suggested that I do a diary. I didn't tell her that I had already started one. After the meeting I went to Olive Morris House then went home for a snack before going to a meeting. Someone is going to collect me at 9am on Christmas morning so that I can help out on Christmas day and be in good company and I have purchased a ticket for a new years eve party. I have also made an appointment to see my old PACE LGBT mental health advocacy volunteer co-ordinator boss, as I spoke to him on the phone in October and asked if I could return as a volunteer and he said no, but that he would write to me and meet me if I wanted him to. So today I told him that I had been detained on a section in hospital and that my son who he has met is in foster care. So we are going to meet up on 13th January 2006 at 11am at his office. He said that he was happy to be supportive and I also asked him for my references that allowed me to get the volunteer advocate post.

Friday 9th December 2005

Dear Yvonne,

Today I slept in until 10am when I was awoken by the phone call of a friend. I had had eleven hours of peaceful sleep and chose to empty the bins and do some light cleaning after I had my breakfast whilst listening to Alicia Keys. I chose to watch 'The importance of being Ernest' on DVD and having watched it I am going to tell you about my ancestors. My mother's grandmother's name was Margorie Williams nee Reid and she was an African and lived in Smithville and was a land owning igler in Jamaica. Her husband's name was Robert Williams and he was a land owner and both he and his wife lived together on a large estate in Smithville and had approximately six children together, who were baptised into the Methodist faith of the family, two of which were girls. The boy's names were Vin, Ezeikiel, Alder, and Lycee who was the youngest and is still alive today and living in Canada. The girls were named Dall and my mother's mother Louise Williams who's married name was Stewart being one of them went to school on horseback and inherited land from her parents. My grandmother's hand in marriage was asked for in her parents home by my grandfather David Stewart, a mixed raced man like my son, but his father was a Scottish man married to a black woman he lived with on a large estate in James Hill. David Stewart who had been baptised into the Seventh Day Adventist faith of his family as a young lad also had many brothers and sisters including an older sister called Sarah and a younger brother called Arthur. David Stewart had ridden his horse from his parents home in James Hill to my grandmother's parents home where she lived in Smithville Jamaica to ask for my grandmother's hand in marriage. He also inherited land from his landowning parents. Both of my mother's parents were competent horse riders. Both of my mother's parents had thirteen children. The boy's names are Leslie, Claudius, Robert, King, Thomas, Alfred and George and the girl's name are Ruth, Catherine, Emily, my mother Lilian, Enid(Madge) and Mary and they all went to school whilst my grandmother stayed at home and embroidered, crochet and excelled as a competent seamstress. My grandfather was employed as a policeman before leaving the force and cultivating his land, and keeping his hand in with the law by reading and writing letters for people in the community and writing to the courts on land law issues.

My mother, like both her mother and father before her learnt Shakespeare and Wordsworth at school and to be honest her reading, writing and maths skills are still superior to my own. When my mother left school she took a job as a nanny and then as a shop assistant in a fabric shop whilst she studied 'Pitman's' short hand typing in the evening before paying her £82.00 fare and boarding the flight to travel to London and stay in her eldest brother Leslie's house with her second eldest sister Catherine in 1960. I met my biological father's mother in Jamaica in 1988 when I went on a fourteen day package holiday to a seaside resort in Montego bay in the country. I spent four days out of the resort especially to meet my surviving grandparents. At that time only my maternal grandfather and my paternal grandmother was alive. My paternal grandmother was residing on her land in Portland Jamaica and introduced me to relatives as well as showing me the two tombs that her two husbands were buried in. Amos, (my father) is buried in Mitcham cemetery. He was a mortgage holder and died when he was approximately 35 in an untimely car accident. He was the driver of his new car and he crashed head on into a bus just after visiting me at my mother's mortgaged property. He died when I was three years of age and I don't remember him. I just know that I was his first child and the only child that my mother and he had together and that I resembled him in facial features plus both he and I share an ardent love for music. Whilst he chose to play discs and was a deejay in the evenings after work and on his days off, I played musical instruments ie guitar and drum kit and was a member of a band in the evenings after work and on my days off. And the other thing that we share in common is the fact that we love to drive. I passed my driving test at 19 years of age and purchased and drove a car one week later. He like me was the life and soul of the party, being jovial and sociable.

Saturday 10th December 2005

Dear Yvonne,

This morning I awoke at 8.30am fresh after having ten and a half hours of peaceful sleep. I went through my usual routine except this morning instead of just eating cereals and toast, I added bacon and a fried egg to the menu before phoning A, a friend of some 16 years. A and myself are the same age and we are also both lesbians, she is not a biological mother but she is a godmother to my son and is abreast of my current circumstances since we spoke about it before going out and enjoying a 'Skin' gig at the students union bar at Kings College together last month. After getting A up to speed with last week's events I set off to a meeting. In my letterbox on my return home was a flyer from South London and Maudsley SLAM NHS trust inviting me to attend a 'Partnership Time Event...Self Management on Thursday 15th December 2005 11.00-3.30pm. The focus: To understand what is meant by 'self management' in its many contexts. To share ideas and suggestions from service users and carers as to what makes good 'self management'. To find ways to support people who want to self manage in the future. I would have loved to have participated in the event but I have my last poetry class for the year taking place and I still have not decided which poem I will allow Cooltan to place on their website. By the way, I've finished reading Kay Redfield Jamison's book 'An Unquiet

Mind'.

Sunday 11th December 2005

Dear Yvonne,

Yesterday after I finished writing to you I went to bed and slept for two hours before going to a meeting in the evening and on my return after my usual night ritual, I went to bed and slept only to be awoken by a telephone call from my Aunt Madge calling at 11.30pm from Canada. After spending forty minutes bringing her up to speed on the events of my life inclusive of the progress with my son, I returned to bed and slept until 9am. I am currently listening to Jeffrey Osborne's 'On the wings of love' it is off the 'Soul Searching' CD I like it because it has 36 classic soul tracks by various artists and on a day like today, when I am feeling sombre, it may be just what I need to hear. Today after reading step 2 in my green and gold plus basic book I rang my sponsor and told him about C and I really came to believe that a power greater than myself could restore me to sanity. As I still text her every day, even though she never replies. I say that this situation that I have built for myself is insane because I wouldn't want her to jeopardise her marriage, not that that is possible when she is not even a lesbian and she loves her husband, When I mentioned that I don't know what I could offer her, except my love, to my sponsor he reaffirmed that I had lots to offer to the right person and anyway it is still early in my recovery and I need to be concentrating on loving myself. Whilst on the phone to my sponsor my mum rang me and after talking to him I rang my mum back and spent over an hour taking to her about life in general as well as expressing my gratitude to her for her input in my life. The next book that I have decided to read is Betty Berzon's 'Surviving Madness' because my mother is the foundation stone on which my survival from madness has stemmed.

When I was a child my mother suffered with depression and was hospitalised in the late sixties to 1979 and ended up in padded cells and endured electric shock treatment (ECT) high doses of medication, massive weight gain which when I was a child meant that she couldn't even watch a television program and understand it, let alone have a conversation without bursting into tears, such was the degree of her trauma. For years my mum could not bring herself to talk about what happened to her and all I could remember was that she had extended absences from me and seemed sad when I saw her. She spent so much of her time struggling with the illness. My mum seemed to find recovery when she turned to her faith, (My cousin Eric has just called and had a conversation with me on my landline and I have brought him up to speed with my life and what is happening about my son.) When I went into hospital for the second time my mum and her husband took me there. They had come to visit me and even though I was not talking my mother bought me something to eat and drink and ate and drank with me, talking to me all that time, hugging me and telling me that she loved me. I had always wanted to know what my mother had gone through and when I found out I was shocked. Every time but my last inpatient admission in October 5th 2005 to 27th October 2005 had me on mixed sex wards. Films such as 'One Flew over the cuckoos nest' staring Jack Nickleson come to mind and still put shivers up my spine. But my mothers strength had become dominant in my recovery, I look to her as a living role model and respect the battles that she has won in her life because I know that these days she is my guide and living testimony that one day at a time a power greater than ourselves can restore us to sanity. These days my mother and myself often laugh with each other about lots of things but sometimes we joke with each other about comments that we have had aimed at us and about us such as 'lunatic on the loose' or 'catch that mad woman' and only we know the depth of despair we both individually felt to be disenfranchised and dismissed by society, isolated individuals imprisoned by our disease and ostrocised by society. Laughing at our lot as we prevail just for today. Our lives are not perfect but we have a life today and we are united by a bond, that is stronger than the things that would tear us apart.

Monday 12th December 2005

Dear Yvonne.

I am listening to the CD 'The very best of Marvin Gaye' having just returned from my weekly group psychotherapy. Next week will be the last time for this year. I had thirteen hours of peaceful uninterrupted sleep last night and today I want to tell you that I am an adult survivor of child sexual abuse. The physical events of it took place whilst my mother was incapacitated. The after effects were played out in my same sex relationships, which became increasingly inappropriate, culminating in domestic violence. I eventually sort help in a twelve step self help programme, whilst attending weekly one to one counselling with a specialist same sex counsellor who recommended the book 'The Courage to Heal' a guide for women survivors of child sexual abuse by Ellen Bass and Laura Davis. I also watched the Steven Spielberg film 'The Color Purple' written by Alice Walker several times at the cinema and gained great strength from it, as well as gaining support from my friends particularly my best male friend Andrew, who is one of my son's god fathers. I was in a very intense, violent and destructive same sex relationship when I left my country for the first time to travel to Jamaica in 1988. Whilst there I met Andrew and became attracted to him, but not only had I been a lesbian since I was 18 years old, but I was also working as a open contracted lesbian hostel worker, making up a percentage of the lesbian quota in a collective and had been doing so for two years previous to meeting him. Although it was platonic, it was a holiday romance and as well as coming out to him as a lesbian it had me question my sexuality and my life. As it was Andrew was born in England and had gone to live in Jamaica when he was young so I wasn't surprised after the holiday when in later months I had a phone call from him saying that he had come back to England to reside. Meanwhile I had started my child abuse therapy and he was at the end of a phone line daily when I went through my angst and revelations. Such was the traumas of what I went through in my recollections that I would walk from Brixton to Turnpike Lane underground to meet my counsellor and return on foot because my emotions were so raw that I didn't want to be confined in the underground or on the buses. I would be crying non stop and many a day rescue remedy was my only tonic. Andrew was a compassionate listening ear and that I truly love him I am in no doubt but for me as a lesbian it would not get past being a platonic relationship.

Tuesday 13th December 2005

Dear Yvonne,

Last night on my way home from a meeting, Stephen, one of my many gay neighbours in the gay and lesbian community that I share a communal garden with, accompanied me on the walk to my home.

He had had his travel arrangement altered due to some problem with the tube and was tired and cold and telling me about it and I told him about the time earlier this year when after a few days stay at my mother's home. my son and myself were caught in the chaos of the 7th July 2005 London bombing and found ourselves walking in the rain from Swiss Cottage to the Elephant and Castle shopping centre. That was quite a tall order for my six year old son but he did it and didn't get carried. I was so sorry for him and the miles that he walked but I am so proud of him as well. Today was I a liability at the stables: I had Bill again today but for some reason I just couldn't seem to remember what I was supposed to be doing and had Ben despairing as to the transformation that had taken place from last week to this. But a few good things took place and one of them was I met a sixty-five year old beginner called Lydia, who has been riding on and off for a year and she was very supportive and in the end I followed that horse that she was riding when she was doing the rising trot. And secondly Lydia mentioned that she was going to change her riding day after the holiday so that she and I will ride at the same time. And thirdly I got off Bill with verbal encouragement only from Ben. Next week I will be having Hughie the horse so this week I gave Bill some carrots that I had brought for him sharing the rest with Lydia for her horse. On my way to a lunchtime meeting after leaving the stables I stopped off in Fortnum & Mason and purchased for my son 'Professor Moles's Machine 'The amazing pop-up book of how things really work.' Last week I gave him a Marks & Spencer's book on the body for children and he liked it so I am hoping he will like this. On arriving home and looking in my letterbox I was pleased to have received another Christmas card, for my son and myself, this time from K and J, E's best friend since childhood, and her son.

Wednesday 14th December 2005

Dear Yvonne,

Today I am listening to Luciano as he is a favourite of mine. Last night I dreamt I was making love to a woman and had an orgasm, the chance in real life would be a fine thing, I was thinking and talking about sex last night but what concerned me about the dream was C was not the woman in it! So at breakfast this morning I wrote the following as a tribute to her.

Love in it's infancy

Love in it's infancy
Careless and abandoned
From a once viewed pair of dialated pupils
Whilst gazing into my likewise
In the mid-morning sun.

Love in it's infancy
I now have a habit
And the drug to which I am addicted
Without doubt is you.

Love in it's infancy
Darn, it's inappropriate
You are married
You love him
And you're not a lesbian too.

Love in it's infancy
My love, I'm now an outcast
Barricades scrawled with prohibited is erect
Between you and me.

I will hand it in to my poetry class tomorrow, so that Cooltan can post it on their website. My gas boiler engineer didn't arrive this morning, and when I phoned to enquire, they said they had been trying to contact me and changed the date to January 7th 2006. I saw my son in another supervised contact. He has had his hair cut. He came later than usual as Lyn, my friend and neighbour, who lives across the road from me with her partner Pete had collected him from his kindergarten and had miscalculated the bus times. Nevertheless it was a good session and I read a 'Wallace & Gromit' comic to him and he made a Gromit model for me to take home out of plastercine. It is quite an odd looking Gromit in all honesty but, I love it because he made it himself. He absolutely loved the book that I purchased for him yesterday in Fortnum & Mason's but, he cried a little when we parted and was as usual reluctant to leave me, but he did go in the end. When I arrived home and looked in my letterbox I found a hand delivered letter from the Co-op which on opening it contained details indicating that I am currently in £326.49

rent arrears as of 12th December 2005. The letter stated that my housing benefit had been stopped since 22nd September 2005. This is the first time in years that I have been in rent arrears and I really don't want to lose my accomodation. So tomorrow after my poetry class I have an appointment with my Community psychiatric nurse and I will hand the case and letter over to him. But for tonight I am going to a Lambeth Lesbian, Gay, Bi-sexual and Transgendered (LGBT) Forum party in Clapham at 7pm and I will be meeting B at sometime this evening there, after she finishes work.

Thursday 15th December 2005

Dear Yvonne,

Last night I had a wonderful night at the Lambeth LGBT forum party. I met a facinating woman who I conversed with for most of the evening. She was born in 1928 and at first I mistakenly mistook her for an aged dyke. But she told me that she was born with both organs and her mother appeased her father by having her wear male clothes and having her grow up as a male, such as the character Stephen in the Radcliffe Hall's book 'The well of loneliness'. This fascinating woman was even in the Royal Airforce with the men as she was made to live as a man, she did not herself realise that she was a woman and even wedded a woman, with whom she lived for years before her partner died. She suffered much torment and anguish and I have nothing but respect for the road of thorns (metaphorically speaking) that she was made to tread bare foot before. Now she volunteers her time to work free of charge with human beings who like her have ambiguous genders at birth. She is a specialist in her field and an unsung heroine in my opinion. B did meet with me at the party after she finished work and we were pleased to be reacquainted. My son and myself recieved two additional Christmas cards and a Christmas present each.

I eventually got to sleep at around midnight. After sleeping for ten and a half hours, I quickly got my act together and went to my poetry class. I was a little late but I was pleased to be there. I put my poems on the www.poetryatyourfingertips.org.uk website. The second poem is untitled but is referred to as dada poem. It is the first poem that I did on my first day at the class and the process was cutting out selected words and making a poem out of them. This is what I made:

The secluded expelled
The deep from the recesses
Odius and drunk canning paradise
Collectors for witches spoken ingredients
Eye the debt from his private works.

Today was the last poetry class session for this year and so we were given £4.00 to put towards our Christmas dinner from Cooltan, which I added two pounds and fifty pence to, in order to purchase my first turkey Christmas dinner this year. I declined the accompanying glass of wine, but accepted the mince pie and ice cream, before bidding farewell to the class until next year and going off to an appointment with my C.P.N. I was thirty minutes late in arriving to my appointment but wasted no time in telling him about my rent arrears. He had forms that I had filled out previously and I completed them and after a chat about my son, poetry lessons, my meetings and telling me that he will be away in India for Christmas so another of his colleagues will be seeing me in two weeks time, he got my medication for me. I popped home briefly after doing my weekly shopping at Marks & Spencers, remembering to buy the milk and biscuits on a separate receipt for the Sunday morning meeting. Before going to Olive Morris house to submit my housing benefit forms and accompanying documents before heading off to a meeting. Last Saturday my sponsor gave me questions to answer for step two and all I have done since is read the step but tomorrow is my day off and all I have scheduled is an evening meeting, so I am going to try to get it all done if the Higher Power is willing.

Friday 16th December 2005

Dear Yvonne,

I have decided to listen to 'The Beatles 27 no.1 singles on 1CD' at the moment because it has on it 'I feel fine' and that is the first song that I ever heard in C's company and as she was singing to it I know she knows the words, or at least some of them. I have slept for eleven and a half hours and feel good and although I am still in my pyjamas I have eaten breakfast and collected the mail from my letter box, which includes issue 889 8 December 2005 of the 'Pink Paper' which headlines with 'Top Cleric Orders Iraqi Gay Murders', I also have a letter from the women only 'Baytree Centre' inviting me to register for a basic computer course which starts in January and ends in April. But I have rung them and asked them to put me on the waiting list to start the course in April 2006 as I have too many commitments to take up the January start date. Today is a very odd day for me as today is the thirteenth anniversary of my last full day of back to back full time employment before wandering in the full wilderness of decline for six months and ending up highly medicated in a psychiatric hospital at the start of my thirteen year history of mental illness and incapacitation. Before this I had an exemplary work record. It is as follows:

I left school in 1978 and went to a sixth form college for one year.
1979-1981 I worked as a nursing aide at 'The Royal Hospital and Home for the Incurables (aka the R.H.H.I) In my spare time my hobby was as a musician, playing guitar and percussion in a group and learning to drive.
1981-1984 I did my practical general nurse training and qualified as an EN(G) at Barnet General Hospital. I was still an active musician playing with the same band in my spare time but I had also passed my driving test and owned my own car. I was living in the nurses home when I was not living with my parents. But in 1983 I moved out of the nurses home and into a Mencap society group home with two down syndrome adults as a voluntary live-in support worker.

1984-1986 I went to work as a hostel manager with the Psychiatric Rehabilitation Association (aka P.R.A). My job was to work with a colleague and to accept long term patients from Frien Barnet Psychiatric Hospital into the group home, rehabilitate them, teaching them to cook, budget and encourage personal hygiene etc and prepare them for supported move on into their own self contained independent housing. Visiting them and shopping with them, and supporting them in the community as well as facilitating them into day time activities and trying to keep them out of hospitals. I was by now a member of a women's only band in my spare time and playing the drum kit as well as still living withing the mencap household. 1986-1991 I chose to move out of the Mencap group home and live in a household of female musicians, came out openly as a lesbian and worked with homeless women in the heart of Soho, hence working at the old theatre girls club, which changed it's name to Fifty-nine Greek Street women's Hostel. 59 Greek Street hostel was a direct access hostel providing accommodation and full board for 41 homeless women. The only criteria was that the person must actually be homeless, aged between 20 and 65 and not pregnant.

A large amount of the women came from psychiatric hospitals and prisons or had histories of drug addiction or alcoholism. 59 Greek Street hostel also got referrals from social services, probation offices and hospitals etc, although many referred themselves simply by arriving at the front door seeking accomodation.

59 Greek street hostel tended to cater for older women and, often, those whom other hostels were unwilling to take.

59 Greek Street hostel's first and main concern was to provide shelter, they did not make any therapeutic interventions and and accepted that women living there were not necessarily trying to change their lifestyles. Neither was there a time limit on length of stay. On the other hand, 59 was very willing to make referrals for psychiatric help, to social services, for rehousing etc and have contact with the relevant agencies and local services.

59 provided a 24 hour cover, with 2 workers on duty at any time, Women going to 59 could expect to share rooms, and the rent was paid by social security.

I was part of the lesbian quota throughout my time working at 59 regardless of which post I held. I started off in the welfare group and my post was lesbian rehousing resettlement worker, before changing to medical worker but finally ending as Admin worker responsible for saleries, inclusive of pensions, union fees etc. Whilst I worked at 59, I obtained a non contributory pension and invested in a mortgage, Buying a three bedroomed house at 9, Highclere Street, Sydenham SE26 in 1988 with a colleague that I worked with. I also started to work at Central London Action on Street Health (aka C.L.A.S.H) whilst I was also working at 59 after retiring from being a musician.

1991-1992 I chose to work for the young homeless women at 'Girls Alone Project' (aka GAP House) still as an open lesbian under contract. I also got married because I wanted to have children. I was also doing a lot of voluntary work in my spare time around HIV/AIDS prevention education. As well as driving mini buses for Camden Community Transport (aka C.C.T). GAP House was my last full time employment and I worked there as a lesbian rehousing manager with special responsibilties for resettlement. The age group of my all female clients were 16-21 years of age. I was responsible for key working, maintaining the lesbian quota, liasing with other agencies and I worked within a small collective, implementing equal opportunities policies. But when I resigned on 17th December 1992 I had grown tired and intended to go back and study to be an educational psychologist. But the rest is history, as they say!

Saturday 17th December 2005

Dear Yvonne,

I had nine and a half hours of peaceful sleep, last night. But I still woke up tired this morning when preparing to attend a mid-day meeting. I am currently listening to Haydn's Andante from Symphony no.94 'Suprise' which is a track off the Classical Masterpieces CD from 'The Classical Collection Cd' set, which I purchased at Woolworth's. Thirteen years ago to the day, I was listening to Jazz fm 102.2 whilst I dressed for work with my resignation letter at the ready to hand in, when I heard the words "No Support!" I looked around the room to try and find out where the words came from, to no avail. But simultaneously, with the words, I also felt physically and emotionally weakened and that seemed to be the start of over a decade of personal challenges with mental illness. The following is my recollection of the six months without funding once I resigned from work and failed to sign on:

One day completely out of the blue, I heard the words "Welcome to the brotherhood, time to know who your friends are" the voice said. I didn't recognise the speaker, I thought that I was alone and scanned the room, I could see no one present. I picked up the telephone to call someone, but as I held the telephone to my ear and waited while it rang, I experienced an excruciating piercing pain in my temples. Debilitated by a splitting headache, as if the back of my head had been blown open, I lay down , each time I tried to get up, the pain returned. I wondered whether I was the unwitting candidate for the television programme 'game for a laugh'? If so, I was in no mood for tom foolery, I tried to make sense of what I had just heard. Was there such a thing as a brotherhood? And if so, wasn't it just for men? More importantly, how did they do that? Talk to me without me being able to locate them. I didn't remember applying to join anything, in fact, I had been so busy working and playing hard, and now that there were only a few days to go before Christmas and I was trying to get some well-earned rest. Only a few days previously, I had handed in my written resignation to my full time employer. I hadn't ever been unemployed in my life and I wasn't worried about it. I had a history of excellent personal health and over the years I had had very few days off from work due to ill health. I had a membership with a gym, I was used to good food and generally took care of myself. I had always lived a full life and that included doing voluntary work on top of my full time employment. I had a mortgage, enjoyed regular holidays abroad, wined, dined, clubbed and partied. I hadn't ever been entitled to any form of financial concessions and I didn't have any personal friends who were out of work or who didn't also volunteer themselves in their spare time. I had a good employment track record and was confident that I would be able to get another job within my field if I wanted, that is if I didn't do the educational psychologist course that I had been interested in for at least two years. I had wanted a slight career change and had become interested in how people learned and why they failed to. It seemed like a great opportunity to pursue my interest.

But with each passing day the world outside of my window seemed as if life carried on as usual. The traffic flow was non-stop and the people from the gas works were digging up the road and so the noise in the day was constant. I on the other hand, was slowly beginning to change on the inside. I just couldn't stop thinking about where that voice had come from. I had never heard of a brotherhood. I was completely puzzled. I knew some people in the film industry and started to speculate about weather they had rigged my abode for a laugh. Within days I had stopped watching television as I thought that perhaps I was being viewed from there. Was it possible that my abode had been rigged up with hidden cameras? I wasn't sure. I turned the television to face the wall, unplugged it and covered it with a blanket. I hadn't ever been a regular television viewer due to work pressures and a demanding social life, so it didn't feel like a great loss at the time. As I struggled to find answers to the mystery voice, I toyed with the idea that perhaps it was the ministry of defence. I had signed the official secrets act, because I had done some regular sexual health and HIV/aids awareness employment sessions in a prison. Could it really be that someone thought that I would really leak inside information? I wasn't sure. I started to listen to the radio instead. Mostly dinner jazz on Jazz fm, but after a time that type of music made me feel sombre. Then I noticed that each time I took a shower or looked in the mirror, the voice commented on how vain I was. It became increasingly difficult for me to make decisions. I felt as if I was being undermined. Each day seemed to have the same feeling about it, almost like waking up to Sunday every day. I tried to get friends to visit me or to go to their abode, my friends could only drop in after work and it was pointless for me to be at their home while they were absent. Friends suggested that I shouldn't be on my own but they were unable to suggest a viable alternative.

For the first time in my working life I was now in between jobs and at home in the days. My busy friends were at work and the best that I could do was to meet them for lunch from time to time. I started to keep my curtains closed day and night, I thought that perhaps that I was being I was being watched from the street or even via satellite although I didn't have a clue why that would be the case. The reality was I had heard the voice and mentally registered what was said and I could not think about getting on with the day to day things that I would have been doing had I not heard it because it just happened out of the blue and seemed like something out of a science fiction movie. I just found myself thinking about it. (In time I was to learn of Rudolf Steiner, Theosophy and Anthroposophy). I gradually started to lose sense of time, hours passed though it felt like minutes. My thoughts seemed to be quickening and as my mind raced through time I sensed that I knew things that I hadn't been aware of before and I began to start to doubt things that I had always felt confident with. I felt a new sensitivity. I began to talk less and was mostly silent. I began to really listen and observe. Food began to have a strange taste to it. I decided to eat less not due to a dis-interest in food, but because it just didn't taste the same. I was losing weight. A friend visited and suggested that I revert to veganism again, so I did.

"Who is your father?" the voice asked. I couldn't think who could be asking the question. I knew who my father is, he is dead, and anyway, who is this faceless voice who wants to know and why? I decided to withhold the information, I didn't think it logical to talk to someone not present. The voice repeated itself "who is your father?" I concluded that who ever it was that was asking the question, could not possibly know anything about me and I wasn't going to make it any easier for them. I decided to tell them nothing. Within days I knew that they, whoever they were weren't going to accept my no for an answer. It seemed as if once they chose me I could not refuse.

I tried not to think, but found that I couldn't conceal my thoughts. My mind refused to stay blank. I found myself combing over my past life to my birth and then beyond. It felt as if I had somehow woken up, matured or come of age. I was experiencing an entirely different perspective, an altered perception which at the time was difficult to articulate. In all my pervious employments I had been both restrained and protected within a climate of professionalism of non-judgementalism and non intervention. Over the years I had cultivated quite a flexible, liberal and sensitive approach within the work environment which naturally spilt over into my personal life. Both client and staff were protected by well thought out policies which were painstakingly implemented. Whilst I was required to think because I didn't know how it felt and couldn't begin to imagine it either. I found that even with the best of intentions I was definitely outside looking in. Now I was faced with first hand knowledge of the inexplicable, the illogical, the incredible and I was to find to my cost that some new skills were needed and that I was quite naturally ill prepared and that if I dared to try to start explaining this new found perspective, which was so new to me that I couldn't even understand it. I would be in danger of being locked up as a crackpot. When my personal life revealed itself to the unseen, my sexuality quite naturally was disclosed and even I was surprised by the response of the unseen presence. It had said "lesbian" as if it disbelieved that it was possible. I know that sexuality can be transient but at that moment in time my sexuality wasn't an issue for me. My woman loving woman lifestyle was not an area of my life that required changes and it wasn't being considered. When my life had been revealed, life beyond was also revealed. The history which preceded my 20th Century existence allowed me to feel as if I were literally present. This was especially so around the time of the witch hunts, and I felt absolutely petrified.

I found this new revelation hard to comprehend because up until that point I had never even thought of reincarnation, never mind believe it and now there I was being given proof that it does exist in memory and believing it. As I passed through time I found that I could keep no personal secrets hidden from an all knowing invisible presence. I understood homophobia and sexism and I hadn't ever knowingly accepted discrimination of that type. My sexuality seemed to become a sticking point. I had been in a very out, monogamous and active sexual relationship with a woman for the last six months but became increasingly unsettled with the thought of being observed whilst in a sexual act with my then loved one and perhaps compromised. A voice kept telling me that there was someone else who really loved me, but who was not willing to share me and that this current relationship that I was in was no good for me. I personally couldn't think who this person could be and at first I wasn't interested anyway but slowly but surely my ardour towards my girlfriend started to cool and I started to speculate about just who this mysterious person might be. I had lived happily within my sexuality for years and felt confident about it but this mysterious presence didn't seem to be impressed by my track record of commitment to my sexual lifestyle, but I was having none of it. I began thinking that perhaps an old girlfriend was playing tricks on me because she wanted me to return to her. But for the life of me I couldn't think which ex girlfriend or potential new girlfriend could be behind this. A voice told me that I had moved far left since he had spoken to me last.

I definitely didn't know what he was talking about. I wasn't particularly politically minded and didn't know right winged politics from left wing and I had no memory of being with this presence before. In my early years I didn't talk about myself much. But I was uncertain how this presence knew I was like that because as an adult I was a lot more open. Another voice which made itself heard said that I didn't know enough. I didn't know what they meant but I thought that I could learn. I was given a warning by yet another voice that I must not be late. I vowed not to be late in my mind and although I didn't really understand the reason why the warning was given I felt a great sense of urgency. Within weeks I discovered that the voice had been right. I did have a lot to learn and although I wasn't certain where it was going to take me I said in my mind that if there were going to be changes then they had better begin with me! The only thing that I was not going to compromise on was my sexuality. It felt as if I was now on a quest and I wanted to succeed in the end. I would let them teach me. I would learn. As time passed I started to notice that if friends in conversation told me to be somewhere or do something at a specific time or on a particular day that within seconds of hearing the instructions, I had forgotten what they had said to me. I just couldn't remember anything like that. I was becoming more caught up in my internal world. I felt like an actor on a stage. I was one step removed for everyone else isolated by my insulation. I felt as if I was being watched and assessed at all times, witnessed by the unseen. I felt conscious of an unseen presence watching my every move and hearing my every word and knowing my every thought and intention. I just couldn't hide twenty-four hours a day. At first it was fun but then I started to wonder how long the assessment would last for and tried to become defiant when I noted that each new day carried on as the day before. I decided to try to out smart the all knowing powers by acting spontaneously. Perhaps if I didn't think about what I was about to do, didn't talk about it but just did it things might revert to how they used to be. It would be totally out of character for me but I was tiring of the continual surveillance. So instead of buying a bus or train ticket and stating the destination, I started to buy a ticket that covered the zones instead.

I no longer felt comfortable in my abode. I started to visit a forty-one bedded intensive high care 24hr emergency hostel situated in the heart of the West End, which I used to be employed at for five years. Because that hostel was the only hostel in the United Kingdom which took women that no one else would take and had a non interventionist policy, consequently women from all walks of life but especially the wageless and vulnerable. I had stopped conducting lengthy philosophical conversations with my friends and family especially on the telephone. I still didn't know what the brotherhood was or who was in it. But my belief was if they, the unseen could talk to me from where ever they were then perhaps they could also see me. I mean what type of advanced technology was there? I started to feel shy about taking showers and my personal hygiene started to suffer. I seldom looked in the mirror these days and seemed to be inappropriately dressed most days. Colours held great significance for me. For instance the colours blue, red, yellow, white, green, gray, pink, purple, orange, I tried to dress in plain clothes with not too many colours, or patterns. Had someone been in my abode whilst I was out? And if so, what for?

Who were the brotherhood? And what did they do? How did they find me and why did they want me to join them? When I hadn't even been aware that they existed. I no longer wanted to be a part of this seemingly one sided affair. A voice told me that it would be the last to leave me. I just didn't know enough and my life had changed beyond recognition. It was a fact that I had felt closer to nature and less inhibited with other human beings. I certainly felt as if on my travels I would be quite safe no matter, what time of the night whilst I was out by myself, star gazing and marvelling at the wonders of creation.

I telephoned a friend who asked me to talk to her mother. The friend's mother advised me to go to church on Sunday. I couldn't believe my ears. I mean church was a place that I hadn't been to for years, not least because I was a lesbian and employed in a management position with a contract for being a lesbian worker. My personal belief was that churches were usually homophobic and as I had no intentions of changing my sexuality it was pointless for me to willingly go anywhere near them. But as this quest entailed identifying my fears and conquering them, I contemplated the prospects of attending church and whilst trying to make my mind up as to which one I would visit, I was going to make a choice between the lesbian and gay Christian Fellowship and the Quakers. I decided to try the Quakers. I didn't know anything about the Quakers and the only reason I had even heard of them because a colleague and friend had told me she was a Christian, which surprised me because she was also having an open sexual relationship with a woman and described herself as a lesbian. When I asked her which church she was with she said that she was a Quaker. I didn't ask her anything else because at that time the only thing that interested me about churches was their architecture. However one Sunday I attended the Westminster Friends meeting house. After I signed in the visitors book and the attendant showed me to the meeting room. I had no idea what so ever that the hour of worship would be in silence. This both suited and pleased me. I had enjoyed going to the lesbian and gay clubs and maneuvering in lesbian and gay circles. Church and religion was the last thing on my mind.

Friends and family were becoming increasingly concerned about me. In between the silences I tried to tell them what was happening but they said that I was unwell. A friend took me to the general hospital casualty department. That hospital transferred me to the psychiatric wing of another hospital. I said nothing, just looked at the ward. I had lost a lot of weight and my friends said that I no longer talked, which was true. The first night I took the single bedroom of a patient who was away on leave. I slept well. The next day I was moved to another ward where I shared a room with two other female patients. I had a single bed and a side cupboard and a window without curtains, which looked out into an enclosure. My quarters were separated from the other women who each had a bed either side of mine separated by a thin curtain. My best friend brought me some clothes to change in to. A pair of green trousers, a green tee-shirt, an off white jumper and some foot ware, which I placed in my locker but when I left the room someone removed them from my locker. As soon as I put on my jumper another female patient on the ward threw a cup of hot coffee on my jumper, while I was wearing it. I had never slept in a hospital before let alone a psychiatric hospital and being in it confirmed my sense of being on a film set. I was reminded of the film 'One flew over the cuckoos nest'. The only thing was, I couldn't find the camera, I hadn't read a script and I hadn't signed a contract. The food was of a good standard but it wasn't vegan, so I didn't eat much. The staff wore no uniform and at first I couldn't tell the difference between the staff and the patients.

They all seemed to be like actors posing as patients and staff. The television would be on first thing in the morning, late afternoon and evening. In the day the radio would be played. The staff asked me if I wanted to do some painting, but not being a good drawer or painter, I declined. There were books on the ward. I tried to read one or two of them but found that I couldn't retain anything that I had read in my mind. Every now and again there would be the drama of a patient, who would make a run for the exit and the staff would charge after them. There would be a scuffle and the resisting patient would be escorted back to their room by the staff. I watched in amazement and observed without making any verbal comment. It seemed so unreal and my altered perception found it hard to believe that this was serious although I would have agreed that it was a challenge. Male patients also shared the ward but their bedroom was the opposite end to mine. I now slept a little more uneasily one more night on the ward. So far I hadn't been given any medication because the staff were still observing me. But on the third day I discharged myself. It was Sunday and there was talk of going to chapel and I didn't want to be around to witness a revelation. I was terrified of church. I didn't think it had the answers to what I was looking for and any unforeseen influence it could have on my treasured sexuality would not be welcomed. I had heard of out gay people who had gone to church and then denounced being gay. I was totally inexperienced when it came to to an acute psychiatric ward. In time I was to discover that the mental health system also had a reputation of homophobia. I didn't know what had made the individuals change but I wasn't going to hang around to find out. I fought hard to be an out lesbian and had tried to be a positive role model to my clients especially in my last employment. After I discharged myself, as I walked down the path away for that psychiatric hospital I knew that the unseen presence had brought me face to face with my Achilles heel. I had no first hand experience of being either an acute or chronic mental patient, I had no employment professionalism to hide behind for protection. And although I knew that this was my first brush on a personal level with the mental health service, what I didn't know was that I wasn't going to be as lucky as this next time.

So far I had lost at least four months of my life or at least there was four months of time that I couldn't account for. I couldn't logically explain why I was so caught up in trying to find the answer to the origin of the mystery voices that I hadn't been getting on with my life. So far the reality was that my electricity was not working because someone had removed the fuse. My shower was not working, my telephone had been disconnected and my gas fires were condemned by British gas. I had last had a full time job four months before. I still hadn't signed on. I was financially embarrassed and owed money for my rent and council tax.

Yvonne, reading the above reminds me of the writer Miguel De Cervantes' book 'Don Quixote' and whilst I was still an inpatient on a section this year in the Maudsley psychiatric hospital, I was given a special pass to attend the White Horse Theatre on Sunday 23rd October 2005 where an adaptation of 'Don Quixote' was performed for it's 400th year anniversary. I had seen the performance advertised in the London 'Time Out' weekly magazine and ordered the tickets to attend escorted with a ward nurse, but the doctors gave me a special dispensation and I was able to attend alone. I enjoyed the performance and was gently reminded of my own life and the seemly never ending quest.

Sunday 18th December 2005

Dear Yvonne,

This morning after having eight and a half hours of peaceful sleep I awoke tired, read my 'Just for today' and 'basic' book, before selecting and playing Watchman's 'Tongues of Fire' CD as it's track 7 'It was me' reminds me of Shaggy's 'It wasn't me' and going on to have a wash, get dressed and proceeded to have my breakfast. Before realising that I had not yet prayed. Needless to say, I stopped in my tracks and remedied the problem before leaving for the meeting, ensuring that I had remembered the milk and biscuits. After the meeting I stopped off for a carrot juice and a decaffeinated cafe Americano hot drink from 'Fresh & Wild' on Lavender Hill, whilst ogling my two additional Christmas cards, one of which I obtained last night from my sponsor and his partner. I reminisced about my full time employment days when I was vegan and used to eat in places like 'Neals Yard', 'Cranks', 'Mildreds', and 'Govinders'. I felt so at home in the organic surroundings of 'Fresh & Wild' that I was reminded of when I would shop mostly in wholefood shops where ever I went. I recalled my trips abroad in Spain, Amsterdam, Cyprus, Berlin, Italy and Paris, where I found it hard to get my needs met. Not least because I couldn't speak or read the language well enough. After I finished my drinks, I made my way home on the bus with the intentions of watching the film 'My summer of love' on DVD. It had been screened at the Ritzy cinema and I had heard that it has a strong religious theme and although I didn't know if that meant like Quentin Tarrentino's film 'Pulp Fiction' as it is Sunday, I thought I would investigate it. But on my arrival all I found that I wanted to do was to eat something and go to bed. Where I slept for two and a half hours and only woke because my phone rang. It was someone responding to my request to do service all day next Sunday. I am going to be collected between the hours of eight and ten on Christmas morning and will be taken to a meeting at the end of the day. I feel that it would be good for me to do service as I have not worked on Christmas day since I left full time paid employment. And although last year my son and myself spent the day with S & S his godparents, the year before I was in the Maudsley Hospital on

Christmas day and saw the new year in as a sectioned patient on a locked ward without a pass. This year without my son here with me I have not put up any Christmas decorations. Without him I feel I'll be better not to dwell on the things that I cannot change and do the things that I can ie doing service for the fellowship Xmas Dinner. I am happy that I am not going to spend the time alone in my abode by choice if only the fact that being around happy families when my son is estranged from me is not something that I can feel comfortable in just for today.

Monday 19th December 2005

Dear Yvonne,

I was just reading the last few words that I wrote yesterday before going to bed. And now I am convinced that my higher power has a sense of humour, because first of all there is a school of thought that says that if you are not grateful for something he takes it away, or better still be careful what you wish for or you might get it. So on the note of... not something that I can feel comfortable in... Last night I had a peaceful twelve hours of sleep only to wake up in a wet bed! I had suffered another attack of enuresis. I first started to suffer from enuresis during my pregnancy with my son, both it and my oesteo- arthritis seemed to have started around the same time and so after going to my GP and being referred by her to Kings College Hospital and getting my bladder checked. I found out that I suffer from a bladder that thinks it is full when it only has a small amount of urine held within it. The medics gave me a host of differing drugs for both that and my hips, plus I had my mental health drugs. Within a year of my child's birth I was to take a trip to Canada and I didn't want the embarrassment of a night accident.

But, thank goodness, the trip went off without event. Since my return I have mostly stuck to not drinking anything after 18.00hrs and that seems to work reasonably well, but it is not full proof as can be seen by last night's accident. I was recently watching The Golden Girls- the complete first series and at some point during the first five episodes, the character Dorothy's mother said the line "I go to the toilet every morning at 7am like clockwork, but the only thing is I don't wake up until 8am" and I laughed feeling a bit relieved that I had been given respite from my own predicament but knowing only too well the implications. But since I can't help it I find that it is another thing in my life that I am powerless over. I take it one day at a time. At the moment I am listening to Luther Vandross' CD of the same title and love it because these days I think of C when I hear track 5 'Say it now' but it is pertinent for today since I have revealed my secret and in common with the late Luther Vandross who may or may not have had a secret if the write ups in 'Celebrating the woman of colour PRIDE' September 2005 and Luther Vandross, 1955-2005 'VIBE' October 2005 is anything to go by. Both magazines topics in common aside from his well know singing ability was his sexual orientation. Also earlier this year whilst my son and myself were having Sunday lunch at 'Southopia' I was reading the 17th April 2005 Sunday Telegraph Magazine and was consumed by April Ashley's cover story article entitled 'Nothing like a dame -Britain's grandest transsexual talks to Nigel Farndale'.

Monday 19th December 2005

Dear Yvonne,

I have just returned from my Monday group and found my BT bill in my letter box and on opening it to find out what sum I have to pay have found that I have a credit balance of £186.23 so I am happy. Plus today at my group, I found out that a member has an English degree, so after the hour session I asked her if she would mind reading my text and inserting the comma's full stops and paragraphs as when I was a child I lived continuously in a childrens home from the time I was still in junior school and was later fostered for a year at fifteen years of age before being returned to my mother at sixteen years old and so my educational achievements are all over the place. But thankfully she very kindly accepted, so Laura will with my permission correct my punctuation. After all my moaning in the group today it is a wonder she said yes! But I am thankful. Today I was having a bout of low self esteem and thinking about these past thirteen years and what I have achieved in them. I have started and stopped just about everything that I have started and I am no closer to achieving a fulfilling career that I left full time paid employment to do and not only that but I have lost new friends that I have made since leaving work to death and the only thing that it seems that I have done full time is to become a medic's case. It is coming up to the third anniversary of L's suicide and she didn't know it but I had had my first mental health relapse since the birth of my son around the same time as she was on the path to a successful suicide. And I was going to tell her all about it over a cup of tea. This is what I wrote a few years ago:

I had hand written a short note to L with my mobile number included in it and posted it first class, quite a few weeks before I decided to just drop in and visit her unannounced. It had been about six months since we had seen each other last. I parked outside the house that she lived in, but when I looked at her house and garden it looked different and indeed as I walked toward her front door the energy that radiated from it felt very strange and unfamiliar. I decided to knock her door only instead of doing my usual and also calling her name through the letterbox. As no one answered I knocked on the neighbours door and asked him if he knew where she was. He asked me if I hadn't heard that she had died. When I asked how, he said that she had hung herself from her rafters just before Christmas and that she had had a well attended funeral and will be sorely missed, because she had touched the hearts of many. Naturally I felt over come by grief in less than a couple of months it would have been ten years since I had first met her. Our tenth anniversary of platonic friendship and our never ending battle with mental health. I loved her and never doubted her love for me. Once again she had gone on ahead and left me for the second time in my life and I found myself crying because she had gone just like she had almost a decade ago.

Almost ten years ago when my family and friends patience had finally ran out, my mother took me and placed me in the mental health social services department at the same hospital that I had discharged myself from only weeks previously after a weekend stay. The doctor assessed me with the social worker present and I was escorted to the ward by both of them. On the way to the ward the doctor told me that my friends and family were allowed to visit. I was still silent. The fact was, I had got no closer to discovering what the brotherhood was and I felt certain that this might give me a clue as to what had happened. Although one of my past employments was as a housing manager responsible for the rehabilitation of psychiatric patients from psychiatric hospital into their own self contained units and I had also worked in more than one job with psychiatrists and doctors, I was completely unprepared as an acute patient on a psychiatric ward. I felt certain that my career was over. There was just no way that I could pursue the educational psychologist course with a mental health label. Potential employers may conclude that I'm unreliable and can't handle stress. I hadn't yet met any professional that truly understood mental health, Which usually meant that in my experience the person who experienced mental health issues was, albeit inadvertently, undermined which compounded the mental health stigma experienced by the individual. I was realising with that what I said and or didn't say or did or didn't do were things that could be monitored but the intentions or reasons vary and is not easy to assess. I had discovered that there were times when words were inappropriate or inadequate in given time, I was to conclude that mental health ie altered perception is a completely idiosyncratic phenomenon which is difficult to treat mainly because it transcends our capacity of understanding. It is not only illogical but it may not follow convention or be considered socially acceptable or even desirable. It may be one of the ways in which social change is introduced in a society. The other ways may be within addiction ie drugs and or alcohol. This was now my second admission into hospital and I didn't know it then but it was going to be about six weeks before I would be officially discharged.

On arrival to the ward I was placed in the same bed in the three bedded side room that I had been in on my previous visit, only this time L was one of my neighbours.

Tuesday 20th December 2005

Dear Yvonne,

I had almost nine hours of peaceful sleep last night, but woke up at minutes to 8am. I had to hurry my morning ritual and leave home without my breakfast, so that I wouldn't be late to the stables. On the Piccadilly train, after I had read in the Metro about the first same sex couple to be wed, I sent a text to C to say, "I love you". A woman opposite gave me a card with her name and phone number on it, as she was promoting beauty products. I said "thank you" and kept the card, not to use it, but because the name written on the card was Blessing and it reminded me of the gay bishop's autograph that he had given me on Saturday 5th November 2005 outside St

Martins-in-the-fields. He had simply written 'Blessings' on my Who's Who of Gay and lesbian History book by Robert Aldrich and Garry Wotherspoon. Today's lesson was a challenge. Not least because I had not ridden Hughie before, and he was hell bent on perpetually stretching his neck! At one point he wondered off in the direction that he wanted to go, whilst stretching his neck. I became frightened and screamed. But Ben tightened Hughie's neck strap and the rest of the lesson was eventful. At the end of the lesson, I was so stiff that I could hardly get off Hughie. But as I walked out of the school gates, I surprised myself by the amount of instructions that I could remember Ben saying to me, such as, Heals down, toes up. Sit forward in your seat with your shoulders back. Have your thumbs pointing to the horses ears, and the same distance apart. Steer into the corner with the hand in the direction that you want the horse to go and use the leg opposite to egg him on. And with rising trot, I am supposed to stand out of my saddle and bend my knees, counting one, two, as I go to keep time with the rhythm. Or at least something like that.

After leaving the stables, I headed off for Waterstones bookshop in Piccadilly. And on my way noticed the billboard of the Evening Standard sensationalising Sir Elton John's stag night pictures, and purchased a Roald Dahl 'Charlie and the chocolate factory' puffin audio book read by David Morris and a Francesca Simon 'Horrid Henry gets rich quick' book and a CD read by Miranda Richardson to wrap for my son's Christmas present. Also 'The rough guide to children's books 5-11 years by Nicolas Tucker for myself so that I can select suitable books for my son. A Christmas present from my son to his foster mother, I purchased 'The Rough guide to children's books by Nicolas Tucker as she has a two year old daughter, and as a present from my son to her daughter I purchased Eric Carle 'The very hungry caterpillar' puffin audio book read by Eric Carle. Before having a spicy peanut butter and bacon granary bread sandwich, a lemon cake and a large decaffeinated coffee at a cafe in Bateman Street W1 and then going to a meeting. On arriving home and looking in my letter box, I found my son and myself had received another Christmas card. This time from S.D, a dear old friend that I trained with in nursing. We have known each other since 1981 and she has recently moved to Edinburgh and knows nothing about what has happened to my son and so has written in her Christmas card "visit me!"

Wednesday 21st December 2005

Dear Yvonne,

Last night I had twelve hours of peaceful sleep, and still wanted more. But got up anyway, after doing my morning ritual. My mum rang me this morning and reminded me to tell my son that she loves him and is thinking about him, and is there for him and that he must think of her as his 'Super Nan'. Later when I saw my son, I told him verbatim what I was told by her and he loved it. Especially the part about 'Super Nan' that bit made him laugh out loud. He gave me a Christmas card in which he signed his name himself and I love it. I am so proud of my son. He is a miracle in my life. I gave him his Christmas presents and after we went to the shop and I purchased a 'Wallace & Gromit' comic and a 'Futurama' comic which we looked at and laughed at. Plus some confectionary and a drink which we ate and drank together. We talked and I hugged him and kept telling him that I loved him and before I knew where I was the hour and a half supervised session was over and it was time for my son to leave. He didn't cry today but he came back for numerous kisses and cuddles from me before he finally left. On my return home I found that I had received another Christmas card, This time from my C.P.N as well as receiving one last night from another friend. I noticed in today's headline of the Evening Standard, on my travels was 'Rocket Man...and Wife' regarding what I took to be regarding the civil partnership of Sir Elton John to David Furnish.

Thursday 22nd December 2005

Dear Yvonne,

I have had thirteen hours of peaceful sleep and have awoken fresh and revitalised and done my morning rituals. I have just had a phone call from Andrew in which he said that he is going to visit sometime soon with Christmas presents for my son. He is also going to get me back on the internet with my computer. Plus he said that both he and his wife are looking into having my son to live with them, if it is possible. But now I have just got off the phone as my mum rang and she has said that she wants my son to live with her and I of course don't want to displease her, not least because she is an aged woman who truly also loves both me and my son. I am currently listening to Kirk Whalum's 'For You' CD and although I am impressed with all the tracks, I can't help thinking of C when I hear track 9 'I want you' C is not the first woman that I have been inappropriate with as I have said as doctor Ros Ramsey was the first and on Sunday 25th April 2004, I wrote the following for her:

Ros Ramsey's Unconditional Love

I love you Ros, so if loving you means hurting me
I am going to die because of it.
It may sound intense, but with each passing day, I discover the day before
was the tip of the iceberg, of the cause of it.
Since loving you means loving me, I don't ever want to recover from it.
Whether or not you feel the same, just do whatever you do,
and there will be no end to it.

Because I am an addict. I am trained to locate, the cause that I have named, as the source of it.
That drip, drip effect, I don't care what the cost, just supply me with it.
I'll cope with the rush, no it wont be too much, it's my euphoria,
so overdose me with it.
I don't seek a cure, because I don't want to cope with the void of it.

I love you Ros
and love is a thing that perfects, as it's work in progress.
All that I know, is I can't let you go.
Perhaps I'm being churlish.
One day at a time, leaves just enough time,
to sustain loves changes.
Just for today, easy does it is the way, I'll maintain it.

I love you Ros and I am an addict.
In my mind and in my heart, you play a fundamental part.
Loves changing me,
though it isn't for you, but for me that I do,
what pleases me.
I am selfish, I must say. And loving you, is one main way,

that satisfies me,
It's lasting effect, means, I just can't forget,
love is leading me.
I love you Ros.

Although I was genuinely frightened to have found myself smitten with a heterosexual woman, not least a consultant psychiatrist, it was really the thing that prevented me from attempting to commit suicide, when I found myself once again in hospital and fighting for my son through the law courts. My heart hardened and I didn't care what happened. But somehow, I developed a crush on Dr Ros Ramsey's professionalism as I didn't know her personally and that saved my life. I wrote a lot around that time including the following, written on Sunday 18th April 2004:

One hundred percent satisfaction

My ultimate personal lesbian theory for individual satisfaction: is to secure a competent, well adjusted professional heterosexual woman and proceed to grow with her as follows. Since I have been immersed in lesbianism from the age of approximately eighteen onwards, my view of the world of men has been one of mental equality. And as such, I have sort to be recognised and respected as an human being equal to males, a best friend, who is platonic. But nevertheless a comrade and a right arm when all is said and done. Growing through the years, learning about women as I also came to know myself. Loving, loathing, respecting and fearing her for many varied reasons, from that time until this my forty-second year. The secret of her total fascination with penetrative coitus has eluded me. And though a comprehensive knowledge had been acquired during my life long held lesbian sexuality, I am aware that I am inadequate to her sexual satisfaction. That if given a dildo to use, would be incompetent to the needs of heterosexual woman, with her feeling perhaps less than one hundred percent satisfied for a greater or lesser proportion of our sexual union. Aside from my own idiosyncratic classification for selecting a mate for such a trial of possible inseparable dominion, the heterosexual woman may if willing, in time also view her sexual history of being on the receiving end of penetration one hundred percent of the time, what ever her station in life, less than satisfactory when comparing it to the equality of opportunities of same sex relations. The steep learning curve in the school of sexuality and personal responsibility as when she teaches me how to please her in such a deeply personal way by demonstrating using such tools as a strap on dildo, learning herself to use her equipment. She not only learns to temper her intolerance for mistakes, but if she manages to arouse me it is a bonus as she may herself also feel likewise, whilst learning to be competent with her tool. Much like virgins, who are attracted to each other and are consenting to each other without a rule book for each persons erogenous zones. Premature orgasm or near virtual rape could be a possibility but instructions from both me the lesbian on the receiving end of the demonstration and my heterosexual woman sexual partner who much like an amputee will be recognising and knowing the given sensation in the absence of the missing limb. Together she and I have reason to converse during love making as with the opposite genders.

The empowering of heterosexual woman in the bedroom can also produce dramatic changes in other areas like compassion, understanding and tolerance. It can give an insight into the plight of man when faced with the opposite gender and mis-read signals as it is my opinion that heterosexual woman does not change her sexuality by engaging in a sexual relationship with a woman who is as myself a lesbian. As there is quite naturally more to lesbianism than what happens during sexual intercourse. Thus in a mixed relationship of one heterosexual woman and one lesbian, I can personally say there are reasons which attract and repel for both parties. But as a 'One track mind' stereotypical lesbian I personally prefer to pursue the options availiable to women although I am aware that males find reasons to be fascinated with me.

Though the teach me to love you so that I can learn to love myself approach may seem rather selfish, for me it is a preservation order on my sexuality. One might ask what is in it for the heterosexual woman? Naturally it is not a question that I can answer. Perhaps she will tell me in time.

Friday 23rd December 2005

Dear Yvonne,

I am refreshed after thirteen hours of peaceful sleep last night and my morning ritual. On looking in my letter box after breakfast, I was pleasantly surprised to have received a Christmas card from

Aunt Catherine for both me and my son and enclosed within was fifty dollars, which was an added bonus. So far I have received eleven Christmas cards this year. Not bad for one that has only been released from a locked ward since Thursday 27th October 2005. I am currently listening to Nancy Wilson's HMV Jazz 'The Nancy Wilson Collection' track 2 'Call me irresponsible' is my anthem to C as with bipolar affective disorder my list of assets seem to be out weighed by my liabilities. Also in my letter box was a copy of a letter sent to my GP, Dr Mark Fisher from Dr Nicola Byrne, the consultant psychiatrist dated 13th December 2005 who I saw recently. It reads:

I met the above for the first time today in the company of her CPN...I am pleased to report that she remains very well since her discharge from hospital. In the circumstances, she appears to be coping well with the situation of her son being in foster care. She now sees him regularly. She is now looking to the future and is positive about an access course for womens studies that she is looking forward to starting.

Yvonne did request that her Stelazine be slowly reduced in order to gauge whether it might be possible to take less on a daily basis. She recalls being well on far smaller doses in the past. She told me today that in the late 1990's before the birth of her son she was well on 3mgs a day, after his birth the dose was reduced to 2mgs and for a year or so she was well on 1mg daily. She recalls only becoming unwell when she actually stopped it all together. Understandably therefore she is keen to see whether she could maintain her current state of health on a smaller dose. This seems an entirely reasonable idea. We did request her patience today to start this process because of the changes currently going on in our service. She agreed that it would be wise to wait until it was established who her new CPN was and she had met and starts to build a relationship with them and her new doctor. At that point a gradual reduction could be initiated and she is amenable to the idea of charting her progress in some kind of diary from that point. For the meantime therefore her medication remains **stelazine 10mgs OD** and this will be reviewed again hopefully within the next few months.

Saturday 24th December 2005

Yvonne Stewart Williams

Dear Yvonne,

Yesterday evening my joyous mood took a turn for the worse and I became melancholic and sad. Added to this the self destructive addict in me metamorphoised itself into the late Isadora Duncan's scarf and tried to put the strangle hold on my recovery. I know that I am suffering from a disease that is cunning, baffling and dangerous and that I cannot afford to let it get a foothold on my recovery. When I isolate I am much like a darkroom and produce the best negatives possible. So much like Chris Tarrant says in the terrestrial television quiz show 'Who wants to be a millionaire' "phone a friend" I chose that as my option and struck lucky. I found strength and comfort. The foundation of why I was feeling sad was that I felt that with it being only two days to go before Christmas that I wasn't going to be anywhere near to see my son open his presents and I generally felt that I had let my son down again. I started to doubt that there was anything in the world that I could do to make it up to him that I would be content with and went into a downhill spiral of negativity. But as I said these last forty two day I have been busy in my recovery and have put in place some useful tools. One of which I used last night when I sent a text out to two friends explaining how I felt. They both got back to me forthwith and the strength and comfort that I gained from their words made it possible for me to stop the negativity in it's tracks. And this morning after ten hours of peaceful sleep, only waking up once for half an hour at five thirty this morning before falling asleep again. When I was on my way to a meeting I met with Johnathan, another neighbour from the gay and lesbian community, who on commenting just how well I looked, asked about my son.

When I brought him up to speed about my son being in foster care and that I was fighting it in the courts he looked genuinely sad and told me that he "admires" me and said that I can go around to his place. When I told him that I was writing my autobiography and asked him if he can help me go through my punctuations, he said that he would be more than pleased to. We then exchanged mobile numbers before parting. After the meeting today instead of getting on my way I stopped with some of the others for a cup of decaffeinated coffee and a chat at the cafe and found it helpful. On arriving at my home and looking in my letter box I found that I had received another Christmas card, this time from Pete and Lyn. I also got 22 December 2005 issue 890 Pink Paper with the headline 'Love, Love, Love' regarding the civil partnership and lastly a Sigma survey to complete, the Lambeth LGBT Matters survey. Lambeth council commissioned Sigma to investigate the social care needs and service use of LGBT people who live, work, study or socialise in Lambeth as well as their experiences of stigma, discrimination and victimisation. I was at the interview of Sigma, Opinion Leader and Stormbreak, the three research teams on Friday 17th June 2005 at the Lambeth Town Hall when they competed for the Lambeth commission. I was there as a volunteer interviewing on the behalf of the Lambeth LGBT forum. To me on the day all of the candidates were top quality and delivered brilliant interviews but to my mind Opinion leader just had the edge but collectively Sigma won and was given the commission. In a bit I am going to watch a few episodes of Frasier just to remind myself that life isn't perfect.

Sunday 25th December 2005

Dear Yvonne,

I had ten and a half hours of peaceful sleep and only woke up once at two thirty this morning for half an hour before returning to sleep. Today is Christmas day and after doing my usual ritual I watched television whilst having my breakfast. I am going to be picked up at 11am today and be taken to Wandsworth where I will be doing service all day and having xmas dinner before leaving. I will also be going to a 7pm meeting tonight, so I won't be lonely and sink into the abyss of negativity.

Sunday 25th December 2005

Dear Yvonne,

I feel so lucky. I arrived for my xmas day service just in time to get a cup of decaffeinated tea and enter a meeting and after doing a little bit of service and socialising I had a delicious Christmas dinner before continuing socialising, sending and receiving texts and phone calls and doing service. I enjoyed myself and did not feel lonely for a moment. I thought of my son but felt that in time once I, one day at a time look after my recovery, I would be able to make amends to him, and not revert to Christmas 2003, when I had spent my

Christmas day and New Years day in a locked psychiatric ward. This year I was in a safe place amongst people who had empathy for how I felt as this was the fifteenth year in a row that a dinner had been put on for free on a Christmas day. By the time I left the Wandsworth site I felt so grateful as not only had I been given a lift to the site but I had also been given a lift home armed with a doggy bag and not one negative thought had passed through my mind. On my arrival home my mum phoned me just to see how I was. She is a Jehovah's Witness and doesn't celebrate Christmas but knows that my son and myself do, and so called to express her love.

Monday 26th December 2005

I woke for an hour and a half at four thirty this morning but had ten hours of peaceful sleep altogether before starting my day. Today I chose to have a small clear out of some excess boxes and papers, whilst listening to 'the greatest 80's Soul Weekender' on volume three. I came across my 2004 diary which reminded me that just after leaving the psychiatric hospital after being on section three, I went to the Old Vic theatre and watched Shakespeare's Hamlet and enjoyed the performance. I had previously read Williams Shakespeare's Macbeth and gained a lot from it and wasn't disappointed when watching Hamlet. I also came across a this year's service users meeting: Helping to shape our service minutes for the 16th March 2005 Boardroom, Maudsley hospital for the psychotherapy department, which I attended. As well as a reminder for LAGNA (the lesbian and gay newsmedia archive) which I committed some of my free time to. I also brought my son to Lagna with me to the office whilst I carried out my voluntary work before it closed in October 2005. I also found a short prose that I wrote with C in mind:

My love for you started out as
a domestic washing machine
ie able to wash ordinarily
And has now developed into an industrial washing machine
transcending most obstacles

After my light spring clean I settled down and watched two episodes of 'Will & Grace' the complete series one and enjoyed myself, before setting off to a meeting.

Tuesday 27th December 2005

Dear Yvonne,

I had ten hours worth of peaceful sleep last night. Andrew rang at ten this morning to say that as the weather had taken a turn for the worst with frost and snow that he would not be driving to London. I was quite naturally disappointed and made a decision to go back to bed for a couple of hours with the intentions of going to the launderette when I got up. I went to bed after I had my brunch. On arising, I started sorting the clothes into colour coded wash piles when Andrew rang again to say that the weather seemed to be okay up his end and that he was going to visit me after all and stay the night. So after finishing the laundry I went to Marks & Spencers and did my shopping for mostly perishable items before returning to my home in anticipation of Andrew's arrival. I had just put my supper on when Andrew arrived. I was so pleased to see him and told him how I felt about my disease, my powerlessness over it, my unmanageability and my insanity and liability. His reply was that I was "his anchor" and that over the years, he has supported in the ways that he could. And that despite bipolar affective disorder I am still the person that he knew always fighting for better not letting anything get me down for long. And when he goes through his low times, he thinks of me and the things that I go through, and it gives him the strength to prevail. I myself was surprised to hear his version and was honoured that I have people in the world that think so highly of me and love me despite my unyielding impediment. It gives 'me' the strength to go on and battle one day at a time forever for my recovery.

Wednesday 28th December 2005

Dear Yvonne,

I didn't go to a meeting yesterday and eventually got to bed at 1.30am but I didn't forget to do my night ritual before going to sleep. I had five hours of peaceful sleep before getting up and doing my morning ritual and waking Andrew, who was asleep on the sofa. I proceeded to make breakfast for both of us, before he left at 8am for his part of the country, and I went back to sleep for a few hours. He gave me Chevelle Franklyn's 'His Way' CD that I am currently listening to. On my way back from seeing my son today I bumped into EA, an associate that I first met in the Maudsley psychiatric hospital on ES3 when it was a mixed ward in 1995 when we were both on a section and lived in each others neighbourhood. I, when meeting him on occasions, used to buy gospel music in his presence. But today EA walked alongside me not five minutes after I got off the bus from Streatham and after giving me the usual salutations told me that he liked how I 'flex'. It was indeed a compliment but since he doesn't know that my son is in foster care and that I had just seen him and wished that my son could be once more living at home with me. I was given a Christmas present by the local authority today as I had an unsupervised contact with my son and phoned my mother and allowed her to say that she loved him to him on the phone and when he heard her tell him that she was his super nan he started to beam from ear to ear. He told me that he had several times looked at a Elmer card with a teddy on it's nose that I had written ' thinking of you mummy ' inside because he was thinking of me over the Christmas and knew that I would be thinking of him and he was right. I was pleased to hear him say he went to the Cinderella pantomine and enjoyed it and thought that buttons was a lovely name. He also told me that whenever he has to leave me it makes him feel like crying. If the truth be known it also makes me feel like crying. Today I am so stiff that I am almost dreading horse riding lesson tomorrow morning but go I will. But for now I am off to a meeting.

Thursday 29th December 2005

Dear Yvonne,

I am currently listening to 'The Picture of Dorian Gray' by Oscar Wilde and read by John Moffatt on volume four. The day so far has been exceedingly good. I started off with eleven hours of sleep before setting off for another horse riding lesson, which was on Hughie today. On the tube I read in 'the Metro' the article 'Hunted to extinction -the common smoker' and realised that for the last six years that I have lost the urge for that particular vice and recalled my romance with it when I was in hospital and even though I shook when I lit it up and inhaled whilst it combined with effects of my medication first thing in the morning and my chest became congested with a solid knot as a result. I could not seem to live without it. In fact to finally nip it in the bud I started to attend a twelve step self help group, which saved my life, because such was my insanity. I am pleased that just for today, I know I don't have to be a smoker and I am grateful. Hughie, me and Ben had a very good lesson today. Not that Ben shouted any less. But somehow things seemed to fall into place and I wasn't stiff. Aside from Ben telling me to hold my hands out in front and closer together and to go faster and to bend my knees in the rising trot and to push up with my tummy and lift myself out of my seat with my shoulders back and to look at the school and not at the floor. I was pleased that I got on and off Hughie's back without a problem and rewarded Hughie by feeding him after the lesson with carrots and patting him. An older woman was there watching a young girl have her lesson and at the end of the lessons she said that since I was doing so well with so few lessons that she herself may have a go. After leaving the stables I went to get my medication from a CPN after which I dropped in to see Lyn and have a cup of tea with her. We spoke about my son and I thanked her for her and Pete's support before returning home and preparing lunch. I am lucky today as I am going to get a lift to a meeting tonight. I asked Johnathan to read my letters and he said that he found then fascinating, which both pleased and surprised me as I had likened it to looking at someones holiday photo's i.e. interesting but tedious after a time.

Friday 30th December 2005

Dear Yvonne,

Today I had twelve and a half hours of peaceful dream filled sleep. As I had selected a temporary sponsor to take me from step four to beyond at last nights meeting, this morning I prayed as usual, read the just for today card, reviewed my gratitude list, read from the big book and rang my temporary sponsor. Before having my breakfast and getting a bath, washing my hair and grooming it. For today is a very special day for me indeed as about six months ago I had booked a place for two to have afternoon tea at the Ritz Hotel in Piccadilly today for my son and myself to give gratitude for the year past. I am trying not to be too pessimistic about it but, the first time that I had made this booking for the same purpose in 2003, months before the very first time that I had been sectioned in the Maudsley hospital, for the first time in my son's life and so he was unable to attend and as I had no pass I was also unable to atten either. Today I will attend unaccompanied and give gratitude just the same and hope that next year my son will be able to accompany me. But just for today I will keep it simple and wear my 'Devotion' designer jacket because I think it suits me, try to enjoy myself and than I will go to a meeting afterwards. I heard it on Radio 4 this morning but it is also covered in today's Evening standard on page 4 under the heading of 'Unmarried couples can adopt' that same - sex couples are legally allowed to adopt together from today' which is a step in the right direction. Although at the same time in the Guardian newspaper today, is an article on page 12 under the heading 'Murder squad trusted by gay community to be disbanded' which saddened me because recently we in the borough of Lambeth had a gay murder on Clapham Common. That shocked me and made me aware that still in 2005 someone's life can be thought of as meaningless just because of sexual orientation and reminded me what Gene Robinson, Bishop of New Hampshire said when I saw him on Saturday 5th November 2005, and that is that he at times has worn a bullet-proof vest and had bodyguards!

Saturday 31st December 2005

Dear Yvonne,

It is 2am and I have been tossing and turning in my bed for the last three hours. I suspect that the problem is that when I ordered my earl gray tea at the Ritz Hotel yesterday that I failed to ask for decaffeinated earl gray like I sometimes drink at home. Nevertheless the overall event is worth a sleepless reflection. I enjoyed the sandwiches and scones and cakes and indulged myself with the tea whilst Louis Armstrong's 'Wonderful World' preceded the several songs played in the background on a piano. I took the opportunity while I was waiting for my tea to brew, to text some of my friends, to share the occasion with them and read their replies. Well today is the last day of this year and thinking back to, thirteen years ago when my life took a change unforeseen by me and lead me into a weekend in the hospital followed a few weeks later by six additional weeks in hospital I then decided that I would have a change of career and that was when on my release from the York clinic, Guy's hospital, I chose to do a media course at the Morley College which started in September 1993. Almost the same time, my ex husband filed for a divorce but as I was still on the drug Stelazine and the dose that I was on was quite high, I was unable to concentrate and had to abort the course before I had even been on the course for six weeks. Fortunately for me, my then psychiatrist reduced my medication to zero and the following year, September 1994, I went to Lambeth College at Knights Hill to do an access to film, media and photography, having spent a few weeks earlier on in the year working on the feature film 'Thin Ice.' I chose to go to Berlin to spend my Christmas and New Year holiday that year and when I came back in 1995, my mental health reprieve was coming to a close. But not before I worked on a short film called 'Thin Walls' finally as a second assistant director and runner and on P.J. Harvey's 'C'mon Billy' pop promo as a production assistant and runner. By the time I had finished both shoots, my mental health reprieve was over and I ended up throwing my guitar amplifier out of my back window onto my neighbour's roof and throwing a hammer through my front window and into the front garden of the same neighbour. Trashing my flat, just like Bruce Willis' charactor in 'Pulp Fiction' in the scene where he is looking for his watch! But unlike that character I ended up being handcuffed on the arrival of the police and taken to the Maudsley hospital, where I was sectioned, re-medicated on Stelazine and hospitalised for about six weeks. When I returned to the community, I chose to declare my illness and do some voluntary work as a volunteer driver for the 'Landmark' a H.I.V/A.I.D.S charity and be a volunteer programme worker for the Y.M.C.A, Young Men's Christian Association, in Lambeth and take a computer course at the Baytree women's centre. But my disease was relentless and from that time until the conception of my son, I was a revolving door case. Going in and out of hospital approximately every six months. Since 2003 I have been more or less back to the six monthly revolving door routine. Last year, when I was at an all time low, almost suicidal and fighting for my son through the courts, there was talk of his being adopted. My psychiatrist prescribed the mood stabiliser Sodium Valporate aka Epilim, the side effects of which are liver failure, drowsiness, fluid retention. pancreatitis, gain in weight, loss of hair, blood changes, effects on nervous system, rashes, vasculitis, toxic skin effects, erythema mutitforme and Stevens-Johnson syndrome (hypersensitivity reactions involving skin and mucous membranes), to accompany my Stelazine and I wrote to Alcoholics Anonymous in desperation to ask if there was such a group in this country or in the U.S.A called Stress Anonymous and sent the following for their perusal, as I felt sure that Step 2, Came to believe that a Power greater than ourselves could restore us to sanity could be of help for someone like me:

THE TWELVE SUGGESTED STEPS

1_We admitted we were powerless over stress that our lives had become unmanageable

2_Came to believe that a Power greater than ourselves could restore us to sanity

3_Made a decision to turn our will and our lives over to the care of God *as we understood Him, Her or It.*

4_Made a searching and fearless moral inventory of ourselves.

5_Admitted to God, to ourselves, and to another human being the exact nature of our wrongs.

6_Were entirely ready to have God remove all these defects of character.

7_Humbly asked Him, Her or It to remove our shortcomings.

8_Made a list of all persons we had harmed and became willing to make amends to them all.

9_Made direct amends to such people whenever possible, except when to do so would injure them or others.

10_Continued to take personal inventory and when we were wrong, promply admitted it.

11_Sought through prayer and meditation to improve our conscious contact with God *as we understood Him, Her or It,* praying only for the knowledge of His will for us and the power to carry that out.

12_Having had a spiritual awakening as a result of these steps, we tried to carry this message to the stressed and to practice these principles in all our affairs.

THE TWELVE TRADITIONS

1_Our common welfare should come first; personal recovery depends upon stress anonymous (S.A.) unity.

2_For our group purpose there is but one ultimate authority a loving God as He may express Himself in our group conscience, Our leaders are but trusted servants, they do not govern.

3_The only requirement for S.A. is a desire to prestress

4_Each group should be autonomous except in matters affecting other groups or S.A. as a whole.

5_Each group has but one primary purpose, to carry it's message to the stressed who still suffers.

6_An S.A. group ought never to endorse, finance or lend the S.A. name to any related facility or outside enterprise, lest problems of money, property and prestige divert us from our primary purpose.

7_Every S.A. group ought to be fully self supporting, declining outside contributions.

8_Stress Anonymous should remain forever non professional, but our service centres may employ special workers.

9_S.A, as such, ought never to be organised; but we may created service boards or committees directly responsible to those they serve.

10_Stress Anonymous has no opinion on outside issues; hence the S.A name ought never be drawn into public controversy.

11_Our public relations policy is based on attraction rather than promotion; we need always maintain personal anonymity at the level of press, radio, and films.

12_Anonymity is the spiritual foundation of our traditions, forever reminding us to place principles before personalities.

(continued)

I took the word **prestress** from the words 'prestressed concrete' written in the Collins plus concise dictionary, the definition is stated as: Concrete contains steel wires that are stretched to counteract the stresses that will occur under load.

I believe that stress (mental, emotional, or physical strain or tension, forces producing deformation or strain in general), is a common human condition which whilst in some circumstances can be alleviated fairly swiftly with the in built human mechanism of the "fright, fight or flight" instinct, in many instances the individual puts in progress a process which compounds that problem that they seek to be reduced, have respite from or abstinence. Unfortunately few people if any are immune to stress, which can have far reaching sometimes detrimental effects and consequences that can be experienced in those from the cradle to the near grave and in all spheres and tiers of human life either directly or indirectly.

In practical terms stress can lead to ineffectual time management and diminished communication skills culminating in loss of or reduced overall productive production capacity, fostering if left unchecked an amalgamating ever increasing amount of counterproductive non-constructive development.

Not only does stress sometimes produce suicidal and or murderous notions within the individual experiencing the emotional psychological extremes of mental distress, but stress can also be a predisposing factor to physical ailments such as in cases like myocardial infarctions, cerebral vascular hemorrhages, the degeneration of the immune system and possibly carcinoma.

Twenty-first century modern day everyday lifestyle ever more sophisticated and demanding even in areas of aestheticism, hedonism and ascetic, but especially in the work place, within educational establishments and in places of learning, amongst the unemployed and in the home, where workload and responsibility has never seemed greater. Whilst endeavouring to keep pace with the cutting edge of development aiming to ensure the professionalism and personal performance of the individual. Within one's area of responsibility, striving to deliver service at a premium whilst developing and maintaining appropriate self-nurturing responses that keep stress to a mimimum.

It is for the above reasons with the individual within management structures in mind at work, rest and play and the inevitable trickle down factor effects may be experienced by family, friends, colleagues, associates and service users in paid or unpaid arenas that I have concluded that the twelve step anonymous recovery programme applied with STRESS as a focus may prove to be advantageous.

Poor performance due to stress can be the difference between satisfaction and dissatisfaction, competence and incompetence, health and illness. Training, discipline, conscious self-awareness leading to effectiveness through confidence advancing to the implementation of befitting exertion would not only be cost effective in the long term, improve the quality of life in the individual and other persons affected by their actions but could perhaps also reduce the risk of life and limb.

The stressed individual has their own idiosyncratic way of dealing with their personal discomfort, which may vary when experiencing stress in excess of their personal capacity. Perhaps stress is the key to substance use, alcohol, drugs, food, sex, gambling, shopping in excess, emotional detachment, workaholicism, reduced work performance, verbal physical emotional abuse, and relationship failure in learnt behaviour and coping response mechanism automatically triggered when stressed.

Saturday 31st December 2005

Dear Yvonne

I finally had one hour of peaceful sleep before getting up and doing my ritual and going off to a 9am meeting and because of the format for this fellowship differed slightly, I did the wrong thing in it, I spoke during the meeting and the only people that are allowed to speak during a meeting are the ones that have done from step 5 onwards with their sponsors. I hadn't done my Step 5, though I only found out in hindsight later when my temporary sponsor told me when I arrived back home, she called me and I told her what it was. Needless to say I won't repeat the same mistake now that I have been told. After I had some lunch I went back to bed and slept for another eight peaceful hours and my cousin Eric rang me on my landline to wish me a happy new year for 2006 as he was getting ready to go to a party. I brought him up to speed on what was happening about my son, plus took the opportunity to get his mother's telephone number off him as I intend to ring her sometime tomorrow. Andrew sent me a text from his wife and children wishing happy 2006 to me and my family to which I replied. I also sent a text greeting to A, who is currently in Atlanta U.S.A and went there with the express purpose of seeing in the New Year. Tonight I, myself will also see the New Year in by going to a party that starts at 9pm and ends at 1am in Holborn. I purchased the ticket a few weeks ago to attend an official fellowship dance where there will be no alcohol on sale. Last year I went to Southopia with my son for the same amount of time and spent the time surrounded by mainly women. This year I decided that my recovery must come first.

Sunday 1st January 2006

Dear Yvonne,

Happy New Year! I have had nine hours of peaceful restful sleep after getting home from the dance at 3am. I thoroughly enjoyed myself arriving just in time to enter a meeting before going out there and taking my chances on the dance floor. To be honest, I am quite shy and, when it comes to dance floors I have since a teenager been highly self conscious and always try to avoid them. First of all, I spent time as a musician playing a guitar and drum kit in groups, creating music for people to dance and sing to. I, myself spent very little time dancing, if but for the reason that I secretly think that I can't dance! Though my son can dance and wastes no opportunity demonstrating his talent. But dance I did last night for all of thirty minutes. Today I am listening to Magic radio station 105.4fm as C quite likes it, and so do I now. But each time that I listen to it, I think of C and as such I feel close to her in her absence. I will be going to a meeting later this evening so I am going to have a nap for an hour or so. I rang my mother and gave her a new year's greeting; I also rang Aunt Catherine and wished her a quick new year's greeting as she was getting ready to usher in her Methodist church. I sent a text with new's greeting to my brother David and my sister Joanne and David replied.

Monday 2nd January 2006

Dear Yvonne,

Today has been a lazy day for me. I spent most of it in bed. I have slept for at least fourteen hours and still feel tired. But I have decided to get up and go to a meeting. At least I have done my suggestions and listened to Magic Fm105.4 whilst I was eating. My cousin Sally, my late Aunt Ruth's offspring rang me on my landline and wished me a happy new year. I returned her best wishes and brought her up to speed on my son when she asked about him. And though she doesn't agree with my sexuality because of her Seventh day adventist faith, I know that she loves me and my son and wants what is best for me. Whilst I am on the subject of family, my mother's second husband who she has been married to for twenty-five years and who I call V.J, is terminally ill and dying from prostate cancer. I love V.J and have many fond memories of him from when I was a child of twelve in 1973. We used to have the kind of relationship that my mother and I now enjoy. That was before mental illness. My illness put a strain on our relationship and each day I have found it challenging to bridge the gap. Before my mental illness V.J and I would spend hours talking together and I even borrowed his jumpers, we looked forward to each others company and he was the first person in my family that I told that I was a lesbian, aside from my mother. And when I told him, he said that in his day, and he was born in 1928, people would have stoned me but, he said that it was okay with him but he would have to see what my mother said about it. As it was, after my mother remonstrated about Sodom and Gomarrah which was in line with her Jehovah's Witness faith, she said that she wasn't going to give up on me as I had stood by her in the days of her mental illness. And stand by me both she and V.J have, even with the news of my son's artificial insemination conception. I love V.J and the unfailing love and support that both, he and my mother, have given me over the years especially in times of crisis has been without compare. But since I have heard that he has incurable cancer, is having regular injections to stem the pain and is dying, I have been fearful. I avoid him and he avoids me and our conversation these days are superficial. It is like he doesn't want to tell me how he feels in case I suffer another manic attack from the stress of it. And I for my part fail to talk to him in detail, just in case he gets wind of my feelings for him and I start to cry and make him weak. The most I do these days, is visit with my son, which V.J loves. Especially as my son's Christian name was chosen for him by V.J at my request and my son loves his granddad. A few months ago V.J fell down the stairs at home at three o'clock in the morning and had to be taken to hospital and by the time I got there the next day with my son, he had discharged himself from the hospital. and gone to play a game of bingo at the Bingo hall. But recently he has been feeling weaker and had been in hospital over night and on his release he has done the same thing. My mother has told me to tell my son's social workers the state of play so that my son will be able to attend the funeral and say his goodbyes, as when my grandmother died in 1976, I was not allowed to leave the country and go to Jamaica with my mother to her funeral as I was in a children's home and my mother's request was denied, even though I was the first grandchild of Louise and David Stewart to be born in England and it was a grave family occasion with Louise Stewart being buried in a vault.

Tuesday 3rd January 2006

Dear Yvonne,

I have had three hours of peaceful sleep and have been tossing and turning for an hour. I have never attended a funeral even when Ishmael aka Al my mother's first husband and my adopted dad died in the same year that the late Princess of Wales died. Dad's death came as a shock to me. I inherited five hundred pounds from him which I spent convalesencing taking a holiday in Italy with a friend and her family and friends. I missed dad's funeral as I was sectioned in the Maudsley hospital and my only consolation was that the nation was also mourning the death of Lady Di and that the funeral was shown on the television. Though on my return from Italy I again found myself sectioned in the Maudsley hospital approximately six months later. My then psychiatrist sanctioned my official referral to the psychotherapy department and I was given a weekly one to one session with a psychotherapist who was also a trained psychiatrist for one whole year and during that time I became pregnant and spent the next few years without incident.

Tuesday 3rd January 2006

I went back to bed and got two additional hours of peaceful sleep and woke up with a start. I was running late to go to the stables so I had to get a move on this morning, but made sure that I had a couple of rounds of toast with bacon and egg and a cup of decaffeinated tea before I left to go to the station. I read my literature on the train and arrived at the stables just in time to put on my half chaps and riding cap. I totally forgot about my gloves! Fortunately it wasn't too cold to ride without them. Hughie was being shod today so I rode Bilbo instead. And today when Ben raised his voice it was to tell me to rise out of my seat or to do rising trot for a bit longer. Ben said that I ride Bilbo better than Hughie even if I can't get off him. Which is true, I felt on Bilbo today like when I was seventeen and had taken a few driving lessons and the initial fear had been overcome and I had gained a little confidence as I instinctively knew what I was doing and it bypassed my brain and went straight to the appropriate limbs. I had a great lesson today and it felt good. and so I asked for Bilbo again next week.

I went to a lunchtime meeting and on my way home I stopped off at Dunning & Co Solicitors to ask for the address of the court and the time that I am supposed to be there next week Tuesday. I have to be at First Avenue House, 42-49 High Holborn, London WC1V 6NP for my son's court hearing but my solicitor will write to confirm the time. Whilst waiting for the bus home I met my old next door neighbour and after giving each other new years greetings, we exchanged telephone numbers. When I got home I rang my housing officer to find out if my rent had been paid by the housing office yet. But she was not in today and I was told to call back tomorrow. I am going to go to a meeting tonight so I am going to have something to eat before I set off.

Wednesday 4th January 2006

Dear Yvonne,

I had nine and a half hours of peaceful sleep last night, even though yesterday my mother telephoned me to tell me that V.J was going to be admitted to Mount Vernon hospital as he was unsteady on his feet, passing blood in his urine, has back pain and is generally feeling unwell. After speaking to my mum yesterday, I made the decision that today, after my supervised access visit with my son, I was going to spend a few days with my mother and give her my support. Before setting off to see my son, I dropped in to see my housing officer and put in a formal application to go on the transfer list for a two bedroomed property for me and my son, or a three bedroomed for a carer in the event of my relapsing. Plus I collected a rent paying in bank book so that I can start paying a contribution towards my now £421.00 rent arrears. I don't want to be evicted before the housing benefit is sorted out. I also gave my housing officer a copy of my keys so that someone would be able to let the gas boiler contractor in tomorrow, as I have a pre booked appointment with them and I will now be at my mother's. I also received a letter from my solicitor today stating that I need to be at the court by 12 noon.

Before I saw my son today I phoned his social worker and told her what is happening with V.J and told her that I was not going to mention anything to my son but in case the worse happens that my mother has requested that my son attends his grandad's funeral. I was late for my appointment to see my son today as I was trying to buy something in Woolworth's and it took longer than I thought. But when I saw my son he was radiant and I was pleased. The session was pleasurable for me and my son seemed to enjoy it, but for me it was over all too soon. After bidding my son farewell I went home briefly before setting off to my mother's home outside London. On arrival there, after eating, I rang the hospital and spoke to V.J. My mother and myself are to visit him tomorrow, I started my period today.

Thursday 5th January 2006

Last night I slept in my mum's bed with her beside me and had eleven hours of peaceful sleep. I did my ritual when I awoke and my mum brought me a pot of tea in bed, before I went downstairs and made myself breakfast. After which I went for a walk around the shopping centre before my brother Paul offered to drive my mum and myself to the hospital to visit V.J. When I saw V.J today he looked perky and was telling me how before he saw the doctor today he was supposed to be on bed rest. But after being caught walking several times by on particular nurse, she told him what he already knew and asked him if he wanted it written down. To which he made no reply and stayed on his bed. I took the opportunity to ask V.J for a hug today and whilst hugging him told him that I love him to which he replied he knows. V.J said that he felt better and his walking had improved.

Friday 6th January 2006

Dear Yvonne,

Last night I had ten and a half hours sleep, and got up and washed and went downstairs before my mum could come up with my pot of tea. I am sorry to say goodbye to my mum, but I can always go back to see her again soon. V.J is meant to be leaving Mount Vernon hospital on Tuesday. I arrived back at my flat this afternoon to find a receipt to prove that my gas boiler has passed it's inspection. I have not been to a meeting for two days and I'm desperately in need of one. So I will go to a meeting that I have not been to before with my old sponsor. I rang the housing benefit office, but my benefit is still being processed.

Saturday 7th January 2006

Dear Yvonne,

I had ten hours of peaceful sleep last night, woke up did my daily ritual, washed, had breakfast and went off to Curry's to buy a memory stick before going to a midday meeting. I found my latest gas bill for £52.32 in my letter box. I will try and pay that next week. I couldn't get my memory stick to work so I went over to Johnathan's flat and he couldn't get it to work either. So whilst I drank a cup of tea, I rang Andrew and he will sort the computer problem out, when he next visits in a week or two. Today I felt quite sombre and felt the lack in my game of working my recovery program. I opted to change my sponsor and get someone permanent as I feel that with my insanity track record that my recovery was too important to dabble with. This evening K, an old colleague and friend from P.A.C.E rang me. K had sent a new years greetings text to me and my son and I had returned the compliments. But when I spoke to her, I told her what had happened to me and my son and as she was, like me a mental heath advocate, she was very empathic. She mentioned a place in Richmond that takes on families, so that the parent and children are not separated when there is a relapse. She is going to look for more information on the net and pass on my e-mail address.

Sunday 8th January 2006

Dear Yvonne,

Today I am toxic with negativity! I had nine and a half hours of peaceful sleep and went off to my meeting and left the milk that I had brought yesterday for the tea commitment and had to pick up a pint on the way. Then for some reason or other I felt under the weather and melancholy. By the time I returned from the meeting, I was thinking about my housing benefit and worrying about when it is going to be paid. God grant me the serenity to accept the things I cannot change, the courage to change the things I can and the wisdom to know the difference. My new sponsor is going to call me today and arrange to meet sometime next week and I am looking forward to her call. In the meantime I am going to read some of my recovery literature whilst I do the laundry and then after I am going have something to eat, have a nap and then go to another meeting tonight.

Monday 9th January 2006

Dear Yvonne,

Last night I had twelve hours of peaceful sleep and woke up refreshed and in good humour. After doing my morning rituals, I went to the post office and exchanged my fifty dollars, added to it and paid my gas bill, before going to my group psychotherapy session.

Tuesday 10th January 2006

Dear Yvonne,

I had just over seven and a half hours of peaceful sleep before doing my usual routine and setting off to my horse riding lesson. When I arrived at the stables I had a message on my mobile from my sponsor giving me her best wishes for today. I was on Bilbo today and the lesson didn't seem to go as well as last week. I seemed to spend quite a lot of it walking Bilbo with Ben shouting for me to do rising trot. At the end of the lesson I patted Bilbo nevertheless and gave him the carrots that I had purchased especially for him. I arrived at the court on time to find Ros Dunning, my solicitor waiting in the corridor of the court. After having a brief word with her and waiting for a few minutes it was time for us to face the judge, who seemed to be in a good mood. This session in court was over within an hour and what I got out of it was the lengthening by thirty minutes of my weekly supervised sessions with my son. I am also to have another psychiatric assessment with a psychiatrist for the court in February and my son is also to have an assessment by a psychiatrist in April. The reason for the assessment is to ascertain if the reunion and estrangement is too much for my son to endure when I relapse and recover. If it is, then he may have to be adopted or put up for long term fostering. If it is not then he can come back and live with me. So the court is putting both options in process so that if the worse outcome is realised then there will not be a delay with my son's care. My solicitor made a appointment to see me next Wednesday 18th January 2006 at 4pm. And after I spent a few minutes talking to my son's CQSW and his court guardian I went home. I am going to a meeting this evening and afterwards I am going to have a coffee with my sponsor.

Wednesday 11th January 2006

Dear Yvonne,

Last night I had eleven hours of peaceful sleep. I woke up this morning to ring my sponsor which I will be doing each morning for ninety days starting today, and then I went back to sleep. Today I had an extended contact with my son, It lasted for almost three hours and went well. He is back at kindergarten after the holiday and was covered in mud from his school's playing field but happy and humming the fireman Sam tune audibly. During the contact I rang my sponsor so that she could have a word with my son and put a voice to the child's name that I think and talk about so much and afterwards I also rang my mum so that she could pass on her grandmotherly greetings in person. My mum also let me know that V.J is now out of hospital and although he is still a bit shaky on his feet he has gone to the bingo hall. I had something to eat before going to a 6pm meeting and on my way home from that meeting, I received a phone call on my mobile from a tutor at Kensington and Chelsea college inviting me to an interview on Wednesday 25th January at 4.30pm. I asked the tutor if she could change the day, or at least the time, but she couldn't. This has put me in a dilemma because it is my contact day with my son and I will not be able to do both things. When I got home I rang the tutor and explained my problem in full and she mentioned that if I was fifteen minutes to half an hour late in arriving she would wait. But the college is in West Kilburn and I know that when my access with my son ends at 3.30pm, an hour and a half won't be enough time to get there in. So tomorrow I will call my son's social worker and ask if she can change the day for one week, if not, then my supervised contact with my son may have to be cancelled for one week. I have been looking forward to this call from Kensington & Chelsea College for weeks and now that it has arrived it has managed to rain on my parade!

Thursday 12th January 2006

Dear Yvonne,

I awoke this morning after ten hours of sleep to my landline ringing at 9.22am. I was greatful for the call as it was Laura saying that she were not going to be at the poetry class today, so I didn't have to meet her. It was a good job that she rang when she did as I had overslept. After ringing my sponsor and carrying out some suggestions, I rang my son's CQSW and she said she was going to try and change the day to Tuesday or Thursday for the week of my interview. Poetry lesson's went well today. I read a bit of the 'King Oedipus', Greek play, and placed two additional poems of mine on the website. one of the poems was 'Unconditional love' and the following titled 'Sorry' which I wrote for C:

SORRY

If I offended
I never meant to.
It's difficult to explain
But I want to.
Remember that first time?
Well I do.
You asked about "...boys?" okay

Remember your name
I can't seem to.
Hear what you say
I don't appear to.
But at the end of the day
I do respect you
And I am sorry if I've caused offence!

I lead a busy life
We both do.
Over stepping the line
I try not to.
but now that I have
Thank you, for telling me I have been

Make amends
I feel compelled to
I have no defence
For having harrassed you
Redeem myself
I have yet to
But only time will tell.

After the poetry class I went to see my C.P.N to give him my disability Living Allowance renewal form, ask him how far he has got with my housing benefit, tell him the lastest of what is happening with the Kensington and Chelsea college and my son's CQSW and collect some more medication. During my conversation with my C.P.N he told me that it was unlikely that he was going to continue to be my C.P.N as he was going to be relocated in Kennington and I was going to be in Norwood within a week or two. I am quite sad about this as I believe that I get on well with my current C.P.N. Anyway he said that he is going to phone me tomorrow. When I arrived home I found a letter from my solicitor in my letter box confirming what transpired on Tuesday. My next court hearing is Monday 15th May 2006 at 11.30am.

Friday 13th January 2006

Dear Yvonne,

I have had ten hours of peaceful sleep. Today is a Friday the thirteenth and I was born on Friday the thirteenth so I am feeling lucky. Today I attended an 11am appointment in North London, that I had made with Guillermo Llorca-Diaz, my old boss, the P.A.C.E Lesbian Gay Bi-sexual and Transgender LGBT Mental health Advocate volunteer co-ordinator last year, so that I could get some feedback on my worth and collect a copy of the references that allowed me to get the post of LGBT Mental health Advocate Volunteer this time last year after completing my intensive training. When I explained to Guillermo where I was at today he said that it was no wonder I was suffering from low self esteem, I had had another bout of relapse in mental illness, been sectioned and my child is in foster care. My Guillermo gave me some valid and positive feedback that I had not been able to see for myself and he said that he is going to write it up in a letter to me. Plus, he said that if I need any help that I must not be afraid to contact him. He is going to refer me on to another of his colleagues, someone outside of his department that works with preparing people to get into work and pass on my telephone numbers. The following letters are the references that were written for P.A.C.E the first one was from Su Glazier, South London and Maudsley NHS Trust, Head of Modernisation, Developing Organisation and Community and the second one was from a personal friend.

Guillermo Llorca-Diaz
Advocacy Coordinator
PACE
34 Hartham Road
London N7 9JL

Dear Guillermo Llorca-Diaz

Re: Reference for Yvonne Stewart-Williams

I must apologise for the length of time it has taken for me to reply to your request for a reference - it was sitting on my desk among a multitude of competing priorities (such is the state of the health service currently). But, my apologies to Yvonne and to you for my tardiness.

I have known Yvonne Stewart-Williams for approximately 10 years. Yvonne can to my attention after recovering from a period of mental ill health when she expressed a desire to become involved in voluntary work in the hospital. She also joined the service user group in the Maudsley, working to influence the Trust to bring about positive change in services for service users.

I learnt from Yvonne that she was a trained nurse and I found her to be a person with many skills both on an intellectual and practical level. The first piece of work that Yvonne did with me was to complete a course in peer advocacy which allowed her to advocate for (and under the instruction of) in-patients who felt they were not having a say in their own treatment and care.

Over the years Yvonne became involved in many projects which she consistently took very seriously and produced good results. She is a flexible thinker and adapts her skills to many situations. She sat on a Police Liasion committed for the Maudsley, giving the service user perspective. She also acted as a "Ward Representative" i.e. liaising very closely with one ward and gaining improvements for the patients there. She helped in the hospital shop on a regular basis. Yvonne also introduced the Pink Paper into the Maudsley wards - ordering it and delivering copies to all the wards every week. Perhaps her biggest achievement was work she did with the hospital Complaints Department which ran a "Talkback" Forum on a 2 monthly basis. Between the 2 monthly meetings, Yvonne visited numerous in-patient and day hospital sites and ran forums wit the patients there, to look at improvements they wanted in the environment and in their care, Yvonne then brought these comments back to Talkback where senior hospital managers agreed an action plan to implement changes. Yvonne's communication skills were excellent -she made summaries of the points made by patients in a constructive and persuasive way.

Yvonne is an extremely level headed and commiteed person, consistently working for equal rights. Once Yvonne takes on a route or task she puts a great deal of dedication into it. Yvonne has had experience of mental health advocacy over the years, understands the mental health system well and the principles of client-directed advocacy. I feel that she would be entirely suitable for the post of volunteer advocate with PACE and would be an asset to the advocacy team.

Yours sincerely
Su Glazier

Reference for Yvonne Stewart-Williams
Post of Volunteer Advocate

I have known Yvonne Stewart-Williams as a personal friend for over 10 years and I believe that her competent and calm disposition suits the role of a volunteer mental health advocate.

I first met Yvonne in early 1993 when I was teaching German in Lambeth. She was an eager, enthusiastic learner and her commitment and passion was evident as we worked together during that year. Our friendship developed over the years and I came to appreciate her genuineness, warmth, compassion and integrity.

Yvonne's own experiences as a lesbian and single mother in the mental health services equip her wit the insight and empathy to advise others in a similar situation. She is organised, efficient and has an excellent rapport with people of all ages. Her communication skills, both written and verbal are excellent. Yvonne is very resourceful - in the face of adversity, she uses her skills to access all possible sources of help, to research legal information and to enlist people and organisations for support.

I have personal experience of Yvonne's capability of guiding other people without judgement or discrimination and maintaining confidentiality and discretion at all times. In 1998, Yvonne founded the Lambeth branch of a self help group and I joined the group to help me. In chairing most of the group sessions, Yvonne displayed excellent listening skills, was sensitive to peoples needs and encouraged their contributions.

In summary, I highly recommend Yvonne for any position or endeavor that she may seek to pursue. She will be a valuable asset to any organisation.

If you have any further questions, please do not hesitate to contact me.

Saturday 14th January 2006

Dear Yvonne,

I had ten hours of peaceful sleep before doing my rituals, ringing my sponsor, talking to her for a time and then setting off to a meeting. I met Lesley and Nell a lesbian couple from the lesbian and gay community on my way to the bus stop. After saying happy new year to each other we spoke for a while about what was happening in my life and with my son and what was happening in their lives. Whilst Leslie, Nell and I were talking Johnathan passed on his bike and I felt not only a sense of community but a sense of real love and fellowship. After the meeting I hung around in a cafe and chatted a while before coming home on the bus and writing a poem for my sponsor as I went, it is as follows:

My sponsor, what you mean to me
I pray I won't forget
the someone who believes in me
and helps me with my steps
that same one that I phone each day
in times of joy and stress
who cares about my recovery
and kick starts my progress.

I have been invited to go to my sponsor's home this thursday to read through step one line by line together and then go to a meeting together afterwards. Today I feel like I am back on the programme and I really am pleased just knowing that just for today, I have a sponsor that believes in me, and wants to help me in my recovery, gives me the faith to grab the bull by the horns and progress with my recovery. My mother also rang me wanting to find out how I was and wanting to have a chat, telling me that she loves me. I truly feel blessed to have people in my life that provide such unconditional love on a daily basis. Today I am listening to Magic Fm105.4 and thinking about when I last saw my son and he remarked that he was bored when I asked him what he did when he was not with me. I was surprised when I heard him use the word bored. When he was at home with me he went to school five days a week from 8.30-12.30 and on Mondays he went to trampoline lessons. Tuesdays it was pony riding lessons. Wednesday it was karate lessons. Thursday it was drum kit practice. Friday it was his day off. Saturday it was gymnastics in the morning and every other week it was also ice hockey practice. Sunday we relaxed in the morning and then went to Southopia for Sunday lunch together. We hardly watched television in the week chosing the option of reading to him instead, listening to the radio and playing games with him. But at weekends I would let him watch children's television and watch children's animations and films.

It is a difficult thing to take a back seat in the up bringing of one's own child but I know that at this moment in time that I cannot do any better. I miss my son everyday, the conversations, the love, the companionship. It sometime boils down to the small things such as a few weeks ago he lost another of his milk teeth, and told me that the fairy didn't get it because he lost it somewhere, perhaps in the carpet and I was reminded that the tooth before that that he lost he had swollowed it during a session in his kindergarten. I love my son and without a doubt to have him is a decision that I don't regret. I rang my Aunt Madge and wished her a happy new year and it was truly lovely to hear from her. Aunt Madge also told me that she loved me and today I feel wrapped in love.

Sunday 15th January 2006

Dear Yvonne,

Last night I had nine hours of peaceful sleep and after having a fifteen minute laze in bed set to work on my rituals, including a brief chat to my sponsor before going to a meeting. After the meeting I went with a few others to 'Fresh and Wild' and soaked myself in the atmosphere of recovery. Someone commented on how well I seemed and I was pleased to hear it as it confirmed my opinion of my state of mind. On the way home I stopped off outside the Battersea Arts Centre (BAC) to phone book a ticket for next months poetry session before getting on the bus and continuing to read the King Oedipus play that I had started in my poetry class. When I arrived home I rang Lyn and arranged to see her for a cup of tea and a chat later on in the afternoon as Peter has gone skiing for a week and it gives me the opportunity to   share my Marks & Spencers lemon drizzle cake and have Lyn co-write a letter to the housing co-op asking if there is any possibility of having a merger of my flat with the flat next door to mine, as the co-op is thinking of amalgamating flats to eleviate overcrowding and the lesbian and gay community doesn't currently have a family unit.

Monday 16th January 2006

Dear Yvonne,

I had ten and a half hours of peaceful sleep last night and woke up at nine thirty and rang my sponsor without getting up or saying my prayers and drowsily spoke to her telling her about my plight with my laptop and the fact that I am having to retype my back dated diary onto my son's computer as I am unable to use the memory stick on my own computer and her filling me with mirth and making me howl with laughter by saying she doesn't understand anything about what I just said because she is still using quills. After my phone call with my sponsor I got on with my morning ritual and just before I ate my breakfast BAC rang and I booked one ticket for an Apples & Snakes pub quiz at 9pm on Friday 27th January 2006 and one ticket for an Something Dark Lemn Sissay at 7.30pm on Friday 24th February 2006. I was also wanting to see Aladdin at the Old Vic with Sir Ian Mckellen but I don't know if I am going to be able to fulfil my wish due to time and finances. Before going to my group psychotherapy I typed up a few days of my diary. At the group I was talking about the situation with my son and the group consensus was one of great sadness. To be honest if it were not for the programme and the fellowship complete with sponsor I don't think I would be able to see the wood for the trees in my life, as so dense and over powering is the trauma in my life and so difficult my choices that each day I literally have to remind myself that only one day at a time can I work with life on life's term. Whilst I was in the group session my mobile vibrated and it was my mother on the line telling me that V.J's cancer is now affecting his spine and that aside from the possibility of a bath rail being fitted to aid his mobility in the bath, a stair lift may also have to be installed. I have decided to visit my mother this Friday and stay overnight returning home on Saturday evening. If suicide were a viable option I think I might be tempted to take it but it isn't. Not least because it doesn't solve anything it mearly removes me from the picture and negates me of my responsibility to exercise choice. My son would be worse off without his beloved mother for the rest of his life and my mum would be without the daughter that she loves and tries to the best of her abilities to support and what of her doting relationship with her beloved grandson? It could send her to an early grave if she were to live the rest of her life without him. What of my friends and family? And all because I don't really want to move from my abode because I don't want to live outside of a lesbian and gay community, yet my son needs his own room and I live in a one bedroomed flat and it is extremely overcrowded. I fear that my worse fear will be realised and my son will not be able to live with me and may be adopted and lost without trace. I fear I may have yet another relapse and jeopadise everything that I am working for. I fear that I am only getting in the way, more a problem than a solution. Yes it is true that my situation is not an enviable one but I have heard it said philosphically speaking that is always darkest before the dawn. I have just telephoned my son's school finance officer in order to make arrangements to pay his school fees as I see that as being my responsibility, as I chose that school for my son and want him to attend as it benefits him and the finance officer is going to call me back sometime on Wednesday.

Tuesday 17th January 2006

Dear Yvonne,

I had eight hours of peaceful sleep before doing my ritual and getting up and getting ready to go off to my horse riding lesson. This morning on the way to the stables, I felt fear dominate me and it was because when I thought back to last week I found that I wasn't confident with myself on the horse. I was powerless over the horse and I wasn't in control. But like my programme I had people with personal experience in what they were guiding me through i.e.

the other riding instructors who had been where I am now at some point in their lives, I had my own one to one session with my own personal riding instructor (Ben) who is much like my sponsor there to take me personally through the process if I take his suggestions. I have other riders such as Lydia and Julia that share a comarradory, giving verbal encouragement and swopping notes, much like the people in the fellowship. And the horse is like life on life's terms independent with a mind of its own, although there are guidelines and tools to use to get the best from it. I am just filled with gratitude for all the things that I have in my life and all the people who care about me. Today at the stables I was on Bilbo and my instructor was Ben and I had a better lesson than last week even though I was fearful that I didn't know what I was doing and at one point I complained to Ben that I cant control Bilbo because I don't know what to do and Ben gave me the benefit of his experience and instructed me and when I took his suggestions Bilbo did what I wanted him to do and not the other way around. After the lesson I went to a meeting. On my way home I stopped off in Olive Morris house and handed in a copy of my tenancy agreement for my housing benefit. When I arrived at my abode I had a bath, had something to eat and went to another meeting, where I met with my sponsor and told her about my feeling and thoughts last night and my progress today. After she listened to me for a while, she spoke and I was grounded by her words. The next time if ever there is such a time I will be sure to talk to her, or have her speak with me because I know that I need never feel alone. I am not alone.

Wednesday 18th January 2006

Dear Yvonne,

I had ten hours of peaceful sleep and did my rituals before phoning my sponsor. I look forward to making contact with her each morning as just knowing that someone is on my side and believes in me, helps me to transcend life's troughs. I also text my sponsor, when I reflect on the gratitude I have for my life and what I am achieving in it from the position that I am in. Last night when I saw my sponsor she lent me 'The Steps We Took' A teacher of the twelve steps shares his experience, strength, and hope with all those recovering from addictions, all who want to recover, and all who love them. Written by Joe McQ, so that I could read step one before

I meet with her on Thursday at her home. Today I rang Foyles bookshop to order a copy for myself. It is going to take several weeks to arrive but my sponsor said I could borrow the book until I obtain my own copy. My sponsor remembers my clean, sober, sane time and I find it deeply touching and humbling as most days I can't even remember it myself and have to look it up in my diary. When I asked her if she would sponsor me, she said she would have to pray about it first before she could give her answer and that she would get back to me in four days. I was bemused, but as I get to know her more I realise that she is deeply spiritual and committed to the programme, and I know I need her in my life to guide me, much like Ben guides me with horses. I rang my son's school finance officer and it is systems all go.

I have been given a bursary of twenty percent discount and I'm pleased so when I receive the standing order, I will gladly sign it and send it back as I feel the school is helping me realise my dream for my son. I rang my housing officer asking if she had read my letter, which she had and thinks that it is a good idea to merge the flats but she has to take it to a management committee meeting. I had a good time with my son this afternoon, in my supervised contact. I had purchased a counting game for him from Oxfam on my way to meeting with him and he liked it. Lyn collected my son from school today and brought him to the local authority meeting point. She said that several of the parents at my son's school had been asking for me and it cheered me up to think that I had not been forgotten. My son was awashed with mud today and was carrying his trousers in a plastic bag as he had slipped over at school. When he spoke to my mum on the phone in my presence and she asked him if he had hurt himself, he said no but he had fun. He was calling his grandmother supernan when he spoke to her on the phone and when he handed the phone back to me, my mother sounded pleased that she could convey how much she loved him and cared. My son remembered to bring the locomotive that I built for him from his K'nex building set and asked me to build him a aircraft which I did, using up most of the pieces in the box and taking most of the supervision time concentrating on following the instruction in the booklet. I also found time to go with him to the newspaper shop and watch him choose a 'Wallace & Gromit' comic, a 'Thunderbirds' magazine and a Cartoon Network magazine. He entertained himself with them and laughed out loud with Wallace and Gromit but shreaked when he saw evidence of the Were rabbit. We shared some sweets with each other that I had purchased for him, knowing that he liked them, at the stables. When he looked at my jacket he was reminded of the stables and told me that he went horse riding too but he didn't like it. As usual he didn't want to leave when it was time to say goodbye and had to be coaxed into leaving, but at least he did not cry, After my son left the local authority building, I had to make my way from Streatham to Camberwell as I also had a meeting with Ros Dunning of Dunning & Co Solicitors, to go over my threshold documents. Ros also told me that my son's court guardian's solicitor had written to her backing my request to see my son somewhere other than an office and for a longer period. I told her about my dilemma with Kensington and Chelsea college and asked her to write to my son's solicitors. I told her about my request to my housing manager and asked her if she could write a letter to them. I also told her that I was back on track with my son's school fees and the outcome of the meeting regarding the bursary. After I left her office I felt lifted with support and sent her an e-mail with my housing co-op's address and went to a meeting. I really want to share my gratitude with someone. I phoned my mum but she said that she is a bit tired. I rang my sponsor but I got her voicemail. A rang but she is still in Atlanta.

I sent a text to my sponsor and when I put my phone down, I got a text from K saying to keep well and that her phone is not working because she is in Trinidad. So I am going to type up one day of back dated diary, put it down on my gratitude list and say it to my higher power in my prayers tonight. I have just typed up 'Way Back When' and recall that it was my first pronounced mental ill health episode, when I was doing film, media and photograpy. All I could think as I was typing it up was, "you wasn't well Yvonne" and "thank goodness, you are not there today!"

Thursday 19th January 2006

Dear Yvonne,

I had just under eight hours of sleep and woke up remembering my dream. It was a using dream that had Mohammed Ali the once world champion boxer and he was snorting cocaine and after watching him do it, I followed suit. To be honest it is unlikely in reality that Mohammed has ever snorted cocaine and if the moral of the story is to warn me that the end is none too pleasant because Mohammed is a man that lives with the disease of Parkinsons then I can consider myself warned! It is my first using dream and although I wasn't distressed by it, I know that using just for today is not a solution or an option. On radio 4 this morning there was talk of cannabis possibly staying classified as a class C drug plus much talk of its possible link to mental illness and so I know with my type of mind, my drug of choice must be sobriety! Also on radio 4 this morning I heard that the country of Nigeria is going to ban same-sex marriages, making sure that it never becomes law! I have a poetry class this morning followed by a meeting with my sponsor at her home to go through step one and then a meeting.

Friday 20th January 2006

Dear Yvonne.

I had nine hours of peaceful sleep last night and woke up to the sound of a text at 8am which was A asking me what the weather was like in London. I dozed off for another half hour before replying to her. I was really exhausted when I went to bed last night, really mentally fatigued. I had started off my activities in the day by going to poetry class. only to leave there before the class started and hot foot it to see my C.P.N as I had rung him from my mobile to ask him to send a letter to my co-op to back my request. He said he was unable to do it because I was going to have a new worker as everybody from that building was going to be at their new work stations as of Monday. He wanted to give me some more supplies of medication, a map with the directions to the new offices that I am going to be frequenting and say goodbye. It is a shame about losing my John Hunt my C.P.N because he is an openly gay man and I found strength from him and a lot of support as a lesbian. The last time I had an openly gay professional working with my case was before my son was born and that was a mental health social worker (CQSW) called Jeremy Walsh and I stayed sane for nearly four years. After leaving John, I went back to my poetry class, where we were comparing women's poems dated from the 1700's and then reading a surreal poem play. With half an hour of the lesson left, we were asked to write a poem dialogue and finish it for homework. I didn't have lunch after poetry with the class as I was going straight to my sponsor's home and had purchased some lunch from Marks & Spencers. On arriving at my sponsor's home I received a phone call from Guillermo asking to see me again as there might be a chance for me to still volunteer as an advocate at PACE. I made an arrangement to see him at 11am on Friday 27th January 2006. I then had lunch and read through step one with my sponsor, collected my step one homework and accompanied her to a meeting afterwards before returning home and going to bed, falling asleep and waking up to the text message sound on my mobile phone, doing my ritual and leaving a message on my sponsors voicemail. I went to my mother's home today on the train and got to her place just in time to accompany her to her GP's where I sat with her while she explained, (our family were treated by his father before him) about wanting a bath rail and a stair chair. Her doctor was very compassionate and sympathetic and instructed us to collect the number for the social services so that V.J could be assessed.

I rang the number and my mother spoke to them before we had lunch and I returned to my abode, writing my poetry class homework on the train. In my letter box I found the letter from my son's school finance officer, completed it and will send it off tomorrow. I found a letter from the DLA department asking why I had not yet replied to the letter they had previously sent and I found a letter from Amy Donovan the LGBT Anti-Hate Crime Coordinator at Lambeth Crime Prevention Trust, regarding www.lambethLGBTforum.org.uk with dates of forthcoming meetings at the Brixton Town Hall the first of which is Thursday 26th January 2006.

Saturday 21st January 2006

Dear Yvonne,

I had nine and a half hours of peaceful sleep before doing my rituals, calling my sponsor, having my breakfast and setting off to a meeting. On my way to my meeting I sent some text messages out to various people and in one of the replies someone invited me out to dinner at a South Kensington restaurant at 9pm this evening and I am looking forward to it. I mentioned that I didn't have any money, but they said that was okay, all I was required to do was eat as it was a restaurant that her boyfriend worked in. I am currently listening to Mariah Carey's Number One US Hits CD on volume two and am going to share with you the poem dialogue that I wrote yesterday on the train. It is as follows:

Jesus Creepers

Sinner-Crikey, here comes Jesus creepers, watch out lads, he'll spot our sneakers, notice we aint no bible preachers, and stop to bend our ears back.

Jesus Creeper-Ar my good man, would you help me if you can, I am a man of the cloth, guiding sinners is my plan, to the path of the lord, making heatherns understand, God is love and he loves you

Sinner-Jez sorry mate, just aint got the time, was meant to be somewhere at eight, and it's now quarter to nine, would have love to have been of service, but it's really not my line. I'm afraid I'll have to desert you.

Jesus Creeper-Hmm hmm, just one minute, thou child of God, refusing God's work, appears very odd. your reasoning is very good, but I'm giving you a prod, as too much of it could hurt you!

Sinner-Put me down, Jesus man, as you don't know where I've been, to hell is half the journey I've trod and lack is what I've seen, a self help recovery group, is helping me stay clean, and I could do without your pressure!

Jesus Creeper-Good lords, it's a sinner, of the most intense kind, I've been praying for one like you, to come into my life, to tax me and reveal the follies of my mind and guide me closer to our father,

Sinner-Oh for crying out loud, I havent got all day, Just tell me what you want, Just say what you have to say, I bet I've heard it all before, but I'll listen anyway, I'll be honest willing and openminded

Jesus Creeper-From the mouths of babes! What did I hear you say, openminded, honest and willing just for today, I've been blind for so long, but this is the answer to my prayers, Thank you lord for keeping me a believer

Sinner-I'm glad your pleased and happy you've found it, the missing pieces to some of life's mysteries, and I am humbled that I have helped you in your discovery, fairwell and have a good day

Jesus Creeper-To think the very one, that I had brow beaten, supplied the wisdom, I had been seeking, prevented me, leaving the Garden of Eden, good day young man fairwell.

Sunday 22nd January 2006

Dear Yvonne,

I had eight and a half hours of peaceful slumber last night, having got to bed at midnight after going out to dinner at Carpaccio at 4 Sydney street, just off the Fulham road. I had a great time eating a three course delicious meal and drinking cocktails minus alcohol, and ending on a night cap of several cups of camomile tea. So this morning I was able to arrive at my meeting for my tea commitment without a hangover and completely compus mentus. On the way to the meeting I wrote a text that I sent to most of my family and friends that I have a mobile number for and it is as follows:

Laughter is my sun filled day.
Smiles are clear skies, shades of grey and or spots of rain.
Tears are darkened clouds or heavy rain.
Grief is my thunder storm, with seemingly no end.
But through it all, what ever my day,
I know that you are there to help me, and it makes life worth living,
Just for today.

I had various replies from my sent text, but Johnathan sent me a text saying that I mustn't forget to put it in my diary/journal. I replied thanking him as I had not considered it before he mentioned it, and he sent a text back saying it was a marvellous turn of phrase. To which I replied that I didn't understand what that meant and he sent the answer back in a text. I feel so blessed to have the people in my life that I have and at times like these I am truly grateful. At the meeting it was decided by the group that I would now have the keys to the doors so that I can get in early and put the urn on for tea. I am so chuffed about being deemed responsible, reliable and trustworthy. I have never had the privilege of being a prefect or a head girl at school but this has made up for it. At the moment I am listening to the Kirk Whalum CD 'The Gospel according to Jazz chapter 1' which is a jazz gospel CD that I love listening to, but seldom get time to do so these days. I am going to make a start on the questions of the first step that my sponsor gave me on Thursday as I haven't looked at them since and I don't want to procrastinate. But I am going to type up another day of my back diary.

Monday 23rd January 2006

Dear Yvonne,

I am currently listening to Mary J Blige's 'Share my World' CD having just returned from my group psychotherapy, having had a productive time there, and deciding within it to get on the buses one stop later and get off one stop earlier for exercise, one of the other participants lent me the film 'Sylvia' on video. It is a film about the poet Sylvia Plath I was going to watch it whilst I had lunch but when I went to put it in the video player I found the film '102 Dalmations' and was reminded of my son who loved to watch it and would have been the last person to have been watching it. Just knowing that Sylvia took her own life leaving children behind in her mental distress has just for today made me to decide to watch Sylvia on another day when I can enjoy her contribution to the world without thinking and reflecting on the chaos of my world!. Last night I had nine hours of peaceful sleep and woke up to my landline ringing.

It was my very first sponsor's fiancé calling to tell me that the reason that he hasn't replied to my calls and texts is that he has had a relapse and is currently in City Roads detoxing. I am sad that my old sponsor had to go through the sorrows of relapse. But I am glad that he has made his way back into recovery quickly. As I love and respect my old sponsor a part of me wants to be a part of his solution and not a part of his problems and his fiancé let me know today that he loves me too. She was just worried that I might become unstable if I knew what has happened to him. But I am just glad that he is not still out there or worse still, dead. After that call I called my sponsor and told her why I was late calling her. During my conversation with her she asked me if I had started my step one questions yet to which I had to reply no as I hadn't. We agreed that I would make a start on it this afternoon. This morning I went to the new offices in Norwood for my health team, spoke to the team leader, explained what I needed done and gave him my DLA letter and the name and address for my housing co-op. He said that my notes had not been unpacked yet but took my telephone number and said that he would ring me. In my letter box today I found my electricity bill £73.19. I will pay it tomorrow. I feel tired today.

Tuesday 24th January 2006

Dear Yvonne,

Last night I had nine and a half hours of peaceful sleep, did my rituals, had breakfast and set off to my horse riding lesson. I rang my son's CQSW before my lesson to find out if I was going to have a supervised contact with my son today, but the someone else answered my son's social workers phone and said that she was in court today and had been in court yesterday. I also rang my sponsor and left a message on her voicemail. I was riding Bilbo this week and Ben took my lesson. Before the lesson this week I wasn't as fearful and asked for riding tips guidance from Ben whilst walking towards the indoor school. All in all it was a better lesson this week. I stayed in rising trot for much longer and felt to myself that I had made progress. Lydia and Julia both said that I looked better on the horse this week, and even though Bilbo at points in the lesson stretched his neck and raised his head in the air I wasn't terrified and after taking instructions from Ben I was able to guide Bilbo to do the things Ben wanted me to have him do. I noticed this week that I trusted Ben more. At the end of the lesson I did my best dismount yet. After leaving the stables I walked to the station with Julia and met Lydia on the platform, we all spoke about riding until it was time for us to each leave the train.

It is so good for me to have that companionship. They keep track of my progress and report it back to me and also give me the benefit of their riding experience. I went to Ray's Jazz the cafe in Foyles bookshop to purchase a sandwich and a soft drink and have them for lunch and took the opportunity whilst in Foyles to go to the Silver moon section on the third floor to buy the latest Karin Kallmaker lesbian romance titled 'Just like that' before going to a 1pm meeting. On my way home from the meeting I started to read 'Just like that' and have decided to read it each Tuesday and leave it with my riding bag. In my letter box on my arrival home I found a letter from my solicitor with a copy of a letter enclosed from my son's local authority solicitors stating that they had given permission for me to have a two hour contact with him today Tuesday 24th January 2006. Obviously I had missed it as I was reading the letter at 4pm. So I rang my solicitor's secretary and told her what had happened and she is going to write a letter back to the solicitors stating what happened. My poor son, I hope he wasn't taken to the meeting point and kept waiting disappointed that he hadn't seen me. How horrible that would have been for him. As for me I am tortured just thinking about it. My solicitor also sent me a copy of the Threshold for my perusal and response. I rang to confirm I agreed to its sentiments. The other letter I received today was one from my old C.P.N which had enclosed within it my DLA application renewal form. So I rang the team leader that I spoke to yesterday and told him that I have them and between us we agreed that I would deliver them to the Norwood office tomorrow. I am going to get something to eat and listen to Erykah Badu's CD 'Mama's Gun' while I do before I get going off to another meeting this evening. I am still feeling tired but not as tired as yesterday.

Wednesday 25th January 2006

Dear Yvonne,

I had ten and a half hours of peaceful sleep last night. I wanted to have a lie-in this morning so I rang my sponsor and when her voicemail came on I left a message and snuggled back up to be only to have my phone ringing a moment later with my sponsor on the line, wide awake, full of beams and offering me suggestions to call my son's social worker and try and arrange a time to see him. By the time my sponsor finished talking to me I was wide awake, so I did my rituals and got up. After breakfast I hand delivered my DLA form in to the team leader. My son's social worker rang me back on my mobile and arranged that I can see my son tomorrow 2pm until 4pm. By the time I returned home and looked in my letter box, I had received a letter from Lambeth a reminder for council tax for the sum of £182.32 to be paid by 29th January 2006 or I will have my installments cancelled and have to pay the balance owed which would be £294.32. I rang my old C.P.N to ask him the name of the benefits advisor that was dealing with it. And then I tried to make contact with her but she had apparently gone to the benefits office. I found out from the team leader that she works on Tuesdays and Thursdays, so I will ring her tomorrow. I also had a letter from my GP's practice inviting me to a patient participation forum, as I had mentioned some months ago when they were doing a survey that I would be interested. It will be on Tuesday 7th February at 7pm. I went to my interview at Kensington and Chelsea college and was accepted. But tomorrow I will have to go to the benefit office and ask them to stamp a letter I was given so that I can get concessionary fees. Whilst I was at the college Guillermo rang and left a message on my voicemail asking me to call him back as he had double booked our meeting and he wanted to change it for a slightly later time. I feel exhausted and ready for bed, which is exactly where I am headed right now!

Thursday 26th January 2006

Dear Yvonne,

Last night I had ten hours of peaceful restful sleep, did my rituals and got up with a slight headache, which seemed to follow me for half of my day. I went to the dss office in Brixton and got my letter signed and stamped so finances are not stopping me from going to college. I left from there and went to Norwood and waited to see my housing benefits advisor who was very helpful and rang Olive morris house and found out that next Tuesday they are going to be processing my claim. She then rang the council tax office and based on the information that she gave them they put a stop on their demands. I left from there and went home and rang the Baytree Centre to tell them that I am now going to be enrolling on a course with Kensington and Chelsea college and so I won't be joining their course.

I rang my sponsor. I rang my son's social worker to ask her to permanently change the contact day starting from next week as it clashes with my new timetable. But she was off sick so I obtained the email address of her boss and sent her an email and copied it to my solicitor. I rang Guillermo and told about my change in circumstances and asked to be excused from being considered for volunteer advocacy. I then collected some toys and clothes for my son that his grandmother had bought for him and went off to my poetry class, where we were reading the writings of William Blake. I arrived at poetry over an hour late and left three quarters of an hour early. Leaving there to go to my supervised contact with my son, who arrived half an hour late. I rang my mother so that my son could speak to her and he did. It was a good session with him, his new tooth can be seen making its way through. My son had a runny sore nose, but he wasn't under the weather. We went off during the session to buy some comics and confectionaries and at the end of the session he did not delay in leaving and neither did he cry. After my son left I got a bus from Streatham to Brixton and went to an internet cafe, where I sent an e-mail to my solicitor telling her about my acceptance on the access course and my thoughts on it. I also sent an email to my Aunt Debbie, in New York, U.S.A. I have known Debbie since I was about eighteen years old when she visited London, England with her husband, my mother's brother George with their then four year old daughter Tangee. Tangee has since grown into a woman and mother of three children. But the affection that I have for her mother has never faded. I have a Lambeth LGBT forum meeting to attend tonight, where a discussion about the David Morley gay murder will take place.

Friday 27th January 2006

Dear Yvonne,

Last night I had ten hours of blissful restful sleep. Did my rituals, had breakfast and about to type up a day of back diary before ringing my sponsor and seeking guidance about some writing for my step one. I am going to go to a lunchtime meeting as I have not been to a meeting for two days and am not going to be at a meeting tonight because I am going to a poetry event at the BAC tonight. Last night at I went to the 'David Morley Verdict' meeting with guest speakers Sue Jacobs (CPS) DCI Nick Scola & Supt Alistair Sutherland (Met.) at Lambeth Concorde 336 Brixton Road, heard about the investigation into the murder and the way the police and crown prosecution service worked in the way they did. In my opinion the meeting was useful. When I sat in the audience a member of the LGBT forum asked me if my son was not with me tonight as he is so used to my son accompanying me to most events, but I told him no he wasn't with me. Whilst at the meeting I purchased a 'Lesbian, gay bisexual, trans history month 2006 badge and picked up a programme for Lambeths first ever LGBT History Month Feb 2006 of which I attended one planning meeting last year with Amy Donovan and Daniel Fitzgerald. I am so happy about my college place. I feel that now I am once again on the ladder to achieving my aims of gaining a qualification and weaning myself off benefits and earning an honest crust for myself and my family ie my son and my mum. Ramona, one of my friends from Berlin, I have known her for eleven years and met her when I was at college doing an access to Film, Photography and media course. Ramona rang me to tell me that she is stopping in London for the night of Wednesday 15th February 2006 on her way to Tobago's carnival. She hasn't been to England since my son was a few weeks old and when she came at that time, we, me her and my two month old baby, went to the Notting Hill carnival. Ramona carried him in a harness on her chest and we all had a good time dancing to the music and watching the floats. I am going to explain what has happened to myself and my son when she arrives

Saturday 28th January 2006

I had nine hours of peaceful sleep last night, did my rituals and left a message on my sponsors voicemail. I started my periods today. A is back from Atlanta and rang me and I brought her up to speed with all the events that have taken place in my life. I went to a meeting and stopped for a cup of tea afterwards. I bought the milk for my tomorrow's tea commitment, a new pair of walking boots to wear in for college and a step counter so that I can find out how much I am walking increase it and get fit. I sent another e-mail to Debbie, telling her about my college course and my son's forthcoming local authority review. I sent several text messages to K in Trinidad explaining about my new student status and I went to another meeting this evening, went to a cafe for a snack and came home.

Sunday 29th January 2006

Dear Yvonne,

I have broken with my Sunday routine of listening to gospel and I'm listening to Aaliyah's Aaliyah c,d this was the last CD that she did before she died in that aeroplane crash. I am not trying to be racey but I am quite smitten still with track 3 'Rock the boat' it seems odd to me that I have no one who seems to be attracted to me the way I am to C, perhaps that is the most obvious sign that I am still sick. My sponsor told me on the phone this morning that she admires me, but in context she admires the fact that I get up and go to morning meetings and anyway it doesn't count as she is my sponsor and to some degree is there to boulster my confidence (I suppose) It is odd that I haven't been in a relationship for so long, not that I am meant to be in one at this stage of my recovery anyway! But I don't even seem to get aroused anymore and seem to be dead to visual stimulus. I blame the medication, I have heard it said long before that it is a liquid cosh and I have lived long enough to be on it and prove that it has made me impotent. don't laugh but even if someone were to make advances I don't think that I could cope with it. I am now living my life just like that character in the long running programme 'Prisoner Cell Block H' I forget her name but she was the lesbian character that went around wearing dungarees, I think her name was Judy but I'm not sure. Meaning that everybody knows that she is a lesbian but somehow she never seems to have a partner, not even for a night.

Monday 30th January 2006

Dear Yvonne,

Today I went to a local authority review of my son. Present at the meeting was his kindergarten teacher that he has had for the last three years, his social worker, his psychologist that he had the last time that he was taken into foster care, his court guardian whom he also had the last time he was taken into foster care, his foster mother, a fostering link support worker and a independent reviewing officer. Lyn and Pete were also invited but Pete came with my son and took him for a pizza lunch. This was the second review, the first was held on 14th November 2005 before I started to have contact with my son. From the review I heard that my son had had a sight, hearing and dental check in November 2005 and that he is going to have an assessment of himself and his family that is going to end on 3rd April 2006 and is going to be done independently of, though in collaboration with his psychologist for the court. I heard that he was distressed when first fostered and that since having contacts with me has become a lot happier including in school. I heard that it was difficult at first for him to go to bed without the main light on, but that now he has a small night light on instead. I heard that he refuses any suggestions from his foster parent and social worker to engage in any after school activities and when karate was mentioned his teacher said he would do it if his mum did it with him. Even swimming stirred no interest in him and he had asked me if he could go swimming and I had booked swimming lessons for him at the Oasis in Camden, which he was supposed to have started a week after he went into foster care. I heard that he was having to wait at school until 2pm after his school finishes at 12.30pm as there was a problem with his collection. I heard from his teacher that he was playing with his hands a lot. she suggested buying playdough for him as he would be able to have an activity to engage in with his hands. I also heard that Lyn and Pete have put themselves forward to apply to foster him if he doesn't come home to me. Generally the reports and feedback that I was hearing was that he is a lot happier since I have been back in his life. The next review will be in six months on Monday 12th June 2006 just days before the court's final hearing on 20th June -22nd June 2006.

Tuesday 31st January 2006

Dear Yvonne,

When I eventually got to sleep last night I had eight hours of peaceful sleep. Today was my first day at the Wornington Road site of Kensington and Chelsea college and I awoke excited and enthusiastic. The other students in the class seem friendly. I introduced myself to them and told them that I was gay and that it is not a secret and they seemed to take it in their stride. I had one lesson today and that was numeracy. We worked on decimals and after the lesson I purchased the book 'Maths The Basic Skills curriculum edition' a nelson thornes publication from Waterstones bookshop because I was given homework to be getting on with from the tutor. Whilst in the lesson I found out that in my English literature tomorrow I will be working on Macbeth and I am looking forward to it. On my way home I purchased some Marks and Spencers perishables. I am going to a meeting tonight. I sent a text message to C today. This is the first text that I have sent C since sending her a text saying that I would be texting her infrequently as I didn't want to bore her.

Wednesday 1st February 2006

Dear Yvonne,

It is the first day of the LGBT History month. It is the first one ever! It was also the second day of my college life, having had eight and a half hours of peaceful sleep last night, I proceed to do my ritual, get ready, have breakfast and proceed to the Hortensia road site of Kensington and Chelsea college. I had never been there before, but armed with my A-Z in my hand I found it without incident. We did read Shakepeare's Macbeth. The class had already started reading it last week so today we started from Act 2 scene 3. It is during this scene that the king is discovered murdered. I read the part of Lennox and stumbled over and fluffed nearly every line. I have decided that I am going to read Macbeth at home from the beginning, and try to improve my oration. I will practice it in my poetry class each week as we take it in turns to read. It seems when I get nervous as I do in such settings I tend to make a hash of what I do, and although I know that it won't improve overnight, I know it definitely won't improve if I don't work on it. During the class we watched the beginning of the film 'Shakespeare in Love' and I loved the scene of William Shakespeare on the psychiatrist couch in search of the the the cure for his writers block, Its just like my ending up in a psychiatrist's chair with a block to life! The tutor gave us details of Southwark Playhouse as it is running Macbeth until February 11th, so I will try and see it tomorrow if I can get a ticket. The tutor also introduced the class to two books that I liked so I purchased them in Waterstones on my way back from the class, and they are 'A million little pieces' by James Frey, it's a non fiction book about drugs and drug taking, My English literature tutor said in class today that she hasn't been able to put it down since she started reading it. And the second book which the other student's in the class couldn't stop reading today was 'Pride and Promiscuity The lost sex scenes of Jane Austen' by Arielle Eckstut. I forgot to call my sponsor this morning and didn't remember to until after 1pm.

Thursday 2nd February 2006

Dear Yvonne,

I had ten and a half hours of peaceful restful sleep last night. Did my rituals and rang my sponsor, leaving a message on her voicemail. After breakfast, I set off to Woolworth's to buy some playdough for my son to play with at our supervised contact session today. And then I went to my poetry class with Cooltan Arts. In the class today we read some of the works of Christian Bok, from his 'Eunoia' publication. We read the work he did using single vowel text and took it in turns to read it out. I put my Jesus Creepers poem on the website. before going off to meet my son. My son enjoyed using the playdough, and didn't look at his Mr Bean comic or eat his sweets because of it. He made me several love hearts and flowers, because he said that he loves me. and at my suggestion he made me a Gromit. I have brought them all home with me. This evening I am going to type up day 17th December 2005 of my back diary whilst listening to a Macbeth audio book performed by Stephen Dillane, Fiona Shaw and full cast.

Friday 3rd February 2006

Dear Yvonne,

Last night I had nine hours of peaceful sleep and woke up with a start as I had overslept. I quickly did my rituals, got ready, had breakfast and dashed off to get the bus to the tube station. I arrived at the stables just in time. I saw Ben on my arrival, and he asked me why I wasn't doing Tuesday. I told him about college being the cause of the day change. I had Bilbo again today and it was just me, Ben and Bilbo in the inside school today. I spent most of the lesson actively engaging in rising trot and today I did my first 20 metres circle in rising trot! At some point in the lesson as I was riding around the school in rising trot Madonna's 'Like a prayer' started playing over the loud speaker system and I was reminded of my son who loves that track. I was really pleased with today's lesson, during it I focused my mind on remembering the rhythm of riding and the techniques. Ben wasn't shouting so much at me today and I believe he was also pleased with my progress. After the lesson I stopped off in the stables cafe for a decaffeinated tea and a couple of slices of marmite toast. Before going to a lunchtime meeting in Soho, stopping off on the way there to subscribe to Amnesty International because I was amongst other things sold on their anti domestic violence. After leaving the meeting I went to West Norwood to collect my medication from a C.P.N. When I finally arrived home I was famished and got myself something to eat whilst watching another installment of the film 'Sylvia'. Because I know that she committed suicide I just can't seem to bear to watch it now that it is coming to the final stages of the film. I am going to do some more work on my step one and then go to a meeting tonight.

Saturday 4th February 2006

Dear Yvonne,

Last night I had nine and a half hours of peaceful restful sleep. And conducted my usual morning routine. After having breakfast I typed up day 18th December 2005 of my back diary, before going to a meeting. After the meeting I went for coffee with some of the participants before coming home and finding in my letterbox a letter from the housing benefits office. Which entails me over the next two weeks going to my mothers home for my passport and driving licence id and getting a letter from my psychiatrist to explain why I didn't respond to the housing benefits requests for do a home visit, I will go to Norwood on Monday morning to try and sort out the doctors letter and give them a copy of my letter. I am currently listening to Jill Scott's 'Who is Jill Scott?' CD. I just love track 8 'It's Love' and I am about to do some more work on my step 1 and type up another day of my back diary, before going to watch a performance of Macbeth at Southwark Playhouse this evening. I have now read the play and over the next few days will go through it line by line with the dictionary out.

Sunday 5th February 2006

Dear Yvonne,

I had eight hours of peaceful sleep last night. I read my 'Just for today and basic book after saying my morning prayer and reading my gratitude list. I then got up and got ready to go to my morning meeting. I chose to get there an hour early so that I heat the urn for the meeting. After the meeting I went with a few of the other participants to 'Fresh & Wild' for a hot drink and something to eat. I went straight home when I left and did some more work on my step 1 before watching the ending of the film 'Sylvia' whilst I had something to eat before setting off to go to an evening meeting,

Monday 6th February 2006

Dear Yvonne,

I had eight hours of peaceful sleep last night, did my ritual and got ready to go to Norwood. I waited around for almost an hour before I was seen by the duty person. She assured me that she would pass the photocopy of my letter and my request for it to be seen as urgent on to the team leader. I also asked her to give a copy of the letter to the housing benefits advisor. After leaving Norwood, I went to see my mum. I had rung her last night, to let her know I would be visiting her. During my visit, we did some grocery shopping, and after lunch my mum spent some time explaining about punctuation and telling me her favourite subject at school was math's and that she liked algebra. After she had finished I spent some time talking my mum through the process of using her computer. On her word pad she typed a letter to my son and saved it under the title 'first choice'. Both she and I were pleased with her progress. And it won't be long before she is confident enough to do it by herself as she was reading the instruction manual. Just before I left, V.J came home, and was as pleased to see me, as I him. On the train home I worked on a poem using only words with the vowel I in them. If it is okay I may put it on the website on Thursday. This evening I worked on my step one, and I have just about concluded it.

Tuesday 7th February 2006

Dear Yvonne,

Last night I had seven and a half hours of peaceful sleep. Did my rituals, and got ready to go to college. I arrived for class half an hour early. So I took the opportunity to text C, ring my sponsor and enquire if the college did a punctuation class, but it does a literacy class instead. After my numeracy lesson, I met with my course tutor and obtained my enrollment documents and officially enrolled on the course. It cost £48.00. On the way home, I stopped off in Marks & Spencers to buy some perishables. I then went home had something to eat whilst I listened to my Macbeth audio book, taking the time to read the play from a book alongside it in parts. I rang several London universities asking them to send me their undergraduate prospectus in the post for my perusal. I rang my psychiatric health team in West Norwood, to see if any progress had been made regarding my letters. But there hadn't been, and I was disappointed. Then I went off to a meeting.

Wednesday 8th February 2006

Dear Yvonne,

I had nine hours of peaceful restful sleep before doing my morning rituals and getting ready for college. Today in English literature I read the part of Lady Macbeth and made a better job of it than I had with Lennox last week. The next book that we are going to be reading is Beloved by Toni Morrison so I am going to try and finish reading it in the next week. I went to my Study skills class for the first time after Eng Lit and my tutor filled out a form for me to attempt to get help with my punctuations, grammer and overall presentation. I then came home, had something to eat and then typed out ten days of back diary.

Thursday 9th February 2006

Dear Yvonne,

Last night I had ten hours of peaceful sleep, did my morning rituals and got ready to go to see my new mental health social worker. My social worker gave me the letter that I requested on Monday and after I left the Norwood office, I tried to submit it in at Olive Morris house but didnt have enough time to do it and not be late to see my son. So I did the contact with my son first. My son was well. I had brought some small pots of playdough for him to use and together we went to the shop and bought a few comics, some confectionaries and a drink. During the contact we read the comics and between us we consumed the confectionaries and drink. I rang my mum whilst I was with my son and they spoke to each other. I also gave my son's foster mother two three piece suits and some trousers that were at my mother's home and asked her to try them on my son and let the legs down if they were too short. At the end of the visit, I went back to Olive Morris House and submitted the documents that they had requested. And left from there and went to a meeting. I am feeling tired this evening. It is my ninetieth day in the fellowship today.

Friday 10th February 2006

Last night I had nine hours of peaceful sleep. I did my morning rituals and got ready to go to my horse riding lesson. Today I had Bilbo with Ben instructing. At first the lesson went without event. I was suprised that I got Bilbo to trot when I wanted him to. It was a cold and icy morning and the air was fresh. Most people hanging around the stable were shivering and commenting on the cold. And even I, myself put my gloves on as my finger tips felt stung with the cold, but when I got into the ride with Bilbo I no longer noticed, and got into my stride, though Ben urged me to quicken my pace. About half way through the lesson Bilbo started to do rising trot in the direction that he wanted to, and at times into the path of oncoming trotting horses. I found that I couldn't control him as he was also stretching his neck, dispite Ben shouting instructions to remedy the situation. I became stiff with fear and after saying the serenity prayer to myself, I told Ben that I didn't want to do rising trot on Bilbo. I only wanted to walk. But after walking and feeling a little bit more confident I decided to do rising trot and Bilbo after a short time started his antics again. I felt as if Bilbo was going to tug me out of my seat and became rivited with fear and so asked Ben to end the lesson.

After I got off Bilbo's back I told Ben that I wasn't going to give Bilbo the carrots that I had bought for him and that next week I wanted Hughie instead. But when I went to the reception desk, and I told them what had happened and explained that I was truly afraid. They persuaded me to get on Hughie and walk around on him for ten minutes today. And I am truly grateful for that suggestion as like they said the negative experience of Bilbo would have gone round and round in my mind and festered more negative thoughts and by next week I would be a bag of nerves which the horse would sense and perhaps react to. At the desk they explained that horses are like us humans and have off days too. And perhaps as it was a cold morning Bilbo got up to some antics. I went out doors with Hughie and found him a delight. I reminded Ben to tighten his neck strap as I remembered him from before. It was the quickest ten minutes of riding such was the degree of my enjoyment. Today I finished my back diary typing.

Saturday 11th February 2006
Dear Yvonne,

Last night I had ten hours of peaceful restful sleep. I went through my usual routine and then got ready to go to a lunchtime meeting. I rang my sponsor from my landline this morning as I only had thirteen pounds worth of credit on my mobile to last until Tuesday. Today she made an arrangement with me to go through my step one with me tomorrow. She is going to meet me in Battersea and then we are going to go back to her home in Parsons green. I have thought about it all day and I am of the belief that I could have offered her the opportunity to get to know me better by allowing her to see where I live for a change. But my place is a caricature of the late Quentin Crisps at this moment in time with dust up to the high heavens and although I am not ashamed of my abode. I have just realised that I rarely invite people back to my place anyway. And even C who I adore waited outside in her vehicle. Anyway I can always alter the destination tomorrow when I meet her, but on top of it I have just paid my son's school fees and my college fees and I am very low on funds, and as such don't know what I would feed her. I am currently listening to Mozart and have decided to leave the problem dusty small flat coupled with whether I will be a host tomorrow on the back burner for now. Johnathan now has in his possession the start of my letter writing until yesterday. I managed to get it on the memory stick and he phoned me to say that he has placed it on a word document and has gone out to buy ink and paper. so that he can read through the first draft of it. I am truly grateful to him.

In my letter box I got some information from the D'Arcy Lainy Foundation an organisation that took over from Pink Parents. I had subscribed to Pink Parents in the past which was for alternative sexuality parents. But what with my son being in foster care, I am going to wait and see what happens before I recommit. I started some of my maths homework last night and was going through my twelve times table on the bus to the meeting today. But when I tried to hurry on to my nine times tables as well, I lost the plot and got muddled. So I will start the whole process again tomorrow and take it a little slower. It's just that I want to know everything that I don't know today and my impatience ruins it.

Sunday 12th February 2006

Dear Yvonne,

I had eight hours of peaceful restful sleep last night, and after doing my rituals got ready to go to a morning meeting.
I met my sponsor in Battersea and as I had rung her last night to ask her to do my step one at my place, that is what we did. We spent approximately two hours together at my abode going through my step one. Afterwards I wondered why I hadn't thought to do it before. I realised at approximately 5.30pm that I had not chubb locked the meeting room of my tea commitment today and so returned to Battersea on two buses, leaving from there to go to a meeting in Brixton. Whilst in the meeting in Brixton I couldn't remember if I had switched the urn off. But fortunately I got a lift there and back to my home. The urn was still plugged in but it was switched off, so I unplugged it. I am just beginning to understand that having the keys comes with responsibility. I have just received a text from Johnathan saying that he has printed the letters that I have written and so far has ninety-five pages! I am going to talk to him about them tomorrow at 10am.

Monday 13th February 2006

Dear Yvonne,

I had Twelve hours of peaceful restful sleep last night. Although I woke up to my landline ringing last night at 23.00hrs. Aunt Madge was on the other end of the line. I told her that I had started an access course. Plus I was now seeing my son for two hours each week instead of an hour and a half. We spoke for a few minutes with her giving me words of encouragement before she told me that she loved me and I went back to bed. This morning after doing my rituals and speaking to my sponsor on my landline, I had breakfast and went to see Johnathan. He told me that he was dAunted by the volume of text and said that he was happy to print it but couldn't do much more than that. I am so grateful to him for that contribution and told him as much. After meeting with Johnathan I returned home and rang my poetry tutor and told her that I was in possession of ninety-five pages of diary text, and asked her if she could help me with my punctuations. She said that I should bring the text into my poetry class on Thursday. I also sent a text to B asking if she could also help me with my punctuations and I am now awaiting her response. I went to my group psychotherapy group today and asked the people present in the group to read the first day of the diary. On my return home I got on with a watching the 'Peace one day' DVD and found it inspirational. plus I did a little bit of maths homework and started reading Beloved by Toni Morrison. It is a book that was given to me about fourteen years ago by one of my clients in my last full time job, which I have not yet read so I am thrilled to be reading it now as it is going to be the book that we will be reading after Macbeth in English literature. I went to a meeting this evening and on the way met the father of a child that used to attend Karate with my son. As the karate sessions are no longer held in the same location I inquired as to where it is now held as my son enjoyed karate and if he comes back to me he might like to attend once more. My mum rang me today and I reminded her that it is her seventieth birthday today, even though she does not celebrate birthdays due to her faith. She is eager to press on with her new found zest for computer skills and I am going to visit her again soon so that she can get some more practice.

Tuesday 14th February 2006

Dear Yvonne,

I had ten and a half hours of peaceful sleep last night. And as it is valentines day today I sent a lot of my friends a valentines text message this morning to cheer them on their way, and have been fortunate to have been receiving replies all day. I sent C a valentine's text message. Today I put some credit on my mobile phone and did some food shopping in Marks & Spencers. I also did my laundary today and whilst waiting for it to dry took the opportunity to read a few chapters of Beloved by Toni Morrison. My son's CQSW rang and told me that her office has been relocated to International House in Brixton and my supervised contact with my son will as from this Thursday be at the Breslass family centre in Stockwell. My housing benefit advisor also rang me and was pleased that I had given Olive Morris house the information that it asked for. She also rang the council tax department for me and they have agreed to hold off asking me to pay council tax for one month until my claim has been assessed. I also hand delivered a letter received by me from my mental health team to my housing manager, which backs my request for my flat to be amalgamated with my neighbours. I am going to a meeting this evening. I have also received from my co-op today a request for my block to have a three day over three weeks treatment of pest control service starting on February 27th 2006. I am pleased about that as I am none too keen on mice. Tonight I received a bunch of flowers for valentines day from a friend.

Wednesday 15th February 2006

Dear Yvonne,

I had eight hours of peaceful sleep before starting my morning ritual. Today I took it easy and after going to Streatham to buy a comic I came home and went to sleep for three hours before going to heathrow airport to wait for Ramona's arrival. I read Beloved by Toni Morrison whilst I waited for her. When Ramona finally arrived we went to leave her suitcase in Victoria train stations left luggage department and came home and ate a pizza. In our journey from the airport to my home we covered the topic of my son and though Ramona was plainly saddened she remained cheery for my sake.

Thursday 16th February 2006

Dear Yvonne,

Last night I went to bed at 1am and woke at 7am. I had six hours of peaceful restful sleep and woke a sleepy Ramona on the sofa when I went in to put the kettle on. Ramona declined breakfast chosing instead a small glass of juice and some perculated coffee. I for my part took the opportunity as usual to indulge in two hotcross buns as well as some juice and a cup of decaffeinated tea. Ramona told me about the openly homosexual Mr Wowereit, the London mayor Ken Livington equivilant, that was voted into office in Berlin, about two years ago and I got Ramona to Victoria train station to collect her suitcase by twenty-five past eight and with ticket for the express train to Gatwick airport purchased on the train for twenty-five to nine. I then went off to my nine thirty Norwood appointment with my mental health CQSW, so that I could collect my medication. I am currently listening to Babyface's 'Face2face' CD on volume two, whilst I reminise about the supervised contact that I had with my son today. First of all I left Cooltan earlier than I was going to because the others were closing the workshop so that they could go to a restaurant to celebrate a pregnant member of staff's leaving to have a baby. So I after picking up some chicken bun and fries lunch I arrived at the Breslass family centre at 1.30pm ate my lunch whilst reading Beloved by Toni Morrison and waited and waited. My son didn't arrive until two thirty, half an hour after my supervised contact with him was supposed to begin. But even though my son had arrived I didn't see him as the person responsible for supervising the contact had not arrived. When the agency was contacted they found that she was apparently waiting a Hopton house unaware of the change of venue. It was agreed with the foster parent that my son could stay on for an extra thirty minutes. But my son and myself was still not in the same building at three forty-five. So the Breslass contact co-ordinator stepped in and supervised my son and my self at three fifty until the agency contact staff arrived at four. In the meantime I took the opportunity to cut my son's toe nails with his baby scissors and whilst I did it he said that it tickled him and he liked it. He also let me cut his finger nails whilst he looked at a transport book. I phoned my mum and both she and my son spoke with each other and at the end of the call my son told her happy valentines. And lo and behold he has lost another of his baby teeth. The one at the top front on the right. So now he looks like a typical six year old with a gap in place of where last week his front teeth were. He also clearly dressed himself today and had his trousers on back to front. The combination made him seem more than just cute, or gorgeous, in my mind he was simply adorable. We played the game 'Frustration' which is like a type of ludo with the dice encased in the centre of the board, which you press to have it change numbers. My son was winning in his own right but he said that he was going to let me win. Then as we were discussing where to put the pins for the ten pin bowling game his foster mother arrived as it was four thirty. It hardly seemed like five minutes in my son's company today and my son didn't want to leave. But at least he didn't cry. During contact my son calls me Aunty a lot and I don't correct him as I know that he knows who he is talking to and being conscious of his wrong labeling may cause him more distress. I am in no doubt about his feelings for me. I know that he loves me.

Friday 17th February 2006

Dear Yvonne,

I had nine hours of peaceful sleep last night and woke up tired. I didn't want to go riding this morning and pondered giving it a miss for one week. But I got up to go to the toilet and before returning to bed decided to get dressed without getting washed so that I would encourage myself to leave my abode. I had very little breakfast this morning, as I just wasn't in the mood. I placed Beloved by Toni Morrison in my riding bag, put my coat on and exited the flat. On the train I read my book and didn't take the opportunity to read the freebies on offer. I arrived at the stable three quarters of an hour before my lesson, and read some more as I waited outside. I had a good lesson with Ben on Hughie. I did rising trot when Ben asked me to and lead rising trot for two other riders, managing to change directions in rising trot. Hughie is a pleasure to ride and is sensitive to touch. I felt physically tired doing rising trot and felt as if I was really riding. Ben shouted stand up out of your seat, higher, use your legs more. tap him on his shoulder, put both reins in one hand and tap him on his rear. Which made Hughie go faster and keep going. Next week Ben wants to take me on a ride and lead out in the woods instead of in the school, so I am looking forward to it and hoping for fair weather. One more thing that gave me joy in riding today was my dismounting. I got off Hughie without Ben holding the reins! When I arrived back at my flat I had something to eat and went to sleep for three hours. My hip is niggling me and it aches when I am at rest as well. I am trying not to pay too much attention to it as the damage to it is irreversible. I am going to a meeting this evening.

Saturday 18th February 2006

Dear Yvonne,

I am listening to Mary J Blige's 'My Life' CD on volume two, having just eaten some spaghetti bolonese - my son's favourite meal, after arriving home from a lunch time meeting. I am on page two hundred and forty-nine of Beloved by Toni Morrison and I am so interested in what is happening in the story that I didn't put the book down while I was eating and have got bolonese sauce on the page. Today was a good day. I had nine and a half hours of peaceful sleep last night and after doing my morning ritual I did an hour of maths homework before calling my sponsor. I received a letter from Ros Dunning, my solicitor asking me to get in contact with her office as, she is trying to arrange a meeting between myself and the psychiatrist doctor Katz, so that I can be reassessed again by her for the court. She assessed me the last time that I went to court because my son was in foster care. She warned me that the likelihood of my relapsing was high, but I didn't take her word for it thinking to myself that she can't be one hundred percent certain as she is not God. But from where I am standing today I am the one who was mistaken. I also received an invitation to attend a Reaching Out, Drawing In: Look at Me focus group in the Education Studio of the National Portrait Gallery at 6pm on Thursday March 9th 2006. The focus group discussion will be audio recorded and the recording transcribed afterwards. I have accepted the invitation. I am going to finish my step one today and continue reading step two. I have been sending out text messages to most of my friends and I have received a few that have touched me. Such as the following:

When we finally
give up the
struggle to find
fulfilment outside
of ourselves, we
have nowhere to
go but within. It is
at this moment of
total surrender
that the light
begins to dawn. We
expect to hit
bottom, instead we
fall through a
trapdoor into a
bright new world.
We rediscover the
world of our spirit!

Once your are
outside your door...
the hardest part of

the journey is
behind you
Hope your day
is a special one

Let us
work as if success
depended upon
ourselves alone;
but with heartfelt
conviction that we
are doing nothing
and God
everything
Have a great day

TROUBLES as light
as air, LOVE deep
as da ocean,
FRIENDS solid as
diamonds &
SUCCESS brite as
gold. Dis is my wish
4u...B blessed
n highly favoured

Sunday 19th February 2006

Dear Yvonne,

Last night I slept for nine and a half peaceful hours, did my morning
ritual and went to a meeting. Today I remembered to turn the urn off
and lock the door on leaving the room. I stopped at 'Fresh & Wild'
for something to eat and drink, with a few of the others, after the
meeting. I am currently listening to Kirk Franklin's 'The rebirth of
Kirk Franklin' CD on volume two, whilst thinking about C. I guess
it is difficult for me to decide what it is about C that attracts me. I
just find her to be so spiritual, honest, open-minded and loving, her
emotional strength is to me breath taking, she is also tall, elegant,
attractive, mature and naturally talented. In fact multi-talented, She
is hard working, healthy and dedicated, with a healthy supply of

willingness. She is intelligent and has a good sense of humour. She looks directly into my eyes when she speaks with me and she doesn't drink alcohol, take drugs or smoke. Has a lovely singing voice and dances well. C has been my muse for the last seventeen months and although it has been brought to my attention that she is not perfect. I am at the stage where C's inperfections are ones that I believe I can live with. I sent C a text today, but it has also been put to me to "Want what I have, not have what I want."

Monday 20th February 2006

Dear Yvonne,

I had ten hours of peaceful sleep last night, rose did my ritual, some maths homework. Got washed, had breakfast and set off for my group psychotherapy, ringing Dunning & Co solicitors and leaving a message to make an appointment before I went. I am currently listening to Wyclef Jean's 'Masquerade' whilst I type out some text that I first wrote around the period that I was sectioned in the Maudsley hospital and my son was taken into foster care on 24th April 2004. It is as follows:

Some of the saddest days of my life

Since the onset of my 1993 mainstream mental health history, I have kept in touch with one lesbian with whom I have always had a platonic relationship, although we have at times shared the same bed and I have known her since 1987. She would describe herself as a black lesbian. Years ago before the onset of my mental health disability, I invited her and her undergraduate law student lesbian lover to dinner at my flat. My mother cooked a meal for the four of us, which we ate together. I had already come out to my mother as a lesbian, some time before and my mother had made the decision not to forsake or abandon me and as such every so often would spend a week or two at a time on holiday at my abode, leaving V.J at home to look after their house. As I was at work and a bit of a workaholic, I would arrange for my mostly lesbian friends most of which were also in full time employment, to babysit my mother, They would take her for instance to hear outstanding women give public talks, Kew gardens, day trips, or to their abode. On one occasion I, myself took my mother with me on a day trip with the young women of Gap House to Alton Towers. When I drove the women aged 16-19 plus colleagues in a hired mini bus in my official position of being employed as a lesbian housing manager, with special responsibility for resettlement. My mother sat at the front of the mini bus next to a young lesbian resident, and happily chatted away to her for the entire journey. It seems that after my mother got over the initial shock of my telling her to her face that I was a lesbian, she took to saying that anyone that I (meaning me Yvonne) love, she loves and she seemed to practice it on a daily basis, even today. However my friend who was an undergraduate and has now earned her degree and who's lover is now a qualified barrister, who were both also present on yet another occasion at my then abode in Penton Place, Kennington. It was for my birthday party. The private invitations went out to lesbians only for that all night birthday party. To my knowledge there were only two heterosexual women invited on that occasion. One of which was my sister and the other was my best friend. It was my friend's idea for me to celebrate my birthday and she offered to pay the cost for providing some of the food for the occasion.

My long distance Bristol based mixed heritage blue eyed lover, who I met only because of my friend and her lover had introduced us, and we got on well together and chose to start dating, was also present that night at my party. That night the building was packed and noisy with women of every shade, who spilled out into the yard at the back and onto the street at the front until about six o'clock in the morning. My friend has also been supportive of me with my struggle with intermittent episodes of altered perceptions since I have moved to my present lesbian and gay community abode in 1993 and reinforced my single-mindedness in steadfastly clinging to my lesbian sexuality within the mainstream statutory hierarchical system even to the point of being overjoyed to learn that I was artificially inseminating, whilst under the watchful eyes of the medical team. My Friend even visited me at the mother and baby unit situated within the grounds of the Kent based Bethlem Royal Hospital.

Within seconds of the birth of my son at St. Thomas' Hospital and the female surgeons announcement that it was a boy. I was mixed with the dichotomous feelings of happiness and sadness that another of my platonic lesbian friends, who would describe herself as a white lesbian, and who I had also know since 1987. She attended my wedding, was also at my birthday party and with whom I had also shared a bed with on numerous occasions, Plus who like me was also 'out' to her mother. In fact the four of us, me, her and both our mothers, went on a day trip to Brighton, we walked the shops and the beach happy in each others companies. Both our mothers happily engaging with one another.

The day was so pleasant that we vowed to do it again. But seconds after the birth of my son I knew that it wasn't ever going to happen. That she would no longer want anything to do with me. Yes she loved me and had been supportive of me even in sickness but she loved girls and boys just did not figure in her life, not even if she loved his mother. She had stated many times before I became pregnant that if I had a boy she just wouldn't want to know. So to then find out after the birth of my son that my black lesbian friend, who is also his official god-mother as she attended both his Seventh Day Adventist blessing and his Church of England christening and is the official name at my son's Montessori nursery and has given her permission for them to use her telephone number if his nursery school is unable to access me and her barrister now ex-lover who has since married a man and has had a child with him, had been covertly discussing the issue of black lesbians and why it is that some of them have chosen to have mixed raced children, behind my back came as a shock and was very painful for me emotionally especially as the information about the fact that they had been doing it was disclosed to me by the white mothered black fathered heritage lesbian lover that my friend is currently living with.

It came to my attention that such is their opposition to mixed heritage that my friend who was also planning to have a child in a same sex union with her current partner was apposed even to the point of not wanting sperm donations from a mixed raced male to represent the partner that she wants to co-parent with. The positive of my friend being okay about my child's male gender didn't make me feel better. So this year when my friend rang my landline leaving a message to say happy mother's day, I did not reply. First of all I love my son unconditionally and I can't forget him so there is a void that makes estrangement from him bring out the worst in me. And I don't do mother by proxy well. At the time of my son's birth I could not have cared less if my child was born a boy or a girl. Black as charcoal, with tightly curled hair and nearly black pupils or white as snow, with straight blonde hair and blue eyed pupils. And neither would my mother. I love my son and my mother loves her grandson and me too. Shortly before I was taken into the Maudsley hospital earlier this year, whilst walking on my road with my son, walking next to me. A man, walking in the same direction in which we were going interjected in a conversation that I was having with my son as we walked. He then slowed his walk to keep pace with mine and my son's and kept interfering by interrupting my conversation with my son.

When I asked the man not to he became surly and then abusive remarking on my half 'caste kid' and was offending me by being offensive to my four year old child. I was then forcibly punched-shoved to the ground by the man who was black. I retaliated by asking him what language was he speaking and who taught him it and was he not on England's soil in the year 2004, Meaning since he was in this latest millennium so opposed to the white man why was he still using his language and in the capital of the country of it's origin. I am not myself racist. I am not inhibited about having a darker pigmentation than some. I care not one jot for favouring someone's pigmentation or facial features or hair texture and as my family have been English language speakers and writers for generations. Jamaica was one of England's oldest colonies and governed by law from London England. And as my family moved to England before Jamaica chose independence. I claim my rightful place as an English woman in my country. If one want's to make a distinction then I am a black English woman, born in London, England and my son is also English being second generation London born and raised in the space of where a grandchild (i.e. third generation) would have been due to my age when I gave birth to him. Anyway about this man that punched-shoved me to the ground. I told him that he was both sexist and primative to act that way to a woman especially with a child present. But when he crossed to the other side of the road and walked comfortably along side an older child not much darker than my son, I knew he was publicly physically demonstrating the verbal sentiments of my friend, overtly in broad daylight.

As his aversion to my son's heritage was so pronounced perhaps he would have been positively hostile towards my sexuality had he know. As even these days the homosexuals life is worth nothing in some sections of the black community. But then my black lesbian friend would know that first hand.

Tuesday 21st February 2006

Dear Yvonne,

Last night I had nine and a half hours of peaceful sleep. But because I dawdled and lazed about in bed, I found myself running late, so I did not do my full morning ritual. I only prayed. After getting washed and dressed, I woolfed down some cereals with warm milk, before leaving to go to college. I had a test in my numeracy lesson this morning and at the first go I answered 16 questions correctly out of 41. I left several of them blank, as I either didn't have a clue or didn't want to guess. At the end of the lesson, I went through some of the questions with the teacher and filled in some of the blanks and my errors. Today I also completed my registration at the college and got my plastic id pass.

I took advantage of the college's computer room and sent an e-mail to Aunt Debbie in New York after checking my mail and realising that she had sent me an e-mail. I also had my first one to one session with the tutor that is going to help me with my punctuations, grammar and general organisation of my work. I wrote a piece of text for him to assess, so next week I will find out what his verdict is. Whilst I was in college Foyles the bookshop rang to say that 'The Steps We Took' by Joe McQ, the book that I ordered several weeks ago had now come in. So after I left college today I went to collect it. And whilst in the shop, I also purchased 'Complete Horse Riding Manuel' by William Micklem, as I have decided to make a commitment to my horse riding and turn up each week for the lesson with some theories that I have spent time reading about.

Since completing book Beloved I have been reading 'A million little pieces' by James Frey, feeling queazy, light headed and faint when reading the gorie bits and being reminded of the time when years ago when I doing my practical nurse training on a male surgical ward and the sister of the ward asked me to come with her and watch her remove some sutures from this man's head who had not been wearing a seat belt and had gone through the windscreen. His sutures were embedded in congealed blood and were difficult to for her to remove. The patient was grimacing and winsing and I for my part at the beginning of my training, became hot behind the curtain at the bedside of the patient with the ward sister and came over hot and faint and had excused myself from the situation and seek solace in the treatment room. On another occasion I was working in casualty and a patient was wheeled in on a wheelie trolley covered in blood and lead into the casualty theatre. I was the trainee that was supposed to assist a doctor to and after preparing the trolley comfort the patient. But when the doctor started working on the patient, the patient grimised and blood started spurting all over the theatre and so the doctor left me with the patient who was lying on his stomach. I was using pacifying words whilst feeling hot and weak and on the point of fainting. And on yet another occasion I was gowned up in theatre watching an abdominal operation and I fainted and when I came too, I was in another room and being offered something to drink! I think I am sensitive to other peoples pain. So I am going to place 'A million little pieces' by James Frey back on my bookshelf and read 'Complete Horse Riding Manuel' by William Micklem until I can handle it.

Wednesday 22nd February 2006

Dear Yvonne,

I went to a meeting last night and I got home fairly early but found it difficult to go to sleep. I finally went to sleep at around 1am. Hence this morning I was still lazing in bed at 8.30am on a college morning, when I would normally have left my abode at 8am. I did get my act together, however and arrived for my English literature lesson twenty minutes before the start of the lesson. The English literature tutor was off sick today, so I left Kensington & Chelsea's Hortensia road site and went to it's Worninton road site early. I spent some time in the study skills centre on the computer, before having lunch and doing some maths homework. Arriving in my study skills class fifteen minutes before the start of my lesson. On arrival to my flat looking in my letterbox I found I have received a letter from the housing benefit office indicating that they are going to pay my rent from September 2005. I also saw Danny a neighbour in my block, who was about to walk the Jake the dog. He told me that just beyond the front door were some flowers that were delivered for me. I couldn't believe my ears and couldn't think who could have sent them. When I took the box up to my flat and looked inside, I found a note that read as follows:

Dear Yvonne

It's never too late to have a
wonderful Valentines Day.
Happy Valentines Day

Underneath the A4 sheet of writing, were the flowers. A bouquet of six beautiful red roses and six milk chocolate caramels in the shape of lovehearts. I am speechless. I am totally overcome. So I am currently listening to Kirk Whalum's 'For You' CD and thinking of C.

Thursday 23rd February 2006

Dear Yvonne,

Yesterday evening I was present at a Lambeth LGBT forum meeting in room 8 of Lambeth Town Hall. I first attended the 'SpeakOut' forum in Vauxhall, April 2005. That public open meeting was laid on to raise awareness of LGBT issues. I decided to become a member of the forum from then on. I have attended meetings several times with my son, in the past and so he is familiar to most of the regular attenders. I started my periods yesterday. Last night I had nine and a half hours of red rose filled sleep. This morning I did my ritual and sent a text to C to tell her that I love her. When my sponsor rang I told her about my roses, she suggested that my mother might have sent the roses to me, but I told her that my mother was the first person that I told about the roses and she was a pleasantly surprised as I was. This morning I purchased a 'Thomas the tank engine' book from Woolworths and a selection of 'Wallace & Gromit' booklets from WHSmiths for my son as well as selecting a variety of sweets from Marks & Spencers for him. Before going to my Cooltan poetry class. Today we continued working on African American writers, but unlike last week when we did Gil Scott Heron's 'The revolution will not be televised', Public Enemy's 'Don't believe the hype', Martin Luther King's 'I have a dream' and folktale trickster tales. This week we did as selection of Langston Hughes and others from the Harlem 1920's genre. I left poetry early to have lunch and get to my contact with my son on time. I arrived at the Breslass family centre ten minutes early and my son and the person who was going to supervise the contact were there already. I was pleased. The two and a quarter hours passed quickly. My son was covered in mud as he usually is on a wet and rainy day like today when he is in term time in kindy. But he was happy and I got to work with reading to him from the Thomas the tank engine book and then helping him to make the pop-out Wallace & Gromit car from one of the booklets. We then played together with a selection of toys before I rang my mother and gave her the opportunity to speak with her grandson. After my contact with my son ended I went straight to my solicitors office to sign some release forms for my , letters, documents, notes etc to be obtained by my legal team, from my general practitioners and my psychiatrists. I feel tired and I am going to have an early night tonight.

Friday 24th February 2006

Dear Yvonne,

I am currently listening to Magic 104.5fm and thinking about C. Last night I had nine and a half hours of peaceful sleep and did my morning rituals. I arrived at the stables just in time for my horse riding lesson, after making a detour to buy some carrots for the horse. Today Hughie was having a day off, so I rode Conan. Conan is taller than Hughie but quieter in temperament. But that didn't stop Ben from shouting throughout the lesson, asking me to keep my shoulders back, rise higher out of my seat and bend my knees. In today's lesson, I don't remember standing up and forwards out of my seat. I only remember standing out of my seat. I as still concerned about falling off my horse and so I wasn't invited out on the hack today as it was a cold morning, and the horses were up for it and I was a bit nervous. The ride and lead hack for me has been postponed until next week. After leaving the stables today on the way to a lunchtime meeting, I popped into Borders the bookshop and purchased the book 'How Your Horse Wants You To Ride Starting Out Starting Over' by Gincy Self Bucklin and I haven't been able to put it down as it is such food for thought for where I am at this moment in time. I have decided today that I am going to start going swimming again, as I need more exercise and swimming was my favourite hobbie before my son was born.

Saturday 25th Febraury 2006

Dear Yvonne,

Last night I went to the Battersea Arts Centre (BAC) and watched Lemn Sissay perform 'Something Dark'. I was truly impressed. I could not help drawing parrallels with him, myself and my son when he talked about being in care. Although my son's life, and his, is chalk and cheese. I am closer to reading the novel 'Borrowed Body' by Valerie Mason-John, about a child that was in and out of care. When I got home after the performance I did my night ritual and went to sleep. I had eleven hours of peaceful restful sleep. After doing my morning ritual I left a message on my sponsor's voicemail. I went to a lunchtime meeting and stopped off after, to have a pot of tea and a chat, with another of the participants. On my return home, I found in my letter box from Lambeth Mind a 'Mind Lambeth Mental Health Directory 2005 Lambeth Mind' and a letter from Amnesty International confirming my details and indicating that their £5.00 withdrawals from my account will be made on the eighth of the month.

Sunday 26th February 2006

Dear Yvonne,

Last night I had nine hours of peaceful sleep, during which I had a dream that involved V.J, who my mum tells me is now walking with the aid of a walking stick, but I don't remember the details. I seem to sleep and not recall dreaming. But in 2004 when my son was last in foster care before being in foster care of late I had the following dream:

Fluffy The Three Headed Dog

Last night Wednesday 2nd June 2004 to Thursday 3rd June 2004, I had a dream and it went as follows: In the dream, I was in the arena of a lion and a human, side by side. But I was facing them, standing about five feet away, though not encircled in a cage. In my right hand I had a stick, which mimicked a club, although it was longer approximately four feet in size with a small bulb on the end, but slim in circumference, The type of stick that could easily cause a lump on the head, but nothing more, In the dream I was having a conversation with the lion only. But I cannot remember what the lion said, although it seems that at a certain stage the talking stopped and I started to aim and swing the club at the front of the lion's head to subdue it. The lion for it's part, moved it's head just out of reach with each swing that I tried to make contact with. I for my part made several attempts at swinging my stick. I do not recall the human saying anything, but I know that in between each pause I felt determined to make contact with the lion's head. On waking from my slumber I immediately realised that in the dream it had been a lion that I was dealing with and that just one pounce from it would have been fatal to me. And that in such a setting only a gun would have been good enough for such foolhardiness or bravado, that is if one had the time to pull the trigger! For such is the speed of a determined lion of which I was certainly no match. It made me feel nervous that a grown adult couldn't see that follies of her ways in the dream, and that the lion was allowing me such luxury without roaring or retaliating. But it most definitely was not docile or old aged. So I started to think in metaphor to try and work out what the lion could represent that I might want to fight with it. and for it to dodge my intended blows. One thought was that the lion was the psychiatric institution and yet another thought was the lion was the legal service system and the last thought the lion was the collective institute of Social Services as it relates to my son and myself. On realising that there were and are at least three possibilities of which each separately would be problematic but when combined they seem positively insurmountable to breach in order to obtain something of worth. Though the dream complete with lion has now only served to remind me of the three headed dog 'Fluffy' in J.K.Rowlings' Harry Potter 'Chamber of Secrets' children's book and movie which has in turn helped me to make sense of my dream.

Monday 27th February 2006

Dear Yvonne,

Last night I had eight hours of peaceful sleep. went to the bathroom and heard a knock at my front door. It was Crystal the pest control company, who placed poison down for hungry rodents and left. I then went back to bed listening to Magic 104.5fm and thought about C for a few hours before getting up, eating lunch and setting off to my group psychotherapy. I mentioned my delivery of roses gift and the group were very supportive of my humbled state of mind. I am just so grateful to have been given these gifts. I am overcome to know that there is someone in this world, besides a family member, who feels about me the way these gifts convey they feel. And I, a mere imperfect person, who's life is in the state that it is in, at this moment in time, am grateful for the love shown. I automatically think of C but there is no guarentee that it is C. I suppose the thing is, I want it to be C because I love her.

Tuesday 28th February 2006

Dear Yvonne,

Last night I had seven hours of peaceful sleep, having gone to sleep and woken with the sound my phone makes when a text comes in going off. Yesterday evening I had sent text to most people on my mobile phone, telling them about my gift of roses and chocolates. Telling them in the text that I was overcome as a result of it and that I was in need of help. I had some verying grounding and interesting replies. Although I had no clues as to the identity of the mystery sender. But at least today I don't feel so dogged with low self esteem. I got to my numeracy class ten minutes before it started and had a fulfilling lesson. The penny is slowly dropping when it comes to maths and I am pleased. This weeks homework is ratios and percentage amounts. I sent an e-mail to Aunt Debbie in New York, from, college today. Also in my learning skills class where I am learning about punctuations. My tutor was fairly pleased with my ability and seems to think that it may take approximately three weeks to iron out my misgivings and boulster my confidence. I am going to a meeting tonight. I miss my son. I miss the conversations that I have with him in our abode, his companionship, Just the communication that a mother has with her six year old son. I miss the things that we do together ie the shopping and the laundry and the things I do for his school such as spend a few hours each week volunteering in his school shop, even snuggling up in bed and reading him stories and hearing him first thing humming in the morning to the world services changing over to radio four. In a way my life feels meaningless without him having an active part in it and just lately even thought I have been in receipt of the most beautiful bouquet of roses that I have ever seen (and I am grateful) I just can't seem to raise my self esteem. At this moment in time I am doing most things that I could be doing with my free time. What with college and poetry classes and writing a daily diary, taking horse riding lessons and attending meetings, plus meeting regularly at group psychotherapy sessions and seeing my son for two hours each week during a supervised contact. But my self worth is at an all time low.

Wednesday 1st March 2006

Dear Yvonne,

I had nine hours of peaceful sleep last night and woke up to a text message on my mobile phone. I said my prayers and then answered the message wishing me an enjoyable day. I arrived at my college an hour before the start of my English literature class and spent half an hour on the phone to my sponsor whilst sitting on my own in the classroom. I read in some more character parts in the Macbeth play and generally the tutor was pleased with my input. We got given a choice of three essay titles in class today and the work is to be completed and handed in by 28th March 2006. In the Study skills lesson this afternoon we did a thirty minute timed essay. I am hoping that we are going to get some more of that sort of practice, as I need it. I sent out some more text messages from my mobile phone today and in a few of my received texts there was mention of my gift of flowers and chocolates from my secret admirer. In one of my replies I pondered the thought of the gifts being from a man. and asked the question what must I do if the gifts are from a man. and the response was PANIC! I just couldn't help but laugh. Tonight I am going to have a chat on my landline with B and she is most eager to know the identity of my mystery admirer. But I am afraid she is going to be disappointed as I don't know who it is. I would like it to be C but she is married, loves her husband and is not a lesbian.

Thursday 2nd March 2006

I feel extremely tired today. I was on my landline until almost half past ten last night after speaking with B for two hours mostly about my secret admirer. B reminded me that there was a woman who seemed to have taken a fancy to me who lives in the area and that perhaps she may be the mystery person. B and myself are going to me up on Saturday 11th March 2006 to start on the punctuations for my diary. For the past few days (Tuesday, Wednesday and Today) I have taken to drinking normal tea. mostly to pep me up because I felt drowsy and wanted to be alert for my classes. But I think that I had better revert back to my decaffeinated beverages and have a few early nights instead. Last night I had nine hours of peaceful sleep but woke up feeling tired. I arrived on time to see my mental health CQSW and after having a chat with her about things in general including a forthcoming C.P.A (Care Programme Approach), my gift of roses and chocolates for valentines (my social worker seemed to think that it was an act of thoughtfulness on the part of the sender) and collecting my medication I left forgeting to book a new appointment for a fortnights time. I arrived on time, to my poetry class. And was happy to see the other participants. I told them about my roses and chocolate gift and they thought that it showed that someone really cares.

I explained to them about my low self worth at this time. But they mentioned that they also felt that way from time to time and that most people suffer bouts of it. I was pleased inside that they said the things that they said and went on to have a great time in poetry today. When I got to the Breslass family centre at 2pm today, my son was already there. He had been there since 1.30pm. In future I am going to arrive for 1.30pm so that if he arrives early, we will have more time together. I had purchased a remote control hovercraft toy, for my son. But he could not play with it as it has rechargable batteries that need to be charged for at least four hours and I didn't have the time to charge them.

So I have taken it home with me and will charge them in time for next week. My son and I shared a Marks and Spensers Bacon sandwich, fresh fruit salad and sweets for lunch. My son also gave me his bread roll that he baked at kindergarten today. He does bakery every Thursday and today is the first time since September that he hasn't eaten his baking first! I cut my son's toenails and fingernails today, he had two odd socks on, and when I asked him about them he said that he didn't know they were two different socks when he put them on this morning. He also had a circle midway between his calf and ankle that looked like a rash/bruise. It was on both of his legs. he said that it was his socks as he likes sleeping in his socks. I didn't let him sleep in his socks and washed his clothes and mine in fairy babies powder, so he didn't get rashes unless he ate seafood or had antibiotics. He told me that Pete had taken him to a graveyard in the day and in the night. And that he had seen five ghosts. But he didn't seem at all frightended. I spent time telling him about himself and what he was like when he was a baby as he asked me to. He enjoyed my report and laughed at little things about his self. I also rang my mother and she spoke with her grandson. At one point in the conversation I heard my son tell my mum that he loves her and that she was cute. Before handing the phone back to me. My mother was still laughing at being called cute by her grandson when she spoke to me. At the end of the session with my son, Lyn came to collect him and he hid himself behind a sofa to stop her finding him. He also asked me why he has not gone home. I told him that I was not well enough. He replied that I (meaning me) am well enough. He is so intelligent and doesn't miss a trick. After my session with my son, I went to an internet cafe and sent an e-mail to my solicitor, requesting that she write to my co-op asking for my abode to be amalgamated with the flat next door.

Friday 3rd March 2006

Dear Yvonne,

Last night I had seven and a half hours. I spent almost three hours speaking with A on my landline last night. We were talking about my roses, my secret admirer and my low self esteem. During the conversation with A I recalled a the love that I had for fifteen years for Hope Massiah and the fact that I still got on with my life. I agreed with A, that I can now stop excluding women from my life. I admitted that my secret admirer has feelings for me, in the way I want someone to have feelings for me. And that I am grateful that that mystery person has shown it in that way they have. Today was a frosty but sunny day. And I arrived at the stables just on time. One of the other beginners told me that they were watching me last week and I looked good when I rode. I admitted to her that there were times when I was nervous. I rode Bill today and Ben my instructor took me out on a ride and lead hack in the woods. It was a lovely day for the event and I learnt a lot from doing it. The mud had ice in it, but the day was pleasant and warm. It has made me all the more determined to do well at my riding. After I left the stables on my way to a lunchtime meeting in Soho. I stopped off in Ray's Jazz Cafe in Foyles bookshop and purchased a decaffeinated sweet chai tea. I am going to a meeting this evening.

Saturday 4th March 2006

Dear Yvonne,

I am listening to Magic 105.4fm and thinking of C. I slept for ten peaceful and restful hours last night. Did my morning ritual and rang my sponsor. I went to a lunchtime meeting and went to a cafe for a cup of decaffeinated coffee after the meeting with a few of the participants. When I arrived home and looked in my letter box I found the minutes for the discussion of my son's review that I attended on 30th January 2006. I then rang my mother, who spent time talking about my son, I mentioned to her that I was going to summons up the courage to go swimming after I finished speaking with her. I then went to the Brixton Recreational Centre and swam breaststroke for an hour. On exiting the recreation centre I took a copy of the pool opening times. On my way home I stopped off in Marks & Spencers to buy some perishables for myself and get the milk and biscuits for my tea commitment.

Sunday 5th March 2006

Dear Yvonne,

Last night I had ten hours of peaceful restful sleep. I did my morning rituals and got ready to go to my morning meeting, where I have my tea commitment. After the meeting I went for a bite to eat and a fresh carrot juice in 'Fresh & Wild' then on my way home, I stopped off in a bookshop and purchased "The Alchemist" by Paulo Coelho and started to read it on the bus home. I did some maths homework, some punctuation homework and started to out my English literature Macbeth essay. I made myself something to eat and I am about to set off to another meeting.

Altered Perceptions

Monday 6th March 2006

Dear Yvonne,

Last night I had twelve hours of peaceful sleep but I was still tired when I woke up to let the pest control man into my abode this morning. So I went back to bed for an hour and he let himself out. I did my rituals and got ready to go to my group psychotherapy. On my way to the group, I met Lyn on my road. She told me that both her and her partner Pete took my son to a children's party which he had been invited to at the weekend which wasn't his usual kindergarten crowd. She said she spent two hours sitting on the steps to the party as he was too shy to go in. But then one of his kindergarten friends came out to get him and once they started playing Lyn and Pete could hardly get him to leave the party. I took him to the birthday party of a six year old girl, this time last year, which was held at Tooting swimming pool. It was a swimming party and my son went in the swimming pool with many of his kindergarten friends and their parents. After they finished paddling, we all had a birthday celebration. On that occasion my son also was reluctant to leave that party.

I am pleased that my son is still able to attend things that he has been invited to. Last October 2004 Lyn and Pete put on a children's Halloween party for my son and a few of his kindergarten friends attended at his invitation, plus some of the neighbourhood children and my son helped Lyn to make the invitations and had a great time at the party. I had a great session in the group today and afterwards stopped for a decaffeinated coffee with a few of the participants. On my return home, I found in my letter box a letter from Christian Aid, an organisation that I donated a small sum of money to a few years ago and letter from the Lesbian Gay Christians inviting me to attend their 1976-2006, 30th Anniversary in Wales, 28th-30 April 2006. Unfortunately I won't be attending. I will be meeting with my sponsor this afternoon in Chelsea to read through step two and attend a meeting afterward.

Tuesday 7th March 2006

Dear Yvonne,

Last night I had eight hours of peaceful sleep. I did my morning ritual and got ready to go to college. I arrived for my numeracy class one hour before it started. Which gave me time to finish off my homework and talk to my sponsor on my mobile. Today in the class we worked on fractions. Most of it went over my head, so I am going to have to dedicated time to it for homework over the next six days. After the lesson I went to the college canteen and ate lunch before going into the study skill centre and positioning myself on one of the computers. I sent a e-mail to Aunt Debbie in New York and was invited to go to my study support class early. I surprised myself with my understanding of sentences. I find, that I do the right thing, without knowing why I do it. I was pleasantly surprised with my work today in the one hour lesson. I am going to a meeting tonight but before I go I am going to have an half an hour brainstorm for my english literature essay, whilst Magic 105.4fm plays quietly in the background.

Wednesday 8th March 2006

Dear Yvonne.

Last night I had ten hours of peaceful sleep but I was still tired when I woke up. But I did my ritual and got ready for college. I arrived for my english literature lesson thirty minutes before it started. We finished reading the Shakespeare's Macbeth play. I left the lesson ten minutes late and arrived five minutes after the start of my study skills lesson. We had another lesson on essay planning. After my lesson ended I went to Waterstones bookshop and purchased some Agatha Christie books and have started with 'The Mysterious Affair at Styles'. I also stopped off at Brockwell Park's lido to enquire about Yoga classes. I have decided to start going to yoga because my sponsor has suggested that it might help me. Today is International womens day and National No Smoking day. I feel especially tired today so I am going to have an early night. Meaning that I aim to be in bed by eight o'clock.

Thursday 9th March 2006

Dear Yvonne,

Last night I had thirteen hours of peaceful restful sleep. I did my morning ritual and prepared myself to go to my poetry class, where I read the works of Kurt Schwitter, before going to my supervised contact with my son. My son himself ate the bread he made today at kindergarten. He was very happy today and sang for most of the session. He told me that he went to someone's house (the party) and he spent time sharing his lunch with me. I rang my mother and she spoke to my son. At the end of the session Lyn collected him and he took the hovercraft home with him. I had charged it and showed him how to operate it. But he wanted to put it in some water. When I my son's session finished I went to the National Portrait Gallery to attend the 'Reaching Out, Drawing In. Look at me focus group' in the educational studio. I spent two and a quarter hours in the focus group and got a lot out of it. The focus group had two men and three women participants and two facilitators. We mostly focused on the 'Look at me' exhibition, which I went to see on Tuesday 1st November 2006, which ends in one weeks time. But we were also talking about the whole gallery. I seem to remember going to exhibition of either Lord Snowdon or Patrick Litchfield at the National Portrait Gallery. I don't remember which man it was but what I do remember was these large elephant portraits that were being exhibited. That must of been some ten years or so ago.

Friday 10th March 2006

Dear Yvonne,

I had eight and a half hours of peaceful sleep last night. I did my morning ritual and prepared my self to leave my abode and go to my horse riding lesson. I rode Bill in the school today and Ben my instructor spent time telling me that Bill was harder to ride because he liked to follow the other horses. I spent the first few minutes of the lesson walking Bill around the school, but when it came time for me to get him to do rising trot, I could only keep it going for a short time. At one stage in the lesson Bill was stood in the middle of the school, not moving! I decided to listen to Ben and use my whip when he instructed me to. I don't usually like to use the whip as I feel a bit timid. But Ben said that I am supposed to be the boss and instruct Bill, not the other way around. I don't like using the whip, because the horse goes off with a start and I don't find that I have time to reposition my hands on the reins. Plus I worry about the horse taking revenge and throwing me off. But today I mostly listened to Ben's instruction and in the end Bill and I did a few circuits in rising trot on the left rein, but I didn't do too well on the right rein. Even though Bill kicked and stomped when I used my crop on him I wasn't particularly nervous today. And at the end of the lesson I got off Bill single handed. All in all, I personally felt I had a real learning lesson today. After the lesson I took Bill back to his stable and put his tack in the right place with Ben's help. I then fed carrots to Bill, whilst stoking, patting and talking to him. Afterwards I watched the lesson of the 'Blazing saddles' a group of eleven women horse riders, who were having a jumping lesson. Last week they syncranised their riding to music. I remarked to their instructor that one day I am going to join them, and she said keep coming and one day you will! After leaving the stables I went to Mary Seacole house in Clapham to get an authorisation for a freedom pass. The authorities had issued me with one, but it was in my old married name. So I brought all the documents and photocopied them for their records and they are going to post the form to me recorded delivery. I feel tired and aim to rest this evening.

Saturday 11th March 2006

Dear Yvonne,

Yesterday evening A rang me and we spent approximately three hours talking on my landline. After I finished speaking with A, I rang B and spent an hour speaking with her. We arranged to meet next week Saturday, so that we can get to work on the punctuations in my diary. After that call I went to bed and slept for ten and a half peaceful hours. I did my morning ritual and got ready to go to a lunchtime meeting. When the meeting meeting ended I went for a cup of decaffeinated coffee and a sandwich with one of the participants before going to Brixton recreation centre and swimming for an hour. I enquired about yoga at the rec and have decided that that is where I am going to do my yoga, so that I can also go swimming afterwards. The next session of yoga for beginners is Monday at 18.30hrs so I will give it a go and follow it with an hours swim. On my return home I had something to eat and rang my mum. We spent half an hour talking about my week including horse riding and swimming, and how my son blew my mother a kiss down the phone line, the last time she spoke to him.

Sunday 12th March 2006

Dear Yvonne,

Last night I slept for night and a half hours before getting ready to go to a morning meeting where I have my tea commitment. After the meeting I went to 'Fresh & Wild' with a few of the participants to have something to eat and drink. When I came home I got to work on some more of my english literature essay. I am going to a meeting tonight.

Monday 13th March 2006

Dear Yvonne,

Last night I had ten and a half hours of peaceful restful sleep. But I did not do my ritual before I set off to my group psychotherapy so I will do it tonight with my night ritual. I came to the realisation that whilst being in the group today that I had taken on a few suggestions. Ie doing my daily diary, going to my poetry class and wearing my step counter each day. I felt good that I had been incorporating changes into my life and it had seemed so effortless that I had almost taken it for granted. After the session ended I stopped off in the cafe to have a decaffeinated coffee with a couple of the participants. When I returned home I spent a hour and a half on my english literature essay. I then had something to eat and ran a bubblebath and languished in it for half an hour. I am going to do an hour session of yoga at the Brixton recreation centre today at 18.30hrs and follow it with an hour of swimming.

Tuesday 14th March 2006

Dear Yvonne,

Last night I had eight and a half hours of peaceful restful sleep. I did my morning ritual and then got up and got ready to go to college. I arrived in the study skill centre were the class were having our numeracy lesson today, as the cookery room that we usually use is out of use for two weeks as there is a cookery exam. Today in maths we did a bit of fractions, then areas and perimeters. I didn't do my maths homework last week, but I am going to do it this week. After my lesson I read my e-mail from Aunt Debbie in New York. Aside from talking about my son and how brave I am to get on a horse, she is hoping that the valentines roses and chocolates are from a woman. In my reply to her I told her that I had been to yoga and followed it by a swim. I also mention the other things that I have been up to this past week. Ros Dunning, my solicitor, also sent me an e-mail. She was clarifying matters relating to my request to my housing co-op for my abode to be amalgamated with my neighbours. I replied. After I had lunch, I went to my punctuation lesson. I have a real problem coming to grips with comma use, but I will keep working on it. At the end of my lesson, I went home, had something to eat and ran a bubblebath and took my Agatha Christie book in with me languised in the bath and read, whilst Magic 105.4fm played in the background. I rang my mum this evening and told her that I had done a yoga class and a swim yesterday, and she was pleased.

Wednesday 15th March 2006

Dear Yvonne,

I had nine and a half hours of peaceful restful sleep, did my ritual and got ready to go to college. For some reason or other I got my travel calculations wrong and arrived at the college, off the Kings road at just after eight thirty. But there was another student, who is also in my english literature class, present and having a hot drink in the canteen. Instead of disturbing them, I went upstairs to the classroom with my almond crossant and camomile tea and after consuming them rang my sponsor. My sponsor invited me to meet up with her after I finished college for the day to read my step two. I accepted her invitation and arranged to meet her at Parsons green station. In english literature today, we watched part of a BBC DVD of Macbeth.

At the end of the lesson, I travelled by the 328 bus to the Wornington road site. Where I arrived for my study skills class ten minutes before it started. Whilst in that class this afternoon, the fire alarm for the college went off and the building had to be evacuated. The study skills class, with all the other classes left the building, and crowded together off the site and across the road, before returning to the building when we were given the all clear. I wrote another timed essay in the class, but I didn't hand it in. And my cousin Sally sent me a mobile text message asking how me and my son were. I sent her a text reply. After the class I set off to meet my sponsor. After meeting with my sponsor I took a bus home and had something to eat and my cousin Eric rang me on my landline. I told him all about my valentine roses and chocolate, and I spoke about my son. Today in my letter box was a letter from Ros Dunning, my solicitor, saying the psychiatrist Dr Katz now has copies of my notes and would like to see me tomorrow morning at 9.30am. I was meant to meet with my mental health CQSW at that time to collect my medication, but I will have to see her after meeting with Dr Katz.

Thursday 16th March 2006

Dear Yvonne,

Last night I had ten hours of peaceful sleep but I was still tired when I woke up this morning. I did my morning ritual and got ready to go to my solicitor's office to meet Dr Katz. I arrived at Ros Dunning's office five minutes before the appointed time and was offered a choice of tea or coffee. I chose tea, white with no sugar and was delighted to be given my cup of tea in a mug with a picture of Henry the eighth sitting dressed in full day robes in bed reading a book entitled 'The joy of Six!' Dr Katz arrived fifteen minutes late and apologised. I was pleased to see her again and during my interview with her I was keen to report that I had started attending a twelve step programme for my 1991-1998 historical cannabis, cocaine, alcohol and nicotine addiction, with the occasional lapse with alcohol at Christmas dinners. When I told her that it was only yesterday that I was with my sponsor working on step two, she asked 'step two, you're only on step two after all this time? She asked if I were ever addicted to heroin and asked me to roll up my sleeves to show her my inside arms. So much for her trust in me! I left Ros Dunning's office at 11am but not before Dr Katz had broken the bad news.

She said that I was a mental health sufferer that had no insight into my chronic condition and that she would be writing that in her report. She said that 'If I were a diabetic on insulin, I would not think about coming off medication, even if my symtoms were not evident' But a diabetic on insulin does not take the same dose of insulin regardless of the amount of sugar in his blood! And That is what I was saying, I felt that, When hospitalised my medication was elevated to 10mgs and remained elevated at 10mgs when I was settled back in the community. Although in hospital all that is available for me to do is rest, sleep and to be cooked for, since I am mostly on the ward without a pass to get out of the ward. Whereas in the community I hold an active life as can be varified in my letters and months later such as is the case now, I am currently still on the same 10mgs of medication that I was placed on at an acute stage in my psychotic illness! She said that she is going to write a recommendation that I get further therapy, but this time in order for me to gain some insight into my condition. She said that that course of therapy is ran at the Maudsley hospital. She said that she could not recommend my son coming home with me as he needs more stablity not less because of the mental health gene in my family.

She said that cannabis can cause mental health relapse or exaserbate mental health problems in a person such as myself who had a weak gene from my mother. Naturally I was crestfallen. When I went to see my mental health CQSW she tried everything to rally me round. She told me that I would be having a care plan approach (C.P.A) at 4.30pm on Thursday 13th April 2006. She said that she would also like a copy of Dr Katz's report so that she can instigate the 'insight' therapy. But she also delivered another blow, namely she is not going to apply for a permanent position with the team, so by the time my final court hearing is held in June she will no longer be a locum for the Norwood team. This may mean that any ideas I have been having about getting a stable team around me so that I could be monitored whilst my medication was reduced would be dashed. Or worse still, it could mean that there could be further delays with the drug reduction therapy. I skipped my poetry class this week and though I missed it I found that I only had just enough time to buy some lunch for my son and myself from Marks & Spencers and some books from WHSmiths for him, before going to the Breslass family centre.

My son arrived a little after two and gave me the bread he made today. It was soft and tasty. My mobile phone battery was almost flat so my son only spent a short time talking to my mother today. He told her that he loved her and his mother. The end of the contact session with my son ended all too soon and Pete came to collect him but not before my son told me that he had been to see 'The Curse of the Wererabbit' and 'Narnia' with Pete. Pete told me that he is going to take my son to see 'Cars' but unfortunately it doesn't come to the cinemas until July 2006. I gave Pete a hug and was pleased to see him. He seems to really be enjoying the opportunity of having a six year old in his life, and that pleases me. This evening I went to my first ever Pilates class. The class started at six o'clock at Brixton recreation centre and was for beginners. I didn't break out in a sweat like I did in yoga, but I was aware of my breathing and my muscles. I followed the class with an hour's swim.

Friday 17th March 2006

Dear Yvonne,

Last night I had eight and a half hours of peaceful sleep but once again I was still tired when I woke up. I did my morning ritual and got ready to go to the stables. I arrived at the stables fifteen minutes before the start of my lesson and when I paid for it, I found out that I was riding Bill again today. I was secretly pleased, as I feel I have made a breakthrough with Bill after last weeks lesson. The day was cold and it started to snow sleet and I went to Bill's stall hoping that I could see him being tacked up, but no one was sorting Bill out so I returned to were the other learner riders were waiting. Only to see Ben turn up with a horse to ride. Ben told me that he was taking me out on a hack as he thought that would make a nice change. I was pleased for the unexpected surprise. So when Bill showed up I got on him. But I wasn't on a lead! I had to literally ride him without Ben holding on to him. It was great. I followed Ben and he weaved in and out of the woods, up and down the hills, and over logs. At one point Ben asked me if I wanted to do a trot. I told him yes reluctantly and so we had a short trot. There were a few times on the hack when Ben was a little in front and waited for Bill and myself to catch up. And because of last weeks lesson when Ben asked me to use the whip on Bill, I complied. I had a really enjoyable ride today and when Bill went back to his stall, I fed him some carrots that I had purchased for him that morning. After my lesson, I went to a meeting. When I got home I rang Mary Seacole house to enquire about my freedom pass authorisation form and was told that it was ready and I could go and collect it. I then went to the post office and updated my feedom pass. It now expires on 31st March 2008. I am going to a meeting this evening.

Saturday 18th March 2006

Dear Yvonne,

Last night after the gay lesbian bi-curious and transgender meeting, I went have a decaffeinated coffee at Costa with a few of the participants. I finally arrived home at 23.00hrs. I had eight and a half hours of peaceful sleep. I did my morning rituals and got ready to 'do a chair' at a meeting in Chelsea at lunchtime. It was the second meeting that I chaired the first was the 'queer' meeting that I go to on friday evening. After the meeting I went with a few of the participants for a cup of decaffeinated coffee in 'Starbucks'. Before making my way to B's house in Lewisham. I got a bus to South Kensington station and made my way to Bank but had to get a bus replacement service to take me from the Bank to Canary Wharf, where I got the dockland light railway to Lewisham. I rang B when I was a few stops from Lewisham and she collected me from the station. When we got to her home, she showed me around, gave some fruit juice and we set to work on my diary. We got to 10th December 2005 before stopping for something to eat. B gave me the film 'Bagdad Cafe' directed by Percy Adlon on DVD for me to take home and watch and gave me some money for me to order Kenneth Williams' diary. Afterwards I got the buses home.

Sunday 19th March 2006

Dear Yvonne

Last night I got eight and a half hours of peaceful sleep but I woke up feeling as if I could benefit from a lie-in. I did my morning ritual and got ready to go to the women's meeting where I have my tea commitment. After the meeting I went with a few of the participants to 'Fresh & Wild' and had something to eat and a decaffeinated coffee. On my way home from Clapham Junction I stopped in 'Ottakar's' bookshop and purchased 'The Kenneth Williams Diaries' edited by Russell Davies. When I got home I made the amendments to the text that I puntuated with B yesterday. Andrew then rang and told me that he had been involved in a car accident, was feeling some spinal after effects and was going to take a week off work. He told me that his car is a write off. I was so grateful not too have lost him to death in the accident. I then rang A and spent three hours talking to her. But I missed a call that I was supposed to be waiting for from my sponsor who is in Geneva on a skiing holiday for a week. But she rang later and we spoke for half an hour, mostly about my sombre mood as a result of what Dr Katz had said. My sponsor told me to put Dr Katz on my gratitude list as I had felt a bit like Bill Wilson one of the founders of Alcoholic's Anonymous when Dr Katz who told me that she has been in her field for thirty years, implied that I was a chronic case, that had no insight into my condition. My sponsor said that she is going to telephone me from Geneva again on Tuesday. I am relieved.

Monday 20th March 2006

Dear Yvonne,

Although I was in bed and asleep before ten o'clock last night and had ten hours peaceful sleep, I was still tired when I woke up this morning to let 'Crystal' the pest control company into my flat for the last time. After they left I went back to bed. and slept for two hours. I was still tired but I decided to get up and do some work on my english literature Macbeth essay for an hour and a half, before setting off to my group therapy. When I got to the Maudsley hospital, one of the group participants of the group said that I looked tired. So during the group today I told them about my meeting with Dr Katz. I told them that I had been waiting for my medication to be reduced for months and that I found it hard to continue with my lifestyle on the high dose of medication that I was on, and that fighting against it would only make me sick. One of the participants suggested that I take responsibility for myself and slowly reduce the dose myself. I said that I had been on 2mgs of Stelazine for two years followed by 1mg of Stelazine for a year before coming off my drugs all together and relapsing. and that was when my son was a toddler up to three and a half years old. Quite naturally I do not want to relapse but I feel the quality of my life is impaired by the dose of medication that I am taking. I may have to stay on 1mg of Stelazine for a few years before testing whether or not I can come off medication but I would like to do it with my doctors blessing not behind their backs. My next C.P.A is not for another month on Thursday 13th April 2006, and my CQSW is a locum who is leaving anyway. I feel so bad sitting in meetings and not remembering what people have just said. Reading and not remembering what I have just read. Feeling constantly tired. Going to sleep and usually waking up tired no matter how many hours sleep I have had. I have decided that tonight I am going to start my own drug reduction therapy as I don't want my body to get so used to the medication so that if I have to go to hospital the dose will have to be elevated still further. I recall the point of when I was first on Stelazine and I don't remember what dose I was one but, it was high enough for my breast to be secreting milk like substance from my nipples, my jaw was locked and I was unable to stop myself from grinding my teeth, My limbs were so stiff that I looked like a puppet and the other patients used to call me Pinocchio, I had terrible limb tremers, twitched and salivated in excess. I couldn't remember a word of what was said to me. It was useless for me to watch television or listen to radio 4 as I couldn't retain the tread of the debate. I ate like a horse and gained suplus weight, and couldn't stop sleeping. I know that my side effects are not as pronounced as in the early days but when I was on 1mg and 2mgs of Stelazine aside from the weight gain life was a bit more tolerable and that was with a small child. I am going to do some numeracy homework and then go to yoga and then swimming and later tonight I will make my first reduction from 10mgs to 9 and a half mgs.

Tuesday 21st March 2006

Dear Yvonne,

Last night I had nine and a half hours of peaceful restful sleep and woke up refreshed and alert. I believe the yoga and swim that I did yesterday helped as well as having nine and a half mgs of Stelazine instead of the ten mgs that I am going to have tonight. This morning I set off to college without breakfast, intending to collect some money from the cashpoint and buy a crossaint on the college site. But when I got to the cash machine and got a printed statement, I found that my money had gone in the bank but I could not withdraw it. On the way to college, I stopped off at Edgeware Road and was waiting at the Abbey National bank when it opened at 9am. I managed to withdraw the cash I wanted and proceeded on to college, but not before purchasing some perishables for breakfast and lunch from Marks & Spencer, whilst on Edgeware Road. I had a great morning in Numeracy, as I asked my teacher if she could teach me separately and slowly as I would be having her next year anyway and she said yes. I also took a draft of my Macbeth essay and gave it unfinished to my english literature teacher, she is going to give it back to me in tomorrows lesson. Plus I gave a copy to the teacher that is helping me with my punctuation this afternoon and he spent half of today's lesson going through my punctuation and talking about my 'subjective' essay. I let him know that it was the first essay that I had ever written and that as he had noticed I had not done a summing up. At about 3pm I became mentally fatigued and was glad to be at the end of another college day. I am going to have an early nights sleep, so I hope that my sponsor, who said she is calling me from Geneva today doesn't call me too late. While I was typing in today's diary, Laura a participant from my group psychotherapy rang and we spent about an hour on the phone. She had her front teeth missing when I last saw her at group on Monday. She told me that her cap fell out and that she had been to the dentist recently to try and get some work done for a new set. She said that she had two injections to stop the pain before the dentist started drilling, but it she could still feel it and it is so painful because it was on the nerve in her tooth. As she spoke to me about it, I recalled 'a million little pieces' by James Frey the book that I stopped reading a few weeks ago when it got to the part about his dentistry.

Wednesday 22nd March 2006

Dear Yvonne,

Last night I had eleven hours of peaceful sleep but I still woke up feeling tired. I took 10mgs of Stelazine last night but tonight I am going to take nine and a half mgs. I arrived for my english literature class half an hour before it was due to start. I took the opportunity to prepare my study skills essay. The tutor did not turn up for my english literature class today, so the class watched the rest of the Macbeth DVD without her and then left. In study skills, the class was asked to do a timed essay. I feel as if I am improving, slowly but slowly. When I got home I found in my letter box a BT credit note. Thank goodness I am still in credit because I am broke. I also found a letter from my solicitor with a letter from Dr Peter Yates, the psychiatrist that is going to assess my son and write a court report based on the report written by Dr Katz. Apparently Dr Peter Yates wants to meet with me for an hour and a half, at 9am on Friday 24th March 2006. So I cancelled this weeks horse riding lesson and rang Ros Dunnings secretary and confirmed that I will be available. I then ate a Marks & Spencer pizza and went to a meeting. I noticed that this afternoon at three o'clock I still felt alert but now I feel tired and so I'm going to have a bath and go to bed, as it is eight o'clock. I am not going to go to my poetry class tomorrow as I need to do some tidying up for Friday morning.

Thursday 23rd March 2006

Dear Yvonne,

Last night I had thirteen hours of peaceful sleep but I was still tired when I woke up. I started my periods this morning. My poetry tutor rang to see how I was today. I explained what was happening in my life and she said that I can call her at home when I find the time as she was missing me. Cooltan is moving to Unit B, 237 Walworth Road, London SE17 1RL. I didn't do very much tidying up and went off to have a supervised contact with my son. He was late to his contact as he had made a crown for himself at kindergarten and he was waiting to get it. He also made a bread roll that was modeled like a belgian bun. He gave it to me to eat, it was hard unlike last week's roll. I tried to call my mother but she was out, so my son didn't get to speak with her this week. My son and myself played with some playdough with a dentist model kit that I purchased for him yesterday at Woolworths. He took delight drilling holes in the playdough teeth and filling the cavities with silver/gray playdough. He also enjoyed looking at his Wallace & Gromit and Spongebob comics that I brought for him yesterday at WHSmiths. Lyn collected my son today and I walked with her and my son to the corner of the road before saying goodbye. I then nipped home to collect my sports bag and went to Brixton recreation centre to do a session of pilates and returned home. I then rang my mum. I feel like just packing my things and moving into my mother's house, with her and her V.J. I still have a bedroom there and so does my son. At least I would be able to be supported in looking after my son. My lifestyle would change and living outside of the capital would be something that I would have to get used to. I know that, I am just thinking like this because, I don't want to be forever parted from my son. I voiced my fears to my mum and she said she would pray for me tonight, all I had to do was go to bed and try and get a good nights sleep. "Just leave it to me, I love you" was my mother's last words to me on the phone

Friday 24th March 2006

Dear Yvonne,

Last night I had eleven hours of peaceful sleep and got up at eight o'clock this morning. Dr Peter Yates was supposed to arrive at 9am this morning, but he did not come. At 9.55am I received a phone call on my landline from my solicitor's office saying that Dr Yates was not going to be able to make it as he had some domestic difficulties and they (my solicitor's) were trying to rearrange another appointment. I decided to go back to bed. I spent the whole day snoozing and got up at 3pm and spent an hour on the phone talking to A. I then ate something and set off to Hammersmith. Whilst in Hammersmith I purchased 'The Valkyries' by Paulo Coelho. I had read the book 'The Alchemist' that he had written within seven days of purchasing it. This evening I, with some other Kensington & Chelsea students went to watch 'Odyssey' the Homer epic at the Lyric theatre in Hammersmith. I really enjoyed the production. I also took the opportunity to tell my english literature tutor that the essay that I handed in to her was the very first essay that I had ever written and that I would very much like to improve.

Saturday 25th March 2006

Dear Yvonne,

Last night I took 10mgs of Stelazine and slept for eight hours. I woke up and decided that I would get a job as a traffic warden and went out for a walk in Brixton to find a traffic warden to ask, how I am to go about it. I met a warden near Brixton market and he told me to get an application form from beside Camberwell bus garage. So I went there on the bus to try and obtain a form. But the man at the reception said that they were overstaffed with traffic wardens at the moment and that I would have to come back in two to three weeks. So not one to be deterred I then took a bus to the west end, had a stroll and came across another traffic warden, and I asked him the same question that I asked the one earlier. He said that I had to go to the NCP car park in Bryanston street, near Marble Arch and collect an application form from there. Which I did, and then got on a bus from Oxford street, home. When I arrived home my landline started to ring, when I answered it my mum was on the line. We spent a few minutes speaking to each other and then my mum told me that she loves me and may Jahovahs blessings be with me and hung up. I continued reading 'The Valkyries' by Paulo Coelho and then had a nap for a few hours. I awoke to the bell of my front door ringing. When I answered my intercom, I found that it was my cousin Eric at my front door. I let him in and we sat chatting for two hours over a couple of cups of decaffeinated coffees. I told him about my plans to become a traffic warden and he immediately asked about my son and my studies. I didn't have any answers. I then showed him what was left of my roses and he said he would throw them out on when he was leaving the building. I am going to have something to eat and then I am going to watch the film 'Bagdad Cafe on DVD.'

Sunday 26th March 2006

Dear Yvonne,

Last night I took nine and a half mgs of Stelazine and slept for ten hours. But I woke up with a start and jumped out of bed because not only is it Mother's Day today but the clocks were put forward an hour and so I was going to be late setting off to my women's meeting tea commitment. I didn't read my daily text this morning or my basic book and neither did I say my prayer but come to think of it I didn't do my night's ritual last night either. After the meeting today I went to 'Fresh & Wild' for something to eat and a hot drink, with a few of the participants from the meeting. Then I went to purchase 'Veronika decides to die' by Paulo Coelho and started reading it on my way to Deptford where I met with someone from my group psychotherapy. He commented that I looked more rested that I had looked last Monday. I told him that I had been sleeping when ever I got the chance. We chatted for a short time and he showed me a drop-in that he goes to, mentioning that I can go there if I need to chat. It was in Watson Street SE8, which is quite a way from my home. I have read the first thirty pages of 'Veronika decides to die' by Paulo Coelho and I am really getting into it. After I finish it I will revert to 'The Valkyries' by the same author. I have read the first seventy-five pages of the book. I was thinking to myself that though I have problems in my life ie what is happening to my son and my enduring mental health condition. My life in many respects is on track and moving locations or trying for a forty hour a week job as a traffic warden is not going to enhance it's quality. But here is a prime example of the type of insane thinking that goes on in my mind. I feel as if I need that person who is on my case each day telling me that this is what you do at each moment of each day. Confirming that I am on track. But on track to where? I seem so insecure at the moment. wanting to simplify my life although the quality of life that I am living is second to very few. I am currently listening to Fred Hammond presents...Joann Rosario 'More, more, more' I have run a bubble bath and I am going to have a soak in it whilst continuing to read 'Veronika decides to die' by Paulo Coelho. A rang and I spent time telling her about having handed in my first essay and feeling worried that it may not be up to scratch. A said that I am at the beginning of my studies and that not everyone takes to it like a duck to water! That I may need time to get into the swing of things. I told her about wanting to give up my flat and live with my folks, plus my canvasing for a job as a traffic warden with an oesteo arthritic hip. She said that I must be careful not to sabbotarge my progress. I agreed that I was on the right track and was trying to find a parent to parent me instead of doing it myself like I had been doing.

Monday 27th March 2006

Dear Yvonne,

Last night I took ten mgs of Stelazine and had ten hours of peaceful sleep. I am getting into the book 'Veronika decides to die' by Paulo Coelho and read a few more pages this morning. After putting it down my sponsor rang. I told her about wanting to give up my flat and move in with my mother and my pursuit with the traffic warden career. She wanted to know what brought that all on. In the end she asked if I had started my step two. "Came to believe that a power greater than ourselves could restore us to sanity." I said no. She told me to start it today. After speaking with my sponsor I got up without doing my ritual got washed, dressed and had breakfast. I then set off to my group psychotherapy, texting C to tell her that I love her on the way. In the group I told them what I had been up to and asked for feedback from one of the group's facilitators. She said that it seems as if I had over the past few days had another manic episode but had regrounded myself. I was inclined to agree with her, because I recognised that when I had relapsed in the past I started to want to look for employment and stopped my state benefit. But the difference between the past few days and other relapses is I kept communication going with other people ie my mum, cousin, friends, sponsor and others. I didn't allow myself to become isolated. I am also aware that over the last few days I havent been doing my morning ritual or my night gratitude list or ritual but somehow I just don't feel like it even though I know that I it is suggested that I am supposed to. I am going to get on with some of my step 2. and then go to yoga later. My mum rang me today and told me that she loved me. She also rang me yesterday as she had not heard from me on Mothering Sunday. She said that she had called me because she had not heard from her favourite. She wanted to know what was wrong. The last time that I did my gratitude list and my night ritual was Tuesday 21st March 2006 and before going to my tea commitment yesterday morning I have not been to a meeting since Wednesday at 6pm. I am going to have to rectify this. It is not good enough, no wonder I lost the plot.

Tuesday 28th March 2006

Dear Yvonne,

Last night I took nine and a half mgs of Stelazine, wrote my gratitude list, did my night ritual and had eight and a half hours of peaceful sleep. When I woke up I did my morning ritual and got ready for college. In maths today we were converting from farenheit to celcius. When I am in the class, I feel as if I might know what I am doing. But left to my own devices I am completely lost. I rang my sponsor and told her that I had done step 2. She said that she will go over it with me at the weekend. I sent another e-mail to my Aunt Debbie in New York before going to my punctuation class. We did a little more work around my commas and soon we will start some proof reading, which I am pleased about. Dominic, my solicitor's secretary rang me today to tell me that a new date and time has been arranged for Dr Peter Yates to see me. The new appointment is 15.30hrs Monday 3rd April 2006 at my place. I am going to have a long soak in a bubble bath, see if I can finish reading 'Veronika decides to die' by Paulo Coelho, eat something, take my 10mgs of Stelazine medication, and go to bed early. I have decided to continue doing my rituals as they are good for me. B rang me tonight. We spoke for about three quarters of an hour and arranged to meet up this Saturday at her home to carry on with my diary.

Wednesday 29th March 2006

Last night I took ten mgs of Stelazine did my night ritual and went to bed. I woke up this morning after nine and a half hours sleep, did my morning ritual and got ready to go to college. My english literature tutor was pleased with my draft essay and spent some time talking to me about it after the class. So I was late getting to my Study Skills class. In Study Skills we did the last of the timed essays. I handed two in to be marked by my peers. My son's CQSW rang my mobile phone and left a message on my voicemail, saying she wanted to know how I am and would ring me tomorrow. I rang her back in her office, she was not in so I left a message saying that I called. I finished the book 'Veronika decides to die' by Paulo Coelho last night and today started on another book of his called 'Manual of the Warrior of Light.' I feel tired today but I am going to a meeting tonight. I am going to meet with my sponsor on Saturday to go over my step 2. So I sent a text to B apologising about having to cancel our arrangement. Or at least postponing it until a fortnights time.

Thursday 30th March 2006

Last night I took nine and a half mgs of Stelazine and slept for thirteen hours, waking once at midnight for half an hour. When I finally woke I did my morning ritual and got ready to see my social worker. I rung my sponsor on the way there. This morning my social worker saw me carrying the book 'Manual of the Warrior of Light' by Paulo Coelho and said that she had read that book and 'The Alchemist' also by the same author. I told her that I had almost finished reading 'Manual of the Warrior of Light' and was on my way to get a book by Carl Jung. She wrote out a timetable of my activities. She said that it was a packed timetable and that I needed to be organised to get through it. She reminded me that I have a C.P.A coming up on Thursday 13th April 2006 and asked me if there was anyone that I wanted to invite. I mentioned that she could invite my son's social worker. I told her about the forthcoming visit from Dr Peter Yates and she reminded me to give him her telephone number and tell him that I have a C.P.A coming up. When I left my social workers office I got on a bus and went to Waterstones bookshop and purchased 'Four Archetypes' by Carl Gustuv Jung. I then went to Marks & Spencers and got some lunch for my son and stopped off in WHSmiths to get a few comics for him to look at. My son arrived to his contact on time. As his kindergarten closed for holiday yesterday he arrived mud free. Instead of being in the basement of the building we were in the top today. He was happy and playing and I spent time telling him about the things that he liked as a baby and toddler, while playing with him, hugging and kissing him. He said that he wanted to go home with me today and asked why he couldn't. I told him that I still wasn't well enough to look after him. I rang my mother and she spent time talking to him and told him that she loves him and he told her that he loves her too. I am going to pilates today and also going to have an hour's swim.

Friday 31st March 2006

Dear Yvonne,

Last night I took ten mgs of Stelazine and slept for ten hours after listening to my sponsor's suggestion of having an over packed schedule and doing did my pilate class but not go for a swim afterwards. My mother rang and I spoke on the phone with her for two hours. She spoke of the current government incentive for people to be encouraged to gain mortgages and reminded me how in 1988 I had also been encouraged to buy by Margaret Thatcher's government, who were reducing the miras on house purchasing from multiple people being able to do it for one property to one. So before the law changed I purchased a three bedroomed house with a female nursing collegue, who also worked alongside me at fifty-nine Greek Street women's hostel. But once we got our mortgage, her boyfriend developed cancer and she wanted out of her financial obligation. So I took over the mortgage and ended up working three different jobs at a time in order to pay the mortgage. Only to be repossessed because the interest rates rose so high that I couldn't keep up with the repayment of them. I wasn't the only person caught up in negavtive equity. Many more single people and families were repossessed and lost a lot of money and their home. My mother spoke of growing up as a young girl and the word 'gay' meaning something different to what it means today. She said in her day it meant happy, joyous but now it indicates homosexual tendencies. She said it is like the word 'wicked' today it means something nice whereas in her day it mean't something unacceptable. She also spoke of wanting a current photograph of my son, so that she can have it enlaged frame it and hang it up. Today I had a horse named 'Flash' to ride on. I liked him and got on well with him. I got on and off him okay and walked and did rising trot okay, although sometimes he started to walk during rising trot. I asked Ben if my feet were positioned correctly today and he said "yes." I followed Flash to his stall and fed him some carrots. I felt tired today so after my riding lesson I came home and went to bed for two hours. I am going to go to a meeting tonight.

Saturday 1st April 2006

Dear Yvonne,

Yesterday evening on my way to the meeting, as I walked down my road I bumped into four of my lesbian and gay community neighbours. I spent a little while chatting with Lesley and Nell, two of the women, who asked about my son, and I said hi to Micheal and Andy R. two of the male residents. Last night I took nine and a half mgs of Stelazine and slept for eleven peaceful hours. I was still tired when I woke up but I did my ritual before getting up and getting ready to go to a meeting. On the bus, on my way to the Chelsea meeting, I did some meditation breathing ie counting my inhalation and exhalation in groups of ten. That seemed to clear the drowsy muffled sensation that I had in my head. After the meeting I went to 'Starbucks' and had something to eat and drink with a few of the participants of the meeting. Then I waited in 'Carluccio's' for my sponsor to arrive so that we could go over my step 2. Whilst waiting for her I helped myself to another decaffeinated hot beverage. When my sponsor eventually arrived and I started to read my step 2 to her, I found that I had written it so formally that it was difficult even for me to find the nurturing qualities of the step. Needless to say I am going to have to re-write some of it, and I will try to be kinder to myself with the redraught. After reading my step 2 to my sponsor, I went with her to another meeting before going home and ringing my sponsor to say 'thank you.' I am so grateful to my sponsor for not allowing me to isolate myself behind formality. It is one way that I seem to use to say everything and nothing. Though I am hungry to be included, I distance myself with walls and barriers of aloofness and conventions and miss out on the welcoming and help I would receive from others if I could only say 'I am afraid' or 'I don't know how to do this.'

Sunday 2nd April 2006

Dear Yvonne,

Last night I took ten mgs of Stelazine and slept for eight peaceful hours. I woke up, did my ritual and got ready to go to a meeting. After the meeting I went to 'Fresh & Wild' for a cup of decaffeinated beverage. Then I came home and got on with my english literature essay.

Monday 3rd April 2006

Dear Yvonne,

Last night I took nine and a half mgs of Stelazine and slept for twelve peaceful hours. I woke up and did my ritual. I also left a message on my sponsors voicemail but I didn't want to get up. I got myself ready to go to my psychotherapy group. After the group I went for a hot drink with one of the participants and went home to get ready for Dr Peter Yates visit at 15.30hrs. Dr Yates spent an hour and a half explaining things and asking questions and told me that he would need to see my and my son together. This may happen at the Breslass family centre this Thursday. He also made another appointment to see me next Monday at 13.00hrs. I told him quite frankly that Dr Katz said she is not backing my claim for my son and that she recommended that I go on an insight therapy course at the Maudsley hospital. He said that his report may be a week late and that he doesn't know if he should put in a recommendation without finding out the results of the insight therapy. After Dr Yates left I ate something and went to yoga only to find out that it had been cancelled. I decided to join the membership scheme so that I would be able to go to the sauna as well as yoga and pilates and pay less for it that I do currently for my yoga and pilate classes only.

Tuesday 4th April 2006

Dear Yvonne,

Last night I took ten mgs of Stelazine and slept for ten hours. I did my ritual and got ready to go to college. My numeracy tutor didn't turn up for the lesson. So I stayed in the college library. I sent an e-mail to Aunt Debbie in New York. I also looked up Carl Gustav Jung on the internet by going to google and typing in wikipedia. In my punctuation and grammer class this afternoon, I worked on my macbeth essay and typed up the alterations after the class. I will hand it in to my english literature tutor tomorrow. When I arrived home today and looked in my letterbox, I found I had received a letter from my solicitor, which had Dr Katz's report with it. It held no surprises.

Wednesday 5th April 2006

Dear Yvonne,

Last night I took nine and a half mgs of Stelazine and slept for twelve peaceful restful hours and missed college. I spent most of the day in bed resting and reading. My son's CQSW rang me and after explaining that she has not heard from me in a while asking me how I was arranged to visit me at home on Friday 21st April 2006 at 14.30hrs. She mentioned that we are back in court on Monday 15th May 2006 at 11.30am. I got my rent statement from my housing association but instead of paying £60.00 each week the housing benefit is paying £47.46 so I rang them and they are going to look into it. I also rang my housing co-op manager and asked about my request for the amalgamation of my flat with the one next door. The co-op manager told me that there is not enough money in the budget for my request to be put forward. Naturally, I am disappointed. I also rang Mind legal to find out if there is anything I can do about this parrallel planning of the court, as I don't want my son to be adopted. They asked if I was happy with my solicitor. I replied yes and so they said that I was to approach her. I also rang Crossroads womens centre and to find out the same thing but they gave me the same advice. I was listening to an item on radio four today, mentioning something about the drug L.S.D and psychiatry, but I was dowsing and didn't hear the discussion properly. I am going to ring B tonight and have a chat.

Thursday 6th April 2006

Dear Yvonne,

Last night I took ten mgs of Stelazine and slept for twelve hours of peaceful sleep. I woke up and prayed this morning but I did not do the rest of my ritual as I was in a rush to get some perishable shopping from Marks & Spensers before going to my poetry class. Cooltan has moved to a new location. They are now near the Wimpey on Walworth road. I arrived at Cooltan at about half an hour after the class started. I went on a tour of the locations and spoke to a few of the Cooltan members before getting on with my poetry. I found out that there will be no poetry class next week, as they are on holiday for the easter break. I left the poetry class about a hour and a quarter before the end of the lesson as I wanted to arrive to my contact with my son on time.

My son arrived for his contact a little late as he was stuck in traffic. But when he arrived he gave me a model with wheels that he had made specially for me. I took the opportunity to cut his fingers and toe nails. I also read to him whilst he ate the lunch that I had brought him. Today he played with some skittles and placed a teddy bear near to observe him knocking over the skittles. Afterwards he knocked the teddy bear over and asked me to make sound effects of the teddy being assaulted. Each time I made the sound effects for the teddy, my son laughed and rolled about on the floor. I rang my mother and she spoke to my son and told him that she missed him and loves him. He told her that he missed her too, and loves her. When it was time to go home my son said that he wished Lyn and Pete were going to pick him up, But instead he was being bought home by the person that supervises us each week. I decided not to go to pilates this evening and instead went home and rang Lyn. Pete answered the phone and I asked if I could drop in for a cup of tea. He said "yes." While I was having tea with Pete he offered me a meal and I accepted. I told him what my son had said and pete told me that he was out with my son having a pizza yesterday. He told me that both he and Lyn collects my son from kindergarten five days each week in term time. I was suprised I didn't know. He said that my son likes his routine and knows that Lyn or Pete pick him up after the contact sessions on Thursday. Pete also told me that his brother is planning his civil partnership with his partner of over twenty-five years soon. I was pleased for his brother and secretly wondered if there would come a day that I would be planning a civil partnership and having a twenty-five year monogamous relationship with C. I also told Pete about my disappointment that the Co-op didn't have enough money to amalgamate my flat with next door and after discussing it with him, went to talk to a few members of the lesbian and gay unit about it. On my way there I met up with Johnathan, and greeting him with a cuddle before speaking with Lesley and Nell, who wrote a letter to the Co-op management committee for me which I hand delivered before returning home. It is as follows:

Dear Management Committee,

As you know, I have a child,... and we are living in a one bedroomed flat. He is nearly seven and we are desperately overcrowded. We do not want to leave the gay community as we are safe here. Since the tenant of flat 3 left, the property has been empty. It is situated on the top floor of..., just next door.

Would the Co-op consider merging my flat and flat 3 to make a 2 bedroomed property so that...I can live more comfortably? This would create the only larger property in this community of one bed flats. I know that BHC has no money for major alterations, but for the time being, it would only involve knocking a through door between the two, and merging the utilities, council tax and rent etc, which should not cost too much. It would be a solution to a problem for my small family and create a larger flat for gay couples and families in future years.

Friday 7th April 2006

Dear Yvonne,

Last night I spent an hour speaking with my mum on my landline. I told her about the letter that my friends helped to write requesting a flat merger. She was pleased and said that she would keep it in her thoughts. We also spoke about my son and the fact that my mother has enlarged a few more of his photographs, framed them, and put them up in her house. I then took ten mgs of Stelazine and slept for ten hours waking up with chest pains. It was a deep penetrating pain, located in the centre of my chest over the area of my sternum. I decided that I may have been overdoing things and took the day off and stayed in bed, sleeping, resting, listening to the radio and reading books. I decided to purchase a yoga meditation DVD from Devotion trading Ltd, so that I wouldn't have to go so long between yoga sessions. I rang the psychotherapy department to let them know that I wouldn't be there on Monday as I have an appointment with Dr Peter Yates at my home.

Saturday 8th April 2006

Dear Yvonne,

Last night I watched the first five episodes of the 'Sugar rush' DVD. It is about a fifteen year old virgin lesbian who has a crush on her unwitting schoolfriend. I enjoyed it as in some ways it reminds me of me and my relationship with C. I took nine and a half mgs of Stelazine and slept on and off for fourteen hours. When I woke up I collected my post from my letterbox and found a letter from Dr Peter Yates confirming that he is coming to see me on Monday 10th at 15.30hrs and a prospectus from the Open University, one that I had requested. I am seriously considering doing my studies at the Open University as I can tailor make the degree that I would like to do. Today I lazed about and slept, listening on and off to radio four. This afternoon I am going to visit B and work on my diary and then I am going to spend an hour doing service on the door of a twelve step party.

Sunday 9th April 2006

Dear Yvonne,

Last night I had a wonderful evening going through my diary with B from Saturday 10th December 2006 to Saturday 24th December 2006. I ate a three course meal with her that she prepared and then left to go to the twelve step party. I was on the door from 22.00hrs to 23.00hrs and arrived at the venue in Camberwell fifteen minutes before I was to do so. It was pleasant being on the door as no one was rowdy or drunk. No alcohol was being sold as no one drank or took drugs and it was hugs all round for the attendents. After my hour shift I spent fifteen minutes chatting to people that I knew but then I went home, without having a dance although I could see that the crowd was hotting up and well into the swing of dancing. To be honest, the venue was a bit too smokey and I feared for my lungs. I arrived home took ten mgs of Stelazine and was in bed by 22.50hrs. I slept for twelve peaceful hours before prizing myself from my bed and hitting the road. I was on a mission. I had dreamt last night that I was once again playing jazz drums. When I woke up, I thought about it and realised that music was my one love. I would spend hours practicing and go to any lengths for music. I just never seemed to tire of it. I thought to myself that I am going to go back to it.

Whilst still staying with the horse riding off course. So I went down the West End in search of a drum tutor for myself. I was looking out for a 'Melody Maker' on the way, but was told that both it and 'Sound' no longer existed and that only 'NME' New Musical Express remained. So I purchased it. But when I looked at the tuition section, there was one advert for tuition and that was not for drumming. I made my way to Charing Cross Road, but the drum shop that I wanted to go to was closed. So despondent I went and had something to eat and drink in Ray's Jazz Cafe. On my way out of the music section I asked where one could find a jazz drum tutor. I was told to go to Footie's in Golden Lion Square, which is a drum/music shop or look it up on the internet. So I looked for a drum tutor on the internet and texted a few numbers and Sarah replied. I said that I wanted to learn jazz drumming, but just like my undergraduate degree course, where I cannot study lesbian and gay studies as an under granduate, Sarah told me that I would have to study some of the other genre's first. I booked my first lesson with her for Wednesday at 11am in Greenwich. She knows that I am 44 and says that her oldest student is 60. I am secretly pleased that she is a woman and hope that her talents and abilities impress me.

Monday 10th April 2006

Dear Yvonne,

Last night I took nine and a half mgs of Stelazine and had eleven hours of peaceful restful sleep. This morning my son's court guardian rang and made an appointment to see me tomorrow at

14.00hrs and would also like to see Lyn and Pete afterwards. He told me that he is going to be at my next contact with my son, which will be this forthcoming Thursday. I am not surprised that he has contacted me as my son's social worker had mentioned him when she last spoke to me to book her appointment date with me. I am almost certain that Dr Katz's report has been had by all the relevent agencies and as it doesn't support my having my son back without insight therapy, the authorities are keen to speak with Pete and Lyn. My sponsor also rang me this morning. She wanted to know what had happened to me as I hadn't rang her for the last few days. She picked up that I was a bit low in spirit and spent half an hour speaking to me. Dr Peter Yates came and when I asked him if he had received that report from Dr Katz yet, he said that he got it on Friday. During the hour and a half with him, I spent time explaining what changes I am going to make and what support I need in order to keep well and look after my son. I also spent time talking to him about the support I got from the twelve step programme that I attend. He told me that he was going to come to my contact with my son this week Thursday, for the last hour. He told me if anything came up during the session that he would need to see me again. He told me that he would be speaking with Lyn and Pete and my social worker. When Dr Peter Yates left and I thought about it, I was non the wiser as to whether Dr Yates is recommending that my son be adopted or not. I am going to have to wait until at least next week Tuesday before I find out what he writes. Thank goodness that I have yoga this evening as I need to take my mind off the issue.

Tuesday 11th April 2006

Dear Yvonne,

Last night I took ten mgs of Stelazine and slept for thirteen peaceful hours. This morning when I looked in my letterbox I found that the postman had left me a note so that I could collect something from the sorting office. When I collected my mail I found that it was my 'Elevation, a Guide to Meditation' and 'The Addictive Personality' Kundalini Yoga DVD's. from the www.Devotion.co.uk website. My son's court guardian came today. A lot rests on what Dr Peter Yates writes in his report. I don't think that my son's court guardian will be coming on Thursday to see my son and myself as the psychiatrist is going to be there. Instead he mentioned that he will perhaps choose to visit us at the Breslass family centre next week. After he left, I sat and watched my new DVD's. My mum rang me this evening and I spent an hour speaking with her about what took place with my son's psychiatrist and court guardian.

Wednesday 12th April 2006

Dear Yvonne,

Last night I took nine and a half mgs of Stelazine and slept for nine and a half peaceful hours. When I woke up, I said my prayers and read my 'Just for today,' got washed, dressed and had some breakfast cereals, toast with marmalade and a cup of decaffeinated tea before setting off at 8.50hrs. My watch had stopped earlier on in the morning at 8.15hrs and I instinctively kept looking at my wrist for the time. I had had my watch a few years and decided to replace it. So I set off to the post office to put some credit on my mobile phone and and proceeding on to Greenwich. Sarah, my drum tutor is located in Greenwich, and as today will be my first lesson with her at 11.00hrs, I didn't want to be late and thought that if I was really early getting there that I would buy my new watch in Greenwich before the start of her lesson. It is a bit tricky to get to Greenwich from Herne Hill at the best of times and today during rush hour was no different. I arrived at Herne Hill station just in time to board a train that was on the platform, which I thought would take me to the Elephant and Castle. There was also another train in the station at the same time, on the other platform but that was going to Victoria. So when the first station that my train stopped at was Blackfriars, I knew I had miscalculated.

I got off the train and took a bus to the Elephant and Castle, then took the underground from there to London Bridge and then took the train from there to Greenwich and walked from there to the Cutty Sark and on to the Cutty Sark pub stopping only in Marks & Spensers to buy a drink and going to the tourist board for directions to the Cutty Sark pub. When I had positioned myself opposite the Cutty Sark pub and seated myself by the large iron anchor, I rang Sarah, who could see me from her building. I really enjoyed the lesson and although it had been almost twenty years since I had last played a drum kit, I felt as if I were doing the right thing going back to live music. Even though I was clumsy with my drumsticks and lacked timing, I felt happy just to be given the chance to drum again. I am only hoping that I won't turn into the late Keith Moon. As well as giving me some written homework of the drum music that I was playing today Sarah also lent me some drumsticks to use. When I left my drum lesson, and got to London Bridge, I purchased a file for my drum music. When I arrived home and looked in my letterbox I found that I had a gas bill, so I went to the post office and paid it. I then went to Argos and purchased a stopwatch watch, which I set to the correct time and placed around my neck. I then brought some perishable groceries from Marks and Spensers and returned home. My social worker rang me to change the time that I am to meet her for my C.P.A tomorrow to an hour earlier as the doctor didn't want to rush the session. I declined as that would have meant my not having contact with my son. So we have postponed my C.P.A until Friday 21st April 2006 at 15.30hrs and I have change the time of my meeting on that day with my son's social worker from 14.30hr to 11.00hrs. I went to a meeting this evening and felt rejuvinated for having done so. Laura rang me this evening and we spent an hour talking.

Thursday 13th April 2006

Dear Yvonne,

Last night I took ten mgs of Stelazine, had eight and a half hours sleep and woke up feeling tired. I prayed, read my daily text, washed, dressed and had breakfast, before setting off to collect my medication from my social worker. When I arrived in West Norwood, my social worker asked me how I was feeling and afterwards spoke about my forthcoming C.P.A. I for my part tried to impress on her just how important I thought that the insight therapy would be for me. She explained to me the terms 'insight' and 'cognative' because I told her I was using the words without understanding what they meant. I thought I understood what she meant when she explained it, but I am so tired now that I have almost completely forgotten her explaination. Even though she spent an hour speaking with me, I can hardly remember a word of what she said. Thank goodness my medication is going to be reviewed in the C.P.A next week. When I left my social worker I went straight to Woolworths to buy some lego's for my son. He had asked me to buy him some last week and I almost forgot. I then went into WHSmiths to buy a Wallace and Gromit, and a Sponge Bob comic for my son. Plus I popped into Marks and Spencer to buy a few perishables for my son and myself to eat. I then got on a bus to Stockwell. I wasn't late to my contact but this week I arrived after my son. My son's court guardian arrived a few minutes after we had settled down in the room. I helped my son make a few Lego models and then rang his grandmother on my mobile. She spoke with him and then started to tell me how things went for her yesterday at her memorial, It was the Jehovah's Witnesses memorial yesterday and Jehovah's Witnesses worldwide were remembering when Jesus Christ was crucified. Not long after my call to my mum Dr Peter Yates came and the court guardian left. My son then decided to play with some skittles. So we tidied away the Lego's and played with the skittles with me doing the sound effects, each time my son made contact with the skittles. Then we played drawing on the blackboard and finally I my son sat on my knee and I read the Wallace and Gromit comic to him. The second hour of the contact went even faster than the first hour and before I knew where I was it was time to tidy away and leave. I didn't tell my son goodbye today and it wasn't deliberate. I just got so caught up in the commotion that I didn't do it and I have been thinking about it ever since. I feel bad about it and like a rotten mother. It is not that I don't care about my son. But somehow it happened. I know that I won't let it happen again.

Friday 14th April 2006

Dear Yvonne,

Last night I took nine and a half mgs of Stelazine and I had a restless eight hours sleep. I kept thinking about the fact that I didn't say goodbye to me son yesterday. I woke at 7.00hrs only to find myself wide awake and thinking about the fact that I didn't say goodbye to my son. I after a further bout of tossing and turning I eventually went back to sleep. When I eventually awoke at 10.00hrs I said my prayers and rang my sponsor leaving a message on her voicemail. I then read my daily text. I had another drum lesson but this time with Dan in East Finchley. After the lesson ended I decided that as I was short financially I was going to give up horse riding. Not least because I have got over my fear of horses and as I hadn't fallen off one yet which is inevitable, I might as well quit whilst I am ahead. Plus I can already do what I want to do, I am able to go on a trek with a horse. I decided that I would return to my first love music and concentrate on drum lessons. For one thing it is something that I can do in my spare time at home on my own, instead of sleeping. It is not high risk. I can join a band when I am good enough or teach in years to come. Thanks to my lesson with Dan, I wasn't on my own this Good Friday. Although I could have gone to a lunchtime meeting. But instead I am going to the Gay, Lesbian, Bi-Curious and Transgender meeting after having something to eat and watching a yoga DVD. I am currently listening to Magic Fm, 'I say a little prayer' sung by Aretha Franklin is booming out through the speakers and I am thinking of C whilst Aretha sings her lyrics.

Saturday 15th April 2006

Dear Yvonne,

Last night I took ten mgs of Stelazine and slept for thirteen hours. I prayed, and read my daily text before getting up, having a wash, dressing and having something to eat. I had made an arrangement to meet my sponsor in a cafe in Chelsea to read some more of step two out of the big book at 16.00hrs. As Brixton underground station is closed until April 17th 2006, I decided to get the 37 & 345 buses to Kings Road and got there an hour early. I took the time to send some text messages before my sponsor came. When my sponsor arrived I ordered something else to drink. I had felt enveloped in a sea of blackness with an overwhelming sensation of fatigue. I spoke to my sponsor about this and she was very helpful. We then went to a meeting together. If I hadn't arranged to meet my sponsor today, I may not have left my home and stayed in bed, isolating and worrying about what was going to happen with my son, as well as what I am doing with my life. Just being able to share honestly what is happening with me, helped to put a little distance between me and the abyss. My sponsor gave me a twelve by twelve book as she had two. I will be able to finish my step two now as this book has the missing answers. Today my sponsor arranged to see me tomorrow and read a bit more from the big book and I am looking forward to it.

Sunday 16th April 2006

Dear Yvonne,

Last night I took nine mgs of Stelazine and I slept for eight hours. I prayed, read my daily text, got up, had a bath, dressed and had some breakfast before setting off to my Women's meeting, where I have my tea commitment. After the meeting I my sponsor bought me lunch and read to me from the big book. She spent a couple of hours talking with me and my dark cloud distanced itself some more. Afterwards I went home and went to sleep for a few hours. When I woke up I decided that I was not going to do drumming lessons. I have planned instead to do yoga and meditation. I need a conscious contact with my higher power as I am insane without it. I had noticed that doing the yoga works with my mind and body and the meditation makes me centre myself. I have also decided that I am going to do a degree in Women's Studies and English Literature at the London Metropolitan University if I get in. As I need to have the support of other students around me and to build up a social network, not to isolate myself off from other people. I went to Brixton meeting and when I came home I dial 1471 and found that Ab had rang yesterday so I rang her. She called me back and we spoke for an hour. I have known Ab for about sixteen years and so I took the opportunity to tell her what I am up to now. I told her about my son being in foster care and I told her my plans for university and yoga. I told her about my ongoing struggle with mental illness. The call ended with her saying that she was going to call me to take me out for an orange juice.

Monday 17th April 2006

Dear Yvonne,

Last night I took ten mgs of Stelazine, slept for twelve hours and then lazed about in bed all day. I started the twelve step recovery program on 12th November 2005 and so I am five months into it. Clean, sober, sane and safe. That means that I can apply to go on the helpline. I rang my sponsor and told her about it and she told me to give her sponsor a call and ask her to explain what it entails. Which I did. I feel I want to give something back and plug myself into the program, especially as my sponsors sponsor is going to attend my

15th May 2006 court hearing with me. I just feel that I am not alone in times of trials.

Tuesday 18th April 2006

Dear Yvonne,

Last night I took nine and a half mgs of Stelazine and slept for nine and a half hours. I then got up and went to put some credit on my mobile phone, plus pay one months instalment on my water rates. I then went to Marks & Spencers and purchased some perishables, went to Woolworths and bought some playdough for my son.. I also went to buy some shampoo, conditioner and hair oil for my hair. I also went to Superdrug to buy some washing powder. When I arrived home I took from my letterbox an envelope with information from the United Kindom Council for Psychotherapy regarding registered psychotherapist. I then proceeded to leave messages on the answer machines of the therapists closest to my abode. I had something to eat and watched 'The L Word' DVD.

I enjoyed watching it as it reminded me about life as a lesbian. I hadn't seen 'The L Word' before and told myself that I needed to start reading my Karin Kallmaker books. One therapist returned my call and when I explained a little about myself to her she let me know that she thought that I could get my therapy on the National Health Service (NHS) and that she was private. I then rang Sarah to postpone my drum lesson with her on Saturday as I am going to a London twelve step convention this weekend. I have the ten pound ticket in my possession as I purchased it whilst at a meeting last Sunday. The London convention is going to be at Friends Meeting House, Euston Road on Friday 21st April 2006 to Sunday 23rd April 2006. But this Sunday I am going to miss the morning program as I have a tea commitment. I also rang B to postpone doing my diary this week Saturday for the same reason. I spent an hour speaking with B and thanking her for her friendship over the years. I told her that I had gone through a black mood over the last few days to do with my son. B reminded me that I had given my son a good foundation. A loving caring home, a Rudolf Steiner education and I continue to do the best I can with my current circumstances. I agreed that I am glad that I brought my son into the world, and that he is a positive bonus.

Wednesday 19th April 2006

Dear Yvonne,

Last night I took ten mgs of Stelazine and sleep on and off for the whole day. I was supposed to do my laundry today but I didn't bother. Instead I slept, listened to radio four, made phone calls and texts and took phone calls and texts. Three therapists returned my call today but were unable to provide me with therapy. One of them gave me the 0207-401-3260 telephone number for the Guild Low Fee Psychotherapy Clinic a sliding scale fee paying for therapists clinic based in London SE1, but the waiting list is full and closed until October 2006. In my letterbox today was a letter from my housing benefits office stating that my £60.00 per week rent is going to be backdated and paid. I am pleased.

Thursday 20th April 2006

Dear Yvonne,

Last night I took nine and a half mgs of Stelazine and slept for ten peaceful restful hours. I woke up and stripped my bed and got my washing ready for the laundry. I had some cereals, toast with marmalade and a cup of tea before I got on with the washes. There were two loads of washes. Whilst doing my wash I looked in my letterbox and found an estimated electricity bill for £59.92. I don't have enough money to pay it this week. I will pay it next week. After I washed and dried my washing, I got ready to go and see my son, stopping off at WHSmiths on the way for some comics and Marks & Spencers for some nibbles for lunch. When I saw my son, he greeted me with six photographs of himself and suprise of all surprises he was wearing spectacles in his pictures. I don't know if he is long or short sighted but if he has glasses then he needs them. He bought his glasses along for me to see them today, but he did not wear them. I asked him if he wears them to Kindergarten, but he said that he didn't. I gave him his playdough and he played with it, making me a train. Then we read from the Thomas the tank engine comic that I bought him. I felt sad today whilst with him. I couldn't help thinking about him and me not being together. I then rang my mum and she spoke to her grandson for a while during which he told her that he had some photographs for her. When my son and mum finished speaking to each other my mum told me that she missed her grandson and was crying because of it. I felt worse to know that I could be responsible for breaking the heart of the seventy year old lady that I love. It was almost to much to bear, especially when things are out of my hands. I asked the supervisor of the contact how she thought it went last week and she said "good" and that cheered me up. When my son was going home after contact, he asked if I wanted a lift with him because he loves me to best. I thanked him for his offer but let him down gently.

Friday 21st April 2006

Dear Yvonne,

Last night I took nine and a half of Stelazine and slept for eleven peaceful restful hours. I then said my prayers and read my just for today book, before getting up. My son's CQSW arrived at 11.00hrs and we settled down with a cup of tea and started to talk about my supervised access. My son's CQSW said that they had gone well and that what she was waiting for was the report from Dr Peter Yates. I told her that I had written a letter to my co-op asking if my flat could be amalgamated with the one next door so that my son could have his own bedroom. She said that it would be good for my son if that could happen. I tried to find out if my son was short or long sighted and she said she would let me know and I asked if I could have telephone contact with my son on a day when I was not seeing him and she said that she would speak with his court guardian and his foster carer and see if it could be arranged. We also had a discussion about my son moving to a mainstream school but I said I wanted him to stay in his school and that I would pay the fees. She told me that she was hoping to have Lyn and Pete assessed as foster carers for my son before we go to court on Monday 15th May 2006. After she left I went to bed listening to 'Wahe Guru' by Carolyn Cowan Karta Kaur. I got up at 14.30hrs and went to my Care Plan Approach (C.P.A) with my social worker and my psychiatrist. After spending many minutes talking to me and reading my report, he reduced my medication to nine mgs of Stelazine each night, and said he would review it in a few weeks. He then rang the Guild Low Fee Psychotherapy Clinic and left a message for them to get back to him so that I could have psychotherapy. Afterwards I spoke to my social worker and told her that I was thinking of changing my horse riding classes for yoga classes. Then I set off to a twelve step London Convention. I arrived there just in time to do service. I was on registration at the front door for the first hour and a half before leaving and going in the main hall and listening to the speakers. I met up with a few friends and went to the Glass Bar with one of them afterwards. We had an orange juice mixed with lemonade before I was given a lift to my door. I rang B to tell her all about my day's event.

Saturday 22nd April 2006

Dear Yvonne,

Last night I took nine mgs of Stelazine and slept for eight and a half hours. Today was a full day at the convention. I gave away my ticket for tonights party as I was feeling tired after today. Instead I came home and worked on my step 2 whilst listening to an 'Anthony C' CD that I purchased from the convention. I also purchased Nicholas Evans book 'The Horse Whisperer' from Waterstones, which I started reading.

Sunday 23rd April 2006

Dear Yvonne,

Last night I took nine mgs of Stelazine and slept for eight and a half hours. I prayed, read my 'Just for today' and got ready to go to my Women's meeting where I have my tea commitment. Afterwards a few of the participants of the meeting went to the convention. But after only a short time there made our way to St Thomas' Accident and Emergency clinic as one of the participants wasn't feeling very well. We spent three hours in Casualty and then I was given a lift home and invited the driver in for a cup of tea. Lucky for me she had driven me to and from the convention yesterday. It is the first time in a long time that I have invited someone in my abode, and I felt glad that I did it. I had become isolated and it was good for me to connect. She told me about an organisation called 'Creative Routes' which is run by and for Survivors of the mental health system, and said that they had a pop in on Mondays, drumming day at the Camberwell Leisure Centre 12-2pm for beginners and 3-5pm for advanced. I am going to go along to it tomorrow. She also lent me her Neale Donald Walsch book 'Conversations with God', which I started reading.

Monday 24th April 2006

Dear Yvonne,

Last night I took nine and a half mgs of Stelazine and slept for eleven hours before waking up, saying my prayers, reading my 'Just for Today' book. I then got up, washed, dressed and had breakfast and set off to 'Creative Routes' I wanted to see what it was like before going to my psychotherapy group which starts at 12.30pm and ends at 1.30pm each Monday. I managed to get myself on their mailing list and collected two of their March newsletters before I left for my group and collected Jason Pegler's book 'A Can of Madness'. In my group today we talked about relationships. I said that I wasn't very good at them. But I had improved with my friendships. During my group a tutor from Kensington and Chelsea College rang to say that he was not going to teach me tomorrow afternoon as he had a meeting about funding for his lessons and could not make it. So as my maths lesson was in the morning and I hadn't done my homework, I decided to take an extra day off college and spend the day languishing in bed. After the group I stopped for a hot drink and a sandwich before leaving the Maudsley Hospital and making my way to 'Creative Routes'. When I arrived for the second time in one day, the time was just gone two and so the drumming was coming to close. But I explained myself to the tutor and he let me just the group and drum for the last few minutes with the others. When the beginners class ended I waited around for the advanced class to start and explained myself to the tutor who signalled for me to join the group. I enjoyed the two hour congo drumming.

One of the group is also a member of my 'Cooltan' poetry class and I was pleased that he sat next to me. The group has a gig coming up on Thursday, I wont be able to attend as I will be with my son. I will however be attending an prop art workshop tomorrow with 'Creative Routes that they are running with someone from the Young Vic Theatre Company and will be arriving at 12pm. After my drumming session today I went for a hot drink in a cafe with some of the participants including my friend from poetry class and spent and hour and a chatting over two cups of hot beverages. I was going to go to a meeting in Deptford at 18.00hrs and then go to dinner with my ex-sponsor and his fiance but I felt tired and cancelled.

Tuesday 25th April 2006

Dear Yvonne,

Last night before I spoke with my sponsor I took nine mgs of Stelazine. My sponsor has arranged to see me at Parsons Green on Saturday at 14.30hrs to go through my step 2. and to start me on step 3. I was pleased but a bit distressed that I won't be working with B on my diary for yet another week. I read step three from my 'twelve by twelve' and from my Joe McQ book as my sponsor had instructed me to, and then I went to sleep at 00.30hrs and slept for ten peaceful hours. I woke up with no food in the house for breakfast and I had to be at 'Creative Routes' for mid-day. So I said my prayer, read my 'Just for Today' got washed, dressed and went out to have breakfast in the same cafe in Camberwell that I had tea in yesterday afternoon. Afterwards I popped into the library to read today's newspapers as I was a few minutes early for my prop art class. I was nervous about going to an art class as I don't see myself as having an ounce of artistic creativity. I was still tired and wondered if it wouldn't have been better for me to just skip the class and return home to bed. But when I went to 'Creative Routes' I met up with the drama group who are meeting on Tues, Weds and Thurs from 12.00-16.00hrs. I stayed with them for a few minutes before going to my class. We made cardboard cut outs just like the ones at the seaside where they have a person in bathing costumes with cut outs where you put your face and hands. I spent time painting my prop and enjoyed myself.

I felt as if I hadn't given art enough of a chance in the past and time flew by so quickly and I lost my sense of tiredness during the activity. The participants and tutors were friendly and one of the participants who I met yesterday at the drumming workshop was taking photographs. I told her that I was dyslexsic with single lense reflex (SLR) cameras and that for years I have been wanting to learn but don't know what to do with the aperture and shutter speed and film speed. I told her that I have a SLR camera and she said if I bring it in the Monday after next she will help me with it. This has greatly pleased me as I have been wanting to learn for at least twenty years! At the end of the class I felt happy with my work and now that the class is going to take place each Friday from 12.00hrs to 17.00hrs I will gladly attend. This evening I went over to Lyn's abode for a cup of tea. It seemed like ages since I saw her last. She told me that Pete was in San Franscisco visiting his son. We spoke about my son and my request for my flat to be merged with my neighbours.

Wednesday 26th April 2006

Dear Yvonne,

Last night I took nine and a half mgs of Stelazine and had ten peaceful nights sleep. I woke up tired this morning and found it hard to drag myself out of the bed to go to college. I arrived in class fifteen minutes before the class started, but my tutor was half an hour late. We started work on Toni Morrison's 'Beloved' after I handed in my 'Macbeth' essay. I was tired in the class and knowing that I had study skills after my english literature lesson didn't make it any easier, though I enjoyed my lesson. At the end of it, I went off in search of my adult learning skills (ALS) tutor as I was eager to find out what was going to happen next Tuesday afternoon with my punctuation class. When I found him he mentioned that the college had overspent its budget and for that area of learning and that a few tutors were given the sack and that even though he hadn't been, he was going to have more students and less time to tutor them, if at all. This news makes me feel more disconnected from my studies as I don't have the confidence and having less time with the tutor, if any at all doesnt help. I arrived late for my study skill class but soon settled in after telling the tutor what caused my delay. I feel really tired today so I am not going to go the LGBT Forum meeting tonight. Even thought it was going to be the conclusion feedback from the research that SIGMA was commissioned to do. I am going to have a lie-down and call B later and speak with her.

Thursday 27th April 2006

Dear Yvonne,

Last night I spoke to B for an hour and then took nine mgs of

Stelazine and went to sleep for ten hours but still woke up feeling tired. I went to West Norwood at 9.30hrs after paying my electricity bill and putting some credit on my mobile. My CQSW was off sick today, so someone else gave me my medication. I took the 68 bus down the Walworth Road and stopped off in Marks & Spencers to buy some lunch for my son and myself. I was about twenty minutes early for my poetry class and felt so tired that I got on another 68 bus and went home. On arrival I went to bed and listened to radio four at 11.30hrs there was a programme with was related to comedy and mental health. It was quite interesting but after it ended I went to sleep for an hour. On waking I set off to see my son at the Breslass Family Centre. He arrived at 14.00hrs.

I had purchased some LEGO, a 'Robots' booklet from the film Robots with both he and I had been to see twice last year. I also bought him a dot to dot book as I feel it will help him to count. When he came in he started looking at the LEGO and then the Robot booklet. Then I set about making the Lego into a helicopter, with his help. He wasn't too muddy even though he is now back at Kindergarten. He gave me the bread that he made today and it was soft and tasty. At 15.30, I rang my mum and my son spoke to her briefly as he was interested in his helicopter. Lyn came to collect my son today and said that Pete had returned today from the U.S.A and was tired and in the car. When I said goodbye to my son, I made my way home. I decided to post my postal ballot for the local elections so I asked Lesley from the Gay Community to witness it and she did. Tonight is the Management Committee meeting and hopefully they will decide in my favour tonight about the amalgamation of my flat.

Friday 28th April 2006

Dear Yvonne,

Last night I spoke to my mother for two hours and then took nine mgs of Stelazine and went to sleep for eleven and a half hours of peaceful sleep. I woke up to the vibration of my mobile phone ringing. It was someone from the fellowship to ask me how I was doing. I told them that I was still asleep. After the call, I rang to find out how my request for a flat amalgamation went. I was disappointed as the co-op said that it had no money and could not go ahead with it. I have since rang back to find out if the co-op can use any of my isms to secure a grant for the venture as a last ditch attempt. I felt bad inside about the flat and decided to go back to sleep, after ringing my sponsor and telling her what was going on for me. I slept for a few more hours, only to be woken by the vibration of my mobile phone ringing once again. This time it was someone else from the fellowship who was fresh back from a relapse and a few days clean and sober. We arranged to meet to go to the Lesbian, Gay, Bi-Curious and Transgendered meeting in Covent Garden this evening. After that call, I went to look in my letterbox and found a letter from PACE (promoting lesbian and gay mental health and well being) promoting a free relationship commitment & civil partnership group, commencing on 8th May 2006. I also received a letter from my solicitor with a copy of Dr Peter Yates report. He does not recommend that my son live with me. But at least he does not recommend that my son be adopted or change school. At first I was gutted that my son not come back to live with me but after ringing my sponsor again and talking it over with her, I began to feel grateful that the recommendation is that he NOT be adopted.

Saturday 29th April 2006

Dear Yvonne,

Last night I took nine mgs of Stelazine and found it difficult to get to sleep as there was a party happening in the Gay Community with loud music that went on until late. I think I got about seven hours sleep. I woke up this morning and found that I had started my periods. I went to my drum lessons in Greenwich at 11.00hrs and my tutor gave me a pair of her sticks to keep. This week we worked on a few rudiments single sticking exercise, which is a single tap with each stick in each hand once ie RLRLRLRL and so on, double sticking exercise which is tapping each stick in each hand twice ie RRLLRRLLRRLLRRLL and so on and flams which is having one stick slightly lower than the other and hitting the snare drum with both sticks with a slight time delay. I also asked to practice the single paradiddle which is RLRRLRLL repeated. First of all I did it with both hands and then I was asked to do it with both feet. I was given written drum music to read and given written exercises to play. I was out of practice and my drum rolls were uneven in sound.

I kept getting it wrong and chose to keep starting again. Sarah my tutor was keen to encourage me and demonstrated when I needed it. I was given homework to take home and practice. After the lesson I went home and dropped off my drumsticks and file with my drum music and had something to eat. In my letterbox was an invitation to service user's psychotherapy department 10th May 2006 from 6-7pm in the boardroom of the Maudsley Hospital. I then packed my bag with my twelve step items. I arrived in Parsons Green on time and took a walk across a park to my sponsors house. After I arrived at my sponsors home I started to blow my now runny nose as I had started to suffer with my hay-fever symptoms. She read to me and I followed in my Big Book. We finished Step 2 and then I read Step 3 and did my Step 3 with my sponsor. I am now on Step 4. I am so pleased. I feel as if I am getting somewhere. After we finished we went to a meeting and I stopped off with her and a few other participants in 'Picasso' on the Kings Road for a hot beverage and a chat. My sponsor told me that she is going to Greece from May 10th to May 17th 2006. Her sponsor will be attending court with me on May 15th 2006.

Sunday 30th April 2006

Dear Yvonne,

Last night I took nine mgs of Stelazine, went straight off to sleep and enjoyed nine and a half hours of peaceful restful bliss. I woke up this morning and said my Step 3 prayer from the Big Book and got ready to go to my Sunday morning women's meeting, armed with milk for my tea commitment. After the meeting a few of the participants went for something to eat and drink in 'Fresh & Wild', Then two other women spent the day together. We went for a walk in Battersea Park this afternoon and then had a meal together before going to a meeting. When I arrived home I received a call from my Aunt Madge in Toronto, Canada. I found out from my Aunt that she was born in March 1946, so she is ten years and a month younger than my mother. She told me that she had left the Jehovah's Witnesses and joined the Seventh Day Adventist. She also told me that she was having trouble lately controlling her diabetes but that she was not yet on insulin. Most of my mother's family are diabetic. They have mature onset diabetes. I told her the latest news about my son and she said that she will pray for me.

Monday 1st May 2006

Dear Yvonne,

Last night I took nine mgs of Stelazine and slept for ten hours of peaceful sleep. I then woke up sent and received a few texts, left a message on my sponsors voicemail and lazed around in bed for the day listening to radio four. I got up at 15.00hrs, said my Step 3 prayer, had something to eat and got on with some of my maths studies. I have a test in my maths lesson tomorrow. When I had nearly finished my studies, my mother rang me and I told her that I was not going to get my flat merger and that my son was not going to live with me. She took it well and said that maybe it was for the best and that she was not going to give up on me. I also told her that Aunt Madge rang me yesterday. My mother told me that she had gone over on the side of her foot two days ago and had sprained her ankle, and was finding it difficult to climb the stairs in her house. She also said that V.J wasn't very well and was still showing blood in his urine. I don't know what to do as I can't live with my mother because I don't want to be away from my son. After I finished speaking to my mother, I set off to Brixton underground station as I had arranged to meet someone and go to the Stockwell meeting with them. After the meeting a few of the participants went for hot beverages in a cafe, me included.

Tuesday 2nd May 2006

Dear Yvonne,

Last night I took nine mgs of Stelazine and slept for nine and a half hours of peaceful sleep, before getting up and getting myself ready for college. My first lesson was maths and I had an exam. It was on ratios, but don't think that I did very well. Other students in the class and even my tutor asked me where I was last week and said that they missed me. I was a bit embarrassed but pleasantly surprised. I decided that I won't take another day off college, except when I go to court. After the lesson, I had some lunch and went to send an e-mail to Aunt Debbie in New York. After which I had my punctuation lesson. My tutor explained that it either he or another tutor will take me for next weeks lesson. When I finished college today, I went to Wordsworth's Bookshop and purchased 'York notes

Advanced Beloved Toni Morrison'. Then on my way home I purchased some perishables from Marks and Spencers. I then posted the six snapshots that my son gave me, off to my mother. But I had missed today's post and it will now be collected from the postbox tomorrow at 17.30. I have been sneezing a lot today but my eyes haven't been too bad.

Wednesday 3rd May 2006

Dear Yvonne,

Last night I spoke to B for an hour and then took nine mgs of Stelazine and slept for ten hours of peaceful sleep, but I still woke up feeling tired. I got myself to college ten minutes before the start of my English Literature class. I drank a cup of perculated caffeinated coffee before going to the class. In the class today we carried on reading about Toni Morrison and was told about a ten minute seminar that we are to each present for one credit. I am petrified as I don't know how to do it, and feel like I don't have enough time. In the following Study Skills lesson we were also told about a ten minute seminar that we are to present in a fortnight. My fear is compounded. My mother rang me to say that she has received the snapshots. I went to two meetings this evening. One in Camberwell at 18.00hrs and the second in Red Post Hill at 19.30hrs.

Thursday 4th May 2006

Dear Yvonne,

Last night I took nine mgs of Stelazine and slept for ten hours of peaceful sleep, but I still woke up feeling tired. I spent the morning sending and receiving texts. I plan to go on a three day camping holiday, Friday 16th June 2006 -Sunday 18th June 2006 in Cornwall, with some people from the fellowship. I will have to get the train there and I am looking forward to the change of scenery, but I am hoping my hay-fever won't get the better of me. Ros Dunning rang me this morning and she and I are going to meet up at 14.00hrs on Tuesday to discuss the medical reports. My mother rang to say that she wants to come to London next week, for the day to see me and bring some gifts for my son. I have asked her to come in a fortnight, so that she can come with me to see her grandson while she is here. It was a hot, sunny and dry day today and I arrived at the Bresslass family centre twenty minutes before my meeting time. When my son arrived I noticed that he had had a haircut. I looked even more cute. He had his glasses in it's case. He showed me a stone that he had found and some beeswax. Today my son was hungry and tucked into the Marks and Spencers lunch that I had bought for him. After he finished eating he played with the K'Nex that I purchased, whilst I built an aeroplane for my son at his request. I also purchased a junior Scrabble and spent some time, explaining the game to my son. It was interesting to hear my son spell phonetically. We spent some time with me tickling him and kissing him and then I rang my mother and she spoke to her grandson. Telling him that she loved his photographs and that she would soon be seeing him in the flesh. Lyn collected my son today.

Friday 5th May 2006

Dear Yvonne,

Last night I spoke to my mother on my landline for half an hour and aside from talking about my son and telling me that she was saving up to buy a new bath, she told me that V.J's condition took a turn for the worst tonight and that he was unable to go to Bingo. He varies from day to day. She said that he was becoming incontinent sometimes with blood in his urine and that she doesn't know where she finds the strength to do all the washing and shampoo cleaning of the carpet. She also let me know that yesterday a rail was erected for her garden steps as now she is seventy years of age, she is not as agile as she once was and when she hangs the washing out, she finds it a bit challenging to decend the steps without a rail. She said that V.J had tried giving up smoking but is finding himself unable to do so. She said that in one of his down moments that he said that he doesn't have long to live and that the medication that the doctors have given him is only going to keep him alive for a short time and that he will soon be leaving her. She said that she doesn't let him foster those types of morbid thoughts and ideas, choosing instead to say that everyone has to go at some point and that until the time comes there is no point talking about it. But to me she says the reason is that talking about it is bad for both of them as she is fearful of how she will cope without V.J. My mother also told me that she has a hacking cough and that she suffers with stress incontinence when her bouts of coughing is severe. She said she only told me so that I can know how things are for her and V.J but when I laughed she said that she wished that I was a little closer so that she could give me a punch on the mouth or a black eye! When I laughed even more, she said that I am not too far away from stress incontinence myself. Anyway the fact is I don't know what I was laughing about I suffer with bouts of enuresis as 19th December 2005 testifies. She then let me into a little secret, and that is that she asked seventy-eight year old V.J if he still felt sexual tendencies, to which V.J said yes but that though the feelings were there he was impotent and his penis remained limp. She said that when they go out together he would say when they are in the company of their friends that he "was dying for love" and the friends would think that my mother was too cruel. I feel as if with each conversation I have with my mother we grow closer and it makes me feel good to think that my mother can turn to me in her hour of need. After speaking to my mother I took nine mgs of Stelazine and slept for ten peaceful hours but I still woke up tired. I got myself out of bed and ready to go to Creative Routes where I spent the day making more props and painting. Afterwards I went to an internet cafe and then to a meeting.

Saturday 6th May 2006

Dear Yvonne,

Last night I took nine mgs of Stelazine and had eight hours of peaceful sleep and woke up feeling tired. But I set off to my drumming lesson in Greenwich. I hadn't practiced my rudiments all week and so was very slow when playing them. We went over last weeks lesson and then Sarah told me the name of each item on the drum kit, before giving me some more sheet music to read and play. This week I also began to use my left foot on the hi-hat. When my lesson was over I met B at the Cutty Sark in Greenwich. We walked in the market and B bought me lunch before looking in a bookshop and buying my son the Charlotte Uhlenbroek book 'Talking with Animals' and me 'Medicines & prescription Drugs' where I found that the side effects of Stelazine aka Trifluoperazine are: sleepiness, vertigo, lightheadedness, unsteadiness, disturbance of vision, rash, hypotension, gastro-intestinal upset, changes to libido, retention of urine, Allergic reactions, dry mouth, constipation, palpitation, sweating, tachycardia, nervousness, heart arrhythmiask conduction defects, Impotence, effects on breasts, weight loss or gain, Tinnitus (ringing in ears), effects on central nervous system, changes in blood sugar, blood disorders. Mania and schizophrenic symptons may rarely be activated, particularly in the elderly. I have the sleepiness, lightheadedness, disturbance of vision, hypotention, changes to libido, nervousness, Impotence, effects on breasts and weight gain, I spent the afternoon doing my diary with B and she gave me a doggy bag to take home with me. When I got home, Eric rang to see how I was and we spent fifteen minutes talking.

Sunday 7th May 2006

Dear Yvonne,

Last night I took nine mgs of Stelazine and had nine hours of peaceful sleep and woke up feeling tired. At breakfast this morning I had a cup of caffeinated Earl Gray tea before setting off to the Battersea women's meeting where I have my tea commitment. Whilst at the meeting I had a caffeinated coffee. After the meeting I went with two others to a twelve step convention in Purley, where they were running a Step 1,2 & 3, 4,5 & 6 workshop in the afternoon. I stayed long enough have another caffeinated coffee and a caffeinated tea whilst listening to the workshops. I managed to listen to the Step 4 workshop before setting off with the others to a meeting in Brixton. I collected my six month keyring at the Brixton meeting. I feel good to be clean, sober and sane. When I got home I rang my sponsor and we have arranged to meet tomorrow go through step four and then go to a meeting in Chelsea. It is now 22.25hrs and I don't feel tired but I am going to have a snack, take my medication and go to bed.

Monday 8th May 2006

Dear Yvonne,

Last night I took nine mgs of Stelazine and had nine and a half hours of peaceful sleep. I then dozed on and off for three hours before finally getting up and setting off to my group psychotherapy session. On leaving my flat, I looked in my letterbox and found that a copy of the 4th May 2006 issue 899 'Pink Paper' had arrived so I took it with me to the group. On my way to the group someone who was decorating a property called out to me as I was walking to the bus stop and I found that it was someone from the fellowship. I spent a few minutes chatting with them about the program before getting on my way. In the group today we spoke about what was in the medical report for the court and the fact that the psychiatrist doesn't think my son should live with me. The people in the group seemed generally sad. I also told them that I had taken to drinking caffeinated tea's and coffee's as I felt so drowsy most of the time. In the group I decided that I would reduce my Stelazine to eight and a half mgs from tonight. After the group I had a decaffeinated tea in the hospital canteen with a few members of the group and one of them, a devoted Christian read my 'Pink Paper' I think the 'Cops Order Christians to Close Hate Site' headlines enticed him. Before he turned the pages and read the articles entitled 'Right wing extremists are on the up, Christians are warned', 'Church inspired by Fashanu kicks off its first service' and 'Bishop bashed for refusing to condemn arch-enemy's hate'. After my hot drink I went home and had something to eat before setting off to my sponsor's home.

Tuesday 9th May 2006

Dear Yvonne,

Last night I took eight and a half mgs of Stelazine and had ten hours of peaceful sleep. I then got up and went to WHSmiths to buy a ring binder for my Step 4 work. I then went to Marks and Spencers and purchased some perishables and after went to Woolworths and bought a couple of games and a jigsaw for my son. Today I didn't feel so tired but I had blurred vision and suffered the ill effects of hay-fever. I went to see my solicitor today and she went over what Dr Peter Yates had written. She wanted me to seriously consider changing my Stelazine to a more modern cleaner drug like the one Dr Peter Yates had mentioned in his report namely Olanzapine aka Zyprexa. The side effects of Olanzapine are weight gain, sleepiness, neutropenia (decline in blood platelets increasing risk of bleeding), eosinophilia (increase in number of eosinophils-white blood cells - usually an inflammatory or allergegic response), weakness, anticholinergic effects, increase, increased appetite, dizziness, fluid retention in peripheral regions, orthostatic hypotention (low blood pressure on standing up), raised blood triglyceride levels ans AST

ALT, akathisia (abnormal condition of agititation and restlessness)
In the end she and I agreed that she could ask the judge to release
the medical reports so that my team can see them. After leaving my
solicitor, I went home and made a start on my Step 4. I also sent and
received some text messages before having something to eat and
going to meet A at the 'Glass Bar' in Euston. When I arrived at the
Glass Bar A, was already waiting for me. We decided to go for a
walk in Regents Park. A, got something to eat and bought me an
orange juice. She said that my facial rash looked bad and that I must
mention it to the doctor. I explained to her that it was the side
effects of the Stelazine that I am on and that my medication is being
reduced, so there is nothing more that can be done about it. As A,
has just returned from a holiday in Atlanta U.S.A we spoke about
that. Plus I spoke of romance and mentioned that I had lost my
libido but that it didn't matter at this stage as I was only six months
into my recovery programme and as it is suggested not to get
involved romantically for the first year, I was okay. A, has a new
woman in the U.S.A that she is smitten with and I am pleased for
her. It helps me to think of C, even though I have no problem
thinking about C and the fact that I love her and still send her a text
every day.

Wednesday 10th May 2006

Dear Yvonne,

Last night I took nine mgs of Stelazine and slept for twelve hours
before waking up, saying my prayers, reading my Just for Today
book, having breakfast and getting on with my Step 4. I then rested
and listened to Radio 4. After a while I decided to have a bath and
get ready to go to my service users meeting for the psychotherapy
department in the boardroom of the Maudsley Hospital. On my
return home I looked in my letterbox and found I had recieved a
letter from my solicitor stating that she had spoken to the local
authorities solicitor and they had said that Lyn and Pete had not
been assessed for fostering yet, and there assessment is going to run
past the final court hearing. She mentioned that the court guardian
was trying to put back the final hearing. After reading the letter I
rang B and she rang me back and I went through my Step 4 with her
and invited her to remind me of any one that I had mentioned
having resentments about. She reminded me of at least seven

additional people.

Thursday 11th May 2006

Dear Yvonne,

Last night I took eight and a half mgs of Stelazine and slept for nine peaceful hours. My sponsor has gone to Greece for a week today so I didnt have to ring her before waking up and getting myself ready to go to see my social worker and pick up my Stelazine medication. We spoke together for half an hour. I told her that I was still tired and that I now had hayfever. I also told her that I had given up horse riding and hadn't been to my poetry class for a while. Since the poetry class has moved it takes me longer to get there and I have to leave at 12.30hrs after arriving at 11.00hrs for the class which ends at 14.00hrs, in order to get to the Breslass centre on time to see my son. After leaving my social worker, I went to Marks and Spencers and bought the lunch, went home and lay down for an hour. During that time my son's court guardian rang and made an appointment to visit me tomorrow morning at 9.30hrs, after his call I set off to see my son. My son arrived at 13.30hrs and seemed lethargic at first but soon settled down into his old self. We started to play a few games and then I rang my mum and she spoke to my son. We then played a tickling game and then a few other games before Lyn came and it was time for him to go. I then went home and lay down for a couple of hours and my sponsor's sponsor rang me. She is going to go to court with me on Monday. I said I would text her tomorrow to tell her which court we will be in. My sponsor rang me from Greece today.

Friday 12th May 2006

Dear Yvonne,

Last night I took nine mgs of Stelazine and slept for nine and a half peaceful hours before waking up and getting myself ready for a visit from my son's court guardian. I felt drowsy before he arrived so I made myself a caffeinated expresso coffee. When he arrived we discussed Dr Peter Yates report and the fact that my son is not coming back home to me. He also recommended that I move as I am currently overlooking Lyn and Pete's abode and if my son goes there he will be looking out the window watching my every move and not settling in. So after the court guardian left, I rang Creative Routes and told them that I would not be going there today and decided to go to view the six, one bedroomed properties that had come up for let in the co-op. Of the six, I thought that one could with a bit of work be suitable and went to view it a second time with Lyn. After which Lyn and I drafted the following letter which I hand delivered to the co-op before heading off to a meeting:

Flat 6, 151 Railton Road, SE24 0LT

12 May 2006

Dear Allocations Committee

I have had a look at available units on offer at the moment.

Of these 66 Mayall Road (basement flat) could be suitable. But it does need work done on it before it is habitable.

These repairs include new flooring throughout, new kitchen units and re-decoration. I also think I would need doors or something similar to close off the bedroom from the rest of the flat.

I look forward to hearing from you, in co-operation

Regards Yvonne

Saturday 13th May 2006

Dear Yvonne,

Last night I took eight and a half mgs of Stelazine and had a peaceful sleep. I woke up and got myself ready to go to my drumming lesson in Greenwich. After going through my rudiments in drumming I drummed to so drum music that I was reading and made lots of mistakes and then Sarah got me to drum to a CD that she played. She asked me to play anything that I wanted and to fill with rolls. I think that I was worse than no good at it. She said that I will get a lot of opportunities to practice like this, so not to worry.

After my drum lesson I met with B and she brought me lunch and showed me some of the sites of Greenwich before we caught the bus back to her place and continued with the rest of my diary up to Friday 10th February 2006, which is the first ninety-five pages of my first draft. I told B about Mayall Road and decided on just moving in without trying to get the co-op to do the work as it is a temparary move. On my return home I spoke it over with Lyn and wrote the following letter and hand delivered it to the co-op:

Flat 6, 151 Railton Road, SE24 0LT

13 May 2006

Dear Allocations Committee

Following on from my letter 12/5/06 re; 66 Mayall Road. On reflection I would like to be considered for allocation to 19c Milton Road.

I look forward to hearing from you, in co-operation.

Regards Yvonne

Sunday 14th May 2006

Dear Yvonne,

Last night I took nine mgs of Stelazine and slept for eleven peaceful restful hours, before getting up and going to my tea commitment womens meeting in Battersea. After the meeting I went to the home of one of the participants and stayed for the afternoon and shared a meal with her before leaving with her and going to the Brixton meeting. My Sponsor sent me a text message from Greece to wish me good luck for tomorrow and a restful sleep tonight.

Monday 15th May 2006

Dear Yvonne,

Last night I took eight and a half mgs of Stelazine and slept for eight hours. When I woke up I got myself ready to go to court for the directives. My sponsor rang me from Greece to wish me good luck and I received a few good luck text messages. I arrived at the court at 10.30am, an hour before the start of the case and my sponsor's sponsor was there waiting for me. We sat in the no smoking waiting room and chatted a while before saying a prayer and the serenity prayer together. When my son's court guardian arrived I told him that I had been to see six properties and had applied for one of them. He seemed pleased and told my son's social worker and I in turn told my solicitor. The judge agreed to an additional date on Wednesday 18th October 2006 being added to 20th June 2006 final hearing, so that we would know the outcome of the assessment of Lyn and Pete and if my son was going to them or another local authority foster parent. After the case my solicitor said that she would have to meet with me sometime next week to go over the threshold document. I then left the court with my sponsor's sponsor and went for a cup of coffee with her in a nearby cafe. When I arrived home I found in my letterbox a letter from the DLA. They have awarded me DLA but it has been reduced and now it won't pay my son's monthly school fee. This afternoon despondent I went to the home of someone in the fellowship and chatted before going to the 18.15hrs Stockwell meeting.

Tuesday 16th May 2006

Dear Yvonne,

Last night I took nine mgs of Stelazine and had eight peaceful hours sleep. When I woke up this morning I got ready to have an inpromtu visit with my social worker in West Norwood. I told her how yesterday's case went. I then told her about my potential move and about my DLA and asked her to appeal. As I will be getting less money I have decided to give up drumming with Sarah for the time being and just do congo drumming with Creative Routes. As I am going to move I have decided to apply to go on a pre-access course if my tutor will let me. Whilst looking through my possessions I came across my single lens reflex (SLR) camera and have decided that I am going to take up photography again and this time master it in black and white without a flash. So I went to Jessops in New Oxford Street and purchased a cable release and an Ilford 400ASA black and white film, to get me started. I am also going to look for my tripod. This evening I went to sleep for an hour and when I woke up I spoke on my landline to my mum for two hours, telling her all that is currently happening in my life.

Wednesday 17th May 2006

Dear Yvonne,

Last night I took eight and a half mgs of Stelazine and had twelve hours of peaceful sleep. My sponsor rang me from Greece and told me she will be back in London this evening. I went to college and handed in two overdue library books, but the librarian did not charge me for them. one of the books were four days overdue and the other three days. I felt grateful. My English Literature tutor rang me and said that she was going to post my Macbeth draft back to me so that I could tidy it up as I was going to get a level three for it. I told her that I was waiting for my course tutor to call me so that I could go on a pre access course starting in September. I then went to dinner with someone in the fellowship and went to a meeting with them after. I failed to send C a text today.

Thursday 18th May 2006

Dear Yvonne,

Last night I took nine mgs of Stelazine and slept for nine peaceful hours. I woke up and got ready to go to Victoria Coach Station and meet my mum from her Luton 757 coach. She arrived half an hour early and rang me on my mobile fifteen minutes before I got there. It was lovely to see my mother. We greeted each other warmly. My mother was carrying two bags of clothes for my son, she said that she is unable to carry heavy loads these days and she is also not able to walk with speed. So the first thing we did was go to the ladies toilet in Victoria Shopping Centre and then we queued up and purchased a one day travel pass for zone 1&2. So that we could catch a train from Victoria to Herne Hill Station. During that time we happily chatted away to each other, while my mother, a woman who is given to wearing make up, looking like a female model out of vogue, applied another coat of nail varnish. I don't have my mother's dress sense. She is elegant and flows and I am not and don't. She wears make up and I do not. She is also taller and slimer than I am. But today when I showed her a small picture I carry everywhere with me of my son, she showed me a small picture she carries everywhere of me! We got the 196 bus from near Herne Hill Station to the Brelass and we were waiting ten minutes when my son arrived. He had picked a flower for me and gave me a fresh bun that he had baked today. When he laughed I noticed that his second front tooth was missing. I asked him how he lost it and he said that it was wobbly and his friend Sebastian punched it out at school. I was agast to think that such things were happening in a Steiner School. But he seem unperturbed so I took him to see my mum who was hiding from him in the meeting room. When my mum saw my son she greeted him with a big hug and lots of kisses and my son hugged her back. It took him a while to start talking chosing to say yes and no by nodding or shaking his head. First I decided to try him in his clothes to see if they fitted him. My mum had bought him a three piece suit which on seeing him dressed in it will fit him properly in about six months time.

She had also bought him some tee shirts which fit and a pair of shorts which fit and three pairs of jeans which were slightly too long, but my son liked them. After fitting him with the clothes we had something to eat and then I played with my son while my mum reminised about when we travelled together and the things we did such as asking my son if he remembered going on a horse on the beach in Jamaica with my mother also on the same horse as he wouldn't go on by himself. My son said that he could remember the man leading the horse which pleased my mum, who had also bought some birthday pictures of my son at his own second birthday party in Florida with my Aunt Catherine. My son said that he loves that photograph. My mum was also saying that my son reminded her of her late brother Robert, when he was a child. She said that Robert was intelligent and went on to pass all his exams and was fun to be with. Robert went on to be a chief superintendent of police in Kingston, Jamaica and was the child that my mother followed in birth. Lyn came to collect my son and offered to take my mum back to Victoria Coach Station and my mum accepted. On my arrival home I found a letter from the department of Work and Pension (DWP) stating that in June my Income Support was going to be reduced by approximately £12.00 each week. I sent C a text to say that I was going to be moving and that I will be texting her infrequently.

Friday 19th May 2006

Dear Yvonne,

Last night I took eight and a half mgs of Stelazine and slept for twelve hours of peaceful sleep. I woke up and got myself ready to go prop painting at Creative Routes. On my way out of my abode I found in my letterbox a letter from Ros Dunning asking me to see her in her office on Tuesday 23rd May 2006 at 15.00hrs to go over the Threshold documents. This will mean missing college and more importantly my punctuation class, which I missed last week. I don't think that I can miss two classes in a row without being kicked off it but it cant be helped. I also found an invitation to Nigel's 60th birthday party on 24th June 2006. He lives above Johnathan in the Gay and Lesbian Community I had a great time at Creative Routes today. I mentioned to them that I am likely to be moving soon and that I need help and they said that they would put it in the newsletter. They may be able to get a posse of people along to help move and decorated.

I also bought my camera along with me today and Nuala looked at it and said that it was a good camera. She said that she had a roll of film for me and made arrangements for me to meet her next week Wednesday 24th May at 17.00hrs at Creative Routes armed with my camera and tripod and she will give me some exercises to do. When she looked through my viewfinder, she saw that my light meter battery was dead and so she asked me to replace it before she sees me next. So after leaving Creative Routes today I went to Jessop's and purchased a new battery and then went to 'First Out cafe bar' and had a cup of coffee. My sponsor rang me on my mobile before I went to the Covent Garden LGBT meeting and arranged to meet me on Monday afternoon, after my group psychotherapy, to do a little bit more of my Step 4.

She told me that she was going to speak with her sponsor to let me know if there was something that I should be working on before I meet up with her. After the meeting I went with a few of the participants to Costa in Old Compton Street for coffee. I met someone there that does photography for a living and she explained to me that the aperture can be used for the field of view. So the larger the number for the aperture ie 22 the further the field of view and the smaller the circle that exposes light to the film. The smaller the number for the aperture ie 3.5 the closer the field of view and the bigger the circle that exposes light to the film. She said that in the park having the aperture stopped at 22 would have clear vision into infinity. She also said that film speed suited the type of day, ie 200ASA was suited to a cloudy day and 400ASA could be used inside at night with or without a tripod. She said that a tripod has to be used for shutter speeds lower than 15. Although if you have a very steady hand you could survive without a tripod at 15. She said that the small flash that I own would be too harsh and could do with a filter. She said that I could get 1600ASA film from Jessop's that could be used at a very slow shutter speeds. She said that I had a good camera so I intend to make photography my new hobby.

Saturday 20th May 2006

Dear Yvonne,

Last night I took nine mgs of Stelazine but because of all the caffeine I drank in the form of espresso's and caffacino's I did not get to sleep until after 2am and I was wide awake at 9am. I got up and typed up the punctuation correction in my diary. I then had breakfast. I was thinking of doing some preparations for my forthcoming move but I felt dAunted by it and aborted the attempt. I rang my sponsor but she was somewhere in the countryside and her mobile had a poor reception and it was difficult for me to communicate with her. I then rang B and made arrangements to meet her in Peckham. When B and I met up we went shopping but I was feeling mentally tired and asked her to buy me a cup of coffee, so we stopped off in McDonald's. We then purchased a few perishable items before catching a bus to her place. When we arrived I asked B to make me another coffee, which I drank while we chatted. B made a loaf of bread today with her bread making machine and after satisfying herself that it had turned out okay she gave it to me to take home for myself. She also helped me to draft a timetable for my weekly activities, so that I can get more rest and have time to prepare for my move. We decided that college had to go, not least because what with my benefit cuts I can no longer afford it and I have no time in my routine for homework with me moving abode. We decided to cut the drumming class that I did with Creative Routes because Monday's was congested with activities.

We decided that poetry with Cooltan had to go because there wasn't enough time for it on Thursdays as it was the day I see my social worker for my medication every fortnight and my son every week and my son had to come first and not see me tired. We decided to place yoga and swimming back in my timetable once a week on Tuesdays. We decided to put a photography session in my timetable on Wednesdays and an art session with Creative Routes on Fridays. We kept the five fellowship meetings in the timetable on Mondays, Wednesdays, Fridays and Sundays and left Saturday's to see B to do my diary punctuation or see my sponsor to do my stepwork and we quite naturally left my Monday group psychotherpy sessions on my schedule. I feel so much better with this new timetable. I had felt that my life was out of control and that I wasn't getting enough time to rest like I am now sitting typing my diary in silence. Next week Saturday B will be in Berlin, Germany so I will take the opportunity to do some more sorting in my flat. I sent C a text today.

Sunday 21st May 2006

Dear Yvonne,

Last night I took eight and a half mgs of Stelazine and slept for eleven hours. Infact I overslept and was late for my commitment at my women's meeting where I have my tea commitment. But I still rang and spoke to my sponsor before I left home. I am so glad that my sponsor is back from Greece because I missed being able to speak with her each morning in order to be grounded. I arrived fifteen minutes before the meeting was due to start instead of an hour beforehand. After the meeting I went for a cup of cappacino in 'Fresh & Wild' with a few of the women from the meeting. Next week Sunday there isn't going to be a meeting in the morning so I have arranged with a couple of female friends in the fellowship to help me do some sorting in my flat. After my hot beverage in 'Fresh & Wild,' I went to a friend in the fellowship's home for lunch and then we both took the 77A bus to the National Portrait Gallery to see the 'Searching for Shakespeare' exhibition, this afternoon, using two complimentary tickets that I had that was due to expire on 29th May 2006. Afterwards we stopped off in an artists shop, as she is a painter, before going for a cappacino in 'First Out' and then walking back to Trafalgar Square and getting on a 159 bus so that we could get to a Brixton fellowship meeting. I feel grateful that I am going to be getting the opportunity to make a new start in my life.

Monday 22nd May 2006

Dear Yvonne,

Last night I took nine mgs of Stelazine and had ten hours of peaceful sleep. I felt tired when I woke up and made myself an expresso before attending my group psychotherapy session. Next week is a bank holiday so there will not be a group and the following week the group will be changing room and within the next few weeks, three new people will be joining. I am looking forward to the changes. After the group, I went to the hospital cafe and had a coffee with one of the other participants before setting off to see my sponsor. I worked with my sponsor for two hours on Step 4 in cafe Nero's and my sponsor bought the cappacinos. I told her about what was happening for me and she was pleased to hear that I was going to be moving. I am please that she is back from Greece. This evening we attended a meeting that she has a treasury commitment in. When it ended, she told me not to procrastinate on my Step 4 as she wants to guide me swiftly through it and to contact her if I get stuck on it so that she can help me.

Tuesday 23rd May 2006

Dear Yvonne,

Last night I took eight and a half mgs of Stelazine and had thirteen hours of peaceful restful sleep. When I woke up I started sorting out my footware and then I went into my waldrobe and sorted that out as well. All in all I found myself putting out four bin liners worth of rubbish, which left three bin liners of my son and my footware and six bin liners of my son and my clothes to arrange to take to the charity shop. I then got myself ready to go to my solicitor's appointment. On the bus I met Helen and her two children Nathalia and Jodie. Helen and her partner Jason is one of the parents who last year used to give my son and myself lifts to school in the mornings. We were pleased to see each other. I arrived ten minutes early and waited. Ros Dunning and I then discussed the threshold document and when I was satisfied I left. I then went to an internet cafe in Camberwell to check my emails. Aunt Debbie hadn't sent me an email, so I was disappointed. I then went to meet a fellowship friend at the Ritzy Cinema in Brixton. She was meeting with her sponsor later on in the evening to go through her step two. I decided to buy a pint of milk, some bin liners and a cake and invite her back to my pad for a coffee. When she was leaving she said that she was going to come back on Sunday and help me with my sorting. Andrew rang me tonight. He is on a five day computer course in London, but such is the intensity of the workload of the course with homework that he is not able to come to see me. I brought him up to speed with what is happening with me and my son and asked him to take toys for his baby daughter, as my son is too old for them and they will be going to the charity shop otherwise. I also asked him to help himself to my books as a fair amount of them will be ending up at a secondhand bookshop. He said that he would try and come down to see me on the bank holiday and that he will be bringing a laptop for me to use so that I can return this computer that I am using back to my son.

Wednesday 24th May 2006

Dear Yvonne,

Last night I took nine mgs of Stelazine and had ten hours peaceful sleep. I woke up and attempted to do some of my Step 4 work but aborted it after half an hour, thinking to myself that I would ring my sponsor and ask her to help me. I then got a phone call from a friend in the fellowship inviting me to lunch with her in Brixton at 13.30hrs, she was paying, and I accepted. I got myself up and out of my dull drums and went up the road to Herne Hill Station and ordered a taxi to take the nine bin liners to Barnados charity shop and did it. I thought it was only going to cost me a fiver but it cost me twelve pounds. When I returned home and looked in my letter box I found the following letter which I handed in to my housing co-op:

23rd May 2006

Dear Mr Hows

Re Yvonne Stewart Willams Flat 6, 151 Railton Rd

I am the children's guardian to..., Mrs Stewart Williams's six year old son. I have been appointed by the court to represent... best interests in the care preceedings which have been initiated by Lambeth social services and to appoint and instruct a solicitor on his behalf. I am writing with Ms Stewart Williams's permission to support her application to exchange her current property for a similar property.

I must make clear from the beginning that nobody within the care proceedings is concerned about Mrs Stewart Williams's care of... outside of those periods when she suffers from mental ill health and she is otherwise considered to be an excellent and insightful mother who always tries to put... needs first. It is likely however that... will be placed permanently with family friends who live directly opposite Mrs Stewart Williams's current property. There is a general concern that it would be very difficult for... to settle in his new home and form attachments to his new carers if he is living so close to his mother who he loves dearly. There is also a strong possibility that in the future... will be able to have overnight stays with his mother and under these circumstances it would obviously be preferable that he had his own bedroom.

If I can be of any further assistance please telephone me on either of the above telephone numbers.

Yours sincerely

Paul King.

After lunch with my fellowship friend, I went window shopping with her in Brixton and then we went to Camberwell for a cup of coffee stopping off at the internet cafe before going to Creative Routes, armed with my camera and tripod to meet with Nuala. Nuala was running late with a previous project that she was working on and so after she finished, we went to a cafe and discussed photography over coffee. She gave me a Jessop 400ASA colour film and suggested that I start my photography projects with colour film as it is cheaper than black and white to develope. She showed me some of her prints and wrote down a few guidelines. She said she was going to photocopy some photography text for me, but before she could go any further I told her that I had to go because if I didn't go I would be late to a meeting. After the meeting I went for coffee with a few of the participants.

Thursday 25th May 2006

Dear Yvonne,

Last night I took eight and a half mgs of Stelazine and slept for eight and a half peaceful hours. This morning I went to see my social worker to have a chat with her and collect my Stelazine medication. I showed her my copy of the letter Paul King wrote for my housing co-op and my letter from the DWP stating that my finances are going to be reduced from next month. She took a copy of both letters for my file. When I returned home and looked in my letter box I found that I had received the following statement for me to sign:

STATEMENT OF FIRST RESPONDENT

I, YVONNE STEWART WILLIAMS of Flat 6, 151 Railton Road, London SE24 OLT make this statement believing it to be true and I understand that it may be placed before the court:

1.   I am the firest respondent in these proceedings and the mother of... I ask leave to refer my response to my resposnse to the threshold criteria document dated 23 May 2006. I do not intend to repeat what is in this document, but would confirm that, with great sadness, I have come to the conclusion that the state of my health prevents me from parenting...

2.   I have read reports by Dr Katz and Dr Yates prepared for these preceedings. While I do not fully accept what Dr Katz says about my insight, I am prepared to attend insight classes. I am currently attending psychotherapy sessions once weekly at the Maudsley Hospital. I am hoping that if I can get through the first year after my most recent discharge from hospital without being readmitted then my state of health will improve.

3.   I have also read what Dr Yates says about my medication. I feel that Stelazine is the right medication for me because it kept me stable for the first few years after... was born. However, it does have to be the right dose. If the dose is too high then it makes me very tired and sleepy. However, I am familiar with Stelazine and would not wish to change to a different medication where the side-effects

are unknown. I have read some literature concerning anti-psychotic medication and I am aware theat no medication is totally without side-effects.

4.   I would wish... to reside with my friends Mr Currey and Ms Medcalf. I realise that my current accommodation is not ideally situated in that I can look into their window. I have approached my landlord and asked for alternative accommodation so that my very close proximity does not destabilise the placement. I understand from my landlord that they are willing to rehouse me a few streets away as soon as acommodation becomes available.

5.   If... is unable to go to live with Mr Currey and Ms Medcalf then I would query whether he has to be moved from his current foster carer. I would not be happy about him being placed with long term foster parents who he does not know.

6.   I would wish for... to continue to attend the Steiner School. I am in receipt of Disability Living Allowance which makes it possible for me to pay for this. Currently I am paying £377 a month but this does include so arrears. I believe the school may be offering me a bursary which would reduce the amount that I have to pay. Whatever happens, I fully intend that I should continue to pay for... to attend this school.

Dated this   day of May 2006

Signed Yvonne Stewart-Williams

I intend to sign the above and hand it into my solicitors office tomorrow on my way to Creative Routes. Today I had contact with my son. He was covered in mud but happy. I bought him a pair of Star Trek slippers which light up when you walk and he liked them. I also bought him a science game for age 7 and above and we took our time and worked on some of the experiments this afternoon. I also gave him his little snooker table for age 5 that I had been saving for him for a few years. He played with it for a bit and then started to build a train track. I rang my mum and she spoke with my son for a while before saying goodbye. My son gave me the bread roll that he made today. I ate it and found it to be soft and tasty. During contact today I was speaking with the supervisor and I mentioned to her that I would like to be a probation officer and after Lyn collected my son today, I went to see a friend in the fellowship and before we went to a meeting in Clapham this evening we went to

Battersea Police Station to find out how I could start training to be a probation officer. I was told to look it up on the internet under a google search so I will do it tomorrow after Creative Routes and before going to an evening meeting.

0.33hrs Saturday 27th May 2006

Dear Yvonne,

Just returned from a late night out. I am going to take nine mgs of Stelazine and go straight to bed.

22.09hrs Saturday 27th May 2006

Dear Yvonne,

I slept for twelve hours and got up and went to Clapham to visit a friend in the fellowship. We stayed chatting with each other for a while and then went to a meeting in Camberwell together. On my way home from the meeting I purchased some batteries for my computerised chess game and on my return home I inserted them and they work. In my letter box I found a letter from my general practitioner's practice, inviting me to a patient participation group on Tuesday 6th June 2006 from 18.45hrs to 20.00hrs. I think I am going to attend. Today was the allocation meeting for the empty properties but since this weekend is a bank holiday, I am not going to know the outcome for a few days.

Sunday 28th May 2006

Dear Yvonne,

I took eight and a half mgs of Stelazine, watched 'The Triangle' on television and slept for ten hours. I was still tired but I got up and prepared myself for a visit from a fellowship friend. She helped me sort through a few of my books and then we went back to her place before going to the Brixton meeting. I sent a text to Andrew asking him if he was going to be able to visit me this weekend. He rang me back and said that he wasnt able to make it this weekend and that he would try and make it next weekend instead. My stop cock to my washing machine is leaking and I can't turn it off, so I asked Pete if he could turn it off. He did his best but said it might be faulty, so I rang the co-op's emergency plumbers and left a message on their answer machine with my telephone mumber explaining the problem and asking them to call me back.

Monday 29th May 2006

Dear Yvonne,

I took eight and a half mgs of Stelazine, watched the second episode of 'The Triangle' on terrestrial television and slept for thirteen peaceful hours. I answered some text messages and went out to Sainsbury and purchased some almond crossaints to eat, left a message on my sponsor's voicemail asking her for help with my step 4 and went back to bed and slept for three hours. I sent a few text messages and received a few before getting up and getting myself ready to go to a meeting this Bank Holiday Monday. On my way to the meeting my sponsor rang my mobile. I arranged to do some work on my Step 4 with her over the phone after attending the meeting. The plumber still hasn't called me back.

Tuesday 30th May 2006

Dear Yvonne,

I took eight and a half mgs of Stelazine and watched the third and final episode of 'The Triangle' on B.B.C1 last night and slept for thirteen peaceful restful hours. The plumber rang and made arrangements to come to my flat tomorrow. I then went to Cash Converters in Camberwell and picked up a 50mm lens for my camera for five pounds. I had forgotten to my mobile at home and when I returned I found Andrew had rung. I rang him back but he said he would speak with me later. I decided to go to a meeting in Stockwell.

Wednesday 31st May 2006

Dear Yvonne,

I took eight and a half mgs of Stelazine and found that I had missed Andrew's call, so I rang him back. He told me that he is not going to be able to come this weekend as he and his wife are separating. I was miserable with the news. They have three children together the oldest is fifteen, the youngest is one and the middle child is nine. I have always found Andrew to be a doting caring father and a loving husband, who doesn't drink, take drugs, sexually abuse, physically abuse, swear, rape, womanise or steal. He goes to work each day, is doing a part-time degree, finances a mortgage and is generally only too willing to be of services to his loved ones. As I have already said I have known him for eighteen years and his character has remained the same.

I am saddened for him as from now on he will be living with his parents, even though he loves his wife and children. I didn't go to sleep until 00.30hrs this morning and eventually got out of be at 13.30hrs, having slept for thirteen hours. Today I went for a ride on the bus and took pictures from the upper deck. I still have black and white film in my camera and on my way home I stopped off at Lyn and Pete's and took photograghs of Ginger their cat and Ben their dog. I heard from Lyn that Pete's mum is in a coma and dying and that Pete has gone away to the Lake District with her brother because, she is not to be resusitated. Lyn said that her Aunt is settling well into her old peoples home even though she wants to go back to her own home. Lyn mentioned that she took my son to Bun, his kindergarten teacher's home to play with the Bun's son Jasper, who left kindergarten last year and is now in year one. My son had a great time skateboarding. Apparently Bun made a big chocolate cake for everyone but because my son doesn't eat chocolate she made a big plain cake as well.

Thursday 1st June 2006

Dear Yvonne,

Last night I took eight and a half mgs of Stelazine and spoke on the phone to B for two hours before going to sleep for twelve restful hours. I then got up and ready to see my son for contact. Lyn bought my son to the contact after having taken him for lunch at McDonald's. He looked well and we played together before I cut his toenails and his fingernails. He then made a twelve piece puzzle by himself before building a train track and naming it Brixton. I rang my mum and she spoke with my son for a while. When Lyn came to collect my son, she bought her digital camera with her and took a few pictures of him. She also told me that Pete's mum died at 4.00hrs this morning.

Friday 2nd June 2006

Dear Yvonne,

Last night I took eight and a half mgs of Stelazine, watched an episode of 'Sugar Rush' on Channel 4 and then slept for eight and a half hours. I then got myself ready and went to Creative Routes. Today we spent from the hours of 13.00hrs and 17.30hrs riding around on an opened topped Routemaster bus, with drummers on board drumming. We went from Camberwell to Forest Hill. Then stopped off at the South London and Maudsley Hospital to give out flyers for the Bonkersfest which is on Camberwell Green tomorrow from 12 noon to 10pm. I went up to ES3 ward and spoke to a few nurses that I knew, as well as going to ES2 ward and AL3 ward before meeting up with the other people from Creative Routes. We then went to the Sainsbury's on Dog Kennel Hill to pick up a few things for a brief picnic in Dulwich Park, where I gave out some more flyers. We then drove down to the Houses of Parliament and Whitehall whilst drumming and stopped at bus stops to pick up passengers and give out flyers before returning to Camberwell, where I got off and took a bus to a LGBT meeting in Covent Gardens. Someone that I was aquainted with from that group had gone back out using and had died on Wednesday. But for the grace of God there go I. I went for coffee at Costa's in Old Compton Street with some of the others after the meeting got two numbers for help in the rehabilitation area of voluntary work from a participant of the group. Mainliners 0207 095 1980 and Turning Point 0207 738 3427.

Saturday 3rd June 2006

Dear Yvonne,

Last night I took eight and a half mgs of Stelazine and slept for eleven peaceful hours. I woke up and on my mobile was a text inviting me to lunch in Battersea. I texted back an acceptance, and went. It was from a friend in the fellowship. Whilst I was at her flat another friend in the fellowship was invited to come with us to the

Bonkersfest on Camberwell Green. We arrived at the Bonkersfest closer to five o'clock and the sun was shining as I was truly a lovely hot dry day, with hardly a cloud in the sky. I was dressed in a tee-shirt and a pair of jeans, plus trainers. There was live music playing and it was well attended. I saw lots of people that I had met from Creative Routes and Cooltan Arts. Plus I met a woman from my Kensington and Chelsea college who was a student with me in my numeracy class. After being on the green a while with my hayfever playing me up, even though I had taken a tablet for it before leaving home. I went to a cafe nearby and had a coffee before going to a meeting in Cambridge House in Camberwell. After the meeting ended I went for a coffee and something to eat with a few of the other participants and got the website www.doit.org for voluntary work.

Sunday 4th June 2006

Dear Yvonne,

Last night I took eight and a half mgs of Stelazine, watched the film 'Wilde' on B.B.C 2 then slept for eight hours. It is my sponsor's first birthday today. She is one year clean and sober so I sent her a text message wishing her happy birthday and many happy returns. I was tired when I woke up to go to my morning women's meeting, where I have my tea commitment. After the meeting I went with a few of the participants of the meeting to 'Fresh & Wild' for a coffee and cheesecake. After which I went back to my fellowship friend's flat in Battersea. Together we went to an internet cafe and tried to log on www.doit.org without success. All that came up was software data. So we did a google search and eventually found the 'Timebank' voluntary work website. Where we both registered ourselves as wanting to be volunteers for fifteen hours each week. I chose the fields of addictions and Lesbians, Gay, Bi and Trans. I said that the skills that I had to offer were as a Befriender and buddy, Mentor and community worker. I then went to a meeting in Brixton, during which my mum rang me on my mobile and left a message on my voicemail saying that she loves me. Over the last few months I have been thinking that I really don't know myself, what I am good at or what I want in life. But today for the first time I each time that I thought about my application to TimeBank I felt as if I had hit the nail on the head and there seems to be a little bit of light at the far end of the tunnel.

Monday 5th June 2006

Dear Yvonne,

Last night I took eight and a half mgs of Stelazine and slept for ten peaceful restful hours. When I woke up today I rang Adaction. They told me that they ran two courses. One of them was for people who are at least eighteen months clean and the other was for people who are three months clean and who have a sponsor and have done the Twelve Steps. As I am only going to be seven months clean and sober on June 12th 2006 and I am only on Step 4, I wasn't eligible to go on either of the courses at the moment. So I rang Acaps and they have given me an appointment to meet with Joanne at 10.00hrs next Tuesday. I went to my group psychotherapy which we had in our new room. Afterwards I went for coffee with on of the male participants. When we finished I went to Battersea for lunch with a fellowship friend and then to a meeting in Chelsea where I saw my sponsor and her sponsor.

Tuesday 6th June 2006

Dear Yvonne,

Last night I took eight and a half mgs of Stelazine and was just dozing off to sleep when Andrew rang me. We spoke to each other until 1.00hrs I then slept until 13.30hrs. When I woke up I rang Mainliners and spoke with Kevin. He is going to send me an application form. My mum rang me to say that V.J was at the hospital and that she was going to see what was going on and would ring me again when she got home. I decided to go to the internet cafe and registered myself on the   www.do-it.org.uk   site for voluntary work. I applied for work with the london lesbian and gay switchboard, Stonewall (a lesbian and gay organisation) and Chipmunks (an organisation that works with mental health and is multi-media) After leaving the cafe I went to a patient's participation forum at my G.P's practice. The Expert Patients Programme free self management course for people living with a long term or recurring illness, was explained to me. The next Lambeth course is on Fridays at the end of June 2006 for six weeks.

Amanda Watson@lambethpct.nhs.uk Tel 020 7411 5697 co-
ordinates the courses and I am going to ring her tomorrow morning
because I want to try and get on the next course. The next patient
forum is going to be held at my G.P's practice in September 2006.
When I got home I rang my mum and she told me that V.J was
admitted into the Luton and Dunstable hospital and put on a drip
because he could not pass urine. She said that she was going to go
up and see him tomorrow.

Wednesday 7th June 2006

Last night I took eight and a half mgs of Stelazine and spent two
hours speaking to A on the phone. We spoke about how it has been
in the news lately that George W. Bush president of the U.S.A has
said he wants marriage to mean a man to a woman and not anything
else. We also spoke about when we were single young lesbians of
twenty-two or twenty-three years of age and went to places such as
'Rackets at the Pied Bull pub on Liverpool Road, Angel Islington.
The Bell pub in Kings Cross and The Entertainer a club on Balls
Pond Road. We said that sometimes we dont know of the struggles
of married heterosexuals with children who suddenly find out in
maturity that they are gay and we find their confidence battle with
us a mystery. After my conversation with A, I rang my fellowship
friend and left a message on her voicemail as well as texting her, as
I hadn't heard from her all day. This was unusual and I thought that
she either didn't have any credit on her phone or she is back out
there using. I decided there was nothing that I could do about it
either way and slept for ten hours. This morning I got up at 9.30hrs
and sent out some text messages. I then left a message for Amanda
Watson to call me on my mobile. Then my fellowship friend rang
me and confirmed that she couldn't text me as she hadn't any credit.
We arranged to meet in Battersea, where we had lunch and then we
went to watch the film 'The DaVinci Code' at Peckham cinema and
then we went to a women's meeting together.

Thursday 8th June 2006

Dear Yvonne,

Last night I took eight and a half mgs of Stelazine and slept for ten
hours. I woke up feeling tired and bogged down with hayfever but I

got myself ready to visit my social worker. Who I spoke to about not wanting to live outside of the lesbian and gay community. She said that next time she sees me she will help me draft a letter to my solicitor. When I came home I rang Luton and Dunstable hospital and asked them how V.J was. The ward sister said that he was still passing blood in his urine but they were going to put up another irrigation. She said that they may want to find out what is going on in his bladder but not just yet. She said that she would tell V.J that I rang. I then went to see my son, who was full of cheer. I took some photographs of him and asked him to sing Happy Birthday on B's answering machine as it is her birthday today and I rang my mum and both she and my son spoke to each other. Pete came to pick my son up today and said that they were going to buy flowers. After my son left I went to visit my fellowship friend and she cooked me a meal. I then walked her to a meeting but I didn't go.

Friday 9th June 2006

Dear Yvonne,

Last night I took eight and a half mgs of Stelazine and slept for fourteen hours then listening to radio 4 dozed on and off for three more hours. I got up and had a bath and something to eat. Then I arranged to meet a newcomer for a meeting that I was going to in Covent Garden this evening. But she didn't turn up at the meeting point and I went to the meeting without her. After the meeting I went with a few of the other participants to Costa's in Old Compton Street for a hot drink and a chat.

Saturday 10th June 2006

Dear Yvonne,

Last night I took eight and a half mgs of Stelazine and slept for thirteen hours and awoke with a splitting headache and cronic hayfever. I got in the bath and got ready to meet B, in Peckham. I left my flat at 13.30hrs and arrived in Peckham at 14.10hrs. B, and I did some shopping before going back to her place and working on my Step 4. I discussed not wanting to move out of the gay community with B and agreed to ask my neighbours at the back if they would do a swop. When I got in I found some of the members of the gay community sitting in the garden. I asked three of them if they would like to do a swop with me but they declined. I am now awaiting the reply of one other. I received an invitation from the Rt. Hon. Tessa Jowell M.P to attend three functions within the next few weeks on of them is the House of Commons. I will accept the invite and post my reply on Monday.

Sunday 11th June 2006

Dear Yvonne,

Last night I took eight and a half mgs of Stelazine and slept for nine and a half hours. I woke up tired this morning but I didn't have a headache and the symptoms of my hayfever wasn't too bad. I got myself up and ready for the Battersea women's meeting. After the meeting I went to have an iced coffee with a few of the participants and then went to my fellowship friend's home for lunch. Tonight I met an newcomer and took her to the Brixton meeting. The person that I was waiting for to reply to my request for an exchange rang and declined my offer.

Monday 12th June 2006

Dear Yvonne,

Last night I took eight and a half mgs of Stelazine and slept for twelve hours. This morning I rang Luton and Dunstable hospital's surgical ward twenty and asked how V.J was doing. I was told that he no longer had blood in his urine and that he was going to be discharged home tomorrow as he was doing well. I rang my mum and told her what I had heard and she was pleased. Then my son's social worker rang me to remind me that his review was at 13.00hrs today. I went and found out that Lyn and Pete's social service fostering assessment is going well and my son will be moving in with them this September. Lyn also told me that the allocation meeting is this Thursday, so I might find out if the co-op have offered me the Milton Road flat this week or next week. All seems to be going well with my son and I am pleased. The next meeting is going to be at 14.30hrs Wednesday 4th October 2006. After the meeting I went to my fellowship friend's abode and had lunch and a chat and then arranged to meet the newcomer at a meeting in

Stockwell. After the meeting I went with my fellowship friend to a dance workshop and enjoyed myself even though I couldn't pay for it. I am overdrawn at the bank and can't get anymore money from the cashpoint and my mobile phone only has 48pence credit.

Tuesday 13th June 2006

Dear Yvonne,

Last night I took eight and a half mgs of Stelazine and slept for nine and a half hours. I went to Turning Point ACAPS and met with Joanna. We filled out forms together and she spoke to me and asked me questions. Then at the end we went to the Job Centre and registered as I have chosen to do the 'Progress2work' scheme instead of the 'Next Steps' scheme. I have an appointment to see Joanna again at 16.00hrs on Wednesday 21st June 2006. After I went to visit my fellowship friend and looked at my e-mails. I had one reply to my Stonewall application. So I rang them and I am going to their office in Victoria at 10.00hrs to do some voluntary work tomorrow. I also obtained the London Lesbian and Gay Switchboard's number and requested an application form for volunteering. B. sent me a text to say that she had lost her purse. I went to a meeting in Stockwell this evening.

Wednesday 14th June 2006

Dear Yvonne,

Last night I took eight and a half mgs of Stelazine and slept for seven and a half hours. I was still tired when I awoke to the sound of a text message going off in my ear. I got up, had a wash ate some cereals for breakfast and set off to Herne Hill train station to get a train to Victoria. The train was delayed so I took a bus to Brixton and got a tube to Victoria, ringing my boss Roy Peterson at Stonewall on the way to tell him I would be late. I also rang Amanda Watson the Expert Patients Programme coordinator to book a place on the next course. She said that it starts on Friday 30th June 2006 and will be running every Friday for six weeks. She said she would send me an application form in the post. At Stonewall I worked on a database. I was basically calling potential delegates and inviting them to a conference that is going to take place on Tuesday

4th July 2006 re Education for all: tackling homophobia in schools. Jim Knight M.P minister for schools is going to be making a keynote speech and Ken Livingston Mayor of London is going to be launching a DVD and people such as Ben Summerskill Stonewall chief executive is going to be there as are many others. I finished work for the day at 16.00hrs and said I would return on Friday. Whilst working at Stonewall today, my sponsor rang me and I spent a short time speaking with her before returning to work. After leaving Stonewall today I went to visit my fellowship friend who had had a coil fitted by her G.P today and sent me a text to say she was in agony. By the time I arrived at her home the pain she was experiencing had subsided to a dull ache and we were able to go to a women's meeting in Stockwell this evening.

Thursday 15th June 2006

Dear Yvonne,

Last night I took eight and a half mgs of Stelazine and slept for twelve hours. I had a phone call from Ros Dunning this morning asking me if I had heard any news about my move yet and telling me that Pete and Lyn's assessment was going well and that my son was going to be living with them. She also told me that next week Tuesday we have one day in court and she was working on another case so a stand-in was going to be there for me. She said that she had mailed a letter to me yesterday but I said I hadn't read it yet. I told her that I was no wiser about my move and that I knew that my son was going to live with Pete and Lyn. I set off to see my son, arrived on time and he was there waiting for me. We cuddled and tickled and joked this week. I also phoned my mum who spoke with him and then told me that V.J was still in hospital and that there was talk at the hospital about him being transfered to Mount Vernon Hospital. Pete collected my son today and afterwards I went to see my friend in the fellowship and we ended up going to a Lesbian and Gay meeting in the West End as I was supposed to do a chair at a mother and baby unit but was blown out at the last minute. I think the nominations of the flats in the co-op was supposed to take place tonight but I'm not sure.

Friday 16th June 2006

Dear Yvonne,

Last night I took eight and a half mgs of Stelazine and slept for eight hours. I then got myself ready to go to Stonewall. I arrived for my voluntary work five minutes or so early. Whilst I was working on the telephones today at Stonewall the news came in that the gay barman (Joe jobroski) that was murdered on Clapham common's two murderers got a sentence of 28 years each in jail. I then rang Amy Donovan Lambeth's anti-hate crime co-ordinator on my mobile and told her the news. She told me that tomorrow there is going to be Clapham Pride and I have decided to attend and to take some of Stonewall's flyers to distribute. I finished working at 14.00hrs today and went to see my fellowship friend. She had found me a lesbian twelve step meeting to attend tomorrow afternoon, and I was pleased. We then went to a meeting. After the meeting we went for a coffee at Costa's in Old Compton Street.

Saturday 17th June 2006

Dear Yvonne,

Last night I took eight and a half mgs of Stelazine and slept for twelve hours. I then got up and got myself ready to go. I rang my mother and she told me that V.J was still in hospital and that she was feeling the pressure as she felt that she had not real support. She said that if the worst happens she knows how to contact me but for now she would like to speak with me every now and again to relieve the pressure. I made arrangements to meet my fellowship friend at 14.00hrs at Clapham tube station but when she arrived and I was ready to set off to the Clapham Pride she said that we have to set off straight away to arrive on time to a lesbian twelve step meeting in the London Friend building in Kings Cross. So off I went to a meeting. Afterwards I went back to her place for something to eat and then we set off to another meeting in Camberwell. After which I did an 22.00hrs-23.00hrs hour on the door of a twelve step disco fundraiser before going home.

Sunday 18th June 2006

Dear Yvonne,

Last night I took eight and a half mgs of Stelazine and slept for eight and a half hours. I woke up and got myself ready to go to the Battersea women's meeting. After the meeting I went to Fresh & Wild for an ice coffee with a few women from the meeting. Then I went with my fellowship friend and another woman to an internet cafe and registered on the gaydargirls website before having lunch and going back to an internet cafe and registering on www.outeverywhere.com to improve my chances of finding a lesbian girlfriend. After which I went to the Brixton meeting and gave someone a year keyring. Then we went for a coffee afterwards. My mum had left me a message on the voicemail of my mobile asking me to call her. So I did and she told me that she needed my help. I don't know what help she needs but I told her I will ring her tomorrow morning.

Monday 19th June 2006

Dear Yvonne,

Last night I took eight and a half mgs of Stelazine and slept for eleven hours of peaceful bliss. I then rang my mother and arranged to visit her on Friday for a few hours. After speaking with my mother my son's social worker rang and said Julian Hows, the chair of my co-op had rung her and said that I had not been allocated 19c Milton Road, but there were two other properties that I could look at. I then arranged to view those properties with Lyn and liked 56A Barnwell Road. I rang Julian and he said I could have it. So I wrote a letter of acceptance and hand delivered it to the co-op. I then rang my son's social worker, leaving a message that I had viewed and accepted the flat and I rang my solicitor and did the same thing. I arrived late to my group psychotherapy and met the new male member that started the group last week in my absence. I apologised for being late and told them what I had been up too. After the group I had coffee with a few of the participants before going home, phoning my mum and telling her about the new flat I had accepted. She told me that V.J had come home today but that he was still not too well and would be going to Mount Vernon Hospital on Friday

23rd June 2006. She said that she may have to go with him, but she was not sure and would keep me posted. I sent a text with my news to my sponsor, A and B. I spoke to B this evening and she and I are going to try and view the property again on Saturday.

Tuesday 20th June 2006

Dear Yvonne,

Last night I took eight and a half mgs of Stelazine and slept for eight hours. I was tired when I woke up and had to prize myself from my bed. I got myself up and ready to go to court. I arrived on the seventh floor of the court house at 9.45am but we didnt go into court 18 until 11.30am. My lawyer, my son's court guardian and solicitor and my son;s social worker and the local authorities solicitor was pleased that yesterday I had found a place that I would be moving to. We spent almost an hour in court and had to come back to the court at 14.00hrs and were in court at 14.15hrs and out again at approximately 14.40hrs. The court heard that Lyn and Pete's social services' assessment had gone well and that they were awaiting Lyn and Pete's police check, plus a report back from their general practitioner. They were also going to be placed before the fostering panel to see if they could be long term foster parents and if they are suited for my son. Lyn and Pete and the fostering panel were also going to be given a copy of Dr Peter Yates report and my son's court guardian's report to read. I am going to have to see my solicitor to read over some paperwork withing the next few weeks.

After I finished in court, I purchased a rechargeable battery charger and batteries from Maplin's which was situated close to the courthouse. I then went home and rang Lyn, who said she was going to ring me and invited me over for a cup of tea and a chat. She told me that next week at my son's school, he was going to have a birthdat celebration, where Bun, his kindergarten teacher, would light a candle for each year of his life and whilst that was taking place some memorable occassion in his life would be spoken about for that year. I said that tomorrow I would call his social worker and ask if I could attend and if not, then I would write something. Lyn also said that her brother and his wife has given my son a four week old kitten of his own, that he is to name. He will go with Lyn to collect it and it will live with Lyn and Pete. After I left Lyn's home I went to visit my fellowship friend and went with her to a meeting in Stockwell. After the meeting we went for coffee with a few of the participants.

Wednesday 21st June 2006

Dear Yvonne,

Last night I took eight and a half mgs of Stelazine and slept for twelve hours. I was so tired when I woke up this morning that I rang Stonewall and left a message on their answering machine to say I wasn't going to be volunteering today, then I went back to sleep. This afternoon I rang my son's social worker and asked her if I could attend my son's birthday celebration at his school next week. After checking she said it would be okay. I went my appointment with Joanna, at ACAPS, Turning Point, today. it went well. I answered a few more questions. Then I told Joanne that I was not confident about my punctuations in writing. So she gave me a test which she said that I passed. She also rang The Hungerford, Turning Point and I spoke to someone who is going to get someone to call me back regarding a project they run called Antidote. Which is for the LGBT community. Afterwards she gave me an application form to take home and read from City Lit regarding voluntary work. I will next see Joanne in two weeks time. I went to the Lambeth LGBT forum tonight in Lambeth Town Hall.

Thursday 22nd June 2006

Dear Yvonne,

Last night I took eight and a half mgs of Stelazine and slept for eleven hours and awoke late for my appointment with my social worker. I rang her and made arrangements to meet her tomorrow at 16.00hrs as she is going on holiday next week. I then got ready to go and see my son. I was pleased to see him. On his arrival he gave me a postcard. I then took a few photographs of him. Tried to teach him to play Chess and cut his finger and toenails. We tried several times to phone my mum but her phone just rang and rang. Marianne the person that supervises the contact did a video of me and my son at play today. I told my son that I will see him at school next week. Pete came to collect my son today. I had forgotten my son's cap with the flap at the back that keeps the sun off his neck. So I told Pete I would drop it round. After seeing my son, I stopped off to buy his skateboard and pads for his seventh birthday. I didn't buy him a helmet as he has one already. So after dropping in to see my fellowship friend and having a meal with her. I dropped the skateboard, pads and caps off at Lyn and Pete's. I then phoned my mum who was sorry she had missed her weekly chat with my son and mentioned that she was looking forward to seeing me tomorrow, I spoke to B tonight about my new flat and the fact that she will be seeing it for the first time on Saturday at 10.00hrs. She reaassured me that I have ample time to get organised before August. She also asked me what had happened about my swimming and yoga.

Friday 23rd June 2006

Dear Yvonne,

Last night I took eight and a half mgs of Stelazine and slept for nine hours. I woke and got myself ready to go to see my mother. When I arrived there V.J was seated in the front room of the house by the telephone waiting for a call to say when he was going to be picked up. He didn't look at all well and had aged considerably since the last time I saw him. My mother greeted me with a big hug and was visibly pleased to see me. I sat near to V.J talking to and listening to him and then went out to buy a Jamaican Cleaner a weekly newspaper. When I asked for it at the newspaper shop the shopkeeper asked how V.J was as he hadn't seen him and knows that he never misses a week without buying both that and the Mirror on Saturday. I told him he wasn't very well and the shop keeper gave his regards. I tried to teach my mother a little bit more on her computer and my brother David had a day off work today and visited her as well and the two of us were taking digital pictures and putting it on her computer. I left my mother's home just after 13.00hrs and made my way back to London. When I arrived I rang to say I had arrived safely and was disappointed that V.J was still waiting to hear if he was going to get his Chemotherapy at Mount Vernon Hospital today. I then made my way to see my social worker, who is going on holiday for two weeks. I told her about my new flat and gave her the address. She told me that my old social worker will look after me whilst she is away. She laughed when I told her I had overslept yesterday and said that it was a good job that I had rung as she would have been worried. She gave me my medicine and I left to visit my fellowship friend and go to a LGBT meeting in Covent Gardens. After which I went to Costa's for a coffee.

Saturday 24th June 2006

Dear Yvonne,

Last night I took eight and a half mgs of Stelazine and slept for ten hours. I woke up and got myself ready to meet B. Today B, and I were going to see the flat that I will be moving into. B was pleased when she saw it. We spent about an hour looking at it and making plans. Then we went for coffee and lunch at the Lounge in Brixton. After which we returned to my flat and started clearing my son's toy boxes. After B, left I took my son's bike to Sam's Wheels and paid for it to be serviced and made road worthy out of the birthday money I got for my son from B. Then I went to a sixtieth birthday party in the garden for Nigel one of my neighbours who lives in the lesbian and gay community but who's entrance to his property is based in Mayall Road.

Sunday 25th June 2006

Dear Yvonne,

Last night I took eight and a half mgs of Stelazine and slept for eight nine and a half hours. I got up and got ready to go to my Battersea women's meeting, where I have my tea commitment. After the meeting I went to my fellowship friend's abode and had lunch and a chat. Then we went to the internet cafe, where I found that I had a message on my gaydargirls email address and several messages on my outeverywhere email address. I didn't have time to answer them today as I would have been late to the Brixton meeting if I had. I rang Andrew today and he said that he may be coming to see me on Saturday.

Monday 26th June 2006

Dear Yvonne,

Last night I took eight and a half mgs of Stelazine and slept for eleven and a half hours and woke up feeling tired and sleepy. I decided to take the day off. So I rang someone from my group psychotherapy and told them that I wouldn't be coming in today and I rang my sponsor to cancel meeting with her at 15.00hrs today. As it was my sponsor had an attack of migraine and was feeling worse for wear anyway. I then went back to sleep. In the afternoon I looked in my letter box and found a reply from the London Lesbian and Gay Switchboard saying that I had been successful in my first phase of applying to volunteer for them and that they were now inviting me to an interview on Thursday 20th July 2006 at 18.30hrs at 356, Holloway Road. I rang them to accept. Then someone from Antidote rang me and left a message to ring them. I rang Antidote and spoke to Tony and explained that I wanted to be a volunteer. They said they didn't have any vacancies at the moment but I should write to them with a C.V and also telling them that I had experience of drug use and recovery. I rang ACAPS and spoke to Joanna and she made an appointment for me to do my C.V tomorrow at 10.00hrs. Lyn rang me today and told me that my son had asked her to tell me to give her his small metal aeroplanes so that he can play with them with his friends. I gathered a few of them together and went over to Lyn and Pete's. I also brought my son's cycle along and whilst I was there I wrapped my son's skateboard and pads in birthday wrapping paper. I arranged to meet Pete and Lyn on Wed at 11.30hrs to go to his school and for Lyn and Pete to say his achievements for his sixth year of life.

Tuesday 27th June 2006

Dear Yvonne,

Last night I took eight and a half mgs of Stelazine and slept for ten peaceful hours. I got up and got myself ready to meet Joanna, at ACAPS. I spent almost one and a half hours doing my C.V and after I had completed it, with Joanna's help I posted a copy of the C.V to Antidote. I saw my cousin Eric in Brixton today. I told him that I was going to be moving and that I needed his help. He said that that was no problem. When I got home I completed my Mainliners application form and I'm going to ask A, and B, if they will write a reference.

Wednesday 28th June 2006

Dear Yvonne,

Last night I took eight and a half mgs of Stelazine and slept for twelve peaceful hours. I got up and got myself ready to meet Lyn and Pete. I had a cup of coffee and a sandwich with Pete and Lyn before setting off to my son's school to celebrate my son's seventh birthday. Once in the school grounds I met with many teachers and parents that I know who gave me a welcoming hug and told me how much they had missed me. In my son's kindy celebration, my son sat next to me and kept kissing my hand and trying to hide under the corner of my blouse. He ceased that behaviour in order to conduct his birthday ceremony with his teacher. He lit seven candles and for each of the lit candles I mentioned a few of my son's achievements. When I got to year six I had already pre-arranged it with Lyn for her to speak about this year, which she did. After which the teacher sliced the cake that Lyn had baked and my son gave a slice to each person in the room including himself. Then my son went around and put each lit candle out. After leaving his kindergarten class, Pete fetched my son's birthday presents from the car and we sat on the grass in the grounds of the school whilst my son unwrapped them. He loved his presents and all the other children gathered around him and wanted to handle them. My son then went off to play with a friend that he was going home with today and Lyn, Pete and myself returned home and I had a cup of tea at their house before setting off to visit my fellowship friend and going to a women's meeting in Stockwell.

Thursday 29th June 2006

Dear Yvonne,

Last night I took eight and a half mgs of Stelazine and slept for eleven peaceful hours. I got up and got myself ready to have contact with my son. He was looking forward to his McDonald's party this Saturday. My son told me that he was going to get a kitten and when I asked him what he was going to call it he said 'Fluffy'. He told me that the kitten was going to be a girl. He seemed pleased which pleased me. I rang my mum so that she could talk to him which she did. I asked Marianne to take some photo's of him so that I can ask Andrew how to put it on my computer. Pete picked my son up today and I went to visit my fellowship friend. Then I went home in time to wait for a phone call that I was expecting from B.

Friday 30th June 2006

Dear Yvonne,

Last night I took eight and a half mgs of Stelazine and slept for thirteen hours. I got up and got ready for A, visit. A, was coming today with her paper shredder so that I could get through my mountain of old paper, ready for my move. Before she came I cleared away some of the excess papers and answered a phone call from my mum. My mum is going to be taken with a Jehovah's Witness convention from Friday 4th August 2006 to Sunday 6th August 2006 and wanted to know if I could go to Luton and stay with V.J as he is not very well, so that she can attend. I told her yes and said that I would see my son on Thursday 3rd August 2006 and go to Luton afterwards. I rang Andrew to ask if he is still coming to London tomorrow. But he said that he has been so busy at work and is on call over the weekend so won't be able to make it. A arrived at 18.00hrs and we sat talking whilst we shredded the papers. A tried to entice me to attend Europride tomorrow but I think I will stay in with the shredder which she has now lent me. Whilst A was with me this evening she transfered some of my telephone numbers from my old mobile phone to a phone that my mother gave me, which pleased me. A, also saved some photographs taken of my son yesterday on to a cd on his computer.

Saturday 1st July 2006

Dear Yvonne,

Last night I took eight and a half mgs of Stelazine and slept for fourteen hours. Got up and went to look at my emails off gaydargirls at an internet cafe in Camberwell Green. I had one email and I replied to it.

Sunday 2nd July 2006

Dear Yvonne,

Last night I took eight and a half mgs of Stelazine and slept for ten hours. I woke up feeling tired but still got out of bed and prepared myself for my tea commitment at the Battersea women's meeting. This morning before I went I prepared myself a bowl of museli ate it quickly and left my abode, just in time to catch the 37 bus. After the meeting I went to Fresh & Wild for a cup of iced coffee with a few of the other participants. Before going to spend the afternoon at my fellowship friend's abode watching episodes of 'Catherine Tate' on her DVD, having something to eat, then leaving for a meeting in Brixton and going for a coffee afterwards with a few of the participants.

Monday 3rd July 2006

Dear Yvonne,

Last night I took eight and a half mgs of Stelazine and slept for twelve hours. I woke up tired and got ready for my group psychotherapy. In the group this week, a new woman joined and I spoke about my feelings of being unemployed and fearing that I may never find suitable employment again especially as my retirement age is presently set at seventy years of age. After the group I went to see my sponsor in Parson's Green to do some more work on my step 4. I met my sponsor's eldest son today. He is a handsome fourteen year old youth. He disappeared off, whilst my sponsor and myself got on with the work. Afterward I went to a meeting in Chelsea with my sponsor. I had a great day today and promised to press on with step 4.

Tuesday 4th July 2006

Dear Yvonne,

Last night I took eight and a half mgs of Stelazine and slept for ten hours. I then got up and started pottering about my flat, sorting out my possessions. I have realised that I am impoverished, Living on the breadline. Last month the bank paid my son's school fee from an unauthorised bank overdraft. They charged me fifty pounds, which they are going to deduct from my money this month on the same day that my son's school fee for this month is being deducted. I have increased my authorised overdraft limit to two hundred pounds and borrowed one hundred pounds from B, Now I am in a panick and wanting to sell the things that are sellable in my flat. I saw my cousin Eric today and I shared a meal with him at his abode, I told him about what is going to happen with my son and he was a bit upset until I told him that the alternative was that my son could have been put up for adoption,

Wednesday 5th July 2006

Dear Yvonne,

Last night I took eight and a half mgs of Stelazine and slept on and off for fourteen hours and each time I woke up I remembered dreaming different dreams. My fellowship friend finally woke me up with a text at 12.30hrs and asked me to meet her in Clapham Junction at 14.30hrs. We met in Cafe Nero's and when my friend asked me how I was I confessed to her about my financial difficulties. I told her that I had been told that I could work for fifteen hours and fifty-nine minutes each week for up to six months and I thought that I could earn up to sixty pounds. She said that we would go to her local Marks & Spencers and get the details of how to apply to work for them part time. We were given a telephone number to ring and a website address. Tomorrow after I have had contact with my son I will go to the internet cafe with her and try to apply. Whilst we were in Marks & Spencers, my mobile phone rang and when I answered it there was a woman from Antidote on the other end. She said that she had read my C.V but didn't have any paid or voluntary work availiable at the moment. She asked if I would mind her keeping my C.V on her files in the meantime and I said I wouldn't mind. My social worker's holiday replacement, who also happens to be the social worker that I had before her also rang me whilst I was in Marks and Spencers to confirm that I would be seeing her tomorrow

Thursday 6th July 2006

Dear Yvonne,

Last night I took eight and a half mgs of Stelazine and spent and hour speaking with Andrew, who had rung my landline. I then slept for eight hours and woke up bright and perky for my appointment with my social worker. I arrived at her office five minutes before I was due to see her. Sat and composed myself. When she came in I noticed that she was visibly pregnant and she said that she would be going on maternity leave in four weeks. I told her about my concerns with my son's school fees and my DLA. Plus I told her that I had an appointment with the job centre next week Wednesday and my plans to go on the net looking for a job. She was very supportive. She mentioned looking on the net to see if I could get some help with my son's school fees. When I left her almost an hour later I went to Book Mongers in Brixton and arranged for them to select approximately two hundred books to purchase on Monday at 11.00hrs. Then I purchased some lunch from Marks and Spencers for my son. When I arrived at the Breslass family Centre my son was already there and was hiding until he heard me mention lunch. I had bought along two books that he owns of Aeroplanes and he sat looking at the pictures. I rang my mother and she spoke with him. Today he gave me two pears that he had scrumped off a tree in his school ground. I spent time tickling him and telling him that I love him. I took a photograph of him with my mobile phone and put it on my phone as a wallpaper for the screen. Lyn collected my son today while Pete stayed with the car. I then went to meet my fellowship friend and later went to the internet cafe. I tried to log on to the recruitment section of Marks and Spencers website after sending an email to a potential love interest/friend in gaydargirls but ran out of internet time and so was cut off before completing my application. I started my periods today.

Friday 7th July 2006

Dear Yvonne,

Last night I took eight and a half mgs of Stelazine and slept for fourteen hours and woke up tired and spent the day in bed. My mum rang me to say V.J had been kept in hospital overnight as he has problems with his blood pressure and is unsteady on his feet. A, rang me and we chatted together for four hours.

Saturday 8th July 2006

Dear Yvonne,

Last night I took eight and a half mgs of Stelazine and slept for twelve peaceful hours. I woke up bright and alert and collect a few things together for my cousin Eric to take to Luton later today whilst he is there to visit my family. After he left I waited for B. Both she and I got to work on my book collection and sorted out the books that I would keep from those that would go to Book Mongers. We also went through most of my old files and stredded most of the contents. Then later we carried my son's toys and books over to Pete and Lyn's.

Sunday 9th July 2006

Dear Yvonne,

Last night I took eight and a half mgs of Stelazine and slept for eight and a half hours. When I woke up I got myself ready to go to the Battersea women's meeting. After the meeting I went to an internet cafe in Battersea and logged on to Gap careers through google and filled out an application online for a part time job at Gap clothing store. Tomorrow I will phone Guillermo at PACE and Su Glazier at SLAM and ask them if they can be my referees. I then went for lunch at the home of my fellowship friend and afterwards I went to a meeting in Brixton.

Monday 10th July 2006

Dear Yvonne,

Last night I took eight and a half mgs of Stelazine and slept for twelve hours. I rang my son's social worker and asked her if I could at the meeting with my son's new teacher at 14.00hrs on Thursday. She said yes. I then rang Lyn and Pete to let them know that I was coming and they invited me over for a cup of coffee and some toast. I accepted and collected some boxes that they had unpacked from my son's toys to pack some new things in. I let Book Mongers in at 11.00hrs and they bought £40.00 worth of books. I then went to my group psychotherapy and afterwards went to the internet cafe and spent four hours there job hunting. I want to call Marks and Spencers tomorrow at 8.00hrs to find out if they have any London

Customer Asistant vacancies.

Tuesday 11th July 2006

Dear Yvonne,

Last night I took eight and a half mgs of Stelazine and found it difficult to get to sleep. I woke up at 8am after sleeping for about five hours. I had a slight headache nearly all day and felt generally larthagic. I sorted my dirty clothes into wash piles but didn't take them to the launderette. Instead I went to visit my fellowship friend and whilst O was with her I went to an internet cafe and noticed that Marks and Spencer had a Customer Assistant vacancie for a temparary worker to work less than 20hrs each week. I tried to apply for it but it had already been taken. When I rang Marks and Spencers they said that they have about 500 jobs but about 10,000 people are appling for them.

Wednesday 12th July 2006

Dear Yvonne,

Last night I took eight and a half mgs of Stelazine, spoke to B, on the phone for an hour and again found It difficult to get to sleep and awoke after seven hours of sleep. I still felt tired but got up because I had an appointment with Raye at the job centre at 10.00hrs. I arrived at the job centre ten minutes before my appointment and I was seen at 10.20hrs. I made it clear that I wanted to go back to work. I said that I wanted a part-time job that didn't affect my income support, housing benefit and council tax. I brought a copy of my C.V and my Maudsley Hospital reference to show her. We did a short job hunt and I found a shop assistant job but it asked for two years retail experience. Raye made ten photocopies of my C,V and gave them to me with an envelope, then she referred me to Yola, and Employment Advisor that works for The GAIN Project in Lambeth. She gave me another appointment to see her at 10.00hrs Thursday 20th July 2006. After leaving Raye I went to see Yola and she gave me an appointment to see her at 10.00hrs Tuesday 18th July 2006 at the Brixton Library. After leaving Yola I went to meet my fellowship friend at an internet cafe in Battersea and did the Marks & Spencer recruitment test over the phoneline. They said that

I had passed the test successfully but all their London Customer Assistant vancancy interviews had been taken, but to keep trying. I had a meal with my fellowship friend and went to a womens meeting in Stockwell.

Thursday 13th July 2006

Dear Yvonne,

Last night I took eight and a half mgs of Stelazine and slept and yet again found it difficult to get to sleep and slept for eight hours. I woke up at 8am and was at the launderette at 8..50hrs but it was still closed so I came back and went to sleep until 11.30hrs. I then got myself ready to go to my son's school at 14.00hrs and meet his teacher. My son arrived at the school with Maria, his current foster mother. Then Pete came a bit later. I was given a picture of my son in his kindergarten class which was taken in March 2006. I spoke to the teachers and parents and found out that it would be possible for me to get a work reference from my work at the school shop. After the meeting with my son's new tutor I played with my son in the school grounds. My mum rang me on my mobile and spoke to my son and me. At 16.00hrs Pete took my son home. I went to visit my fellowship friend when I left my son's school. Together we wrote a covering letter for my C.V that I am going to try and post out tomorrow when I see Joanna at ACAPS asking for paid employment. Tonight B rang and she helped me to earmark the organisations that I am going to send my C.V's to.

Friday 14th July 2006

Dear Yvonne,

Last night I took eight and a half mgs of Stelazine and spoke to B on the phone about my plans for my job search for almost two hours. I then went to sleep for thirteen peaceful hours. I woke up to a phone call from Andrew asking me if I was going to visit his home in Coventry tomorrow. I said I would and made arrangements with him to collect me from the coach station. I then got ready to go to ACAPS. When I arrived there I told Joanna of my plans. She helped me to tidy up my letter and then we printed fifty copies. I posted thirty-six copies today and look forwards to the response. I then went to the home of my fellowship friend and chatted and prepared seventeen additional letters and after leaving posted them. My coach leaves at 8.30hrs so I am going to get an early night. I am looking forward to travelling further afield than Luton or Kent as I haven't for over ten years.

Saturday 15th July 2006

Dear Yvonne,

Last night I took eight and a half mgs of Stelazine and failed to go to sleep. I tossed and turned but no sleep came my way. In the end at 4.30hrs I got up and had a bath, I decided to get an earlier coach to Coventry. In the end I got the 7.00hrs coach and arrived in Coventry at 9.30hrs. Andrew collected me from the station and I spent three and a half blissful hours in the company of him, his wife and three children.

Sunday 16th July 2006

Dear Yvonne,

Last night I took eight and a half mgs of Stelazine and went to bed at 20.00hrs and woke up late this morning at 8.50hrs. I arrived late for my tea commitment. This afternoon I gave Lyn and Pete my son's computer and I have now started to use my new computer. Today I also spoke with my mother and promised to give her a short visit tomorrow after my psychotherapy group.

Monday 17th July 2006

Last night I took eight and a half mgs of Stelazine and spoke to A, for three hours. By the time A, and I ended our conversation at 00.28hrs, I found I could no longer sleep. So I played some Will Young and Dennis Brown songs on my new computer and recorded them on to the real player. I finally went to sleep at 4.30hrs and woke up at 8.30hrs and went to the launderette. After I finished my wash I went to visit my mother for a few hours. Before I arrived at her home she rang me whilst I was on the train to ask me when I would be arriving and when I got there she gave me a tight hug. She told me that V.J was having a good day, the best that he has had in quite a few days as he had been having bouts of being doubly incontinent and listless due to his medication. He had found a new lease of energy today and was out taking a walk. She said that the nurse visited V.J on a regular basis and was monitoring the situation. She herself said that she felt very tired and I noticed that at 14.30hrs she was still dressed in her night attire. She had just eaten lunch and taken her blood pressure and diabetic tablets. She asked me to do some grocery shopping for her and gave me some money to shop with. She wanted some skimmed milk, fresh orange juice and potatoes from the local Sainsbury's supermarket. When I came back with the goods, she thanked me and we chatted together for the rest of my visit. Just as I was getting ready to go back to London, V.J came home and although he seem frail he was happy to see me.

Tuesday 18th July 2006

Last night I took eight and a half mgs of Stelazine and spoke to B, for half an hour and then went to sleep at 20.30hrs. I woke up at 9.15hrs this morning and got ready to go to Brixton library, where I was going to meet Yola, my employment advisor from The Gain Project. After having a wash and getting dressed, I set off to without breakfast (I didn't have any food in the flat or any money) to the cash point and then bought a takeaway breakfast at McDonald's, arriving ten minutes late to see Yola. We filled out some forms and Yola mentioned the possibility of my being able to do some voluntary work for Lambeth council. She said there were ten places available and asked me if I was interested. I said yes and she said that she would give her colleague a copy of the C.V that I gave her to put forward to Lambeth. She also said that I might like to take advantage of some free computer courses that are available in Lambeth. I agreed. She said that she will phone me tomorrow morning with the telephone number of one of them. After leaving Yola, I went to visit my son's school charity shop in Balham, which was busy. When I left, I went to visit my fellowship friend who was also being visited by another fellowship friend. The three of us walked to Specs Savers in Clapham Junction and helped her choose two designer glass frames. We then went to the other friend's home and went on the internet. Together we changed my profile on the gaydargirls website. I also checked Marks and Spencers website but the London part-time jobs that they had advertised were for 20-30hrs per week. Tonight I went to a meeting in Stockwell. After which I went for coffee.

Wednesday 19th July 2006

Dear Yvonne,

Last night I took eight mgs of Stelazine and went to sleep for eight hours. When I got up I rang my solicitor to get a copy of the court guardian's report. I rang my mental health social worker and made arrangements to see her at 11.30hrs on Friday. I rang Yola and obtained Threshold's telephone number which I then rang and booked myself on their computer course of which the induction starts 10.00hrs Thursday September 7th 2006. I then also rang TBG in Brixton and arranged to go on their computer induction course next Wednesday at 9.30hrs to 16.30hrs. Then I went to pay my gas bill at the post office. On my return, when I looked in my letter box, I saw that I had received two replies from my 14th July letter with C.V, neither was able to offer me a position. One was from Women's Link, who advised me to have a look in the Guardian newspaper as that is where they advertised their posts and SANE, who said they advertise their posts on www.sane.org.uk Two of my fellowship friends came to my flat today and helped me to purge my kitchen dinning room. One of them will be coming back on Friday afternoon to start on my bedroom. Today I got rid of nine black bin liners full of clutter. This evening I went to a women's meeting in Stockwell.

Thursday 20th July 2006

Dear Yvonne

Last night I took eight and a half mgs of Stelazine and went to sleep for nine and a half hours. When I woke up I had a wash and ate a bowl of cereals before setting off to the job centre for a 10am appointment with Raya. I told her that I had sent off forty-six c.v's last Friday and had two replies. She asked made another appointment for me in two weeks time. She also asked me to fill out a form for which the information will tell her how much money I have to make before I make more money than I get paid in my benefits. After leaving Raya, I went to see Yola at the Gain Project. I took the opportunity to go on the internet and looked at the Marks and Spencers website but only found a Fenchurch street customer assistants post for 20-30hrs each week in London. I looked at Sane's website but they only had volunteers post. Yola told me that my c.v had been sent to Lambeth council and I will have an outcome next week. I bought lunch for my son in Marks and Spencers and went home to rest for an hour. During my hour of rest, I received a phone call on my mobile from Central and Cecil House inviting me to do some voluntary admin work at their head office. They also informed me that they had a seven hour a week Saturday job going at Colliers Wood. They said that they would send me the information via e-mail. They invited me to an interview next Wednesday at 15.00hrs at their head office. This afternoon I saw my son and gave him the remote controlled car that Andrew had sent for him. I also rang my mum and both he and her spoke. Lyn and Pete are in Chester this week and so Marianne drove my son home to his foster mother at the end of our two hour session.

Friday 21st July 2006

Dear Yvonne,

Last night I took eight and a half mgs of Stelazine and slept for ten hours. When I woke up I went to see my social worker. I told her that I had started applying for jobs. I asked her if I could look at my e-mails to see if I had an email from Central and Cecil. When she said yes I looked but could find nothing from them. I then rang them and arranged to collect the application by hand. But when I arrived at the office, the person responsible was at lunch and they asked me to leave my name and address so that they could send it out in the post. Today a gay male fellowship friend rang me to tell me that he would not be meeting up with me today as I had arranged because he had just found out that his younger brother had hung himself in his stairwell in Germany and he was arranging to fly there to bury him. I was naturally sad for my fellowship friend and after talking about it with the fellowship friend that I normally spend time with, we arranged to meet with him in Fulham Broadway and go to a meeting there. After the meeting I went with him back to his place in Vauxhall for a coffee.

Saturday 22nd July 2006

Altered Perceptions

Dear Yvonne,

Last night I took eight and a half mgs of Stelazine and slept for eleven and a half hours. B, visited me at home today. We walked up Brixton Hill and arranged for someone from a record shop to come and view my records. When he came he collected quite a few and paid me one hundred pounds. I also got myself on the pay as you go internet. B, friend D, came with her car and bought some flat pack boxes.

Sunday 23rd July 2006

Dear Yvonne,

Last night I took eight and a half mgs of Stelazine and slept for eight and a half hours. Today I got to the Battersea women's meeting on time. Afterwards I went back to the home of my fellowship friend. I then went to the internet café. I had no messages in my gaydargirls box. I then went to a meeting in Brixton. Before the meeting started I rang my mum and told her that I would be visiting her tomorrow morning before my psychotherapy group. After the meeting ended I went for coffee afterwards with a few participants.

Monday 24th July 2006

Dear Yvonne,

Last night I took eight and a half mgs of Stelazine and after finding it hard to go to sleep, slept for six hours. I placed myself on the 7.45hr train to Luton. I arrived just in time to have breakfast with my mother. She told me that V.J was having a bad day and she was going to the doctors for him. After breakfast I went upstairs, woke V.J and spent some time speaking with him. He conveyed to me that he felt dizzy when he got up and generally felt weak. I let him know that I will be back to see him next Thursday and staying until Sunday. This pleased him. He asked if my son would be with me. So I told him he wouldn't be. I arrived back in London in time to go to my psychotherapy group. One of the facilitator, the female, is going to be away from next week for three weeks. And the male facilitator will be taking the group next week but will be away for the following two weeks.

Tuesday 25th July 2006

Last night I took eight and a half mgs of Stelazine and slept for twelve hours and went to a 14.00hr ACAPS Turning point workshop on C.V's in Brixton. Whilst I was there, I received a phone call from MHM (Mental Health Media) asking if I would like to do some voluntary work for them. I said yes and they sent me some information via email. After I finished the workshop I got some help with my Central and Cecil application form. I will try and get it finished tomorrow so that I can hand it in when I go for my interview with them at 15.00hrs. I went to see my fellowship friend and was told that she had seen a professor today who said that she had psorosis of the arteries. She is going to be on medication for life. Her diet is going to be permanently altered and she has to give up smoking cigarettes and she is only thirty-nine years of age. She was in shock. We went to a meeting in Stockwell and afterwards went for a coffee.

Wednesday 26th July 2006

Dear Yvonne,

Last night I took eight and a half mgs of Stelazine and slept for twelve hours. A, rang and I spoke to her. Then I got on with my application form. I arrived for my interview fifteen minutes late but with my finished application form in hand. I hope that the interview went well. I was interviewed by two people and man and a woman. After the interview I went to visit my fellowship friend, who was still in shock. We had something to eat together as she hadn't eaten all day and neither had I. Then I went home and spoke with B, on the phone for an hour and then rang and spoke with the fellowship friend, who's brother had recently committed suicide. He is flying off to Germany tomorrow and won't be back until Tuesday.

Thursday 27th July 2006

Dear Yvonne,

Last night I took eight and a half mgs of Stelazine and slept for eleven hours. I woke up feeling tired. I received a telephone call on my landline from Mental Health Media inviting me for an interview at 10.00hrs on Tuesday 8th August 2006. Looking in my diary, I have noticed that I have an 14.00hr appointment with Raye at the Job Centre. I will have to postpone it. Today A, rang me on my landline and we spoke together for almost four hours. She had found out yesterday that she was Dyslexsic. My mother also rang me, thinking that she had missed her phone call from my contact with my son this week. I had forgotten to inform her that I am seeing my son on Friday this week instead as he is going on an outing.

Friday 28th July 2006

Dear Yvonne,

Last night I took eight and a half mgs of Stelazine and slept for seven hours and woke up and sent a text message at 06.30hrs to my fellowship friend in Germany. He rang me back and told me that he had been to see his brother's body. He said that it was a surreal experience and that he had spent ten to fifteen minutes with his brother's body and kissed him goodbye. He said that the he was being well supported and that the funeral was at 09.00hrs German time tomorrow, which is an hour later than England's time. He said that today he was going to speak to the priest to make the final arrangement and to try to be allowed three tracks of music to be played at the funeral. One of the tracks is Tears in Heaven by Eric Clapton and Beautiful Day. Today at 15.30hrs I was waiting for my son to arrive but he was stuck in traffic and didn't arrive at the Breslass Centre until 16.55hrs. He gave me two sticks of rock from Littlehampton and a small box of raisons and currants. We shared one of the sticks of rock together and I am saving the other one for his grandmother with his permission. I rang my mother and he told her that he had something for her but that it was a secret. I told her that I had eaten mine and she not knowing what it is asked if hers will still be okay. I told my son that I will be visiting my mother for a few days after I see him next week. The session with my son was extended until 18.00hrs.

Saturday 29th July 2006

Dear Yvonne,

Last night I took eight and a half mgs of Stelazine and slept for ten hours and woke up tired. I took a few things over to Lyn and Pete for my son and stayed to have a cup of coffee and a chat. B, came at 13.30hrs and we spent the next few hours until 19.00hrs packing boxes. I then went to visit Eric and had a cup of tea with him.

Sunday 30th July 2006

Dear Yvonne,

Last night I took eight and a half mgs of Stelazine and found it difficult to get to sleep. In the end I slept for four hours before getting up and getting myself ready for my tea commitment. After the meeting I went for an iced coffee at 'Fresh and Wilds'. Then I went for lunch at the home of my friend in the fellowship. This evening I found out that my mountain bike has been removed from it's storage in the neighbours in Mayall Road's cellar. I spoke to Johnathan and he suggested that I write to the co-op about it. I spoke to Lyn and Pete about it and they agreed to help me draft a letter tomorrow. I then went to a meeting in Brixton.

Monday 31st July 2006

Dear Yvonne,

Last night I took eight and a half mgs of Stelazine and yet again found it difficult to get to sleep. I woke up to my landline ringing at 09.55hrs after having eight hours sleep. It was someone from the Gain Project letting me know that Lambeth Council was in the process of looking at my C.V and may be interviewing this week. I was asked if I would be available and I told them that I would be available until the end of Wednesday. I was then told that the interviews may then take place early next week. After that call I rang the Marks and Spencer's recruitment line only to find out that I was ten minutes too late to obtain an interview for a customer assistant post in Marble Arch. Naturally I was gutted. I then got ready to go to my group psychotherapy. Once there I told them about my forthcoming interview with The Mental Health Media and the fact that if offered the position I would be away from the group for at least three months. After the group I had coffee with a few of the participants and then made my way to my fellowship friend.

Whilst I was there I tried to call Central and Cecil to find out where I failed in my interview. But after a few unsuccessful attempts at calling them on my mobile phone and pausing I received a call on my mobile by Threshold, the Brighton based women's project that works with mental health. They had read my C.V and were interested in the idea of paying me fifty pounds a week if I worked for them in an administration role for two days each week. I asked them if they could pay for my fares to and from London and the woman that I spoke with said that she would have to speak with her director as they were suffering from funding shortages. She said that she was impressed with my C.V and that I seemed to have worked with a variety of vulnerable people. Quite naturally I am hoping they will be able to take me on. When I got home I rang Lyn and Pete and went over to their place for a cup of coffee. Pete was out taking my son to the cinema to see Cars but he returned before I left. I spent time telling them that when they return from their holiday in a week's time I will try to start my photography hobby

Tuesday 1st August 2006

Dear Yvonne,

Last night I took eight and a half mgs of Stelazine and slept for eight hours. When I woke up at half past nine this morning I rang Raya at the job centre and she confirmed that I had an appointment with her this afternoon at two. I then went back to sleep until 13.00hrs. When I arrived at the job centre Raye was at lunch and when she came she said that she had the flu. I told her I had had an interview last Wednesday and that I have another next Tuesday with The Mental Health Media. I told her that Threshold seemed interested in me and asked if there was any thing that she could do to help with the travel costs. She said that she was unable to help me with the travel costs. We left it that I would contact her in the future and make an appointment to see her. When I left the job centre I went to visit my cousin Eric, who after making me a cup of tea said that I looked shaky and made me something to eat. I spent about an hour and a half with him before going home and returning to bed. I went to a meeting in Stockwell this evening and then went for a coffee afterwards.

Wednesday 2nd August 2006

Dear Yvonne,

Last night I took eight and a half mgs of Stelazine and slept for ten and a half hours. I woke up at 11.00hrs and got ready to visit my fellowship friend. When I arrived there almost two hours later, my friend said that I still looked tired and that my eyes were sunk into the back of my head. To be honest I felt distressed as tomorrow I will be going to Luton to look after V.J in the absence of my mother and I am apprehensive about it. Plus I was aware that it was the second of the month and I still had no job with the targeted fifty pounds income to put towards my son's school fees. I hadn't finished packing my possessions and I didn't have a move on date. And last but not least I haven't done any work on my step four for weeks even though my sponsor rang and spoke to me on Sunday morning. My fellowship friend took me for a coffee in Café Nero and listened to my problems. She suggested that I call Threshold. But when I did I didn't get a reply. Afterwards we went to see if there were any vacancies in Debenham's and a shoe store nearby in Clapham Junction. She then went food shopping in ASDA's with me in tow. When we arrived back at her place, after having another coffee I rang Threshold, who explained to me that they were unable to pay my fares. I told them that I was still interested if they were willing to pay me fifty pounds each week. They invited me to an interview on Monday at 15.00hrs and I accepted. Tonight B, rang at 20.00hrs. She was still at work and so it was a short call. She told me that she had deposited my son's school fees into my bank account plus some extra money for the purchasing of shelves etc and removals. I am so grateful and feel an overwhelming sensation to try and repay her but I just don't know how at this time. Maybe when I get my full time job.

Thursday 3rd August 2006

Dear Yvonne,

Last night I took eight mgs of Stelazine and slept spoke to A, for an hour before going to sleep for nine and half hours. When I woke up this morning I got myself ready to go to see my social worker. When I brought her up to speed with what I had been doing. She said that she will phone me next week to find out how things have worked out. Then after speaking to me for a while she got me my medication. This afternoon when I saw my son, I noticed that he had a cold with a runny nose. Aside from that he was in good humour. I rang my mother and she spoke to my son. Then my son built a railway line and played with a few trains. When I asked him if he enjoyed 'Cars' the film, he said that he did. After my contact with my son ended I came to Luton.

Friday 4th August 2006

Dear Yvonne,

Last night I took eight mgs of Stelazine and slept for eleven and a half hours. When I got washed and dressed and made my way to the kitchen, my mum was just finishing her breakfast. V. J called to me and asked me to go to his G.P to get a repeat prescription of the 400mgs of Ibuprofen tablets that he is taking one of three times a day with or after food and is running low on. He had last been dispensed with 84 tablets on 11th May 2006. As well as this he is on Ferrous Sulphate 200mgs one to be taken twice a day with or after food. Bicalutamide 50mgs one to be taken daily. Proscar 5mgs one to be taken each day. Prazosin 1mg two tablets three times a day. Movicol 13.8g sachet, powder for oral solution (effective relief from constipation) 1-3 sachets per day. The tablets that my mum is taking is Glucobay/Acarbose tablets 50mgs. Metformin 500mg tablets. Bendroflumethiazide 2.5mg tablets. Enalapril 20mg tablet. Cardura XL 8mg tablets. Gliclazide 80mg tablets. Mebeverine 135mgs tablets. Nizatidine150mgs tablets. Adalat retard/Nifedipino 20mg tablets. Chlorpromazine 25mg tablets. I don't know how many times each day she takes them, but her tablet bag is always near her at meal times. She also takes Pharmaton capsules for relief of daily fatigue. V.J also asked me to buy him some brown sugar, which I bought at Coop after ordering his medication which is due for collection on Monday after 14.00hrs as it takes 48hrs to order them. Whilst out one of my mother's old friend recognised me and called me by name. She spoke to me for a while and asked me if I recognised her. I told her that her face looked familiar. She told me that she hadn't seen my mother in a while and sent her regards. She told me her name was Dee. When I told my mother she said that Dee knew my mother when she was still married to my adopted father and living at 104, Old Bedford Road, Luton. I must have been about two or three years old at the time.

Saturday 5th August 2006

Dear Yvonne,

Last night I forgot to take my stelazine, slept for eleven hours and woke up with a headache. After getting washed and dressed V.J gave me ten pounds to spend and told me that he wanted some toothpaste, Radox body soap and his Mirror newspaper as it has the weekly t.v guide. He was aided with a walking stick and said that he was going to the town and wouldn't be back until 4 o'clock. My mum had told me that sometimes he goes to Bingo and comes home in a taxi, so I let him leave. As I was on my way down the road I saw V.J catching the bus to town. I went and purchased the few bits and on my return did some hoovering as my mum had requested and then took my eight and a half mgs of Stelazine.

Sunday 6th August 2006

Dear Yvonne,

Last night I took eight and a half mgs of Stelazine and slept for ten and a half hours. I spent the whole day with V.J he cooked the sunday lunch with my help and kept me entertained with dialogue for the day. My mum returned at 18.30hrs and I left for London. Both my mum and V.J said that they were sad to see me go.

Monday 7th August 2006

Dear Yvonne,

Last night I took eight and a half mgs of Stelazine and slept for ten hours. I woke up and got myself ready to go to my interview at Threshold in Brighton. I was dressed and ready to go when my landline rang. When I answered it was Threshold cancelling the interview and saying that they were on holiday and would contact me in September. I felt so disappointed that I was ready to put myself back to bed. But I decided against it and went to pay my electricity bill and afterwards spent the day with my fellowship friend. When I arrived she spoke to me for a while and then we went to Lambeth College and I decided to take a beginners photography class. I went with her to my job centre and obtained a letter to say that I was in receipt of Income Support. Which I will submit when I apply for the course on Wednesday. I hope there will be enough places left as my fellowship friend said she will join the course as well.

Tuesday 8th August 2006

Dear Yvonne,

Last night I took eight and a half mgs of Stelazine and found it difficult to get to sleep before 2am I woke up at 07.30am and got myself ready to go to my Mental Health Media interview in Holloway road Islington at 11am. I got there fifteen minutes before eleven and met with Sara Chew, the person who first contacted me. She said that I was going to work with the open up team and introduced me to Kelly Cheshire who heads the team. I was interviewed by both of them and afterwards I signed a volunteer contract. Then Sara took me around the offices and introduced me to the other workers. Then she gave me an induction and showed me the mango computer diary. After she finished with me, Kelly took over and showed me the open up website which she wants to up date. Then she played to open up DVD for me to watch before I left the office for the day. Whilst there I received a call on my mobile phone from Woodfields/Central and Cecil inviting me to an interview tomorrow at 11am in Colliers Wood. I am going to start working at Mental Health Media on Monday 10.30am to 16.30 and each Monday there after. In a few weeks I will be working every other Wednesday. After I left Mental Health Media I went to Lambeth College to try and register for the beginners photography course but it was all booked up and I was placed on the waiting list. I also placed my fellowship friend's name down on the list. Afterwards I met with my fellowship friend and another fellowship friend who had just returned today from Naples and had relapsed. Together we went to a meeting in Stockwell.

Wednesday 9th August 2006

Dear Yvonne,

Last night I took eight and a half mgs of Stelazine and spoke to A, on the phone for an hour after briefly speaking with my mother. Then I slept for eight hours and got up and prepared myself to go to my interview. When I arrived there I was pleasantly surprised to find that the staff was jolly and the clients seemed happy. It is a day centre and my job entails going to Morden at 8.45am on Saturday mornings, going in a mini-bus and collecting ten elderly house bound clients from their home and escorting them to the day centre. Entertaining and feeding them for the day and then returning them home at 15.30hrs. The people that interviewed me said that they liked my c.v and that I did a good interview and they were recomending that I be employed. All that needs to happen now is for them to obtain my references and give me a start date. On exiting the building I rang PACE but was told that my old boss is on two weeks annual leave. I also tried to call Su Glazier but she was not going to be in her office until the afternoon. I went to see my fellowship friend and went to a meeting in Stockwell.

Thursday 10th August 2006

Last night I took eight and a half mgs of Stelazine and spoke to A, and told her my good news about finding a job. She was pleased as she also started a new job on Monday. But her job is a full time supportive housing manager for a housing association in north London. After speaking with her I slept for nine hour and when I woke up I rang Lyn and Pete, who had returned from their holiday a few days ago. Lyn told me that my son was going to be going to Butlins tomorrow for a long weekend and that neither she nor Pete would be collecting him today. After I spoke to Lyn I went back to sleep for three more hours. Got up and prepared myself to see my son. This week when I purchased his lunch and sweets from Marks and Spencers I also bought him some strawberries and he had told me that he likes them. When I arrived at the Breslass centre today none of the fulltime staff were there. Their office building was being painted. A woman who was situated in the basement of the office building let me in to the building where I meet my son and I waited for him. He soon arrived. He didn't have a runny nose this week and quickly set to building his train track. I then rang my mother who spoke with him for a while. I cut his fingernails and toenails this week whilst he flicked through the pages of a wildlife book. Afterwards he ate some of his strawberries. We played the tickling game and the two hours just flew by. He went to the toilet about three or four times today but although he ate his sandwiches he didn't seem to want to drink anything. After my son left, I went to visit my fellowship friend. When I arrived home, I rang the Loot newspaper to put in a free ad for my three piece sofa to be removed for fifty pounds. Buyer Collects. The ad will go in on Tuesday. Today I rang my sponsor and she is moving house tomorrow. She was pleased to hear about my jobs but was displeased to hear that I hadn't finished the piece of work that she had set me on my step 4. She asked me to call her again on Sunday evening and mentioned that if I wasn't going to do my step work then perhaps I should let her go so that she can help someone else who is more desparate. Quite naturally I didn't like the sound of that option. So instead of watching 'Bad Girls' I got some more of my step work done.

Friday 11th August 2006

Dear Yvonne,

Last night I took eight and a half mgs of Stelazine and slept for nine hours. I woke up to a phone call from The Gain Project, telling me that I have an interview with the council on Thursday 17th August 2006 at 11.30am. I said I would attend and called my social worker and rearranged meeting her until Friday 18th August 2006 at 11.30am. But on reflection I will not be attending as Mental Health Media provides ample opportunity for me to gain voluntary experience. I went to a pre arranged 3pm appointment with Joanna at ACAPS and she was pleased with my job news. I will see her next on Friday 1st September 2006 at 3pm. After leaving ACAPS I went to the Gain Project but it was closed so I will have to contact them next week. I went to bed for two hours this afternoon and a fellowship friend gave me a lift to a meeting at the CDP(community drug project) in Coldharbour Lane, Brixton where I did a chair at a meeting. After the meeting I went to the home of a fellowship friend in Streatham and spent a few hours there talking before being given a lift home.

Saturday 12th August 2006

Dear Yvonne,

Last night I took eight and a half mgs of Stelazine and slept for eight hours. Then I went back to bed for six additional hours. When I got up I went to Sainsbury's and purchased some light groceries and came home and spent three hours speaking on the phone to A. Then I slept for two more hours before spending an hour on the phone with my mother, after which I settled down and got on with my step work. I was not able to complete my work and left a message on my sponsor's voicemail for her to get back to me. I am nine months clean and sober today.

Sunday 13th August 2006

Dear Yvonne,

Last night I took eight and a half mgs of Stelazine and slept for nine hours. I woke this morning and got ready to do my tea commitment at the Battersea women's meeting. After the meeting I went to the home of my fellowship friend and had lunch. We then went to the internet cafe and went and paid five pounds to update my profile at gaydargirls for a month. My fellowship friend say's that I must start actively looking for a girlfriend and leave C in peace. I think differently but there is no harm in looking at what's on offer. Even thought I know deep down in my hearts of hearts that I sincerely love C. My fellowship friend chose two women from gaydargirls website and wrote to them. Afterwards we went to a meeting in Brixton. On the way I met Angelika, the woman who is currently living in the flat which I will be moving in to. She said that she had been told to move out by tomorrow. We arranged to meet on Tuesday. When I arrived home after the meeting Andre a member of my psychotherapy group rang me on my landline and we spoke for about an hour.

Monday 14th August 2006

Dear Yvonne,

Last night I took eight and a half mgs of Stelazine and slept for eight hours. I then woke up and got ready to go for my first day of work at The Mental Health Media. I arrived there fifteen minutes early and my boss Kelly Chester was there to welcome me. There was office moves going on and so not all the workers were in. I was shown how to get my emails and shown the data base. It's all new to me. Kelly sent me emails from her computer for me to correct and send. I lost the data several times but Kelly patiently helped me with my work. The day went quickly after lunch it only seemed like minutes before I was given my fob(an electric key that lets me into my office) and asked to return in a fortnight on Tuesday as Kelly will not be in next week. After work I went to see my fellowship friend and was a sounding board for her while she completed her DLA form.

Tuesday 15th August 2006

Dear Yvonne,

Last night I took eight and a half mgs of Stelazine and slept for eight hours and then all morning and most of the afternoon before going to my fellowship friend's home and then on to a meeting at Stockwell. I left early and went to see Angelika who informed me the shelves would cost £115.50. I offered her £100.00 and she said that she will consider it and get back to me on Sunday. B is back from her holiday and I spoke to her for an hour and told her what I had been up to in her absence. She said that she will be coming to visit me and help with more of the packing on Saturday. I spoke with A on the phone for two hours.

Wednesday 16th August 2006

Dear Yvonne,

Last night I took eight and a half mgs of Stelazine and slept for eleven hours. I woke up to my mobile phone ringing and it was Toyin from Central and Cecil telling me that I had been successful in my care assistant job application and that she would now be sending off for my references and my police check. I went for lunch with my fellowship friend and then went to Parson's Green to meet my sponsor and do a bit more on my step four. Afterwards I went to a meeting in Chelsea with my sponsor.

Thursday 17th August 2006

Dear Yvonne,

Last night I took eight and a half mgs of Stelazine and slept for twelve hours. I then got up and got myself ready to have contact with my son at the Breslass family centre. On his arrival he presented me with a large stick of Butlins rock and a keyring with Mum written on one side and 'Mum we have a special bond between us that makes us more like friends. You're always there to listen, and that's what makes you the perfect mum' on the other side. I kissed him on his cheek and thanked him. This week as well as purchasing strawberries for him from Marks and Spencers with his sweets and sandwiches plus drinks, I also bought some grapes. I spent this contact tickling him and asking him about his trip to Butlins. He kept telling me about his ghost train ride and the red coats. He seemed to have enjoyed himself. I rang my mother and she spent time speaking to him. Then he asked if Pete could collect him today and asked me to call him. He spoke to Pete on the phone for a while but Pete didn't collect him this week Marianne, the person that supervises my contact took him home. Afterwards I met my fellowship friend and shared a meal with her and two other fellowship friends at her home.

Friday 18th August 2006

Dear Yvonne,

Last night I took eight and a half mgs of Stelazine and went on the internet. I looked at Carolyn Cowan's website and read some of her articles before going to bed. One of them was on sexual abuse and after reading it I found she is going to be running a yoga workshop around the issue on October 14th and 15th 2006. Although I have had counselling for my sexual abuse, I am interested in doing the workshop as I feel that lately my creativity has dried up. I seem to have writers block in that department and feel that revisiting the issue may release my artistic energy. After unsuccessfully trying to book a place on the workshop, I slept for about eight hours and then went back on the internet and started to read Carolyn Cowan's weblog. Today she had written that her internet connection has been down since Wednesday and she was addressing the issue of death as a topic. I was pleased to see this subject broached as since V.J's diagnosis, I have been almost fearful. I used to fear what would happen to me if my mother died, thinking that I would be all alone with no one who loves me unconditionally. It is not just the death but also the impact that it has on the people that are left behind. I started to wonder again just how my mother will cope if V.J dies before her and what my new role will be. The thoughts around the subject seemed all too much so I went back to bed and woke up three hours later and set off to collect my medication from my social worker in West Norwood. I had an appointment with her this morning at 11.30am but now the time was 14.30 and I was just arriving.

Needless to say she wasn't in her office and the duty social worker had to give me my medication instead. When I arrived home I set to work on the next part of my step four, and after calling my sponsor four times to seek clarification I came to the final part of step four which was my letter to God. After going through my resentments with individuals, and institutions. I did my principals. Then I had to write down 'Everyone I have ever been physical sexually with' Then 'Everyone that I have ever fondled, kissed, cuddled and flirted with' but I wrote that one wrong and my sponsor told me that it included people I had manipulated, Then I had to write about Attitudes I have had during my life. and write a paragragh on 1) How I was raised. 2) How the attitude of my family affected me and the way I was treated. 3) What I thought and believed. 4) What I thought others thought of me. 5) Judgements I made and why. Then I had to write about What do I think is a sane and sound ideal for future sexual partners and last but not least my dear God letter. Tonight I went to the lesbian and gay meeting in Covent Garden. Afterwards when I arrived home I asked A to list my attributes and she said the following. Good organisational skills, have a lot of ideas, done a lot of different things and some amazing things in the face of needing help myself. Very helpful and considerate.

I texted my fellowship friend and she said "I love you and you are my best friend. You are loving, loyal, understanding, kind, patient, funny, broadminded, great company, outgoing, honest, affectionate, giving and hard working" I told her that I can't believe that she is talking about me. But she said that she is describing me.

Saturday 19th August 2006

Dear Yvonne,

Last night I took eight and a half mgs of Stelazine and slept for twelve hours. I am so pleased that this round of my step four is over. It has taken me about four months to do it as I was reluctant to do my house cleaning, metaphorically speaking, whilst I was preparing to move, in financial hardship and looking for a job. Having done step four now I know that I could have done it in less time and procrastinating with it didn't help me feel any better whilst not doing it. B, visited me today and helped me to pack a few more items. I was glad of her company. She is a dear friend, whom I love very much, and when I take the time to speak with her about how I feel emotionally I feel so much better.

Sunday 20th August 2006

Dear Yvonne,

Last night I took eight and a half mgs of Stelazine and slept for eight hours. I woke up at 8am and got ready for my tea commitment at the Battersea women's meeting. I had just purchased my McDonald's breakfast and coffee in Brixton and was waiting at the bus stop at 9am when I noticed that my mother had called my mobile phone. When I rung her back, she told me that she had just returned from the Luton and Dunstable hospital. Apparently V.J had become ill in the night and she had to call the emergency services. During the conversation she asked for my support and if I could come and live with her. I told her that I was on my way to a meeting and that I would ring her back later and ended the call. I sent a text to my sponsor and my fellowship friend telling them what had happened. My sponsor rang me back and told me that she would meet me at the meeting. I met my fellowship friend at the local shop where I buy the milk for the meeting. After the meeting I decided to go to my sponsor's home and do my step five. In the evening after doing my step five with my sponsor in Parsons Green I went to dinner at a fellowship friend's home in Streatham. I rang my mother on the journey there but she was out, but she rang me back when she returned. She told me that after speaking with me in the morning she went back to the hospital with pyjamas etc for V.J. She told me that it was discovered that V.J is now a diabetic and that they were going to keep him in hospital. I told her that I couldn't leave my home in London because I felt I needed to be near my son. I said that I would visit her regularly and that she could visit me. We agreed that I would visit her twice a week. she said that she couldnt visit me whilst V.J was around. We agreed that I would visit her on Tuesday's and Friday's.

Monday 21st August 2006

Dear Yvonne,

Last night I took eight and a half mgs of Stelazine and slept for nine hours. I woke up and got myself ready to go to my group psychotherapy. The hour session was extremely productive. One of our member's comes to group from a secure locked unit. A lot of the people in the unit have been placed there by the courts and could be there for years without release. Afterwards I went to an internet cafe and started to read the backlog of Carolyn Cowan's weblog and found it facinating. I arrived just after 15.00hrs for the local authority meeting about my son. Maria, his current foster mother was present. So was his court guardian, social worker, psychologist, me, Pete and Lyn. We agreed to meet again September 21st 2006 at 12noon to plan how we are going to tell my son that he is moving to Lyn and Pete's. After the meeting I went to visit my fellowship friend.

Tuesday 22nd August 2006

Dear Yvonne,

Last night I took eight and a half mgs of Stelazine and slept for eight hours. I was woken up by the vibrating sound of my mobile phone at 06.30hrs. It was my mother asking me if I could bring her some flowers when I visit her. I got up at 09.00hrs and went to the florist and purchased some flowers for my mum on my way to Herne Hill train station. I didn't have to wait long for the train and was in Luton Town and at my mum's home by 12.30hrs. My mum loved the flowers and gave me the money for them and said that each time I visit her I am to buy her some flowers as it helps her to feel better. We shared some lunch and then my mother went to the hospital to visit V.J. Apparently V.J suffered with heart failure yesterday. I stayed at home and helped my mother with some housework. When my mum returned she said that V.J had been sleeping and had to be gently woken by the nurse. She said he wanted to talk to her so she stayed but he began to vomit and couldn't stop. She told me that the nurses told her that he had been washed and shaved by a male nurse this morning as he wasnt well enough to do it himself. She told me that he was attached to all sorts of monitors and drips. I told her that I would visit him on Friday when I go back to visit her. We ate a meal together and then my mother prepared herself to go to a Jehovah's Witness meeting at the Kingdom hall and I returned to London and went straight to a meeting in Stockwell. I arrived there late but after the meeting I spent time talking to a few of the participants.

Wednesday 23rd August 2006

Dear Yvonne,

Last night I took eight and a half mgs of Stelazine and slept for ten hours and went to the home of my fellowship friend. Together we went to the Brixton road job centre to get a letter confirming I am on income support to take to South Thames College to enrol on a twelve week photography course. I am also going to see if I can enrol on a beginners Bridge course. The photography course will be held in Roehampton college, near the university. I went to a women's meeting in Stockwell this evening.

Thursday 24th August 2006

Last night I took eight and a half mgs of Stelazine and slept for eight hours. When I woke I got ready to go to The Gain Project for a review interview at 09.30hrs. I arrived on time and after letting them know about my voluntary job and the pending seven hour, one day a week paid job. I signed a few forms to that effect. Afterwards I met my fellowship friend and went to the Putney branch of the south thames college to sign on for the photography course in Roehampton and another one in Battersea. After we finished we went for coffee and I went to meet my son at the Breslass centre.

His court guardian arrived before he did, and we spent the time speaking about how my son was and my forthcoming move. Then my son arrived but his contact supervisor said that she wasn't feeling well this week and had had to stop the car and sit on her way to contact with him. She said that she had felt faint. She sat quietly throughout the contact and seemed better at the end. This contact, my son kept calling me Yvonne and I kept saying it's mum to you, and tickle him until he said mum. But when I stopped tickling him he would start teasing me again and call me Yvonne. He told me that his grandad was in hospital and asked if he was going to pass away like Pete's mum. I told him that his grandad was seventy-eight and not too well and that I didn't know if he was going to pass away. When I asked my son how old he thought Pete's mum was? He said twenty-nine. He spoke to his grandmother on the phone and put the phone in the hand of his court guardian. After the contact ended and there was just me and the court guardian left behind. He asked if I wanted my son to visit my step dad. He said he would be in agreement and call my son's social worker;'s boss as she is currently on holiday, and say he had no objections with my son visiting his grandad in hospital. I said that I would assess the situation and call her as well.

Friday 25th August 2006

Dear Yvonne,

Last night I took eight and a half mgs of Stelazine and slept for nine hours. I bought my ticket bound for Luton at 09.36hrs and arrived in Luton at 11.00hrs. My mother was out on field service. But she came home after 12.00hrs, bagged some clothes up to give to the charity shop, had something to eat and went up to the hospital. When we arrived in the CCU V.J was sitting in his chair. He had a drip going and a line going into his chest and a catharter in. He seemed weak but in good spirits. Today was his birthday. He was a bit short of breath but after a while the doctor came in and said he was making good progress and would be transfered from the CCU in ward six on Tuesday. I asked about his diabetis and the doctor said he is controlled on tablets. V.J said that he was worried about the amount of medication that he was now on and that he felt he couldn't remember which ones to take as there were so many. My mum tried to say that she was also on a lot but that didn't help him. After leaving V.J my mum and I went grocery shopping, then we went home ate and I went back to London. I arrived home at about 21.10hrs I was shattered.

Saturday 26th August 2006

Dear Yvonne,

Last night I took eight and a half mgs of Stelazine and slept for fourteen hours. I woke up and got ready for B,s visit at 14.00hrs. When she arrived we spent time talking before we finally got to work. By the time she left some six hours later, I was shattered.

Sunday 27th August 2006

Dear Yvonne,

Last night I took eight and a half mgs of Stelazine and slept for nine hours. I woke up and got myself ready for my tea commitment at the Battersea women's meeting. On the way there I stopped off at my fellowship friend's home after buying a jar of coffee and some fresh milk from Sainsbury for the meeting. After the meeting I went for a coffee at Fresh and Wild with a few of the participants from the meeting and then went to the internet cafe with my fellowship friend to look at the gaydargirls website. This evening I went to the Brixton meeting and stayed for the business meeting and was voted in by the committee to be Brixton's H&I (Hospitals and Institutions) rep. I rang my sponsor and left a message on her voicemail today.

Monday 28th August 2006

Dear Yvonne,

Last night I took eight and a half mgs of Stelazine and then after I had settled myself down to bed. My mother rang at 22.30hrs and told me that the Luton and Dunstable coronary care unit had just rung her to say that V.J's condition had deterioated. I told her that I would visit her first thing in the morning but afterwards I rang her back and said I would try and make it to Luton straight away. By the time I got myself organised and walked to Brixton it was after midnight. I then got on a N2 night bus and went to Victoria. I arrived just in time to see a 757 coach getting ready to leave but it was not stopping at Luton Town centre, it was only going to Luton Airport. I eventually got a coach for Luton at 01.30hrs and arrived in Luton, where I rang my mum and took a taxi to my mum's at 02.45hrs rang the hospital ward and went there by taxi. When I arrived V.J's condition had stablised and he was asleep, but he was nil by mouth as his abdomin was distended and needed to be x-rayed but the hospital were unable to do it as he was too ill earlier that evening. He was on a insulin drip and having hourly blood sugar tests. His heart was rigged up to an electro cardiagram monitor and he still had his catherta in. Plus he was wearing an oxygen mask. I sat with him holding his hand for two hours. When he woke and asked me the time I told him it was 03.00hrs which it was. The nurses looked after me well and offered me coffee and biscuits, a foot stool and a blanket. I left the hospital at 05.00 and took a taxi to my mum's. She was awake and on her way to the toilet when I arrived. We spent some time talking and I told her that she didn't need to be at the hospital until around 11.00hrs as that would give V.J time to be seen by the doctors and possibly get his x-ray done. I left my mum's at 06.00hrs and walked to the coach station and took the coach to London. I arrived home a 08.30hrs and went to bed. I got up at 12.30hrs and went to visit my fellowship friend taking my list of charactor defects with me to work on. I went to a illness in recovery twelve step meeting in Battersea this evening and the feeling it left me with was acceptance.

Tuesday 29th August 2006

Dear Yvonne,

Last night I took eight and a half mgs of Stelazine and slept for eight hours. I woke up and got myself ready to go to work for the day at Mental Health Media. I arrived there half an hour early after stopping off at Brixton's McDonald's for breakfast. The day went by quickly as I was getting used to the database. Reading my email's and getting to know the computer. My boss Kelly's desk has been moved into another room as the office has been decorated. Kelly said that other volunteer's are going to be working for the project and she needed my fob back as we are to share the quota. Kelly asked me if I could do another day's work this week and I said I would do Wednesday afternoon. After finishing work, I went to see my fellowship friend and went to a meeting in Stockwell. I didn't get to bed until 23.30hrs and asked my fellowship friend to text me awake at 08.00hrs

Wednesday 30th August 2006

Dear Yvonne,

Last night I took eight and a half mgs of Stelazine and slept for eight hours. I was woken at 08.00hrs with a text from my fellowship friend. I felt like staying in bed but got up and noticed that my mobile phone needed charging. It was too late to charge it and I hoped that I would be able to get through the day with it as it was. I had a bath and got dressed. I got on a bus and met my fellowship friend in Battersea we went on our way to the South Thames College and signed up for a Spanish language course. I also rang the Loot and put in an advert to sell my sofa, tumble dryer, books and some children's toys. It cost me ten pounds to advertise for a week. I then rang Brixton Housing Co-op and spoke with Glenda, who told me that I could collect the keys to my new flat next week Monday. She said that I would be given two weeks to move in. I then tried to ring my job referees without success. Then my fellowship friend and myself went to Wimpy's for brunch and then I set off to work. Whilst at work my mobile phone kept ringing but I didnt answer it as my battery was almost expired. When I got to work and saw the tasks I was faced with I felt like going home. I want to be perfect without practice. I stayed and found that I improved and at the end of the day I felt satisfied with my input. My boss thanked me for coming in and said that she would see me on Monday. To go home I took the tube from Holloway road to Kings cross and then got a bus to Euston and then a 68 bus to Herne Hill. On my way my phone rang and it was my mum but after it rang twice the battery died.

When I got home I rang her and she told me that she had been calling me all afternoon because V.J took a turn for the worse and had died. She asked me to come to Luton and support her. I was supposed to see my social worker tomorrow morning and get a top up of medication. Plus see my son at my place in the afternoon. My mum said that I must see my son in the afternoon. I've never been to a funeral before. I left three voicemail messages. One to B, one to my sponsor and one to my fellowship friend. I told Pete on my way to the train station.

Thursday 31st August 2006

Dear Yvonne,

Last night I took eight and a half mgs of Stelazine and slept for eight and a half restless hours in my mother's bed. After eating the breakfast my mother had prepared for me and leaving a message with my mum's name and telephone number for the bereavement officer of the hospital to call so that my mum can obtain the death certificate, Rung my social worker and my son's social worker with the news. I set off to London. I collected my medication from my social worker in West Norwood. I rang my housing officer and arranged with her that I could collect the keys to my new flat on Monday and take three weeks to move in. Then waited at home until 13.50hrs I rang the Breslass centre and found that there was a booking for me to meet my son there today instead of at my place as I had thought. I was an hour and fifteen minutes late arriving for contact with my son today due to this and the fact that the 196 bus was on a diversion and I hadn't remembered and was waiting for it to arrive in Brixton. My son was pleased to see me. I apologised for being late and after explaining my reason told him about his grandad. My son started to cry and cuddled me and I placed him on my knees. Naturally the contact was very short today and when I tried to call his grandmother she was wasn't in. After the contact ended I went to the home of my fellowship friend and gave her the keys to my Sunday morning tea commitment as I had rung the treasurer on my way to London this morning, explaining what had happened and she said that she would do the tea commitment for the next two weeks. After visiting my fellowship friend I took the train to Luton.

Friday 1st September 2006

Dear Yvonne,

Last night I took eight and a half mgs of Stelazine and slept in my mum's bed for eight hours. I woke up for about an hour at 02.00hrs and after going to the toilet I just lay resting until I fell asleep again.

My mum wakes up at 05.00hrs each day and reads her daily reading and her bible and prays then she goes to the bathroom and has her bath and gets dressed, after which she has her breakfast. I woke up at 08.00hrs and lazed about in bed for half an hour. I then got up, washed and dressed and went downstair and ate the breakfast that my mum had prepared for me. Namely fruit and nut fibre cereals with skimmed milk. Orange juice. cottage cheese toasted sandwich, a boiled egg and a cup of tea. After I ate I washed up the breakfast dishes, whilst my mum sweep the dinning room floor. Then we set off to Luton Register Office armed with the death certificate that my mother had collected yesterday afternoon from Luton and Dunstable Hospital. We arrived on time for the ten o'clock appointment that my mum had booked when she rang them yesterday. Whilst there V.J's death was registered and we were given a death certificate which cost £3.50, a form for the social security office and two forms for the undertakers (one was so they can remove V.J's body from the hospital and the other was for the funeral). Whilst my mum was there she broke down when she was speaking about the last time she saw V.J alive. Which was Wednesday morning. She said she had been conversing with him whilst stoking his hand. After a while he said that he was tired and she said that she was going to wash and iron his pyjamas and return the next day (Thursday) as she was going to her meeting and wouldn't be up to visit him Wednesday evening.

As she was leaving him she blew him a kiss and she said she saw a twinkle in his eye. She said after leaving the ward she went shopping and then went home. Where on her arrival she received a telephone call from the ward telling her that V.J had taken a turn for the worse and that she was to rush to the hospital by taxi and to hurry. She said when she arrived he had already passed away but that "he looked so sweet" he looked so peaceful. His skin was smooth. When we left the register office, we went to the bank and presented them with the death certificate and they wanted to see V.J's will. So we went to the Social Security and gave them the form and registered for my mum's pension to be looked at and V.J's to cease. We also applied for the bereavement fund and took a form home with us to help us with the cost of the funeral. Then they rang the pensions department and they said they would phone my mum or write to her and come and look at her benefits and help fill out the form to help her apply for the funeral cost. After the Social

Security we went to the undertakers where I found out for the first time that V.J is going to be cremated because that is what he wants. The funeral is going to be on Wednesday 13th September 2006 at 13.00hrs. There is going to be a herst and one limosine. Both are going to arrive at my mum's home at 12.30hrs on the day. After leaving the undertakers my mum and myself went home for lunch. Then we went back to the bank with the will but the bank wouldn't accept it without the solicitor's stamp so we went to the solicitor's and got one with a stamp and handed it into the bank. After that my mum felt like taking a long walk, which she did and on the way home she she told the newagents where V.J used to get his newspaper that he had died and that from now on she wouldn't be having the papers but she would have a copy of the 'Radio Times' each week and will collect it on Tuesday or Wednesday. When we arrived home my mum's cousin Noel(Bobsie) from Derby rang to say he would be coming to the funeral and her brother Alfred from California rang to say he was unable to come to the funeral. I am physically shattered. My mum rang one of her Jehovah's witness brothers who confirmed he will be doing the service for V.J and she rang one of her Jehovah's witness sisters who is going to do the flowers for the coffin. It's not yet 22.00hrs but I'm going to bed.

Saturday 2nd September 2006

Dear Yvonne,

Last night I took eight and a half mgs of Stelazine and slept for ten peaceful hours. After I woke up I found I had started my periods, I got up and had my breakfast and washed the dishes. I put two loads of washing out on the line to dry. Then I tidied up and set off with my mum to the undertakers to tell them who was going to be conducting the service and doing the flower. After leaving we took the bus into town and went into Debenhams to try and find an outfit for the forthcoming funeral. I found a jacket and my mum found a dress. Afterwards I went home and took the washing in from outside, whilst my mum did some food shopping in Sainsbury's. When she came home we had some lunch. Then Alvin, one of my mum's cousins from Canada who is currently on holiday in Manchester rang to say that he will be coming to the funeral.

Sunday 3rd September 2006

Dear Yvonne,

Last night I found that by eight thirty I had a headache and decided to be in bed by 21.00hrs. I took eight and a half mgs of Stelazine and slept for ten hours. I got up and had my breakfast that my mum had prepared for me, did some dusting and hoovering and then set off to get the train to London. On my way there I received a phone call from someone who saw my ad in the Loot and was interested in buying the dryer. I said I would meet him at my place. When I arrived he was there and bought the dryer for ten pounds. I then met my fellowship friend in 'Fresh & Wild' in Clapham Junction. I went to Brixton meeting tonight. I was introduced as the new H&I rep. After the meeting I made arrangements with a guy to move my things to my new place next Sunday.

Monday 4th September 2006

Dear Yvonne,

Last night I took eight and a half mgs of Stelazine and slept for eight and a half hours. I spoke to my mother, who asked me to bring a torch for her on my return. Then I spoke to my fellowship friend that had recently lost his brother to suicide. After that conversation I got myself ready to collect the keys for the new flat. Once I had them I went to the flat and had a look around with the Tim the maintenance worker for the co-op. The previous tenant also came and kindly left some curtains and plants for me. The gas fitting needs a new bayonet fitting so Tim said that he would sort that out for me. After leaving my new flat I went back to my old place and started to make phone calls to British Gas, B.T, Thames water and so on to let them know I am changing my address. I also rang my son's social worker's boss but she was busy so I left a message with the date and time of the funeral, his grandmother's address and the time he should be there. I then rang my referees and was told that they would be sending the references off by fax. When I had finished making my phone calls I made my way to my fellowship friend's home. Whilst there my mum phoned me and told me that her brother, my uncle King was with her. When I spoke to him he said that he wanted to see me and said he would stay the night at my mum's and wait to see me tomorrow. I went to a meeting in

Stockwell this evening then after the meeting me, my fellowship friend and two other fellowship friends went to see my new abode.

Tuesday 5th September 2006

Dear Yvonne,

Last night I took eight and a half mgs of Stelazine and slept for seven hours and got up took the train to Victoria and then the 757 Greenline coach to Luton bus station. I then took a number 10 bus to my mum's. My uncle was asleep in front of the television and my mother was upstairs sleeping on her bed. They were both pleased to see me. My uncle hadn't been to my mum's home for almost twenty years as he has been living in Jamaica for years and the U.S.A before that. I last saw him in Jamaica when my mum, my son and myself were in Jamaica for a holiday three or four years ago. After spending some time speaking with me my uncle King took me out to lunch and then left for London. He will return tomorrow and then I will go to London.

Wednesday 6th September 2006

Dear Yvonne,

Last night I took eight and a half mgs of Stelazine and slept for ten hours. I had breakfast when I woke up and left the house with my mum. We briefly looked in B.H.S (british home stores) and then I got on the coach home. When I arrived I went to sleep for two hours and then went to the home of my fellowship friend.Whilst there someone rang me regarding my advert and is coming tomorrow morning at 09.30hrs to have a look at my
sofa.

Thursday 7th September 2006

Dear Yvonne,

Last night I took eight and a half mgs of Stelazine and slept for nine and a half hours. After I had been awake for half an hour a man came to look at the sofa but he didn't buy it. I went back to sleep for two hours and was woken by someone from British Gas who wanted to read my meter. I then went to Marks and Spencers and did some perishable food shopping for lunch and took it with me. When I saw my son he was full of joy and spent time being tickled. I told him that he would be going to the funeral next Wednesday with Lyn and Pete. He wanted me to read to him a lot today, which I did and before I knew where I was it was the end of the session. This evening I went to see my fellowship friend and when I came home I spoke to B for a while and then to a few members of my psychotherapy group.

Friday 8th September 2006

Dear Yvonne,

Last night I took eight and a half mgs of Stelazine and slept for eight hours. I got up and went to see my fellowship friend. When I arrived home I spoke on the landline to A.

Saturday 9th September 2006

Dear Yvonne,

Last night I took eight and a half mgs of Stelazine and slept for eleven hours. B and Doris came today and helped me to take some books and some toys to Wandsworth Oasis in Mitchem Lane. They also helped me to move some of my things into my new flat and took a few books away to store them for me. I was so happy to have them around today that I almost didn't want them to go in the end.

Sunday 10th September 2006

Dear Yvonne,

Last night I took eight and a half mgs of Stelazine and slept for ten hours and got ready to move into my new flat in 56A Barnwell Road, Brixton London SW2 1PW. By the end of the day and two van loads later I was about seventy five percent there. I have to arrange another day to move within the next two weeks. Tonight at Brixton meeting I said that I was the H&I rep there.

Monday 11th September 2006

Last night I took eight and a half mgs of Stelazine and slept for seven hours in my old flat as the bed is still here and got ready to go to the job centre for a letter confirming my national insurance number and so on. After leaving the job centre I went to Central and Cecil and gave in my documents ie my passport, two bills and a bank statement, plus I handed the completed CRB(Criminal Records Bureau) form back to them. They said that they will write to me. This afternoon I went to the home of my fellowship friend and she came with me to Chelsea where I did a chair for my sponsor. Afterwards my sponsor took me for something to eat and the three of us chatted. Then not long after my sponsor's sponsor arrived I left.

Tuesday 12th September 2006

Dear Yvonne,

Last night I took eight and a half mgs of Stelazine and slept for ten hours and went to Luton.

Wednesday 13th September 2006

Dear Yvonne,

Last night I took eight and a half mgs of Stelazine and slept for ten hours and woke up at 8am. Pete and my son arrived at 11.00hrs and soon after uncle King arrived and then cousin Andrea and her son Tavaray arrived and then uncle Noel(Bobsie) and his sons Godfrey and Lennox. Then the hearst arrived and the limosine and my mum, me and my son. Plus Andrea, Tavaray and uncle King got inside to follow the coffin and Godfrey drove behind. I felt emotional almost as if I would start crying at any minute. The service was a good one and it was well attended. It was the first funeral that I or my son had ever attended. My son took it in his stride. I hitched a lift back to London with Pete and my son and asked to be dropped off in Victoria. I took the train to Clapham Junction and met my fellowship friend in cafe Nero.

Thursday 14th September 2006

Dear Yvonne,
Last night I took eight and a half mgs of Stelazine and slept for eight ten hours. I woke up and got myself ready to have contact with my son. He was full of smiles and hugs. He had gone back to school today and started in class one. His social worker rang me to tell me that Lyn and Pete had been accepted by the panel to foster my son and that he was going to be moving in with them soon. The panel also asked her to tell me that they admired my courage in this situation and the fact that I had put my son first. I took my first spanish lesson today with my fellowship friend. Andrew rang me on my mobile to tell me that he is coming to London tomorrow. He also told me that his wife is expecting another baby, which is great news. I told him that V.J had died and was buried yesterday and that I was in the midst of moving.

Friday 15th September 2006

Dear Yvonne,

Last night I took eight and a half mgs of Stelazine and slept for eight hours. I was woken up by the B.T(British Telecom) engineer calling me on my mobile and telling me he was outside my new address. I told him I'd be five minutes and went there and let him in. One hour later and my landline was working with my old number as I had requested. I went to see my social worker today. Afterwards I went to visit my fellowship friend.

Saturday 16th September 2006

Dear Yvonne,

Last night I took eight and a half mgs of Stelazine and slept on and off for twelve restless hours. I was going to do some more packing in my old flat when I woke up but my mother rang me and told me that her bedroom ceiling had collapsed and that when I visit her on Tuesday to go with her to see her G.P(general practitioner)she wants me to help her to clear the room. I feel dAunted. I decided to visit my fellowship friend.

Sunday 17th September 2006

Dear Yvonne,

Last night I took eight and a half mgs of Stelazine and slept for nine hours and got up and went to my tea commitment. followed by going to the home of my fellowship friend. I did my Spanish homework with my fellowship friend and went to the Brixton meeting which has been running for nineteen years and did my H&I commitment.

Monday 18th September 2006

Dear Yvonne,

Last night I took eight and a half mgs of Stelazine and slept for ten hours and when I woke up I rang Kelly at Mental Health Media and asked her if I could take two more weeks leave. She said I could and told me to call her next week. I also rang my cousin Eric and asked him to help me to do some of my move this evening and he said yes, he'll be at my old flat at 18.00hrs.

Tuesday 19th September 2006

Dear Yvonne,

Last night I took eight and a half mgs of Stelazine and slept for eight hours. I went to see Lyn and Pete this morning before I went to Luton. Lyn told me that they had to do a presentation when they went before the panel. My mum had to go to sort out her pension at her old workplace today (Vauxhall) then she went to her doctors appointment. and then after going collecting her weekly tv guide she went to a meeting this evening and I returned to London. I am writing this after spending the last hour on gaydargirls exchanging emails with a woman who's user name is alto and say's her name is Ger. she wants to meet me. I told her that would be possible in a few weeks. I am on my way back to Railton road.

Wednesday 20th September 2006

Dear Yvonne,
Last night I took eight and a half mgs of Stelazine and slept for eight hours. Today I started my photography course. Lots of homework. Back on gaydargirl exchanging messages with alto.

Thursday 21st September 2006

Dear Yvonne,

Last night I took eight and a half mgs of Stelazine and slept for eleven hours. I went to a meeting regarding my son. Lyn, his psychologist, social worker, foster carer, court guardian and me were present. I am going to be present tomorrow when we tell him that he is going to be going to live with Lyn and Pete. After the meeting I went for a cup of coffee and a cake with Lyn then I met with my son and took him to see the property I am moving from and the property that I am moving to. He asked me if I was going to take his toys with me but I said that they are at Lyn and Pete's. This evening I went my Spanish lesson and later I exchanged messages with alto, who suggested that I dismantle my futon base and reasemble it in my new flat.

Friday 22nd September 2006

Dear Yvonne,

Last night I took eight and a half mgs of Stelazine and slept for ten hours. On waking, I took my futon base, in two trips and placed it in my new flat. I then went to see my fellowship friend, who had been told that she had possible coronary arteries and was distressed. I left her and went to the meeting with my son, Lyn, Pete and the psychologist. Today he was told through a story using toys that he was going to be living with Lyn and Pete. I think it was a bit much for him to take. He wouldn't listen and kept moving around the room and I felt sad that this was happening to my son but happy that he was going to be with people who love him. After the hour long session, I met with my fellowship friend, who had been having a bad day and thinking of 'going on the piss' fortunately it was a passing thought. We ate together and went to the internet cafe and read a message on gaydargirls from alto to me. I then sent a message back. Alto is in Ireland this weekend and it seems strange to log onto gaydargirls and not having her send me messages.

Saturday 23rd September 2006

Dear Yvonne,

Last night I took eight and a half mgs of Stelazine and slept for ten hours. I then got up and did my laundery. I moved a few light items from my old flat to my new flat. Then I went to have something to eat at the home of my fellowship friend. Alto sent me some messages from Ireland. We had our first misunderstanding tonight when she asked me my bra size after going out with her sisters for a meal and drinking three Vodkas and diet cokes. I told her what it was as she told me hers but I told her that I want to take things slow.

Sunday 24th September 2006

Dear Yvonne,

Last night I took eight and a half mgs of Stelazine and slept for eight hours. I reread my gaydargirls messages from last night to and from alto and found that she had sent me her mobile number. I sent her a text and she replied even though she was getting ready for mass! I moved most of my things from my old flat to my new flat with the help of another fellowship friend who owns a van. Just bits and pieces left for me to collect. Went to a meeting in Brixton and stayed for the business meeting. Alto left me (at my request) a voicemail and I left a voicemail on her phone. So today was the first time either of us had heard the others voice.

Monday 25th September 2006

Dear Yvonne,

Last night I took eight and a half mgs of Stelazine and slept for nine hours. When I woke up I found that I had two texts on my mobile. One from my fellowship friend and the other from Alto. After making a few phone calls I went back to bed until 15.00hrs. I rang my sponsor today, who wasn't impressed with my Alto decision.

She asked me what I had to offer in a relationship? I believe that I have a lot to offer Alto. My sponsor also told me to write a two week timetable. I went to see my fellowship friend today and together we went to a meeting in Kennington.

Tuesday 26th September 2006

Dear Yvonne,

Last night I took eight and a half mgs of Stelazine and spoke to A, for an hour then slept for eight and a half hours. I woke up at 08.30hrs and made a decision to send a text message to Alto as we didn't speak last night. But while I was writing it, I received one from her. I spent the day in Luton with my mum today. I arrived just in time to accompany her to the undertakers to collect V.J's ashes. I carried the ashes back to my mum's home. It felt strange. Really weird, as I kept fluctuating between happiness because of alto and sadness because of V.J. Today my mum and myself cleared V.J's waldrobes of shoes and clothes. My mum said that she would look through them at her own time and decide which ones are to be binned and which are to go to the charity shop. Today she was just clearing the room ready for the decorators, who are coming on Friday. Since my mother wakes at 5am, I asked her if she could start calling me on my landline early in the morning as I want to get back in the routine of having a longer day. She said that starting from tomorrow, she will start calling me between 06.30-07.00hrs. Maybe I can start the day off by finding out how my mum is, each day. Tonight my son will be spending his first night at Lyn and Pete's.

Wednesday 27th September 2006

Dear Yvonne,

Last night I took eight and a half mgs of Stelazine, spoke to B, for an hour and then exchanged gaydargirls messages with Alto. I then went to sleep for eight hours and my mum rang and woke me up this morning. I had two good photography lesson's today. By the end of them I felt as if I was grasping something. This morning Fiona Cunningham-Reid, director of the UK's first lesbian feature film 'Thin Ice', that I worked on and was credited with, came to my digital photography class. She sat next to me. She told me that she now has an MA in script writing and is working on another script to film. I mentioned that I would like to work on her forthcoming film. She said it would be in two years time. We exchanged telephone numbers.

Thursday 28th September 2006

Dear Yvonne,

Last night I took eight and a half mgs of Stelazine and slept for eight hours. At 08.20hrs my son's court guardian arrived at my door for a prearranged appointment. Afterwards I went to see my social worker who suggested I tell Alto that I'm a mother and that I have Bi-polar. On the way to my contact with my son I sent Alto a message to say the content of what my social worker and myself discussed. When I saw my son today he rode on my back and called me 'Smudgeley' and 'Furby' two ponies that he used to have riding lessons on when he was five years old. Pete collected my son today and after the session I went to see my fellowship friend and from there to Spanish class. I hadn't done any homework and that mustnt happen again. When I got home I read the message from Alto and she was okay about both subjects. The thing she found shocking was that my son didn't live with me.

Friday 29th September 2006

Dear Yvonne,

Last night I took eight and a half mgs of Stelazine and spoke to B, for an hour then went to sleep for eight hours. My mum rang to wake me up this morning like she has since Wednesday but unlike the other days this morning I went back to bed until noon. Today is the day my son goes to live with Lyn and Pete. I moved more pieces of my possessions from my old flat with Eric's help. Alto's temparary contract expires today.

Saturday 30th September 2006

Dear Yvonne,

Last night I took eight and a half mgs of Stelazine and slept for eleven hours. B, came in the afternoon and we got the clothes housed, the the kitchen floor cleared of bags. We emptied three boxes and at least eight bin liners.

Sunday 1st October 2006

Dear Yvonne,

Last night I took eight and a half mgs of Stelazine and slept for ten hours. My mum woke me up at 07.30hrs. I slept until 08.00hrs and then got ready to go to my Battersea women's meeting. I purchased some milk on my way there. After the meeting I went to the home of my fellowship friend and then later I went to the Brixton meeting.

Monday 2nd October 2006

Dear Yvonne,

Last night I took eight and a half mgs of Stelazine and slept for eight hours. My mum woke me up at 07.15hrs this morning. I told her that Aunt Madge had left a message on my answering machine yesterday, when she was trying to get hold of my mum. My mum has asked me to return Aunt Madge's call, as she cannot locate her phone book at the moment due to the decoration of her room. But my phone books are packed in a box somewhere so I'm no better. I returned to Mental health media this morning and it came as a surprise to know I had forgotten what I had learnt. I spent the day on the computer looking at anti-discrimination websites for my boss. The information was interesting. By the time I left the office for the day I felt quite tired. But in Brixton underground I bumped into my cousin Eric and went to his place for something to eat. He then took me on a trip to PCWorld in Collier's Wood. But I didn't buy anything as I am broke.

Tuesday 3rd October 2006

Dear Yvonne,

Last night I took eight and a half mgs of Stelazine and slept for eight and a half hours. I went to Luton to visit my mother today. She had a decorator doing her bedroom. She sent me out shopping for light groceries in the town centre. When I returned she sent me down to the newsagents to collect her Radio Times but it wasn't in yet.

Wednesday 4th October 2006

Dear Yvonne,

Last night I took eight and a half mgs of Stelazine and slept for nine hours. Before leaving for my photography class I had a phone call from my son's social worker. We arranged to meet today at 13.30hrs with her boss. When I arrived I was told that they are wanting me to see my son once a month instead of once a week. Quite naturally I felt gutted and rather helpless. From there I went to my son's review which went well. He seems to be settling in with Lyn and Pete. I rang my solicitor to arrange to meet with her before I next see my son's social worker and her boss on Tuesday morning at 10am. I also rang my sponsor, who rang me back and spoke to me for quite a while.

Thursday 5th October 2006

Dear Yvonne,

Last night I took eight and a half mgs of Stelazine and slept for eleven hours. My first appointment today was with Joanna at ACAPS. She has booked me on a Mental health day at the business centre for Wed 1st November 2006 and a Learning difficulties day at the same place on Wed 22nd November 2006. Then I met with my son for two hours and had a great time talking to him and reading to him. Lyn collected him at the end of the contact. Today I told my social worker about what happened yesterday and she rang my son's social worker. I have also got an appointment with my solicitor for Tuesday at noon. Had a great time in Spanish class today. My fellowship friend didn't come this evening.

Friday 6th October 2006

Dear Yvonne,

Last night I took eight and a half mgs of Stelazine and slept for twelve hours. I got up and did some laundery today and whilst there

I read the coop's newsletter and found out that one of my son's godparents sons had been murdered and his funeral was today. I was shaken as he was only 25 years old and used to babysit my son with his brother. I went to the wake and his father told me he had been stabbed by someone he knew. I gave his mother a huge hug. I am lost for words. I went to a meeting at CDP, Brixton.

Saturday 7th October 2006

Dear Yvonne,

Last night I took eight and a half mgs of Stelazine and slept for ten and a half hours. I got up and went to a meeting in Stockwell and met up with my fellowship friend and followed her to Harrods then I went to another meeting in Soho. When I got home I spoke with my sponsor.

Sunday 8th October 2006

Dear Yvonne,

Last night I took eight and a half mgs of Stelazine and slept for nine hours. I did my tea commitment at the Battersea women's meeting, but there was no urn so I was unable to make tea or coffee today. Alto rang me today and we spoke together for the first time. This evening I did my H&I rep stuff at Brixton meeting.

Monday 9th October 2006

Dear Yvonne,

Last night I took eight and a half mgs of Stelazine and slept for eight hours. I went to Mental Health Media today and received a phone call from my son's court guardian, my solicitor and my son's social worker. The professionals are all going to meet on Thursday at 16.00hrs to discuss my contact arrangement with my son. I am going to see my solicitor tomorrow at noon. Went to see Mousetrap today.

Altered Perceptions

Tuesday 10th October 2006

Dear Yvonne,

Last night I took eight and a half mgs of Stelazine and slept for eleven hours and went to see Ros Dunning at noon. She drafted a statement which I went back to sign at 17.00hrs. She told me that the meeting had moved from Thursday to Tuesday. This evening I spoke to B, on the phone for an hour and followed that call by speaking to my sponsor then having an early night. Today was world mental health day.

Wednesday 11th October 2006

Dear Yvonne,

Last night I took eight and a half mgs of Stelazine and slept for twelve hours. I then got up and read my step 8 from the big book. Then I went to my old flat a collected a few more of my belongings. Afterward I went to see Glenda, my B.H.C housing manager and arranged to collect my tenancy agreement. I then went to Olive Morris House but it had closed at 13.00hrs I then went to the dss but I needed to go to another office with id that I didnt have. I then filled out a change of address form at my G.P's and met with my fellowship friend, had something to eat then went to a meeting.

Thursday 12th October 2006

Dear Yvonne,

Last night I took eight and a half mgs of Stelazine and slept for ten hours. I then went to see my social worker and spent an hour speaking with her. She is going to the meeting on Tuesday morning at ten. I also had contact with my son this afternoon and he seems brighter since living with Lyn and Pete. He spoke to his grandmother on my mobile today and was very cheerful. Lyn collected him and brought along his scooter. Lyn said that they went to the lake district but it was a little too far. I met with my fellowship friend for coffee and then went to my Spanish class.

Friday 13th October 2006

Dear Yvonne,

Last night I took eight and a half mgs of Stelazine and slept for eight and a half hours. It's my forty-fifth birthday today. I was also born on Friday the thirteenth. I then went to visit my mum in Luton. After spending the day with my mum I came home and went to the cinema to watch Meryl Streep in the film The Devil Wears Prada. On my return home I met Lyn walking Ben (the dog) on my road. She was armed with a birthday card from my son, her and Pete. Today was a very special day as I heard via text or phone call from all my close friends for my birthday, I had a lovely day with my mum and my son remembered it was my birthday.

Saturday 14th October 2006

Dear Yvonne,

Last night I took eight and a half mgs of Stelazine and slept for twelve hours. Then B, visited me with a card and a cake to celebrate my birthday. We went out shopping in Brixton and ended up having a meal at an Eritrean resturant. On my return home I unpacked a box with my lesbian books and DVD's and placed them on the shelf in my bedroom.

Sunday 15th October 2006

Dear Yvonne,

Last night I took eight and a half mgs of Stelazine and slept for ten hours. My mother didn't wake me this morning so I rang her. She told me that she thought I was tired and decided to give me a lie-in. But I asked her to wake me at 8am on Sundays in future. I arrived at the Battersea women's meeting in time to put the urn on in time for the meeting. My sponsor came to the meeting today and we went to a Cafe Nero's to read step 8 and have a chat. I went to a meeting in Brixton this evening.

Altered Perceptions

Monday 16th October 2006

Dear Yvonne,

Last night I took eight and a half mgs of Stelazine and slept for eight and a half hours. I got up and got myself ready to go to Mental health media. Kelly, my boss, wasn't in today. She left me an email detailing work that she wanted me to get on with. I had a great day at work and sent my boss an email at the end of my working day. Then went to a meeting in Stockwell.

Tuesday 17th October 2006

Dear Yvonne,

Last night I took eight and a half mgs of Stelazine and slept for ten hours. Today it is the meeting of the professionals where they sort out contact with me and my son. I lodged two cheques from the Norwood and west dulwich labour party lottery for 42.50 then I changed my address with the bank. I then went with my fellowship friend to see her new flat off lavender hill. Then at six I help some of the men in my old building empty my flat of most of the furnishings and placed them outside the front for the council to collect tomorrow.

Wednesday 18th October 2006

Dear Yvonne,

Last night I took eight and a half mgs of Stelazine, was in bed by nine and slept for eleven hours. I arrived at the court at the same time as my solicitor and the outcome of the meeting was that I see my son once a fortnight in term time and once a week outside ie Christmas, Easter and summer holidays. The judge praised me for my courage. After the case I felt as if the world as I knew it had ended. My son in long term foster care without me to guide him through his growth. Mother by proxy. I went home and slept for two hours then went to my photography class and had a great time. The tutor helped me to put my photoshop on my computer. I texted my sponsor and she both texted and rang me back.

Thursday 19th October 2006

Dear Yvonne,

Today was the last time I saw my son for weekly sessions. When I told him he held a faraway look in his eyes. I told him that I will be calling him on the phone next week.

Friday 20th October 2006

Dear Yvonne,

Today my sponsor called me and asked me to get a move on with writing my step eight list of amends. She asked me to call her some time next week so that we can meet up and prepare for step nine.

Saturday 21st October 2006

Dear Yvonne,

Today B, visited me and brought along some gifts for my bathroom. We also went shopping where she purchased pots and pans and a broom for me. Then we went out for a meal at a Thai restaurant.

Sunday 22nd October 2006

Dear Yvonne,

Today I did my tea commitment at the battersea womens meeting and my H and I commitment at the Brixton meeting.

Monday 23rd October 2006

Dear Yvonne,

Today I did a day's work at mental health media. My boss was back and seemed quite pleased with what I did last week.

Tuesday 24th October 2006

Dear Yvonne,

I spent the day in Luton with my mum and stayed overnight.

Wednesday 25th October 2006

Dear Yvonne,

I took it easy today. I went to a SW GSR ASC meeting in Brixton tonight, where I purchased where to find for the Battersea womens meeting and was an honourary GSR for the night and was able to vote. Lyn rang to ask me to call my son on her mobile phone tomorrow as they are not going to be at home. She also told me that she, Pete and my son had spent some time with her brother and his family and he had helped my son to do doggy paddles.

Thursday 26th October 2006

Dear Yvonne,

I went to acaps at 09.30 this morning I found it hard to get out of bed but got up at the last minute and went anyway and whilst there rang Central and Cecil regarding the Saturday job. I left a message on the answering machine. I then went to see my social worker who informed me that I was going to have a review with the psychiatrist soon. I then went to the dss and changed my address and then to the housing benefit office and changed my address. I then rang Central and Cecil again who told me that my references had cleared but my crb had not but they were going to send me a contract next week. I rang my son at six this evening and spent seven minutes speaking with him. He said that he would like to go to London Zoo to see the parrots and the Science Museum another time. He has been to both before. He told me that he loved me and let me know that he had been doggy paddling up to his chest in water. He said that he was frightened but he did it. I rang my sponsor and made an appointment to meet with her tomorrow at noon. Spoke to A, for two hours tonight.

Friday 27th October 2006

Dear Yvonne,

I found it difficult to get out of bed today. I just felt tired but I got up and went to my sponsor's home. I did my step eight and now I am on step nine. Whilst I was there Central and Cecil's day centre rang and confirmed that I will be starting work with them next saturday and offered me sundays starting 26th November, which I accepted. The contract is in the post so I will sign it and return it via hand delivery. I went to a meeting in CDP in Coldharbour lane this evening and whilst there recieved a call from someone that is going to help me set up a web log blog.

Saturday 28th October 2006

Dear Yvonne,

Last night I took eight mgs of stelazine and slept for twelve hours. I got up and went to photography in Waterloo. Where I was meeting my Wed evening tutor and the class. We took photos on the South Bank and at the Eid festival in Trafalgar square. I chatted online with Alto a bit this evening and I watched a DVD of Oscar Wilde's An Ideal Husband.

Sunday 29th October 2006

Dear Yvonne,

Last night I took eight and a half mgs of Stelazine. In the morning I went to my tea commitment at Battersea women's meeting. I spent the day with my fellowship friend and in the evening I went to do my H&I rep commitment at the Brixton meeting.

Monday 30th October 2006

Dear Yvonne,

Last night I took eight and a half mgs of Stelazine. In the morning I got ready and went to Mental Health Media for the day. Afterwards I went to a meeting in Stockwell.

Tuesday 31st October 2006

Dear Yvonne,

Today is Halloween and two years ago Pete and Lyn held a halloween childrens party for my son at their house where he invited his friends from kindergarten. It went well.

Wednesday 1st November 2006

Dear Yvonne,

Last night I took eight and a half mgs of stelazine. I went to a Mental Health day seminar and workshop in Islington at the business design centre and collected information whilst I was there for www.openuptoolkit.net I got the ticket to go from Joanna at Acaps. I went to my photography class this evening and we spent most of it in the darkroom.

Thursday 2nd November 2006

Dear Yvonne,

Last night I took eight and a half mgs of Stelazine. Today I met my son at Brixton station with Marianne and we went to London Zoo. My son was unfortunate because the zoo didn't have any parrots but he got the chance to feed a barn owl. Eric rang me today. Elaine rang me this evening.

Friday 3rd November 2006

Dear Yvonne,

Last night I took eight and a half mgs of Stelazine. Today I went have a dummy run with my new job then I went to the housing benefit office and declared that I was going to starting work on Sat 4th November 2006

Saturday 4th November 2006

Dear Yvonne,

Last night I took nine mgs of stelazine. I got up at seven and set off to work at 7.50. As an escort in the minibus I almost choked one of the clients with the seat belt. Another of the clients nearly ran off from the bus. While I was playing penny bingo with a group of clients one woman kept removing her dentures and playing with them. I started my induction and forgot my fire drill notes. By the time I got home I was tired and took an hour long bubble bath in a candlelit bathroom.

Sunday 5th November 2006

Dear Yvonne,

Last year on this day I was at St Martins in the field participating in a service celebrating ten years of inclusiveness with the openly gay American anglican Bishop. It was also the 400th year aniversary of Guy Fawkes failed attempt. On this day in 2004 I was attending a fireworks display with my son and his kindergarten friend Louis Hugo, Carolyn Cowan's son at Lyn and Pete's house. The next evening my son and my self went to dinner at Carolyn Cowan's house and enjoyed a fireworks display with her family and friends.

Monday 6th November 2006

Dear Yvonne,

Last night I took nine mgs of stelazine. I went to mental health media. The lifts to the office was out of order this morning and it was three long flights up the stairs. Five minutes after I had arrived in the office I was still breathless. The job centre rang me while I was at work and asked me if I wanted to go to an interview for a job at Sainsbury's in Streatham. I said no. I went to a meeting in Stockwell today. I started my periods today.

Tuesday 7th November 2006

Dear Yvonne,

Today I rang my mum and cancelled visiting her and stayed in bed for the day. I felt better for it.

Wednesday 8th November 2006

Altered Perceptions

Dear Yvonne,

Today I went to my new G.P's practice to see the nurse and when she took my blood pressure it was 133/95. She took the reading twice and because it was high, she said that I must go to see her in two weeks. She also said that the practice is unable to do my medical for my central and cecil job, as I have not been with the practice for two years. So I took the papers to my old G.P's.

Thursday 9th November 2006

Dear Yvonne,

Today I went to see my social worker, who will be going on holiday in two weeks. We had a good long talk and I feel better for seeing her. We were discussing the fact that it has been just over a year since I have left hospital, my new job that I started on Saturday and my high blood pressure. Whilst with my social worker Central and Cecil rang to say that they will get their occupational health department to do my medical as my old G.P's couldn't do it as they are not my current G.P. When I returned home I found I had received my CRB in the post. I slept this afternoon. I rang my son at 18.00hrs. We spent thirty minutes talking. He asked me why he can't live with me and I told him that I don't know if I am going to go into hospital again etc and that he is loved where he is and that I am near and love him too. I told him that next week when I see him I will be taking him to see STOMP. I asked Lyn to explain a little bit about it to him.

Friday 10th November 2006

Dear Yvonne,

Today I spent most of the day in bed. Resting, sleeping, taking phone calls, reading. I went to a meeting at CDP (community drug project) Harbour and then went for a meal at Fujiyama in Brixton.

Saturday 11th November 2006

Dear Yvonne,

Today was my second day at work. I took the mini bus that had the largest round. I played penny bingo again this week and genuinely had a good day at work. After work I went to visit my gay male friend Micheal. He placed a photo of me on the gaydargirls website in my profile. I also asked him about sorting out a blog site for me. He is going to do it but not just now. He cooked for me and I ate whilst chatting to him and watching the X-Factor. My sponsor rang and told me that she is coming to give me my year medalion at the Brixton meeting tomorrow.

Sunday 12th November 2006

Dear Yvonne,

Today I went to do my tea commitment at the Battersea women's meeting. But there was no urn. I gave up my commitment this week and will no longer be doing it. This afternoon I went to High street Kensington with my fellowship friend and she bought me lunch. This evening my sponsor gave me my keyring at the Brixton meeting and then we went for a diet coke and a chat at the cafe in the Ritzy cinema.

Monday 13th November 2006

Dear Yvonne,

Today I spent the day working at Mental Health Media. I felt tired as I didn't go to sleep straight away last night, and tossed and turned until I finally fell asleep in the small hours of the morning. I was pleased when lunch time came. My boss Kelly told me today that she is going to be leaving. She said that she will work up until Christmas but may not return after the Xmas break. After work I met my fellowship friend in a cafe and went to the Stockwell meeting. I again celebrated my year birthday but this time my fellowship friend brought me a cake.

Tuesday 14th November 2006

Dear Yvonne,

Today I went to my mum's for the day.While I was there I did some hoovering and shopping for her. I then did my step nine amends just as I was about to leave and it went well. When I returned to London and went to a meeting in Stockwell. I met a potential sponsee there. I am going to give her a call tomorrow after I speak with my sponsor.

Wednesday 15th November 2006

Dear Yvonne,

Today I spent the morning in bed dozing in between phone calls as my appointment with ACAPS was cancelled as Joanne is off sick today. I spoke to my sponsor, who spoke to her sponsor and was thrilled that I had a new sponsee. I then spoke to my son's social worker and finalised the details of tomorrows trip to the theatre to see STOMP with my son. In the afternoon I returned my old set of key's to my housing co-op but kept the key to the mail box so that I can collect my mail for now. I went to a meeting in Camberwell this evening and afterwards had dinner with my fellowship friend. A, rang me at 22.30hrs and we stayed chatting on the line until 02.00hrs.

Thursday 16th November 2006

Dear Yvonne,

I didn't get to sleep until about four this morning and I almost got up and did some writing in my diary. I was thinking about my new sponsee and didn't want to oversleep and not hear her ringing me on my vibrating phone. I woke up at 08.50hrs and waited for her call. She rang. It was the start of my new life, giving a direct service to someone. Whilst speaking to her I tried to remember the things my sponsor said to me. The disease of addiction kills! So I want to be a good sponsor. After speaking to my sponsee and asking her to try and get to a meeting today and get there at least five to ten minutes before it starts. I rang some other new comer in the fellowship that is only just two weeks clean and sober. I said that I could only keep what I had by giving it away! I then sent a text to Alto, it was a quote and she replied. I then rang and spoke to my fellowship friend, who was on her way to a meeting. This afternoon I went to see Stomp with my son and Marianne after the show we went to

Pizza Hut for something to eat and then returned home at 18.30, one hour after the time we were meant to have got home. B, is going to call me tonight and I am looking forward to it.

Friday 17th November 2006

Dear Yvonne,

Today I had a lie in. Then I went to a meeting in another fellowship where I met my sponsor and collected my year keyring.

Saturday 18th November 2006

Dear Yvonne,

Today was my third week at Woodlands and I escorted the Wimbledon clients to and from the day centre. My manager gave me a list of training dates. I finished work early as we were two client down. B, and her friend Doris plus Hanine her daughter came by with a mattress that B, bought for me. B, and Doris look around my flat and discussed how they were going to put up my shelves so that I can unpack my boxes. It is A's birthday. I sent her a text. This evening my sponsee told me she had just found out she was pregnant and that she had had just asked her boyfriend to buy a bottle of wine.

Sunday 19th November 2006

Today I went to Croyden's IKEA with B. We were there until it closed at 17.00hrs. We saw the sofa B wants to buy for herself. I liked it too, I went to a meeting in Brixton this evening and went for coffee afterwards. My sponsee told me she had relapsed on alcohol. She said that she is not going to turn up for her greeting commitment at Brixton tonight. I said I'd meet her at a meeting in Stockwell tomorrow. Alto is in Budapest.

Monday 20th November 2006

Dear Yvonne,

Today I went to mental health media and worked on two

spreadsheets instead of one. I also made phone calls and answered the phone on occasions as well as sending e-mails. I feel as if I am progressing all be it slowly. Tonight I went to a meeting in Stockwell. My sponsee said that she was unable to make it. This evening I sent a multimedia text to myself and am now able to send and recieve them. I was speaking on the phone to A at the time.

Tuesday 21st November 2006

Dear Yvonne,

Today I went to visit my mum in Luton. She had me hoovering and shampooing the carpet. She was very pleased to see me and told me so. I enjoyed my day with my mum and arrived home at 19.00hrs.

Wednesday 22nd November 2006

Dear Yvonne,

Today when I went to see the nurse, my blood pressure was back to normal and at 124/80. The nurse was pleased and so was I. Then I went to see Tamara Webb, my care co-ordinator and mental health social worker. She helped me to fill out a community care grant form which I handed in to my local benefit office. Unfortunately my medication hadnt arrived so I might have to collect it tomorrow or Fri. After leaving Tamara, I went to get a set of keys to my home cut for B and Doris to use for when they come to do my shelves. This afternoon I went to see Joanna at ACAPS. my next appointment with her will be in one months time. Then I went to the dss to tell them that I was going to be starting additional hours on Sunday. This evening I visited my fellowship friend.

Thursday 23rd November 2006

Dear Yvonne,

Today I spent most of the day in bed. I slept mostly and when I woke I sent and received texts. I rang my son at 1800hrs and spent about ten minutes on the phone with him. I spoke with B, at 20.00hrs and spent an hour talking to her. Then I watched Catherine Tate on B.B.C2.

Friday 24th November 2006

Dear Yvonne,

Today I did some of my laundery. I sent a text to Alto yesterday and she still hasn't replied.Getting to know someone from scratch can be so tricky. I've taken on my second sponsee today.

Saturday 25th November 2006

Dear Yvonne,

Today I went to work and found out that one of the clients had died on Monday. I had a good day at work and was given my payslip, my first for fourteen years. I went to see the film 'Borat.' I was not overly impressed.I spoke to A, on the phone when I returned home. I went online and had a conversation with Alto and she has booked a date to see me on Tues 19th Dec 2006 for a bite to eat.

Sunday 26th November 2006

Dear Yvonne,

Today was my first day of care assistant work on a Sunday. I met a gorgeous client of eighty four years that I have fallen in love with. She is so cantankerous! This morning she hid her wig and refused to come to the day centre without it on. She had two homehelps searching high and low for it for over an hour. We found it in the end and she reluctantly came. After work I met up with my second sponsee and went to the Brixton meeting. There was a business meeting after tonight's meeting and I stayed for it. My sponsor rang me and we spoke for a good little while.

Monday 27th November 2006

Dear Yvonne,

Today I went to Mental health media. My boss didn't come to work today, it was her thirtieth birthday. She is leaving in a few weeks so she took the day off. I was tired all day today. After work I went to a meeting in Stockwell and met my second sponsee there. When I rang my mum, she was glad to hear from me. She told me that her diabetes has got out of control and her doctor called her in to tell her to get back on her diet. She also had a leak from the ceiling in her sitting room and blockage in one of her drains. She got someone from her kingdom hall to sort it out.

Tuesday 28th November 2006

Dear Yvonne,

Today I was at Central and Cecil's head office in Waterloo. It was the start of my training days. I was fifteen minutes late arriving and was tired all day. The day started at ten and ended at 16.30hrs. There is a lot to study and I don't know how I am going to do it but I must. Tonight I came home and it wasn't long before I was in my bed and asleep.

Wednesday 29th November 2006

Dear Yvonne,

Today I spent a second day training at Central and Cecil's head office. The tutor said that because we were new, we didn't know enough. So instead of us coming in next Wed and Thurs we will have it postponed until Jan 9th and 10th 2007. I was pleased. My boss rang me and asked me if I would like some overtime. I said yes. She will ring me tomorrow to obtain the days. This evening I went to a meeting in Camberwell but missed the chair so I then went to a women's meeting in Stockwell.

Thursday 30th November 2006

Dear Yvonne,

This morning my boss rang and I arranged to go into work on Wed and Thurs of next week on the Pollards Hill route. I then went to the dss to submit my payslip and do the same at the housing benefits office. Afterwards I met my son at Brixton underground station with Toyin a different supervisor as Marianne was on leave as her sister-in-law had recently died. I purchased some sandwiches for my son from Marks and Spencers and we set of on a 345 bus towards the Science museum. We went to the 'Game On' exhibition and had a go on lots of the computerised games. My son didn't want to leave and asked if he could go there again next time. I will gladly take him. When I got home it didn't take me long to go to bed. I woke up for an hour to speak with B, who is coming with Doris on Saturday to try to do my shelves.

Friday 1st December 2006

Dear Yvonne,

Today was a rainy day but it was a lovely one spent with my mum. We went food shopping as she is going to be cooking a meal for some of her kingdom hall brothers and sisters. She showed me the work that was done and seemed to be in good spirits.

Saturday 2nd December 2006

Dear Yvonne,

Today I did the escort for the Wimbledon side of the day centre. Whilst I was at work B, and Doris was at my flat erecting shelving, my big mirror and a bathroom cabinet. When I came home in the evening I was pleased. So I started to unpack a few more boxes. B, and Doris will be coming back next Sunday to finish the work off.

Sunday 3rd December 2006

Dear Yvonne,

Today I was again on the Wimbledon side. My boss rang me at work today to ask me if I want to do overtime on Monday, so I told her that the overtime that I do can only do voluntarily as I don't want it to have an adverse affect on my state benefit. She offer me the chance to think about accepting a full time post and said that she would speak to me again on Wednesday, when I am next at work. I told her that I couldn't do Monday. I went to a meeting in Brixton this evening.

Altered Perceptions

Monday 4th December 2006

Dear Yvonne,

This morning when the alarm went off I kept putting it on snooze until it was too late. I rang Mental health media and to say I wouldn't be in today. Then I slept until noon. After I woke up I went to the dss and wrote a statement to say that I work eight hours a week at £6.38 a hour making it a total of £51.04. I then went to the housing benefit office and told them the same. Then I went to see my social worker to collect my medication. Then I went to see my fellowship friend for a cup of tea at her house and after I went to a meeting in Chelsea and then was taken out for a meal with my sponsor and her sponsor.

Tuesday 5th December 2006

Dear Yvonne,

Today I went to see my mum in Luton. She told me that her diabetes is high and almost out of control. She said that she had gone off her usual diet since V.J's death and that was why. She told me that she will go back on it. Today I bought my son's xmas present.

Wednesday 6th December 2006

Dear Yvonne,

Today on my escort job I was working the Pollards Hill side and the second client that I went to collect, stumbled on the way to the bus and fell in the road and cut his head open. I called 999 and the ambulance came and took him to St Heliers hospital. It wouldn't be so bad but he is ninety-one and has a pacemaker. His head wound was pouring blood. and I put a dressing on it from the first aid box. I rang and told my boss and she called his next of kin. When I arrived at the day centre I filled out an accident report. It was busier at work today and I enjoyed it. But I still feel a bit shook up about this morning's incident it happenend at approximately 09.40hrs. After work today I booked a ticket at clapham cinema to watch the animation film 'flushed away' next week Thursday with my son. B rang this evening and we spoke for an hour.

Thursday 7th December 2006

Dear Yvonne,

Today I went back to my escort job and the client that fell yesterday was reluctant to come into the day centre. He had a black eye, stitches covered with a dressing on his forehead, bruised ribs and a bruised hand. But he did come in in the end. Whilst I was on my lunch break, Lyn rang me on my mobile and asked me to call my son at 19.30hrs tonight as they are going to be out christmas shopping earlier than that. My boss said that she will pay me for eight hours each week. Tonight I spoke to my son for twenty minutes. He has seen 'Flushed Away' before but said he would see it again with me.

Friday 8th December 2006

Dear Yvonne,

Today I visited my social worker. She told me that she was going to be on holiday in a fortnights time. At 16.30hrs I went to the Angel Islington to have xmas dinner with Mental health media.

Saturday 9th December 2006

Dear Yvonne,

Today I started my period. I escorted the Wimbledon side today.

Sunday 10th December 2006

Dear Yvonne,

Today was my first day at work to go to work and help the manager. I finished work at four. When I arrived home B and Doris was still working on the shelving at my place. In fact they were getting ready to leave. I am so pleased about my place. I went to the Brixton meeting this evening.

Monday 11th December 2006

Altered Perceptions

Dear Yvonne,

This afternoon I went to visit my sponsor in Parson's Green to make a start on my step ten. After we read it I went to a meeting with her in Chelsea.

Tuesday 12th December 2006

Dear Yvonne,

Today I went into work at Mental health media. I also had my review. At lunchtime I did a step nine with A. After work I went to visit my fellowship friend. Alto and I had our first real misunderstanding on the phone and she hung up without saying goodbye. I rang B and spoke to her for an hour.

Wednesday 13th December 2006

Dear Yvonne,

Alto didn't ring today. Today was the day centre's xmas party and I worked from ten until four.

Thursday 14th December 2006

Dear Yvonne,

Today I went with my son to watch 'Flushed Away' at the cinema in Venn Street, Clapham. Afterwards I went to visit my fellowship friend. When I returned I rang A. Still no word from Alto. We are ment to be going out for a bite to eat on Tuesday. I am going to send her an online message, tonight.

Friday 15th December 2006

Dear Yvonne,

Last night Alto's reply to my online message was that it is all over. Today I spent the day with my mum in Luton. This evening I went to see my fellowship friend and when I returned home I sent some online messages to some new contacts on gaydargirls and got one response.

Saturday 16th December 2006

Dear Yvonne,

I was on the Mitchem side to escort today. My boss brought in some orange cake that she had baked. This evening I went to have dinner with B at a Thai restaurant in Brixton after she helped me with some more unpacking of boxes.

Sunday 17th December 2006

Dear Yvonne,

This morning I was tired for work and only just managed to arrive on time. After work I met my fellowship friend in Brixton and went to the Ritzy for a coffee and then we went to a meeting.

Monday 18th December 2006

Dear Yvonne,

Today I was twenty minutes late for mental health media. My boss Kelly and her boss Anne will be leaving on Wednesday. Today Kelly tried to give me all the information that I will need. I gave out Christmas cards. This evening after work on the 137 bus in Clapham and woman that had two babies in a double buggy screamed for help whilst I was talking on my mobile phone to my fellowship friend. One of her babies had stopped breathing and he was only 15 months old. Myself and two other passengers turned the baby upside down and I squeezed his stomach and he started breathing again. The bus waited for the ambulance to arrive and then drove off. I felt emotional. I felt choked up and wanted to cry and didn't start to settle until I arrived at my fellowship friend's home. To think that I may have helped to save someone's life just one week before Xmas.

Tuesday 19th December 2006

Dear Yvonne,

Today I went to work voluntarily at Woodlands Day centre. My boss told me that I didnt have to go to work on Friday. So I think I will have a lie in and go to my mum's a bit earlier. Today at the centre we had Karaoke and all the staff had to sing including me! After I left work today I went to see my fellowship friend.

Wednesday 20th December 2006

Dear Yvonne,

This morning my mum rung me at 08.10hrs and we chatted for fifteen minutes. I then got up and prepared myself to go to my first day on the NA helpline. Whilst there the time passed so quickly that I was suprised that the ten to noon shift was over so soon. I didn't work the phones, I only read the procedure file. Afterwards I went to the dss regarding the fact that they have stopped my Income support. I wrote a statement and hope that they will restart it again. When I had finished I went to an appointment with Joanna at ACAPS. She said that she will see me again Fri Jan 19th 2007 at 14.00hrs and make a plan for next year. I told her that I needed to be in full time employment by 2nd November 2007 and the salary must be of a sum that can pay for my son's school fees. I went to see my fellowship friend and than went to a meeting in Camberwell. B, rang tonight and we spoke for an hour and a half. A letter arrived today from the housing benefit office to say that my claim has been suspended.

Thursday 21st December 2006

Dear Yvonne,

I had a lie in this morning. Then I met my son at noon. Today he had a stiff neck but his cold had gone. He gave me a Christmas card and two presents. One of which I opened in his presence and the other I am keeping to open on Christmas day. Then we went to see the film 'Happy Feet' at Clapham Picture House. The cinema was packed with children. Afterwards we went to buy a SD(secure digital) card in a photography shop in Brixton. Then we went for some Chicken Chow mein without veg for my son and a sweet and sour chicken for me to eat at Speedy Noodles. When we finished eating we took the bus and went to my flat so that I could pick up my CF(compact Flash) and then we returned to the photography shop where I printed fifteen prints for my fellowship friend and took my son home. After I went to meet my fellowship friend, who was at her old abode with her old neighbour. We took the bus together to her present abode, where I had a cup of tea and went home. I tried to phone my mum at least four times today but she was out. When she returned she left a message on my answering machine and my voicemail. But she was too late to speak with my son. The only thing that consoled her and my son today was that they are both going to see each other next Thursday when I take my son to Luton on the train. My mum says that she is going to bake him a pizza.

Friday 22nd December 2006

Dear Yvonne,

This morning I went to West Norwood to get my medication. On the way there I saw a lorry that had been too tall for a bridge it went under stuck under it, with the police closing the road off and re-diverting the traffic. It was the bridge nearest to where I get my medication at David Pitt house. Tamara Webb, my social worker was on holiday, so I saw a duty social worker. Then I went dss to try and find out weather they had my new details for my claim. But I came away non-plus. Then I went to the housing benefit office at Olive morris house and gave them a copy of my latest dss letter, 13th Dec 2006, which stated that the recent changes to my benefit had not affected my income support. I then went back to my flat and unpacked three more boxes and had a bath. I then went to my 15.00hr appointment at the Tate Library in Brixton with Learn Direct. I was there almost two hours and got a level two for my english. I have another appointment next Wednesday at 14.00hrs. After leaving the library I went to my mum's in Luton.

Saturday 23rd December 2006

Dear Yvonne,

Last night I spent the night in Luton and slept in my mum's bed, with my mum. I woke up this morning with a headache so my mum told me to stay in bed whilst she made me a cup of tea and got me some soluble paracetamols. I took one and my headache shifted. I then got up and was company for my mum for the rest of the day.

Sunday 24th December 2006

Dear Yvonne,

Last night I again slept in Luton in my mum's bed. I left for London at 16.00hrs I went home dropped my bag off. My fellowship friend called me on my mobile to say that she was in the area. She called for me and we went straight to the Brixton meeting.

Monday 25th December 2006

Dear Yvonne,

Last night I didn't get to sleep until 02.00hrs. I spent my time reading my twelve step literature and watching Catherine Tate DVD's. Just before I went to sleep, I opened my christmas present from my son. It was a pocket notebook. I said my prayers before I went to sleep tonight and again when I woke up. I made sure that I was in the bath by 09.00hrs. I went around to the Brixton meeting, where I waited for my lift at 10.30hrs and went to the Wandsworth twelve step dinner. It took place at the same spot as last year but this year I didn't do service. My fellowship friend met me there. I had a great day eating and drinking and I was in time for the meeting. I received and sent loads of text messages. While I was eating lunch, I got a call from my son. He thanked me for his christmas present and I thanked him for my present from him. Pete also said that I can collect him at 11.00hrs instead of noon this Thursday. I rang mum and told her that I would be having my son one hour earlier. She was pleased. After the dinner I got a lift to a meeting in Stockwell and after that meeting I walked home. It has been a great day.

Tuesday 26th December 2006

Dear Yvonne,

Today I was meant to go to visit my mum in Luton. But when I got to Herne hill station the ticket office wasn't open. So I took a bus to Brixton underground and went to Kings Cross and walked to the overground station. But they said that there was only a bus going as far as the A1, and I would have to take a taxi from there. So I got the tube to Victoria coach station, but the 757 greenline coaches was only going to Luton airport today and the driver said that I would have to get a bus from the airport. So I rang my mum and told her that I will see her on Thursday when I visit with my son. I then rang my fellowship friend and arranged to meet her for a lunchtime meeting in Soho. After the meeting I went with her to another fellowship friend and had a meal that she had prepared for us and yet another fellowship friend. Then in the evening the four of us met up with another fellowship friend that was driving and we went to an meeting in Bermondsey as the meetings that we had intended to go to in Clapham and Stockwell were not on on Boxing day.

Wednesday 27th December 2006

Dear Yvonne,

This morning I went to do service and be inducted on the NA helpline. After I finished my two hour stint I went to Olive morris house to the housing benefit office and informed them of my forthcoming rent rise from £60 to £70. Then I went to the Gain Project but it was closed. I then rang my sponsor and arranged to meet with her this forthcoming Friday. Then I went to Learn Direct and spent an hour and a half there. I will return this Friday to do a three hour assessment. I met up with my fellowship friend afterwards in Clapham Junction and went for a coffee in Cafe Nero's. Then after having some retail therapy we went to a meeting in Blackfriars then when it was over, on the train on the way back to Brixton, I bumped into Ismail, an old collegue from C.L.A.S.H and the Angel Drug Project. I took his mobile number and he told me he had bumped into Esther earlier on that day. Ismail got off at Vauxhall and my fellowship friend and myself went for something to eat in Speedy Noodles Brixton and I came home. I have been saying my prayers each morning and night since Sunday night. I have also been reading my big book and my just for today and daily reflections books.

Thursday 28th December 2006

Dear Yvonne,

This morning, I slept until 10.30hrs and then got up, washed and dressed and there was a delivery for my neigbours at number 54, Barnwell Road. I signed for the packages put them in my flat and then went to pick up my son at 11.00hrs. We were lucky and got the 11.08hr train to Luton and caught a number 10 bus when we got there. My mum was thrilled to see my son and when she hugged him she lifted him off the ground. She had baked a pizza and two cakes. My son loved the cheese and the base of the pizza, but he didnt like the filling. He loved the cake. We took photographs and made a video and later on an elder and his wife from my mum's Jehovah's Witnesses religion came to visit my mum. My son and I retired to my bedroom and read some of his books that he has at my mum's house. Then we left for London. I arrived back at Lyn and Pete's at about 17.45hrs. My son is lovely and kept telling me that he loves me. He was is happy and healthy. When I came home, my neighbour came by to collect her packages.

Friday 29th December 2006

Dear Yvonne,

This morning, I slept until ten, prayed and then read my 'As Bill Sees It', 'Just for today', and 'Daily reflections'. Got up washed and dressed. Ate some cereals and then left for my Learn direct course. I arrived at 11.00hrs and left at 13.30hrs. I will return on Friday 5th January 2007 at 11.00hrs. I went for lunch in Speedy Noodles popping home briefly afterwards and then set off to Parsons Green, where I did my step eleven with my sponsor and followed it with a meeting in Chelsea.

Saturday 30th December 2006

Dear Yvonne,

This morning I woke up said my prayers, read my literature and got ready for work. I was on the Mitchem run today. There was fifteen clients in the day centre. After work I went to visit my fellowship friend. She wasn't feeling too well and had spent most of the day in bed. Whilst I was with her another fellowship friend rang and read step one and two from the green and gold book. When I got home my mother rang and I spoke to her for over half an hour.

Sunday 31st December 2006

Dear Yvonne,

This morning, I found it difficult to wake up. I said my prayers and read my literature and got up anyway and got ready for work. I arrived on time to the day centre. I worked a little more closely with my manager today and finished at 16.00hrs. I went to a meeting in Brixton. When I got home I got a phone call from Andre, a participant of my psychotherapy group. We were on the phone talking for over an hour. In the new year, we are going to go for a pizza and watch a film.

Monday 1st January 2007

Dear Yvonne,

This morning, I still found it difficult to wake up, but I still got up prayed and read my literature. I arrived on time to do service at the twelve step helpline. On the way there I rang someone in the rooms who is over eleven years clean and sober and asked her to be my shadow sponsor and take me through the steps in the green and gold. She accepted. But when I spoke to my sponsor and told her what I had done, she said that she would have to speak with her sponsor and tell me if it is acceptable to her or not. I spent the afternoon with my fellowship friend and went to a meeting near Charing x road this evening.

Tuesday 2nd January 2007

Dear Yvonne,

Today I went to Luton to visit my mum. She was having her front garden repaved. She seemed in good spirits. On my return to London I went to a meeting in Stockwell and read step eleven. I shared about my sadness about the issue of my sponsor.

Wednesday 3rd January 2007

Dear Yvonne,

This morning I slept until twelve noon, said my prayers, read my literature and ran my sponsor. She said that she was okay with me having a shadow sponsor and was happy for me. We arranged to meet this Friday, so that I can complete my twelfth step, after which we will go to a meeting that my sponsor is the secretary of and which her sponsor will be chairing. Quite naturally I was elated and set to work reading my twelfth step. I also briefly spoke to my fellowship friend on the phone and arranged to meet with her in the afternoon. Today was my son's review at Lyn and Pete's home. He wasnt there. He was at a school friend's home, as it disturbs him. His social worker, myself, Lyn, Pete and the reviewing officer was there. The review went well. My son has now been living with Lyn and Pete for three months and seems to be getting on well. He still wants to live with me and is also sad after seeing me each week. Lyn and Pete are paying for my son to go to an after school club each friday at his school so that my son can play with his school friends, which he enjoys. They are also paying for him to attend a classical percussion lesson workshop at the ...Allen girls school in Dulwich on Saturdays the lessons are two hours a session. Plus they are going to pay for him to go on holiday to Ibiza in Spain to visit Pete's brother who lives there. The social worker also told me that since the last three weeks of contact with my son has been unsupervised and has gone well that from now on I will be having unsupervised contact with my son. After the review I met my fellowship friend and a few other 12 step members in Clapham Junction at Cafe Nero's. I followed her home and she cooked me a meal. She also gave me some recovery books. We went to a meeting tonight in Islington.

Thursday 4th January 2007

Dear Yvonne,

This morning, I had a lie in until 10.00hrs. I then said my prayers, read some recovery literature and then got washed and ready to go to see my social worker in West Norwood. As I left my flat I met my new neighbour Anthony. He lives upstairs. He seems very friendly. As usual I was happy to see Tamara Webb and we spent the half an hour we had together evaluating last year. I am grateful to have a social worker like her. She is so warm and spiritual. Plus she has great empathy. After leaving her, I picked up my son from Lyn and Pete and went to Speedy Noodles for lunch with him. Then we went to Webster's shoe shop in Brixton and purchased a pair of shoes for him. His foot size is one and a half G and I also purchased a pair of trainers for him in a size two. My mother had given me the money to pay for his footware on Tuesday. So afterward when we rang her, my son told her thank you. This afternoon my son and I went to see Mary Poppins in Old Compton Street in Soho. He enjoyed it and so did I. it started at 14.30hrs and ended at 17.15hrs with a short interval. After I dropped my son home, I went to see my fellowship friend.

Friday 5th January 2007

Dear Yvonne,

This morning I again slept until 10.15hrs, prayed, read and got myself ready to go to Learn Direct. I arrived there just after 11.00hrs and left at 14.15hrs. I went to lunch at Speedy Noodles then went to my sponsors home. I did step twelve with her today and then went to a meeting with her.

Saturday 6th January 2007

Dear Yvonne,

This morning I was tired when I woke up but said my morning rituals and got ready for work. When I got to Stockwell tube there was an announcement that all trains from Kennington to Morden was cancelled. So I got a train back to Brixton and took the 118 bus to Morden. I got to the meeting point ten minutes late. When I got home I rang Laura and wished her a happy new year and chatted for a while. I tried to call my mum but her phone was engaged. I then got on with writing a few pages of Step one from the green and gold. Then I rang my fellowship friend and spoke with her for a while and was asleep by 21.30hrs.

Sunday 7th January 2007

Dear Yvonne,

This morning I woke at 08.20hrsand still felt tired. So I went back to sleep and rang work to say that I wasn't going to work today. I then spent the rest of the day sleeping. I got up at 17.00hrs and went to a meeting in Brixton. I was in bed by 22.30hrs.

Monday 8th January 2007

Dear Yvonne,

Today I had Basic first aid training for Central and Cecil. I arrived at 9am and left just after 3pm. I went to a meeting in Stockwell this evening and rang B, on my return home. I got a letter from my housing benefit office saying that they are going to pay my £70 per week rent.

Tuesday 9th January 2007

Dear Yvonne,

Today I had a Common Induction training day for Central and Cecil.I arrived just after 9am and left at 16.30hrs. My income support wasn't paid into my bank today. I was given £20 from Eric (my cousin) who I went to see after completing my Listening skills entry level three at Learn Direct tonight. I sent a text to B and asked if she could loan me some money. She offered £250 but I took £100.

Wednesday 10th January 2007

Dear Yvonne,

Today I had the fourth and last Common Induction training day for Central and Cecil. I arrived just after 9am and left at almost 5pm. This evening I went to a 12 step meeting at the Gorden hospital, Victoria. It was the H&I (Hospitals and Institutions) committee meeting. I takes place on the second Wednesday of every month. It was my first attendence.

Thursday 11th January 2007

Dear Yvonne,

This morning at 10am, I went to see Tamara, my social worker in West Norwood. She rang the dss. After we finished talking she gave me my medication. On my way home I went to the dss. They said that they have changed my benefits to incapacity benefit and are waiting for the income support department to send them my details. Then I will be paid. I then picked my son up from Lyn and Pete's at 2pm as he is now back at school. He was waiting at the front door for me to arrive. We took the bus to Brixton. popped into Marks and Spencers and bought some snacks to nibble. My son had already eaten some sandwiches. We then took the underground to South Kensington, so that we could go to the Science Museum. My son wanted to see the airplanes so we took the lift to the third floor and took a look. Then we went to the second floor and looked at the sailing vessels and then finally we went to 'Game On' where my son played a few computer games. Then we left to take the train back stopping off at a shop to buy a couple of doughnuts at my son's request for him. We spoke to my mum on the phone arrived back at his home at 17.30hrs. I was really happy to see my son.

Friday 12th January 2007

Dear Yvonne,

Today I went to visit my mum in Luton. On my return in the evening, when I switched my bedroom light on, I heard crackling sounds. When I looked at the light bulb, I saw water so I turned the switch of and lit two tea candles. I then wrote a note for my neighbour who wasn't in, telling him that he had a leak in either his bathroom or kitchen. This evening I washed one load of washing and did some more unpacking, then went to bed at ten.

Saturday 13th January 2007

Dear Yvonne,

Today I went to work and was on the Mitchem escort side. I had Gina the driver for the second time in my career, the last time I had her was last week Saturday. We joked happily with each other and when I told her that I was gay she told me that her best friend was gay! This evening was to be my first Saturday night on the helpline as a commitment but when I got home after work this evening, I found plaster on the ground floor of my flat and on my spiral staircase. When I went up to the bedroom I found that the plaster had come from my bedroom ceiling. My bed was wet and in a mess with the debriss and water was dripping from the ceiling. My neighbour wasn't in, so I rang the co-op and got the emergency number for Julian, who came within the hour to see what the problem was. I also rang B, who said that I could spend the night at her place. I then rang my workplace and told my manager what had happened and said I would not be going to work on Sunday. When Julian arrived he had his son Dillan with him and when he saw the problem he went to get Vic, who is the chair of the maintenance committee. When all four of us had viewed the damage, and Julian had broken into my neighbours flat and found out that the fault was with a washing machine connection. It was decided that I could not stay in my flat as it would be too dangerous. So I went to Lewisham to stay with B. Vic said that he would have an emergency meeting with Tim, the maintenance worker and Julian on Monday and prioritise the work to be done. I was asked not to return to sleep at my flat until at least Monday. I gave Julian my keys took a few things and then left. I arrived at B,s at 22.00hrs.

Sunday 14th January 2007

Dear Yvonne,

I stayed up until 01.22hrs watching t.v and talking with B, last night before I went to bed. I had a good sleep although I had forgotten to bring my medication. I woke up at 09.00hrs had a bath, got dressed and sat quietly in my bedroom until B got up. We then had breakfast. I was unable to charge my phone as my charger had got wet in my flat and was no longer working. B, and I went to Lewisham shopping centre and she purchased a new charger for me and put £20.00 credit on my phone. We then went to Doris' house and together the three of us went to my flat. More debris had fallen and there was plaster covering the spot where I usually sleep on the bed. The matteress was soaked and stained and we put it on it's side to start drying out of the way of the point of the leak. My little t.v was leaking water so that will have to go and so is my four pin plug. I got my computer and camera plus some underwear. I also took my step working guide with my written work even though it was a bit wet and went back to B's.

Monday 15th January 2007

Dear Yvonne,

This morning, I started my periods but I still went to the housing benefit office at Olive Morris house to give them a copy of my this December payslip, but I will have to return as I didn't have my bank statement with me. On my way to my group psychotherapy I stopped off at my flat and was pleased to see that they had started work by partially stripping my ceiling of plaster board and sound proofing. I also so saw Lyn briefly and told her what had happened. At my group today I met five participants that I hadn't met before. I got the telephone number of two of the women, Michele and Lena. It was strange to be back at the group and people seemed curious about my artificial insemination. After the group I went back to my flat and packed a small case. I then set off to take a train from Vauxhall station to the country, where I did my first step in the green and gold book with my sponsor and went to a meeting. I got to bed about midnight.

Tuesday 16th January 2007

Dear Yvonne,

This morning B, woke me on her way out to work at 08.20hrs. I got up and had breakfast before setting off to see my mum. I felt tired today and slept on the train on the way to Luton. I really feel like a commuter living in Lewisham. My mum was really pleased to see me. After me telling her all my news and she telling me that she had purchased two pair of gloves for herself, she asked me to clean her cabinet and I did. My mum also mentioned again that she wanted a cat. So I rang a cat rescue centre in Luton and she made an appointment to view some 18 month old cats on Saturday evening, with a view to taking on home. She gave me some money to buy a cat litter tray and some litter. A feeding bowl and a poo scooper, which I did. She told me that she is going to buy some Whiskers cat food whilst she is out shopping on Thursday. I arrived back in London at 18.30hrs and tried to take my wet bedclothes to the laundry at 18.55hrs but it was closed.

Wednesday 17th January 2007

Dear Yvonne,

This morning B, woke me at 08.00hrs so that I could have my breakfast and set off to Mental Health Media in Islington in good time. I arrived there at 10.15hrs and Mina wasn't in this morning. So I didn't stay after telling Rosie what had happened. I went to my flat got my latest bank statement and went to the housing benefit office with it. Then I went to the JobCentreplus and rang Incapacity benefit and told them that my money didn't arrive last week or this week. They took my number and rang me today. They said I will be getting a giro on Friday and the rest of my money will be paid into my account. I then went to my flat and put my bedclothes into a service wash. It cost £17.00. Afterwards I went to a meeting in Hinde Street and met with my fellowship friend and she bought me lunch at Speedy Noodles in Brixton. Then I collected my service wash and showed my friend my flat.

Thursday 18th January 2007

This morning B, woke me up at 07.00hrs so that I would leave by eight. I arrived at Woodlands for my moving and handling training. The tutor was Luigi. He took us last Monday for the basic first aid training. In my breaks I went downstairs to visit the day centre. It was a very windy day today and the large garden shed, which belongs to the day centre was blown over the six foot fence and into the adjacent park. Plus a large tree was uprooted and fell lying across Cavendish road. I was tired all day today but stayed up long enough to ring my son at 19.00hrs and my mother afterwards. I went to bed at 20.00hrs.

Friday 19th January 2007

Dear Yvonne,

I slept until 10.15hrs and so was too late to get two buses from

Lewisham to Brixton for 11.00hrs for my learn direct appointment, so I rang them and made another appointment for Thursday 1st February 2007 at 12 midday. I then went to my flat and Anthony, my neighbour was at home, so I showed him my flat. He was very apologetic and said he would replace my t.v and is willing to clean and paint. He gave me a sorry card with a candle as a present. I then went to the gain project and did a few lessons of Mavis Beacon's typing lesson. I then went to have lunch at Speedy Noodles. Afterwards I went to my flat and filled out a housing benefit form which came yesterday. I was ten minutes late for my appointment with Joanna at ACAPS. We did a year plan together and updated my C.V, plus I sent off for an application form for a Mental health job in Westminster. After leaving Joanna, I went to Olive Morris house and handed in the form. I went to a 12 step meeting at Brixton Harbour and then I took the buses back to Lewisham.

Saturday 20th January 2007

Dear Yvonne,

This morning B, alarm clock that she leant me woke me up at 06.30hrs. I left the flat at 07.20hrs and arrived in Morden at 08.30hrs. I had a good day at work and afterwards went to my flat to see if my giro had arrived but it hadnt. An application form for a job had arrived.It's closing date is 2nd Feb07. I read through it and will try to get Joanna at ACAPS to help me with it. I rang my mum from my flat and she told me that she was now the proud owner of a four and a half month old male kitten. It's name is Angel. My mum said that it was love at first sight and that she has fallen in love with Angel. He cost thirty pounds and will need to be doctored in March. Tonight I did my first Saturday shift on the twelfth step helpline. I started at 20.00hrs and finished at 22.00hrs. I got back to B's at 23.00hrs.

Sunday 21th January 2007

Dear Yvonne,

This morning the clock alarmed at 07.00hrs but I didn't get up until 07.45hrs. So I missed having breakfast.I arrived in Colliers Wood at 09.10hrs and my line manager was pleased to see me. Today she took me through a fire drill test and showed me where the gas and electricity meters are. I left work at 16.50hrs. I went to my flat and phoned my mum to find out how Angel was. She told me that she had got up at 01.00hr to see it he was resting okay, last night. Tonight I went to Brixton meeting and the meeting was finished by 20.55hrs. Someone gave me a lift to Peckham and I got the 136 bus straight away and arrived home at 21.30hrs. B, was home to greet me. She hadn't been here for the last two nights. She has lent me another £20.00 as I only have one pence in my purse.

Monday 22nd January 2007

Dear Yvonne,

This morning I had a lie in until 11.15hrs and then rang the helpline to see if I could get keys to the building and was told that I didn't have to go in this Saturday as my colleague is unable to attend, but I would have the keys Sat 3rd Feb 2007. I also rang Joanne at ACAPS and made an appointment to see her so that she could help me with my application form at 14.00hrs today. I went to my flat first to pick up my application form and then I went to my psychotherapy group. Today there was only three participants. Liz, Lena and myself with Wil and Jack the facilitators. It went well. Then I went to see Joanne, who photocopied my application form and talked me through some of the questions. I went to a meeting in Stockwell tonight.

Tuesday 23rd January 2007

Dear Yvonne,

B, woke me at 06.45hrs and I left at 08.00hrs to get to Waterloo for 09.15hrs for my Central and Cecil Food Hygiene training. At the end of the day we did a multiple choice test. If I get twenty out of thirty right, I will pass and get a certificate. Julian rang me today to say that my flat will be ready on Thursday. I went to Lewisham and was in bed at 19.30hrs. I woke for the toilet at 02.00hrs and did some more work on my application form and then went back to sleep until 07.00hrs

Wednesday 24th January 2007

Dear Yvonne,

B, woke me at 07.00hrs and told me to look at the settled snow out of her bathroom window. I was bemused. Getting to Mental Health Media in Islington from Lewisham today was stressful. The train kept being delayed and was packed by the time it got to Lewisham and when I got to London Bridge I had to take the 17 bus, as there was no service on the Jubilee line and a poor service both ways on the Northern line. I arrived at work at 10.30hrs. I like MHMedia. I am interested in the work they do and I like the people that work there and I feel that what I do is worthwhile. Anti discrimination and anti stigmatisation of people with mental health really turns me on. Whilst at work today I watched two MHMedia videos 'Working Partners' and employment video and 'Families and Friends' both showed empowering of people with mental distress. I went to a meeting in Dulwich tonight.

Thursday 25th January 2007

Dear Yvonne,

I woke up at 07.30hrs today and got ready to get to West Norwood from Lewisham. I took the buses. I arrived to see Tamara at 09.30hrs and waited until she arrived. I told her about my ceiling and about the Job that I am trying to apply for and she helped me to see my assets so that I could begin to understand how to get the questions answered. I made an appointment to see her again for help with my application form at 16.00hrs on Monday. I went to my flat afterwards but Julian didn't appear. He rung to say he will finish up tomorrow. I spoke to my neighbour Anthony who is a gay man and gave him my front door key so that he can start to clean and place things back in my bedroom. I will get my keys off him or his boyfriend Glen tomorrow evening when I return from Luton. 14.00hrs I collected my son from Lyn and took him to the Aquarium near the London Eye. We had a great time together. I gave him some trousers and sweatshirts that my mother had purchased for him from 'Adams' and when he spoke to her today he thanked her. They both spent time today talking about their cats 'Fluffy' and 'Angel'.

Friday 26th January 2007

Dear Yvonne,

Today I spent a few hours in Luton, with my mum. I left at 14.00hrs as I felt tired and have Central and Cecil tomorrow. My mum was cheerful and was expecting two of her witness sisters to visit her this afternoon. I didn't see Angel whilst I was at my mum's, even though I walked about my mum's home calling out his name. I went to my flat when I got back to London and was pleased to see that Anthony had made good his promise to place my belongings in my bedroom. He also left me a note. I have decided to move back in tomorrow.

Saturday 27th January 2007

Dear Yvonne,

Today I was on the Mitchum side with Gina as the driver. I had a great day at work and afterwards went to Lewisham and got a black cab at the station and went to B's home to collect my belongings. She was in when I got there so she helped (reluctantly).

Sunday 28th January 2007

Dear Yvonne,

I had a lovely sleep in my own bed last night and got up at 08.00hrs ready for work. I had another great day at work and afterwards I went to a meeting in Brixton.

Monday 29th January 2007

Dear Yvonne,

Over the weekend I recieved my payslip from Central and Cecil (my boss only paid me for seven hours each Saturday instead of the eight hours that she had promised.) I also recieved my bank statement through the post. This morning I took them both, plus my work contract to the housing benefit office. Then I went to my group, where there were six participants. Afterwards I had a coffee with two of them, Lena and Liz. Later this afternoon I went to see

Tamara, my care co-ordinator and mental health social worker. I discovered that I am on an Enhanced Care Programme Approach (C.P.A) Both of us went through my job application together and I put her down as a referee for the ThamesReach post. I went to a meeting in Stockwell this evening and then went to print off my job application at my cousin Eric's.

Tuesday 30th January 2007

Dear Yvonne,

This morning I had a lie-in and when I got up I went to The Gain Project, where I was lucky to see Yola, who is usually on secondment. She looked at my application form and I tidied up one or two things and sent it off. I then went home after having a meal at Speedy Noodles.

Wednesday 31st January 2007

Dear Yvonne,

Today I spent the day at Mental Health Media. I put myself down to go on a course that they are running for service users, which starts next Wednesday in Waterloo. There are five sessions to it and it takes place every other week. I went to a meeting in Camberwell this evening and the had a meal at Speedy Noodles with my fellowship friend.

Thursday 1st February 2007

Dear Yvonne,

This morning I had a lie-in and then I went to Learn direct at Brixton Library. I did my level one in writing. I have a test to take next week Friday.

Friday 2nd February 2007

Dear Yvonne,

This morning I had another lie-in, in between doing my laundary.

This afternoon I went to see Joanna at ACAPS Turning Point. Joanna, earmarked two more jobs for me. One was a dual diagnosis drugs/Enhanced C.P.A but it was in Brent and the other was in Lambeth, but it was Drugs/Alcohol.

Saturday 3rd February 2007

Dear Yvonne,

Today I did the Mitcham side again, as there was an agency driver on who did not know the route on the Wimbledon side. I worked with Gerry today. After work I went to a meeting in Soho and then went to do service on the Helpline until 10pm.

Sunday 4th February 2007

Dear Yvonne,

Today I told my boss that I wont be working next Sunday, as I have training on Tuesday and Thursday next week. I finished work at 4pm today and went to the Brixton meeting this evening.

Monday 5th February 2007

Dear Yvonne,

This morning I stayed in bed until 10am. Then I got up and went to the housing benefit office. Afterwards I collected a job application form from Joanna, of ACAPS and went to my group psychotherapy. People in the group seemed a little negative today. This afternoon I met Linda, my shadow sponsor in Vauxhall and did my step two with her. Afterwards I went to visit my fellowship friend and went to a meeting in Stockwell.

Tuesday 6th February 2007

Dear Yvonne,

Today I spent the day in Luton with my mum. I met Angel, her kitten today. He is so cute and bigger than I thought. My mum told me that she is going to get on with some interior and exteria painting when the weather gets warmer. When I got back to London I went to the culture meeting in Stockwell and afterwards I had a meal with a fellowship friend.

Wednesday 7th February 2007

Dear Yvonne,

Today I started the first of five training days for mental health anti-discrimination faciltated by Openuptoolkit.net (mental health media) At the beginning of the day, I felt shy but by the end of the day I felt as though I fitted in. This evening I did a chair at the detox in Springfield hospital, Tooting Bec

Thursday 8th February 2007

Dear Yvonne,

Today there is several inches of snow on the ground. But I still went to collect my medication. Tamara was off sick today so I spoke to the duty social worker. Today I got a phone call from Thames Reach, inviting me to an interview on Tuesday. When I said that I couldn't make it due to being on a training day, they changed it to Wednesday at 10am. I had a lovely day with my son today. We went to the Museum of London. On the bus home he said to me "Let's have Sex" when I said where did he get it from he told me his friend Declan. I told him that it was inappropriate and he must tell Declan not to say it to him. I was secretly shocked to think that two seven year olds could be so bold. I spoke to my mum this evening and B

Friday 9th February 2007

Dear Yvonne,

Today I did a mock level one literacy test at Brixton library and got 36 questions out of 40 right. I will book the real test next Friday. Lunchtime I spent some time with my cousin Eric and then I went to my appointment with Joanna (ACAPS). Her team manager asked me some interview questions to prepare me for my forthcoming interview. I arranged to see Joanna again on Monday at 17.00hrs.

This evening I went to a meeting in Chelsea where I had a meal afterwards with my old sponsor and her new boyfriend.

Saturday 10th February 2007

Dear Yvonne,

Today I worked with Gina, the driver, and we exchanged mobile phone numbers. I worked on the Wimbledon side. Today my colleague was on annual leave so I was on the shift with an agency staff. My boss gave me a new contract to sign but I didn't sign it. It was a proposal for new pay scales. My pay is now going to be £6.02 per hour instead of £6.38. Considering that I get paid seven hours a week, the missing £2.50 is quite a lot. I also asked my boss if I could have tomorrow off as I will be on training day two days next week. After work, I arrived at the Helpline thirty minutes early for my shift because I wanted to pick up my keys and code to the building. I had wanted to go to the Soho meeting before my shift but the Charing Cross side of the Northern line was out of service both ways, so I went home first. When I got home I spent an hour and a half speaking on the phone with A. I arranged to speak on the phone to her again Sunday at 17.00hrs so that she could help prepare for the interview.

Sunday 11th February 2007

Dear Yvonne,

Today was my day off. I had a lie-in and my mum rang me at noon. We spent about half an hour chatting and then I relaxed and watched a bit of television before getting myself ready to visit cousin Eric for a bite to eat at 14.00hrs. When I arrived I sat on Eric's computer reading the Thames Reach Bondway website. I was impressed. I arrived home in time to phone A. She was very helpful and we spent about thirty minutes with the preparation. I went to Brixton meeting this evening.

Monday 12th February 2007

Dear Yvonne,

Today I arrived at eleven forty-five, fifteen minutes late to see my social worker and found that she was busy with someone who was in a crisis. I didn't go to group today. I went to see Sara Northey at 15.00hrs. My son and Lyn was also there. We are going to do a life story for my son. This happens for children in care. It will take about six to eight weeks. The next time we meet I must provide my son's baby pictures. At 17.00hrs I met with Joanna, who gave me a test interview. She seemed pleased with me overall and wished me luck.

Tuesday 13th February 2007

Dear Yvonne,

Today was my mum's seventy-first birthday. But as she doesn't celebrate birthdays or Christmas, I didn't draw attention to it when I spoke to her on the phone today. Today I had a Corparate Induction day at Central and Cecils head office. I met the chief executive, amongst others and I was one of the first of a group of employees to see the companies new mission statement and aims. It was a worthwhile day. My social worker rang me and spent time over the phone trying to prepare me for my forthcoming interview. This evening I ate a chinese takeaway, had a bath and went to bed at 19.00hrs. I feel really tired.

Wednesday 14th February 2007

Dear Yvonne,

This morning I woke up at 07.30hrs and heard on the clock radio that Aldgate tube station was closed and that a lot of Whitechapel has been cordoned off, because yesterday afternoon part of a building collapsed. I decided to use the Aldgate East station instead. A and B sent text messages wishing me luck. I left my flat at 08.00hrs and arrived in Whitechapel where my interview is going to take place at 10.00hrs at Thames Reach Bondway's head office at 09.30hrs. I was given a cup of coffee while I waited. There was a test and an interview and the whole thing took one and a half hours. I left the building at 11.30hrs and went straight to Mental health media. Whilst working I kept looking at my phone but it didn't ring. When I got home at 17.30hrs I had no messages on my landline so I rang my mum and told her that I didn't get the job. Then I started to look in today's Guardian at the job ads to see if there was another that I could apply for. I saw one and picked up the phone ready to dial for an application form and the phone rang in my hand. It was Thames Reach saying that I had the job subject to references. I was overjoyed and rang my mum back to tell her. What a Valentines day present! I also rang my friends and my sponsors. Tonight I went to an H&I Committee meeting. Tonight Andre rang and we spent about two hours talking He is an old member of the monday psychotherapy group. He said he will ring me again tomorrow.

Thursday 15th February 2007

Dear Yvonne,

Today I had a Central and Cecil Health and Safety training day. During my break I went to the cashpoint and found that my son's school fees had been paid but my incapacity benefit money didn't arrive and I have only got £2.00. I rang my social worker and told her about my interview and asked her to reply to them quickly when they ask for my reference. I also told her about my finances and said I was going to the benefit office tomorrow. I rang mental health media and asked them also to be quick with my reference. I spoke to B tonight and told her about my benefit situation and asked her if she could lend me some money. She said that she will put £100 in my account tomorrow morning on her way to work. Andre rang again tonight and we spoke for about fifteen minutes.

Friday 16th February 2007

Dear Yvonne,

This morning I woke up at 08.30hrs and decided to go to the dss before my learn direct appointment but it doesn't open until 10.00hrs on Fridays. So after making my appointment with learn direct to have my test next Friday, I went to the dss and rang incapacity benefit. They informed me that I now get paid fortnightly so my next payment isn't going to be until Tuesday. I then went to Luton. My mum has a cold and was trying to get an appointment with the doctor. She went up to the doctors and had just arrived back minutes before I arrived. She then ate something. She said it was her first wholesome meal since she became ill and set off to the doctors again at four o'clock to be in time for the six o'clock surgery. I was hoovering and didn't see sight or sound of Angel.

Saturday 17th February 2007

Dear Yvonne,

Today I worked on the Wimbledon side with Gina as my driver. My line manager told me that she has recieved the letter requesting a reference from Thames Reach. She said that she will write it and send it tomorrow. I asked her if I can read the letter that they sent her and she was agreeable, but requested that I do it tomorrow. I have rung my mum three times since seeing her yesterday. She is now taking medicine and says she is feeling a lot better than she was. I am working on the helpline tonight. Today I started my periods.

Sunday 18th February 2007

Dear Yvonne,

Today, I had a good day at work. Natalia, my line manager and supervisor wrote my reference. She will be flying to Portugal tomorrow and will not be at work next weekend, so I will take next Sunday off. I spoke to my mum twice today and she seems to be improving. She still has quite a bad cough. Elaine rang me on my landline and sent me a text message today. We spoke briefly and exchanged email addresses and sent each other an email tonight. This evening I went to a meeting in Brixton.

Monday 19th February 2007

Dear Yvonne,

This morning, I had a lie-in until 10.30hrs. I then spoke to Joanna from ACAPS, who congratulated me on my successful interview. I will meet up with her next week Monday afternoon. I rang my mum, who is still not well then got ready and set off for my group psychotherapy via getting some credit for my mobile as I am down to 99p. Andre came to the psychotherapy group today to tell everyone why he was leaving. I also announced that I would be leaving by the end of March. After the group I went to Chelsea with Andre and watched a film 'Music and Lyrics' I then came home and rang my mum.

Tuesday 20th February 2007

Dear Yvonne,

Today I went to Luton to visit my mum. She still has a cold and is taking her antibiotics. I saw Angel the cat in my mum's dining room today.

Wednesday 21st February 2007

Dear Yvonne,

Today I did the second day of a five part anti- stigma anti-discrimination open up workshop. I got to know someone called Jaz a worker of Mind on the course a little better. I feel as if I am getting somewhere with the information that I am getting. This evening I went to two meetings. One in Camberwell and one in Waterloo. On the way to the first meeting, I met Lyn on the bus and she told me that my son had had a friend over to play today. She told me that my son only knew two days of the week Thursdays because he has contact with me and Saturday because he gets 50p pocket money.

Thursday 22nd February 2007

Dear Yvonne,

This morning, as I was getting ready to leave to see my social worker, my mum rang me. She told me that she was improving but she wasn't going to go out today, unless it stopped raining. We spent about ten minutes speaking with each other and then I left home. When I got to my social workers office the receptionist shook my hand and congratulated me on getting my job. When I saw Tamara Webb, my social worker this morning, she said that she was still in the process of completing my reference. Tamara also let me know that she would be leaving at the end of March 2007. She said we had started working together from February 2006. Quite naturally, I am sad to hear that Tamara is leaving. Today I took my son on the London Eye. This was his second time. The first time was was two years ago when he was five. My son told me today that he was afraid of heights but not in the London Eye. When I got home this evening I found that I had received a drawing in the post from my son and I rang him and thanked him. This evening I spoke to my mum on the phone and B

Friday 23rd February 2007

Dear Yvonne,

This morning I had a lie-in and then went to do my test at Learn Direct. I got 35 out of 40 right in the test and so passed. I also went to Hopton House social services department and informed them that I have moved from Railton Road.

Saturday 24th February 2007

Dear Yvonne,

Today I was on the Mitcham side for my Woodlands Central and Cecil escort job. I worked with Jason the driver today. Josephine was in charge at the day centre. I heard that another of the day centre's clients, a male, had died yesterday. This evening I worked on the Helpline.

Sunday 25th February 2007

Dear Yvonne,

This morning I was having a lie-in when my mum woke me up with a phone call at 09.30hrs I chatted to her for about twenty minutes and then went back to bed. When I woke up later I went on the net and found that I had received an email from Elaine. I replied to it and sent an email to Linda, my sponsor, inviting her to meet with me so that I could go through my Third Step with her. I rang my mum and spoke to her for twenty minutes and then went to a meeting in Brixton.

Monday 26th February 2007

Dear Yvonne,

This morning I had a lie-in and then I got up and went to my group psychotherapy. Thames Reach rang me and asked if they could obtain a reference from PACE, I said yes. I then rang PACE and informed my old boss Guillermo that I have him as a referee. This afternoon I met with Joanna of APACS and she tried to contact an organisation to get some clothes for me to wear to work. I met with my old sponsor and her sponsor this evening and then went to a meeting in Chelsea.

Tuesday 27th February 2007

Dear Yvonne,

Last night I had a dream about V.J in it he had moved down the road from where he lived when he was alive to a house numbered eleven. It was smaller and newer and he said that he didn't want to do the work needed like my mum has on the old house. He told me that this new house is what he is leaving to me and my son. I also dreamed that Lyn was stressed looking after my son and social services couldn't give her anymore support even though they could see she needed it as an older parent. I offered to look after my son on Sundays and said that I would contact his social worker to say I wanted to have two days contact instead of one. But then I realised that I couldn't do it because of my work with Thames Reach. As I sometimes work until 21.00hrs on Sundays. I was glad when my mum woke me up with a phone call at 08.30hrs. Today I spent the day in Luton with my mum. She was slightly improved in health and is now going to start a seven day course of antibiotics. We to a short walk to Bury Park this afternoon when the rain paused for a bit and then we took a bus into town. We did a little bit of food shopping and then caught the bus back. Joanna rang me this afternoon to tell me that I have an appoinment on Thursday at noon to hopefully get some clothes. Another of the contacts for clothes that Joanna rang yesterday also called me and said that I need to go to the dss and they will refer me. I went to a meeting in Stockwell this evening and then dined out with two of the participants.

Wednesday 28th February 2007

Dear Yvonne,

Today I felt sluggish but still went to Mental Health Media. I had a great day and for the first time wrote a letter on a word document, saved it and sent an email with it as an attachment without any help. O2 rang me today and gave me some bolt on treats for my mobile phone I went to the psychotherapy users forum this evening in the Maudsley Hospital Boardroom and it was well attended by users. When I got home I rang my mum and spoke for about thirty minutes.

Thursday 1st March 2007

Dear Yvonne,

At 10am this morning I went to see Joanna, at ACAPS so that she could give me the address of 'Dress for Success' and she did. I arrived at 11.50am and was back on the road by 12.30pm with a suit, blouse, shoes and handbag. I am pleased. As I had some time on my hands, I took buses back from North London to Brixton and popped home briefly before setting off again to Learn Direct. This evening I spoke to my son on the phone for thirty minutes. He seemed happy, which made me feel happy too.

Friday 2nd March 2007

Dear Yvonne,

Today, Thames Reach rang me to say that my reference from Pace had not yet been received and could I try to speed things up and forward Pace's telephone number to them which I did. Then 3pm I went to see Sarah Northey, my son's psychologist and met up with my son and Lyn. I had brought to photographs of my son and other people from his birth to his present day, for us to collectively make a book about my son's history. Lyn told me that my son had been missing me lately and also the people that he used to see. During the hour and a half that we spent today in the session, I made much of him. My son took a few of the photograghs away with him when he went.

Saturday 3rd March 2007

Dear Yvonne,

Today I was on the Wimbledon side and the driver's name was Joseph. I had a great day at work and a productive evening on the Helpline. But before I went to the helpline I stopped off at my cousin Eric's for something to eat.

Sunday 4th March 2007

Dear Yvonne,

Today at work I met my line manager's brother. I had another great day at work and went home and spoke to my mum on the phone who told me she had been out to a service today. Then I spoke to B, and told her that me and my former fellowship friend and irretrievably fallen out. I then went to the Brixton meeting.

Monday 5th March 2007

Dear Yvonne,

Today I took the day off and slept on and off all day. During the afternoon, I rang Pace and left a message to let Guillermo know that I had given Thames Reach his email address and telephone number on Friday. I also rang Thames Reach and they told me that they had called Guillermo this morning and left a message but that he had not returned their telephone call yet. This evening I spoke to my mum, who told me that Angel went to the vet to be doctored today. Andre rang me and we had a ten minute conversation He told me that he had bought the latest Bryan Ferry CD. He said that it had something to do with Bob Dylan.

Tuesday 6th March 2007

Dear Yvonne,

This morning I had a lie-in. When I got up, I found that my future line-manager at Thames Reach had left a message on my mobile. So I rang her back and left a message on her answering machine. I then met my son at 2pm at his home. Pete made me a coffee and I heard that Fluffy had given birth to four kittens last night after I drank my coffee I set off with my son. On the way to Green Park, we stopped off at Marks and Spencers in Brixton to get some lunch and speak to my mum on my mobile. When we got to Green Park, the Big Bus Company bus was just parking. We got on and took a seat upstairs at the front. It was a pleasant day with no rain. We came off at Tower Bridge, stop number 19. We then took the river cruise back to Westminster bridge and took the number three bus home. We got home very late 18.30hrs. I spoke to my mother this evening.

Wednesday 7th March 2007

Dear Yvonne,

Today, I went to the Open Up workshop. I feel it was another productive day. After I finished I went to have a meal at my cousin Eric's home.

Thursday 8th March 2007

Dear Yvonne,

This morning, I went to see my social worker and asked her if I could call PACE to see if my reference has been sent. I rang but didn't get to speak to Guillermo, so I left a message. I also rang my son's social worker to find out if I can see my son once a week for his easter school break. She said that she will speak with her boss (Toni Rietig) and get back to me. My social worker told me that she might be staying on for two weeks extra because of the Easter holidays. After leaving my social worker I went to Brixton Library to do some work on my Literacy with Learn Direct. This afternoon, I did most of my Step Three with my sponsor in Starbucks in Vauxhall. I am going to seek out a church that I can pray in and ring my sponsor so that we can finalise it over the phone. My sponsor has asked me if I would do a chair at the Covent Garden meeting tomorrow evening and I told her that I would. After leaving my sponsor, I went to visit a fellowship friend that lives in Vauxhall. This evening I spoke to B on my landline. It was international womens day today.

Altered Perceptions

Friday 9th March 2007

Dear Yvonne,

Today I spent the day in Luton. Angel and my mum are close and he seems shy of visitors. My mum went out on Field Service today and didn't get home until mid-day. I rang Thames Reach today to see if they had got the reference. They said that they had and that Emma, my future line-manager will be calling me to discuss my start date. I am relieved and excited. Just before I returned to London, I followed my mum up to her G.P's practice so that she could collect her prescription. This evening I did a chair at the Covent Garden meeting. When I got home I rang Andre and spoke with him and then I spent over an hour and a half speaking with A, on the phone.

Saturday 10th March 2007

Dear Yvonne,

Today I was on the Mitcham side with Gina driving. At work today I broke a glass in the dishwasher and Maureen, my kind colleague cleared it up. This evening I went to my commitment on the Helpline.

Sunday 11th March 2007

Dear Yvonne,

Today I told my colleagues at Central and Cecil, Woodlands that I will be leaving. At 5pm today I rang Emma, my future line manager and have agreed to start full time work at Thames Reach on Tuesday 10th April 2007. I have also arranged to go to her office in Strutton Ground, Victoria tomorrow at 10.30am to hand in my completed Criminal Records Bureau form and show the relevant i.d. After speaking with Emma, I rang Natalia, my line manager at Central and Cecil, Woodlands day centre and told her that my last working day there will be Saturday 7th April 2007. This evening I went to a meeting in Brixton.

Monday 12th March 2007

Dear Yvonne,

This morning I went to Thames Reach in Victoria and handed my CRB form to Ken (my line manager's line manager) as Emma was not at work today due to having a migraine. I met a few of the office staff. I spent about ten minutes there and then went to Leicester Square to the Notre Dame De France church next to the Prince Charles cinema to try to complete my Step Three, but I couldn't get hold of my sponsor. At lunchtime I went to my group psychotherapy and told them that my last day there will be Monday 2nd April 2007. Afterwards I went to Central and Cecil, Woodlands and handed in my formal resignation to Janet, the Manager of the Day Centre. She said that if things don't work out I can come back. Then I went to a meeting in Stockwell. This evening I spoke to A on the phone for almost three hours.

Tuesday 13th March 2007

Dear Yvonne,

Today I spent the day in Luton with my mum. When I returned I spoke to B, this evening.

Wednesday 14th March 2007

Dear Yvonne,

Today I handed in my notice at Mental Health Media. My last working day will be Wednesday 4th April 2007. This evening I went to do my commitment at the Hospital and Institutions (H&I) Committee. I announced that from next month onwards I will be working shifts so wont be able to attend every meeting.

Thursday 15th March 2007

Dear Yvonne,

Today was my day off, so I had a lie-in and then got up and did some cleaning and washing. At 6pm I rang my son and spoke to him for twenty minutes. He told me that he went to 'Crufts' with Lyn's neice last Thursday. He also told me that he will be able to hold his cat Fluffy's kittens in the middle of next week. We agreed that next week when we are together, we are going to visit 'The London Dungeon'.

Friday 16th March 2007

Dear Yvonne,

This morning I sent a text message to my sponsor to tell her that I was outside the Nostra Dame De France. She rang me back and I went into the church and my sponsor lead me through the Step Three prayer. Afterwards I went to Oxford Street to buy a pair of cowboy boots for my forthcoming employment. Then I went to visit a fellowship friend and his new boyfriend from New York for lunch. After lunch I watch the Oscar winning Helen Mirren in 'Queen' and then we watched 'Borat' on DVD and when they ended we went to a 12step meeting in Fulham Broadway.

Saturday 17th March 2007

Dear Yvonne,

This morning I listened to the 11th Step meditation and some affirmations on CD before going to work. Today I was on the Wimbledon side and worked with Joseph the driver. When I got home B, and Doris were here working on putting together a sofabed that B, had purchased for me as a present from IKEA. They said that they will return after Easter to complete my shelving.

Sunday 18th March 2007

Dear Yvonne,

Today is Mother's day and I had a lie-in this morning. My son left a message on my mobile, with Lyn's help, wishing me a happy mother's day and told me that he loves me. I rang him back and spoke to him for a while. During the conversation it was decided that the London Dungeon might be too frightening for him at this time and so I will take him to Hamleys toy shop in Regents Street instead. I spoke to my mum today and she said that she was visited this morning by my brother David, who gave her a card with twenty pounds in it and he also gave her a card from my sister Joanne, and she gave her a bottle of perfume as a gift. This evening before I went to the Brixton meeting I went to my cousin Eric's home as he had invited me to dinner.

Monday 19th March 2007

Dear Yvonne,

This morning I had a lie-in and then I got ready to go to my group psychotherapy. After the session I rushed home and was just in time to meet the man that did my gas safety check.

Tuesday 20th March 2007

Dear Yvonne,

Today I spent the day in Luton with my mum and when I returned to London I went to a meeting in Stockwell.

Wednesday 21st March 2007

Dear Yvonne,

Today I did day four of the five day open up workshop and afterwards I did a Step six chair in Blackheath.

Thursday 22nd March 2007

Dear Yvonne,

This morning I went to see my social worker who told me that she will be working until the end of April 2007. At 2pm I took my son to buy a pair of sandles and wellingtons, tee-shirts and shorts. We stopped off in Hamleys in Regents street before I returned him to Lyn. Today Lyn told me that his teacher had told her that he is not working at school. choosing instead not to do as he is told. Lyn said that he is going to have his pocket money reduced if he does not comply. Today my mum slipped in her bath and banged her head hard. Though she remained conscious she was shaken.

Friday 23rd March 2007

Dear Yvonne,

This morning I had a lie-in and then I went to see my Pan Fellowship sponsor and read through the first step. This evening I went to a meeting.

Saturday 24th March 2007

Dear Yvonne,

Today I was on the Wimbledon side and Linda was the driver. This evening I went to my commitment at the Helpline.

Sunday 25th March 2007

Dear Yvonne,

Today I lost an hour because the clocks went forward. It is now British Summer time. I had to escort on the Wimbledon side this morning because Rui turned up an hour late. This evening I went to have dinner at Eric's home. Afterwards I went to the Brixton meeting, tired.

Monday 26th March 2007

Dear Yvonne,

This morning I had a lie in and then I went to my group psychotherapy. Today is the last day that I am going to see Will the female therapist. I am saddened as she was the one that intereviewed me for the group in the first place. I then went to collect the twenty pounds that my son's social worker (Anneka Fouche) owes me and then I went to see Sarah Northey, Lyn and my son. Lyn told Sarah what had been happening to my son at his school and we agreed to meet once a month and just play. We will do the life story at a later date. After we finished Lyn, my son and myself went for a coffee in Cafe Nero's in Brixton.

Tuesday 27th March 2007

Dear Yvonne,

Today I spent the whole day sleeping, on and off.

Wednesday 28th March 2007

Dear Yvonne,

I spent the whole morning sleeping but took a walk this afternoon to Herne Hill and back to buy a pizza. I then went back to bed. Later I noticed that I had received mail from Thames Reach. It was my contract and some policies. There was also some information informing me that the clients that Thames Reach works with may have TB and Hep B so I must get myself vaccinated by my GP. When my mum rang this evening I told her I had got my contract.

Thursday 29th March 2007

Dear Yvonne,

This morning I arose fresh at 10.30am. My first stop was to make an appointment at the G.P's surgery. They gave me an appointment with the nurse for Monday at 3.15pm and told me to ring the surgery tomorrow at 8.45am or 2pm for an appointment to see my doctor for a prescription. Then I went to the Jobcentreplus and told Molly Hamilton that I was going to be starting a full time job 10th April 2007. She gave me an appointment to see her tomorrow at 2pm and said she would try and make an appointment with Instant Muscles, a disability organisation, to see that I get my entitlements. I then went to the housing benefits office and told them about my forthcoming job and asked for extended benefits. Then I went to Learn Direct and told them about my forthcoming job. Then at 2pm I went to see my sponsor and read through my Step One. I also did one Step Ten but I am going to add to my Step One this evening. When I returned home I changed my bedclothes, took a bath and spoke to my son for thirty minutes whilst I soaked in it. Today my son wanted to tell him about when he was born and why he is not allowed to live with me until he is an adult. He also wanted to know where I was going to take him next week. After speaking with my son, I finished having my bath and then did some laundary.

Altered Perceptions

Friday 30th March 2007

Dear Yvonne,

This morning I went to the doctor's surgery and got a 11.30am appointment to see Dr Hartmann, who is my personal G.P. He gave me a blood form to take to Dulwich hospital on Monday to see about the Hepatitis B and blood sugar, plus colesteral. He asked me to go to Kings college hospital and make an appointment for a TB check. He said that I must see him again in three weeks. After seeing Dr Hartmann I went to see Maria at Instant Muscles and filled out some forms so that I can gain £100.00 when I start work. Then I went into Wallis' in Morley's in Brixton and chose some work clothes for the sum of £100.00, had a coffee and cake in Cafe Nero's and went to see Molly at Jobcentreplus. She gave me the token that I needed to collect the clothes from Wallis' and said that she will see to it that I get £100.00 in my account from the dss. She said that she would work out if I am better off at work and ring me when I have settled in. After seeing Molly I went to Wallis' and collected the two blouses, one cardigan and pair of trouser. Then I went to Woolworth's in Camberwell and purchased the animated DVD of 'Charlottes Web' I then went to Kings college hospital and left my contact details for someone from the TB clinic to get back to me. One my way home I posted my signed and dated contract Thames Reach to them and went home and watched the 'Charlottes Web' DVD

Saturday 31st March 2007

Dear Yvonne,

Today four escorts showed up for the buses for Woodlands. The drivers Gina and Mike were stunned. I rang Natalia my line manager and she asked me to leave Rui and Maureen on the buses. Ask the agency escort to go home and for me to come straight into Woodlands. I got my payslip from Woodlands today. When I got home from work, I found that I had received a letter from the child benefit agency, stating that I am not entitled to child benefit as my son is not living with me, and they want me to pay them back £1002.20 Quite naturally I was insensed and set to work drafting a letter to reply to them. I finished at 8pm and went to my cousin

Eric's to print it off. Then I posted it to them on the way to the helpline.

Sunday 1st April 2007

Dear Yvonne,

Today I forgot my mobile phones at home on the way to work at Woodlands and decided not to turn back to pick them up. I told the clients that I would be leaving next week. They asked me why I was leaving and some said that I did not like them. I spoke to my mother today and she told me that it is her Jehovah's Witness memorial on Monday. Tonight I went to a meeting in Brixton and when I came home A, rang me and we chatted for two hours.

Monday 2nd April 2007

Dear Yvonne,

This morning, when the radio alarm clock woke me up at 7am, I was still tired. But I got up and was waiting in the queue to have my blood taken in Dulwich hospital at 8.05am. There was quite a crowd. About thirty people. When I finished there I went to see Joanne at ACAPS, who informed me that although my case will be supervised for the next six months, it may not be by her. Apparently ACAPS may be downsizing and some people may be deployed and one of them may be Joanna. Today Joanna photocopied my Thames Reach contract and gave me a pep talk as well as reminding me that I need to give ACAPS a copy of my first and third payslip. When I finished at ACAPS, I went to the jobcentre in Josephine avenue and rang the child benefits office and asked for an appeal form to be sent to me. Tamara Webb rang me today to say she is on duty this Thursday, so wont be able give me any quality time. She offered to reschedule but I decided to tell her what I was up to on the phone instead. After I finished speaking with Tamara, I went to the Brixton Advice Centre on Railton road regarding my recent letter from the child benefits office. The person at the advice centre said that she will help me to fill out my appeal form when it arrives. I also rang the Disability Rights Commission to find out if I could get any help. Today was my last day at my South London and Maudsley (SLAM) group psychotherapy sessions. After today's session, I was treated to a coffee from Lena. Afterwards I went to Kings College Hospital, armed with my letter requesting my have a TB vaccination from Thames Reach and went to the chest clinic again. This time I was asked to wait in the waiting room. The nurse then came and told me that the clinic is for appointments only and they don't usually do cases such a mine but she took my date of birth and doctors name and address. She then said that she would send me an appointment in the post. This afternoon I watch the film 'Amazing Grace' at the 4pm viewing at the Ritzy cinema in Brixton.

Tuesday 3rd April 2007

Dear Yvonne,

Today I attended the fifth and last session of the Open Up workshop. After the session a group of four of the participants went for a coffee together. Then I did some work on Learn Direct. Tonight I started to read a book 'Conversations with God' Book One by Neale Donald Walsch

Wednesday 4th April 2007

Dear Yvonne,

This morning I went to Mental Health Media. It was my last day and I decided not to stay for the day. I received a box with an easter egg filled with truffles and a good luck card signed by members of the team. This afternoon, I collected my medication. This evening I did a Share at the Camberwell meeting.

Thursday 5th April 2007

Dear Yvonne,

This morning, I went to see Joanna at ACAPS and wrote a short statement of my progress for the forthcoming Thurs 3rd May 2007, open day. Then I went to do a mock exam at literacy level two at learn direct.

Friday 6th April 2007

Dear Yvonne,

This morning at 11.15am, Good Friday. Birgit, Doris and Haneen, arrived at my flat to work on sorting it out. At 11.45am I set off to collect my son from Lyn and Pete's and bought him to my flat briefly, to see B, Doris and little Haneen. I took a few photograghs of him and them both he and I set off to Luton. At Kings Cross thameslink station, my son found two pence and when we arrived in Luton and was walking towards the bus station, my son found a folded twenty pounds note on the ground. My mum was pleased to see him and he my mum. Angel, the cat on the other hand hid. Eventually we found Angel but my son didn't get to stroke him. I took a few photographs of my son and my mum. I eventually got my son to his home at about 7.45pm. My hayfever started today.

Saturday 7th April 2007

Dear Yvonne,

Today was my last day at Woodlands central and cecil. My driver was Malcolm and I was the escort on the Wimbledon side. Natalia wasn't at work today as her dad has died and she was in Portugal. Josephine was in charge and Maureen was the escort on the Mitcham side. Michael, mysponsor rang me and asked if I could sit his pet cat Audi and dog Stan for four days, whilst he services a Pan Fellowship retreat, starting Wednesday 18th April 2007. I said yes. Today I rang Anna, my sponsor and tried to arrange to meet up with her tomorrow, but she said it wasn't going to be possible. This evening I did my service at the Helpline.

Sunday 8th April 2007

Dear Yvonne,

Today is Easter Sunday, I had a lie-in and slept on and off for most of the day, I also spent time speaking on the phone to my mother and Annette. Sonia an open up participant also rang me today. I finished book one of conversations with God.

Monday 9th April 2007

Dear Yvonne,

Today is Easter Monday and as such it is a bank holiday. This is my last day off and tomorrow I will start full time work. I spent the whole morning sleeping and listening to radio four. I got up at midday and had a bath and something to eat and then I took the bus to Vauxhall to meet with Micheal, my sponsor. On the way there I rang Linda, my sponsor and she said she would call me back at 7.30pm tonight. I read out my step one to Michael and then read step two from the Deep Soul Cleansing book. Afterwards I walked with Michael when he took Stan for a walk and then I went home. My mum had rung me on my landline whilst I was out and also on my mobile, but I missed her call. I will ring her later on tonight, after I have written my step two.

Tuesday 10th April 2007

Dear Yvonne,

Today was my first day of full time employment in fourteen years. I arrived fifteen minutes early to start at 10am and my line manager greeted me. Today I was given keys to the building and shown the fire exits. I met the whole team, just about!, but was given each Tuesday as my day off instead of each Thursday. As soon as I found time I started to call Lyn, my son's social worker and his psychologist to tell them, but I was unable to do anything but leave them a message. I found out that I only do earlies (9-5) on Saturdays and Sundays so it wont interfer with my Na commitments. This afternoon I spent the time reading policies. Molly from the job centre rang me to find out how I was getting on on my first day and wanting the name and number of my boss so that she can call her tomorrow. On my way home tonight I stopped off at learn direct to book my literacy level 2 test. It will be at 9am this Saturday. When I got home I received a phone call from my mum asking how I got on today. I am on earlies for the next two weeks so I am going to go to bed early tonight, so that I will be at work on time for my 9am start.

Wednesday 11th April 2007

Dear Yvonne,

This morning, I got to Brixton underground and found that the trains on the Victoria line was experiencing severe delays, so I took the number 2 bus, and arrived at work 8.55am. I was the first person there, so I used my keys to open up, I also switched the lights on and made myself a cup of coffee. This afternoon, I went to the head office and gave Tarrance a copy of my bank statement for my criminal record bureau (CRB), my p60 and employment details and a copy of my EN nursing certificate. I had a look around Gem House with Tarrance and took a seat downstairs and at 3pm I met with Rob. Rob gave me a talk on Resettlement. I finished work at 4pm. Tonight I went to my commitment at Gordon Hospital in Victoria to attend the H & I committee. I felt tired and didn't want to go, but it's my commitment so, I made the effort.

Thursday 12th April 2007

Dear Yvonne,

Today I forgot my mobile phone and as I had left home early, I went back for it. But on my return to Brixton tube station, I was met with the announcement that "due to a train in Green Park, there is no service between Brixton and Warren street on the Victoria line." I and two train full of underground passengers made our way to the bus stops and I missed three crammed buses before I decided to walk up the road to the Fridge and board a no2 bus from there. I arrived at work at 9.30am. I was meant to have been there at 9am, but I wasn't the only person who came late this morning. Today my boss took me in her office and said that she had given my Tuesday days off some thought and decided against it as that would mean that I wouldn't be able to have two days off together and after six months I would be tearing my hair out. So she has given me every Monday off and Sundays. Whilst I was at lunch I rang Will and Jack, my psychotherapist and asked them if I could come back to group therapy. They were not in work, so I left a message. I then sent a text message to Lyn and called to tell my son's social worker and his psycologist. I also rang the child benefit office to see what had become of my appeal. They said they would stop the debt collection and I was to do nothing until I next hear from them. This evening I spoke to my son on the phone. He seemed in good spirits and is going to the lake district on Saturday morning and returning on Monday night. I told him that I had started my new job and he wanted to know what it was. I told him that I was a mental health, floating support worker. I asked Pete this evening if one of my son's kittens could go to my mum as she had asked for one. Pete didn't know what the situation on the kittens were and couldn't be sure if they had already been taken. I have decided this evening that instead of taking the train to work, I am going to get up at 6am, have a bath, have breakfast and leave my house at 7.30am and take the no2 bus to Victoria. I rang B this evening and got her up to speed on the events of my working life and asked her if she could deposit £50.00 in my account she said that she would deposit £100.00 tomorrow, but next time could I give her a few days notice.

Friday 13th April 2007

Dear Yvonne,

Today at six I stayed in my bed and didn't get up until 6.45am. I left my home just after 7.30am and was on a no2 bus at 7.45am. I got to work peaceful and serene at 8.30am. Today I went to the cinema with three other collegues and one client. when I got to the Clapham picture house in Venn st I met up with someone that I know from the 12 step meetings. We met and greeted each other with a hug and I spent time speaking with him. He I found out was is living in Thames Reach shared housing. The film we viewed was 'Sunshine' Two of the other staff members returned to the office instead of staying to watch the film. When I got back to the office, I reported the fact that I was friends with a client of the organisation. This afternoon, Emma, my line manager gave me my log on details so I was able to log on to the computers and I now have an email address. but I don't remember what it is. Tonight I went a meeting in Brixton and was asked to do a Share. I did. On my way home, I purchased some fresh fruit and All Bran cereals.

Saturday 14th April 2007

Dear Yvonne,

Yesterday was the start of three days of 12 step convention in London and another 12 step convention in Brighton. But I am not going to either even though my sponsors will be at them. Instead, at 9am this morning, I did my City and Guilds literacy level 2 test and got 36 out of 40 questions right. I passed. I then did my laundery and changed my bedsheets and pyjamas. I then made myself some breakfast and had a fresh fruit salad. A, sent me a text asking how my week went. I then took a twenty minute rest on my bed and then got ready to see my (PF)sponsor. When I got to his place in Vauxhall, he told me that he would like to take a walk with me along the thames river. So we took Stan, the dog and walked to Blackfriars Bridge and back. I was a beautiful dry, and sunny day and there was lots to see. I then went with him to buy a chinese takeaway and then went straight to do my commitment on the helpline. Lots of calls this evening.

Sunday 15th April 2007

Dear Yvonne,

This morning I had a lie-in until 8am. I then got up and made my way to Luton. I arrived at my mum's place at about 10.30am. She was still in her nightclothes as she was feeling a bit under the weather, but she took a bath, whilst I made myself some breakfast. I spent time hoovering and washing up my breakfast stuff and chatting to my mum. My mum then got herself ready to go to her Jehovah's Witnesses meeting and I left before she left for her meeting. When I got home home I got into my pyjamas, lay on my bed and spoke to A, on the phone for three hours and then afterwards I got ready and went to the Brixton meeting.

Monday 16th April 2007

Dear Yvonne,

This morning I slept until 11am, then I went to see Maria Logan at Instant Muscle for my £100.00 and then went to my group psychotherapy. The members were pleased to see me. I went to have lunch in the hospital canteen with one of the members and then went to see Tamara, my social worker and care co-ordinator. Today is the last day that I will meet with Tamara as my care co-ordinator as she will be leaving in two weeks. She introduced me to Grace, my new care co-ordinator and social worker. Afterwards I went to Brixton to get some underarm deoderant, toothpaste etc and some shampoo, conditioner and hair oil then I came back to my flat and had a bath and washed my hair. I then got something to eat and got into my pyjamas. I rang my mum.

Tuesday 17th April 2007

Dear Yvonne,

Today made one week since I started my full time job at Thames Reach and it started off with me being on office duty at 9am and then leaving the office with Mike my colleague and going to Ladbroke grove, to St Charles hospital, to take part in a CPA after which, I had a brief lunch in Paddington station with my colleague and then going to Harrow Road to witness the same soon to be client of Mike's sign his tenancy agreement for a Stadium housing association property. The tenancy starts on Monday 30th April 2007 and then the client will be Mike's. Today I was given the rota for May, June and July and I took time out to log my shifts and my on call time in my diary. At 7.15pm this evening I did a chair at a meeting in Waterloo.

Wednesday 18th April 2007

Dear Yvonne,

This morning I got up at 6.15am took a piriton tablet for my hayfever (the start of which was Good Friday when I spent the day in Luton with my son.) I then had a bath, had my breakfast and then rang my mum at 7.15am and spoke to her for about five minutes. She asked me to take some time out before I went to work to read Psalms 23 (which I did instead of reading my Just for today and daily reflections. For the last few weeks in my head I have been saying thank you to the God of my understanding and trying to make myself genuinely helpful without expecting rewards. Today I didnt feel as drowsy as yesterday but still stopped off at McDonalds in Victoria for a strong coffee. Today in work I was given my work phone. I spent time putting in all the team's mobile numbers. This afternoon I went to Maida Vale and met my colleague Dick there. We went to see one of Dick's clients whom he hadn't seen in two weeks. The client was in and spoke to us at the door but would not let us enter the flat. He was passive and recalled correctly the date of his next CPA. Whilst we were at the same building we met up with another colleague Sue and her new client. The same client that I may be going to visit with Sue next Wednesday. This evening after work I went to My sponsor's flat in Vauxhall and walked his dog and feed both his cat and his dog. I will be sleeping at Michael's until Sunday night. I will try to keep you updated as to my progress with this new set of responsibilities.

Thursday 19th April 2007

Dear Yvonne,

When I woke up this morning, I found that I had received a text message on my mobile phone from my friend Andrew. In it he said that his wife Jackie had given birth last night atBy 6.20am this morning, I was out walking Stan the dog and, my hayfever was in full swing. I had had a peaceful restful night's sleep, intermittently interupted with my need to take a piriton tablet for my hayfever and the ClassicGold radio station of Michael's radio alarm gently and quitely going off at 6am. Stan and Audi, slept on the bed with me and I felt so serene. When I returned from walking Stan, I fed both him and Audi and set to work getting a shower and having breakfast. I left for work at 8.20am and got a no3 bus to the Houses of Parliament and walked down to my workplace in Strutton Ground. I arrived at 8.55am. I spent most of the day in the office, looking at Policies and client's files, answering the phone and generally helping out. My hayfever was just awful today even with the four hourly doses of Piriton. So when I got to Michael's place after work and walked Stan and fed both him and Audi, I went to bed and was in bed by about 6.30pm. Wheezing and sore eyes.

Friday 20th April 2007

Dear Yvonne,

Last night, I had a restless sleep. I was thinking about my work and worrying that I was not going to do everything expected of me. So today when I woke up at 6am, I decided that I would write a to do list each working day. Today at work Linda, my sponsor rang me and spent time speaking with me. We arranged to meet next week

Wednesday morning at 10am in Vauxhall on a day when I am on a late shift. Today at work my line manager revealled to me that she had also suffered a nervous breakdown in the past and had pyschotherapy and a social worker. I feel better for knowing that. In supervision, she told me that I shone in the interview and that I was definitely wanted for the post and had been chosen out of a lot of applicants and had some very stiff competition. She said that my specialism for the team will be to work with my colleagues Dick and Dionne to produce a client led/involvement aspect of the team. I feel that I got a lot of work down today and learnt new things.

Saturday 21st April 2007

Dear Yvonne,

Today was my day off but I got up at 6am to walk Stan. I then fed him and Audi and then after I had my breakfast I swept and mopped Michael's flat, cleaned Audi's litter tray and then I went to Learn direct and started my computer course. This evening I did my commitment on the helpline. It has now got two unconnected computers, so it won't be long before I will be trained to use them. I started my periods today.

Sunday 22nd April 2007

Dear Yvonne,

Today was the London marathan and this morning was the last time that I walked Stan before setting off to work. I had a geat day in work. My line manager showed me how to make appointments on my computer calender and ran through how to do a risk/needs/support assessment. I don't know how I am going to do it but I am determined to learn. Michael came back from Brighton this evening and I tried to meet him at Starbucks in Vauxhall but the was no underground trains running between Brixton and Victoria and by the time I had got the no2 bus to Vauxhall, I had missed him. This evening I have come home to my pet free place. Rung and spoke to my mum, Andre and Annette.

Monday 23rd April 2007

Dear Yvonne,

This morning I stayed in bed until 12.30pm. So I missed my group psychotherapy and rang leaving a message with the department. I arrived at Kings College Hospital at 1.40pm and waited until 2.15pm for my heath test. I then went to my appointment with Sarah Northey, my son's psychologist. My son was in good spirits today and very affectionate towards me. Todays session with Sarah may be the last but one and in it we played a psychotherapy game. Lyn invited me for a coffee at Cafe Nero's in Brixton afterwards and I accepted. My son was very well behaved. This evening I went to a meeting in Stockwell. I spoke to Anna, my sponsor on the phone this evening

Tuesday 24th April 2007

Dear Yvonne,

This morning although my clock radio alarm went off at 6am, I didn't get up until eight. Then I quickly got myself ready and went to my one day Protection of Vunerable Adults (POVA) training with Thames Reach at 55 Bondway, Vauxhall. My colleagues Sue and Dionne were also on the course. It was a day well spent. Afterwards I spent half an hour on my computer course at Learn Direct and then I went to my cousin Eric's place for a bit to eat before coming home. I am going to wash, oil and twist my hair this evening.

Wednesday 25th April 2007

Dear Yvonne,

This morning at 10am, I was in Vauxhall, phoning Linda my sponsor. She invited me to her workplace, where she gave me some Step Four handouts. She was on her way to the House of Parliament so I didn't stay long and decided to go straight to work even though I was not supposed to start until 1pm. I did my first late shift today and I am on call for the first time tonight. My on call duty started at 9pm tonight and doesn't end until 9am tomorrow. Tonight when I arrived in from work, I was pleased to find that my CRB check had arrived. I will take it to work with me tomorrow. My mum rang me on my mobile tonight and has not put her phone back on the hook properly and so I can't get through to her. Also today at work I got kitted up with a computer terminal at my desk.

Thursday 26th April 2007

Dear Yvonne,

Today I went to get the result of my heath test and was told that I have an excess of TB virus. Kings college asked me to take a chest X-ray, which I did today. I had no calls while I was on call last night. I was on another late today.

Friday 27th April 2007

Dear Yvonne,

Today I was on an early. I also successfully secured some complimentary theatre tickets for six of my Thames Reach clients and two members of staff to see a performance of 'African Snow' at the Trafagar Studios in Whitehall at 2.30pm on Saturday 5th May 2007. I will be one of the members of staff that will be going to watch the performance with the clients. Today I got paid and went for an orange juice with some staff members after work at 'The Riverside' in Vauxhall. I spoke to B tonight.

Saturday 28th April 2007

Dear Yvonne,

I worked today and for the first time since I first heard about it, I felt as if I knew what a risk assessment was. I had finally understood the concept of risk assessment, needs assessment and support plan. Risk assessment was the element of danger that the individual presented to themselves, others or staff. Needs assessment was what the individual needed help with and support plan was how we as professionals were going to meet those needs. This evening I worked for two hours on the helpline and finished at 10pm.

Sunday 29th April 2007

Dear Yvonne,

This morning I went to visit my mum in Luton. She was up but still in her night clothes when I arrived at 11.20am. She soon got herself in the bath and ready for her Kindom Hall meeting, whilst I did some hoovering. I ate a meal that she had prepared for me before I left for London at 1.30pm. When I arrived in London, I purchased some fresh fruit from Marks and Spensers in Brixton and then spoke to Annette on the phone for over and hour before setting off to my H and I rep commitment at the Brixton meeting. When I arrived home at 21.30hrs I rang Annette again and spoke to her for another hour.

Monday 30th April 2007

Dear Yvonne,

This morning at just after 9.30am I was in West Norwood at the David Pitt house speaking with Tamara Webb. Today was her last day. I am going to miss her. Grace was on a training day and will see me in two weeks. It was so refreshing to speak with Tamara, and the hour flew by quickly. I then took a bus to Brixton and paid £140.00 (two week's rent) and £115.00 (one month's council tax) I then went to Olive morris house and wrote a letter and handed it in saying that I would be paying my rent and council tax from Tuesday 10th April 2007. I then went to my group psychotherapy and was delighted to see that Mav was back. I hadn't seen him since last year July 2006. After the group I went to collect my son and take him to 'The Tate Modern' near Blackfriars unfortunately when we got to the Tate they had dismantled the slide and there wasn't much there to hold my son's interest. So we went to Pizza Hut on the Walworth Road and ate garlic bread and a margarita pizza and drank a diet pepsi. I also had a salad bowl. During a break in our meal, I rang and spoke to my mum. When I got to my home this evening, I had received an appointment re my TB to attend a respiritary clinic on Thursday 24th May 2007 at 9.45am. Fortunately for me, I am on a late that day. They want me to bring in a list of the medication that I am taking.

Tuesday 1st May 2007

Dear Yvonne,

This morning at 10am, I rang a newcomer in the twelve step programme and then I went to Brixton library to do an hour and a half worth of computer studies before setting off to work for a late shift. Today at work, I met one of my clients at her home with a colleague who told me that they are a recovering alcoholic and is eight months sober. They told me that they had gone into a rehab after being given the sack from their last employment. They told me that they goes to 12 step meetings but not as often as they should. I told my colleague that I go to 12 step meetings too and that I would be happy to accompany them to 12 step meetings in the area. They accepted my offer. This evening after work, I rang my mum and then I rang Annette and spent two and a half hours speaking with her. I hung up before it came to an hour and rung her back so that the call would be free.

Wednesday 2nd May 2007

Dear Yvonne,

This morning I slept on and off listening to Radio four until 11am then I got ready for work. I had a 13.30hr appointment with a client at a cafe near the Royal Oak tube station. He didn't show up. But then at 15.15hrs I had to attend a crisis meeting with the community mental health team (CMHT) and the Crisis team at his home. He unfortunately left before the Crisis team arrived. If he doesn't engage with the Crisis team, he may be sectioned and hospitalised. I didn't get back into the office until after four this afternoon.

Thursday 3rd May 2007

Dear Yvonne,

This morning when my alarm clock went off at 6am I stayed in bed until 7am because I felt tired. I got to work at 9.10am after missing three number 2 buses to get there. Tonight I went to a meeting and saw my first sponsor and took his number.

Friday 4th May 2007

Dear Yvonne,

Again this morning, I stayed in bed until 7am when the clock went off at six. I got to work at 8.45 and my boss was already in. We had an internal audit today and we had improved on six months ago, so my boss was pleased. I was supposed to take a client of the project to watch 'Spiderman 3' with the meaningful employment cinema club, but he did a no-show. Instead I tried to ring around a few of the theatres that I had written to on 23rd April 2007 to see if there was any chance of getting complimentry tickets for our clients. I wasnt in luck. Today I bought the book 'The Devil Wears Prada' and started reading it. It's funny. This evening I went to a NA meeting in Loughborough Junction and was asked to become the meeting's tresurer, but I dont think I can as I've got too much on at the moment. When I got home I found that I had received a letter for the housing benefit department saying that I owe them £770.00 from the eighth of January 2007. I will ring them tomorrow.

Saturday 5th May 2007

Dear Yvonne,

This morning I stayed in bed until 6.45am and then got up. I was on duty at work this morning and none of my colleagues were in until after 9.10am so I rang the housing benefits office and spoke to a man called Mel. He looked at my case and said that he is going to speak to head office about it as he cant see why I owe the money. This afternoon I went to the Trafalgar Studios in Whitehall to watch 'African Snow' with four clients and my colleague Liz. It was a great performance, and the clients also enjoyed it. This evening I went to see my sponsor Michael. I read out step two and read step three. I've now got to write my step three.

Sunday 6th May 2007

Dear Yvonne,

Today was my day off and I slept in bed until 2pm, then I got up and put a wash on, took a shower, ate and then took a bus to Clapham Junction and went to 'Fresh and Wild' and bought something for my hayfever. I then went to Woolworths and bought the DVD 'The Devil Wears Prada' and popped into Marks and

Spencers and bought a weeks supply of fruit and took a bus home. This evening I am going to the Brixton meeting.

Monday 7th May 2007

Dear Yvonne,

Today was my other day off, and I slept in bed until 3pm. I then got up, ate, and brushed my flat. I rang my mum and she told me that she was unable to call out on her phone. I rang Virgin Media to try to sort the problem and they rang her. When I rang her back, she told me that they had told her that her failure to pay her last bill was the cause of why her phone was set to incoming calls only. We spoke for almost two hours today. My friend Laura, rang me this afternoon. This evening I spoke to my son on the phone for twenty-five minutes.

Tuesday 8th May 2007

Dear Yvonne,

Today I was back at work, I had to go to the drop-in at the Hudson House site, which is near Stockwell on the Landor road corner. I enjoyed my hour and a half there and met one of the Westminster clients and helped to give her an email address. I then went to do a shadow visit with my colleague Rob in Harrow Road W9 and afterwards returned to the office. This evening I went to a meeting in Waterloo. It is looking for a GSR and I am tempted but two commitments and a full time job is enough. My mum told me today that she paid her bill minus ten pounds as Virgin hadnt sent her a statement and charged her ten pounds extra. She also wants to return to British Telecom. She still has incoming calls only on her phone.

Wednesday 9th May 2007

Dear Yvonne,

Today I was on an early at work. I got to work at 8.50am armed with my strong coffee purchased from McDonald's in Victoria. My line manager is off sick today. I accompanied my colleague Stephanie, who is leaving this month, to visit one of my clients. At first the client didn't want to let me in but she changed her mind and we spent over an hour talking. After work today I popped into ACAPS and gave the team leader my payslip to photocopy. in three months time I am to have ACAPS photocopy my July payslip. My mum's phone is still on incoming phone calls only. This evening I attended a H & I committee meeting. I feel as if I am getting in the swing of things and the penny is beginning to drop.

Thursday 10th May 2007

Dear Yvonne,

This morning I was too tired to get to my Learn Direct lesson at the library for 10am. I arrived there at 11am and stayed for just over an hour. I was on a late today and after my team meeting I went to St Mungos at 217 Harrow Road to meet a client. He seemed a lovely man, though sadly he said that his next move wont be to the housing that his social worker has in mind for him. It will be the streets.With Ken's help, he is my line manager's line manager, I was able to mailmerge an invitation letter to our clients inviting them to participate in user centred service. This evening my mum got her phone put back to normal and she was able to phone me. I am on call tonight.

Friday 11th May 2007

Dear Yvonne,

This morning I got up at 6.45am and got to work at 8.45am. I slept like a baby last night and I didn't get any calls. I got to work packing the letters (all 66 of them) into envelopes and stamping them. I posted them on my way out to keywork a client in Royal Oak. This afternoon, I was on office duty. My line manager is still off sick. I miss her energy around the office. I left the office just after five this evening but I didn't hand over which was a mistake and so one of my colleagues called me on my mobile to get the information from me. This evening I went to Loughbour Park meeting and took on the treasurers commitment. I took some telephone numbers and told them that I will be on a late next Friday so I will not be able to attend. I now have three commitments and a full time job.

Altered Perceptions

Saturday 12th May 2007

Dear Yvonne,

At work today, me and my colleagues Sue and Ricky from the other team helped me to assemble my desk, but it was 6.45pm when I finally left work. So I went straight to the helpline.

Sunday 13th May 2007

Dear Yvonne,

I got up at 8.30am and set off to visit my mum in Luton. When I got to her house at 11.15am, she had two workmen there. They were working on the floor and walls of her dining room. My mum took the day off going to her meeting and I slept from 11.30am to 1pm and then my mum made dinner for me and we chatted. I set off back to London at 4.15pm and went to collect my eighteen month medalion at the Brixton meeting tonight.

Monday 14th May 2007

Dear Yvonne,

Today I got up at 11.15am and got ready to go to my group. After the group at 3pm I went to my son's review. Present was his teacher, his social worker, her boss, Lyn, Pete, My son for part of it, Me, my son's psychologist and the social services reviewer. The review went well and afterwards I took my son for something to eat at McDonald's in Brixton. Tonight B, rang and I spoke with her for an hour.

Tuesday 15th May 2007

Dear Yvonne,

Today I was on an early and I met another of my client. Tonight I went to the Waterloo meeting.

Wednesday 16th May 2007

Dear Yvonne,

Today I was on another early, but I was also on duty this morning. This afternoon I went on a Link Essential training at Gem House. Link is the database that Thames Reach uses for its clients. Today's course was to show me how to use it. Tonight I went to the Camberwell meeting and then after I went to visit my cousin Eric.

Thursday 17th May 2007

Dear Yvonne,

Today I was on a late, so I had a lie in.

Friday 18th May 2007

Dear Yvonne,

Today I was also on a late and met with Grace, Tamara's replacement, at Cafe Nero's in Brixton, before I then went to Learn direct for an hour.

Saturday 19th May 2007

Dear Yvonne,

Today was a work day and after work (I was told by Dick, my colleague that I could leave work and go home at 16.30hrs instead of 17.00hrs), I rang Annette and spoke to her for over an hour. I popped home briefly and then went to do my commitment on the 12 step Helpline. I rang Linda, my sponsor and she rang me back. We spoke for a while about my affirmations and she told me to call her on Monday. I find that I am able to write my step four whilst working at the helpline.

Sunday 20th May 2007

Dear Yvonne,

Today I was in Luton at 10.30am. Having had to go to Kentish town to catch the train. My mum has had her dinning room floor done and was pleased with it. She seemed in good spirits. No sign of Angel. This evening I went to do my H&I commitment at the Brixton meeting. Afterwards, I rang and spoke to Annette for two hours.

Monday 21st May 2007

Dear Yvonne,

Today I slept on and off until 2pm. Waking only long enough to ring Linda, read the devil wears prada (I am nearing the end of the book) and cancel today's group. I didn't want to get up at two but I had an appointment that I couldn't cancel with Sara Northey at Clams at 3pm. Lyn, Sara and myself met today and planned the next five meetings. Sara is leaving Lambeth and going to work in Westminster at the end of August. I will miss her, but I may meet up with her in my present job. After the meeting ended, Lyn and I went for coffee at Cafe Nero's and then I went to Camberwell to do the start of a three day creative writing course at Creative Routes. I enjoyed the hour that I spent doing the writing.

Tuesday 22nd May 2007

Dear Yvonne,

Today I was on an early. After work I went to Creative Routes.

Wednesday 23rd May 2007

Dear Yvonne,

Today I was on an early and after work it took me an hour to leave the Victoria area as there had been a fire in Bermondsey. I got to Creative Routes at 6.45pm. Too late to do any work so I had a cup of Camomile tea and a chat before going home.

Thursday 24th May 2007

Dear Yvonne,

Today I was on a late and before I went to work I went to Kings College Hospital for my 9.45am appointment with the TB clinic.

They said that I had been in contact with TB at some point, but they don't know when. The doctor said that if I was fifteen years younger they would treat me for it, but not now. He said that I don't have TB now. He sent me off to get some blood tests, which I did at the hospital. I took my first set of minutes for TR and typed them up this evening. I had help with it from Sue and I finished at 8.45pm this evening. My boss returned from sick leave this morning but had to go home sick again and so I didn't see her and she couldnt help me with the minutes.

Friday 25th May 2007

Dear Yvonne,

Today I was on an early. I purchased just over twenty-eight pounds worth of perishables for Westminster TR's first service users participation meeting. unfortunately no service users arrived. Emma, my boss came back to work today and I was pleased to see her. This evening I went to Brixton meeting were I have my Tresurers commitment. I am on call tonight from 9pm.

Saturday 26th May 2007

Dear Yvonne,

Last night I was woken up on call at 3.30am 3.45am and again at 5.15am I was on an early today and I was shattered. I started my periods this morning. I and my colleague Mike took six clients bowling this afternoon at Queens in Bayswater. I did my helpline commitment tonight but because I was so tired I left at 9.30pm.

Sunday 27th May 2007

Dear Yvonne,

Today was my day off and I went to Luton to see my mum. I arrived at my mum's home at 10.45am. I left at 1.30pm and went home to bed at 4pm. I rang Annette and left a message on her answering machine and she rang me back. We spoke until 6.45pm. I went to Brixton meeting where I have my H & i rep commitment. We had a business meeting tonight.

Erotomania & Me - A love addict and Sexual Anorexic's story

2009, started off wonderfully. I was employed full time and I was one of a few people present in the Prime Minister's private office, who witnessed Prime Minister Gordon Brown sign a pledge to show his support of the *Time to Change* http://www.time-to-change.org.uk/ national campaign to end mental health stigma and discrimination. I posted a photo of me doing this on my http://onthecuspofmadness.blogspot.com/ blog I also witnessed David Cameron MP and several other MP's elsewhere in the House of Commons sign to pledge their support. This was the first national campaign of this type to take place in England.

Amongst other things, I had made a short documentary film with Mental Health Media titled *Experience Strength and Hope* for *Rethink* http://www.rethink.org/ outlining some of my mental health journey. I had also been featured in several of the 2009 *Comic Relief* http://www.comicrelief.com/
Red Nose Day http://www.rednoseday.com/ fundraising and awareness campaign.

At that time I had no idea that I would also be spending several weeks on remand, as a prisoner in HMP Holloway Women's Prison, due to Erotomania.

Erotomania is a diagnosis with which I had no prior knowledge, until Thursday 6th August 2009 whilst sitting in a holding cell of South Western Magistrate Court. I was waiting for my case to be heard. It was the final hearing and I was handed the following court report dated 15th July 2009.

1. Introduction

1.1 This report is prepared at the request of the South Western Magistrate Court from this hearing on the 2nd July when Ms Stewart-Williams was remanded to HMP Holloway, The charge was harassment without violence between the 29th June 2009 and 1st July 2009 of the complainant, Caroline Hugo.

1.2 I can confirm that I treat Ms Stewart-Williams in my capacity as a Speciality Registrar in General Adult Psychiatry with the South

East Lambeth Recovery and Support Team. I am a member of the Royal College of Psychiatrists and I am approved under the section 12 of the Mental Health Act. The consultant responsible for Ms Stewart-Williams' overall care is Dr Harvey Wickham and her care coordinator is Grace Isiaka.

1.3 In order to prepare this report I interviewed Ms Stewart-Williams at HMP Holloway on the 15th July for 50 minutes. In preparing this report I have had access to the following information:

Electronic and paper hospital records from the South London and Maudsley NHS Foundation Trust

A 17 page fax from the National Probation Service detaling the charges

Information provided by Beatrice Lamptey the named social worker for Yvonne's fostered son James

Conversations with her care coordinator Grace Isiaka, and also Professor Bebbington and Mark Landy from the Mental Health Liaison Team at HMP Holloway and discussions with the wing staff.

1.4 As there were no specific Instructions enclosed with the request I will address the following points in this report:

Diagnosis of any identified mental health conditions and comment on current treatment.

Summarise Ms Stewart-Williams's response to a mental health diagnosis and treatment and compliance.

I will provide an opinion as to the prognosis for Ms Stewart-Williams mental health in terms of possible relapses in the future.

I will give an opinion on possible disposal option.

1.5 I have obtained Ms Stewart-Williams' consent to providethis report and she understood that the usual limits of confidentiality do not apply in reports that will be shared with the courts.

2. Index Offence

2.1 Ms Stewart-Williams is charged with harassment without

violence towards Caroline Hugo. She was arrested on Monday 29th June and again on the 1st July for breaching the harassment warning, which was issued to her on the 29th June. In the police file it states that she had known the defendant since September 2004 and their children attended that same school. Ms Stewart-Williams started to send Mrs Hugo gifts and letters alonside emails, text messages and posting s on Internet blogs over a five-year period. On the 29th June Mrs Hugo called the police as the situation had escalated as Ms Stewart-Williams arrived at her shop attempting to give her a DVD which apparently showed footage of the shop, she than gave the DVD to Mrs Hugo and refused to leave upon which time the police were called, she was issued with a warning which she understood. However, at four o'clock in the morning on Wednesday 1st July emailed Mrs Hugo stating that she was going to visit the shop later, again stating her lover for her ahd her two children, Louis and Isadora. At eleven o'clock the following morning she arrived at the shop, placed her bag on the counter and refused to leave when asked, and was arrested when the police arrived.

3. Psychiatric History

3.1 Ms Stewart-Williams first presentation to mental health services was at the age of 31 in 1993. At the time she was known as Yvonne Siddiqui following a brief marriage, but described herself as a single homosexual woman during the admission clerking. Her first presentation was on the 28th March 1993 when she had self presented with a friend to the A&E department complaining of being woken up by noises, gradual decline in personality, personal functioning and perplexity. She went absent without leaver during the evening and was to be followed up at the Monroe Clinic in outpatients.

3.2 She presented for the second time in June 1993 via the accident and emergency department with history of rapid decline in self-care and behavioural disturbance over an approximately 6-month period. She had sleep and appetite disturbance, had resned from her hob as a hostel worker for homeless young women and had been turning up at friends' houses in a perplexed state often with a mute presentation. She had recently shaved all of her hair off and had persecutory delusions, as she believed she was being monitored and that people could hear her, and had thought insertion from the television. She had written such things as "I am a princess" and much of her writing showed evidence of thought disorder. On mental stated examination she showed evidence of thought bock, poverty of speech, thought disorder, perplexity, and persecutory delusions. She also had auditory hallucinations. She was admitted informally between the 2nd June 1993 and the 6th July 1993 and was treated with Trifluoperazine (also know as Stellazine) 15mg twice a day and 30mg at night, together with Procyclidine 5mg twice daily for side effects. She was given a possible diagnosis of paranoid schizophrenia (in view of the fact that the duration had not yet met diagnostic criteria) and followed up b the Shore Day Centre.

3.3 She mad a good recovery and was maintained in outpatient care and was discharged in January 1994.

3.4 Her next admission was in 1995 via the emergency clinic on a section 4. At the point she was living on her own and was noted by neighbours to become increasingly agitated. One night she smashed her window and threw out an amplifier. According to the admission summery prepared by Dr Raffi she then attacked a social worker who was called by the neighbours and during an assessment by social services she expressed the belief that her flat was cursed and she was being affected by computers. She was therefore placed on an emergency section four and adnistted to the Maudsley Hospital. It was recorded that she did not smoke nor use drugs and in psychosexual history given that she said "she sleeps with anyone" and her first sexual intercourse was with men but this was "too early and against my will". She said that in 1991 she married a Pakistani man and divorced 3 years later. She described herself as having long and meaningful relationships with women although she was single at that time of the assessment.

3.5 Here next admission was from the 5th June to the 24th June 1996 after she had disengaged with Community Mental Health Services. She had been placed on a section two as neighbours had again noticed her becoming increasingly agitated and throwing things out of her window. She had visited her general practitioner several times in a week and become increasingly bizarre during the consultations, handing out leaflets on HIV and assaulting a fellow patient in a completely unprovoked attack. An ASW (approved social worker) who also tried to speak to her was kicked and Ms Stewart-Williams apologised saying she was terrified he was going to section her again. Although she denied any abnormal perception she was very agitated and thought disordered at the time of the admission. It is recorded that she had attacked two people in the street before that admission in unprovoked episodes. She had been non-compliant with her Trifluperazine (10mg twice daily) and had amassed large stores of tablets in her home. At that point she admitted to using one to two units of alcohol per week and occasional cannabis when she visited Amsterdam. During that admission her Trifluoperazine dose reinstated and increased to 15mg twice daily, after with her mental stated improved and she was discharged back to community care.

3.6 Her next admission was from the 8th August 1997 to the 23rd September 1997 to the Maudsley hospital. Prior to that admission she had been maintained on Stelazine 5mg on alternate days but her mental state had deteriorated gradually since May 1997 after the death of her father. She stopped attending the Shore Centre and was aggressive, and erratic at attending appointments. When her CPN attempted to visit her at home, she locked the door and refused to let her in. It was reported that there were no clear-cul psychotic phenomena but the behaviour pattern was typical as witnessed in previous episodes. She refused to disclose any symptomatology when assessed in hospital but some bizarre behaviour was noticed, including talking to the wall in the emergency clinic and ritually visiting the toilet several times especially at night.

3.7 In between her admissions she managed to function quite well working with the Southside Rehabilitation Association, which is a supported employment scheme.

3.8 In June 1997 she began to attend Group Psychotherapy at the Maudsley Psychotherapy Unit.

3.9 She was followed up in outpatients during 1998 was maintained on 4 mg of Trifluoperazine per day and was active in the hospital user group, worked in the Maudsley hospital WRVS (voluntary shop work).

3.10 In 1998 she became pregnant with her son; she described having inseminated herself using a donation from a male friend. She was referred to the perinatal psychiatry team at sixteen weeks pregnancy in December 1998, her plan was to continue taking medication during the pregnancy and she was offered an elective admission to the mother and baby unit after her delivery because of the concern about high risk of relapse during the perinatal period. It seems that she remained well throughout the pregnancy and during the post-natal period.

3.11 There is a gap in the correspondence available for the period between 1999 and 2002 but from the information cited in later summaries it appears that this was a period of stable functioning in the community, and she was maintained on low dose Trifluoperazine.

3.12 In the autumn of 2002 there were concerns from Yvonne's general practitioner suggesting that she might be suffering from a relapse of a mental illness. It appeared that in September 2002 she attended the A&E department at the Whittington Hospital claiming her son was dehydrated and was unable to give adequate reasons why she had travelled so far across London. She was becoming increasingly preoccupied by her sexuality and was concerned about the spelling of her name. She began sending numerous emails to her general practitioner mainly correcting the spelling of her name and raisin issues about her sexuality. In a meeting with her general practitioner, psychiatrist and social worker, Clare Saxon, on the 11th December 2002 she was found to be belligerent and suspicious in manner and increasingly angry. She was preoccupied by sexually orientation asking the doctor "what can you do for lesbians and gays?" She was assessed and placed on a section 3 of the mental health act on the 19th December 2002, and admitted to ES3 ward. It appeared that she had become non-compliant with her medication, and on the ward elevated mood was the main presenting feature. She was discharged in January 2003 on Trifluoperazine 10mg at night. She made a full recovery, and by the time she was reviewed in clinic in June 2003, had regained insight and was maintained on a dose of 5mg Trifluoperazine at night.

3.13 By November 2003 she had deteriorated again, and contacted her general practitioners requesting that she comes off her benefits and speaking in a loud and angry manner about her sexuality, poor communication and irritability, she was offered home treatment, but would not allow them contact or access. She then had an extensive meeting with her community consultant Dr Rifkin, and the care coordinator who appears to have fully complied with medication and follow-up appointments after this.

3.14 On the 5th March 2004 Yvonne was admitted to the Maudsley Hospital under section three which was precipitated by her decision to leave her son James in the care of his nursery on the 1st March 2004. In the notes at the time, her care co-ordinator, Clare Saxon, noted that the decision was made of of Yvonne's care and concern for his well-being and any impact her mental health difficulties might have had on him at that time. Has remained in local authority foster care since then. She had a brief admission lasting 2 months responding well to Trifluoperazine, which was increased to 10mg, and Sodium Valproate (a mood stabilizer) and she was discharged on the 4th May 2004

3.15 In July of 2004 she wrote approximately six letters to Dr Ros Ramsey who had been her ward consultant psychiatrist, one ended "My dear Dr Ros Ramsey I do so miss you and still to date I am unsurprisingly spellbound by your mysterious alluring charm much like a Rubik Cube in the possession of a tanacious persevering novice, lucky me". After receiving several such letters Dr Ramsey handed Yvonne's care over to Dr Larry Rifkin. The letter writing then stopped.

3.16 In July of 2004 there was a statutory 'Child Looked After' review of her son James' placement, and Ms Stewart-Williams was commended for being child focused, committed to her son and contributing to the foster placement working well. The decision was made for him to be returned to his mothers care.

3.17 However, her mental state again deteriorated and she was readmitted ES3 on the 5th October 2005 and there were concerns that her son had not returned school after the end of the summer term. She was discharged on the 7th November 2005 on 10mg of Trifluoperazine at night and during the admission insisted that she had wanted her son to be placed in adoptive care.

3,18 Between 2005 and 2009 Ms Stewart-Williams remains

extremely well and was seen regularly by a care coordinator on an enhanced CPA register and at the time of her review by Dr Davis (the previous team consultant) in February 2008 Trifluoperazine 8mg daily and Procyclidine 5mg once daily. He noted that she had previously been well maintained on doses as low as 2mg and at that point reduced the dose from 8mg to 6mg daily.

3.19 I first met this lady for a CPA on the 1st July of last year (2008) and at that point her mental health had remained stable. She was paying £300 per month for James to go to a Rudolf Steiner school in order to promote his long-term attachment to a teacher as they don't change classes, and she recognised that his attachments to adults had been disrupted because of her illness. She was working full time for Thamesreach Broadway as a support worker in housing in the Westminster area. There were no psychotic or affective features on her mental state and she was fully insightful and wished to continue with her plan of reducing the Trifluoperazine towards a lower maintenance dose of 1-2mg.

3.20 On the 27th April this year I saw Yvonne when she presented to the duty worker saying that she had a buzzing sensation in her head and felt generally dazed and fuzzy. She felt that this had been precipitated by heavy workload in organising a trip at work and had called in sick and wanted to take a little time off work to recover, she declined an increase in medication. I gave her a sick note for 10 days and she returned to work after this, and when next seen by her care co-ordinator she reported that she had improved later that month.

3.21 Her care coordinator, Grace Isiaka, received a telephone call on the 2nd June form Beatrice Lamptey of the Children Looked After Team and said that the foster carers of Yvonne's son had expressed their concerns about Yvonne's mental state and worried that it might be deteriorating. There was some behavioural disturbance in that she had been turning up without an appointment to see James but then not arriving to scheduled meetings. They decided to suspend contact for the time being as they were worried about the impact on James who had started bed-wetting. When I reviewed Ms. Stewart-Williams on the 5th June her version of events was that there were difficulties with the relationship with the foster parents, for example over their decision to book a family holiday to a house with a swimming pool and Ms. Stewart-Williams objected to this on the grounds that James is unable to swim and he was regularly sleep walking. There were no overt features of psychotic or affective disturbance during the review appointment.

3.22 On the 19th June Grace received a telephone call from Carl Todd, Yvonne's line manager, to say that at work they noticed some difficulties in the way Yvonne interacted with other people since her return from sick leave. I saw her for a further review on the 23rd June, to which she had arrived 30 minutes late, with was unusual for her. Yvonne denied any problems at work, said things were fine and although she was talking prominently about issues around sexuality said that she had been assigned this as a specific project area at work. However, I noted that she was talking about colleagues bullying her in a homophobic manner and seemed somewhat paranoid compared, given that she had previously spoken of them as being extremely supportive. The concerns from different parties were reflected to Yvonne and a strong recommendation made for her to increase back the dose of Trifluoperazine. She refused to do so, although she did agree to a further meeting to discuss it the following week.

3.23 I enclose the text of my clinic review in full as follows;
"I reviewed Yvonne urgently in clinic today (30th June) following concerns about potential deterioration in her mental health. The information to hand before her appointment came from the Social Services framework system, which suggested that there had been problems with them not being able to contact her and Yvonne not returning calls. There was also an incident with another parent at her son James's school yesterday that had resulted in her arrest by the police for harassment.

3.24 "I saw Yvonne jointly with Grace Isiaka, her care coordinator and Yvonne reported that things had gone quite well at work, although she had a session in supervision with her manager who said that he had been concerned about potential deterioration in her mental health a few weeks ago but said that the first draft of her LGBT project had been going well. She reported that it was James's birthday on Sunday and she had sent a CD and DVD she made for him, but had attended a 12 step meeting on the day because she is not currently allowed contact.

3.25 "She then described the incident with the Police unprompted by us. She said that she had gone to 15 Hildread Street in Balham a few days ago and took a picture of a shop and uploaded the video onto Flikr, the online file-sharing site. She said that it is a shop that sells clothes and items connected with spirituality and she was doing a project on forms of worship. She said that she went to the shop to present the DVD to the shop owner. She then claimed that she did not know that woman, who I will refer to as (CH) was there, who is a parent at her son's school. She said that this lady used to give her lifts and they have eaten at each other's homes and formed a friendship some years ago although CH is a heterosexual married woman. Yvonne described that during the friendship she had begun to have strong feelings for CH, and about 4-5 years ago had written a letter to say that she adored her. The lady had explained to Yvonne that the feelings were not mutual and she would have to distance herself and so arranged for her husband to drive the children to and from school to reduce her contact with Yvonne.

3.26 "Yvonne said the first time that lady had admitted to her that she felt that Yvonne's contact was harassing was four years ago and at the time Yvonne was sending her text messages and gifts. She said that she had tried to 'make amends' and had met some 'amazing' women since, but said 'no woman seems to compare; it's not because she is unobtainable, it's the quality of the person'. She said she had declined other people and had been celibate for years since this. She said that she did socialise with women, but none had been the same. She recently sent an email to CH about the *Time to Change* campaign she was involved in, and CH sent her an email back saying that she was glad that Yvonne was doing well. Since then, Yvonne has shopped online at the store, which she disclosed to me that CH owns and called her about a work related issue and it was then that CH said that she felt that the harassing was beginning again.

3.27 "Yvonne said that she had got some correspondence from the online store after having returned from a Britney Spears concert and had emailed to explain her position. She said that she had never touched CH or been alone with her or had not made any threats etc. She said as far as she was concerned, CH would perceive it as unwanted gifts only. She said 'I read her web blog, and read that her children had been vomiting and wrote a letter to her wishing them speedy recovery and sent that care of the shop'. She then said she was arrested yesterday and was charged with harassment. She said 'I did not dispute it, it's a fact, I am not remorseful and that sentiments still carries'. She said that she has conditions not to go to the shop, the worm's home or approach her children; but could buy things online from the store. If she breaks the condition, she will be taken to court and the consequences of that she was not sure about. She has a meeting with her manager scheduled later today and does not think as the situation stands now, it will affect her work, but future charges may show up on her CRB check.

3.28 "She describes a previous attachment with her previous female consultant, Dr. Ros Ramsay when she was an inpatient on ES3 in 2005. She said she sent her letters and gift, she said that this was before meeting CH. She said that the gifts were returned to her, and her Community Consultant Psychiatrist read the letters. She said that that the feelings subsided and it was easier because she did not really know Dr Ramsay. She says the difference with CH is that she knows her well.

3.29 "I asked her why the situation has arisen now and she said that it was difficult to say and went on to mention that the woman's husband was a Sikh; and that she did not think that they wanted her attention. She then said 'I sincerely believe that CH is my soul mate from many lives past. She encompasses things that I value deeply, not just about her physical state but many things about her and it is coming from a place of sincerity. I care unconditionally for her. It had added on from the experience with Ros Ramsay and I feel like I am giving her something back, because I love her and know her so it will continue'. I asked her if the love was likely to die out and she replied, 'No because I adore her and I can live with that'. She said because she was not able to have contact with her, she would re-read that woman's web blog and could watch her DVD's and Yoga videos that she had made.

3.30 "After her assessment, I reviewed that paper notes that we have. During her mental health act assessment on 22 September 2005 prior to being admitted to ES3 the ASW wrote on the form; 'she had a fallout with another parent at her son's school in relation to her feelings for the woman who is said to be married. When the school informed her key worker of crisis, she interpreted it as being homophobic'. At that point she had also become erratic in her behaviour and towards her son with missing appointments around that time he was fostered. As far as I can tell, I cannot see any references to any episodes of harassment in the risk assessment nots that we have, but I have requested a full copy of her old file and will contact the Consultant concerned to try and get more details.

3.31 "In the meantime, the impression must be that this behaviour of harassment has previously been seen in a context of a relapse of her mental illness and on mental state today, she has presented as irritable and tense although there were no other delusions, thought disorder or hallucinatory experiences. During the interview she said she was going to a Stonewall debate tomorrow, and implied that she would bring up our questioning of her behaviour as an example of homophobic bullying. She reluctantly agreed to an increases in her medication from 1 to 4 mgs, which she will commence today and will be seen by her care coordinator next week. I have scheduled a review with myself on Friday 17 July and she has given her verbal consent for us to continue to speak to her employer so he can feedback any concerns; and given her assent, although not active consent for me to refer her to the Forensic team to do a full risk assessment of her risk of stalking and harassment given her position working with vulnerable adults".

4. Personal and Family History

4.1 The records indicate that Ms Stewart-Williams mother lives in Luton. She appears to have been suffering from mental illness, maybe schizophrenia and is being treated with depot injection. She has been supportive towards Ms Stewart-Williams at times, has taken care of her grandson when Ms Stewart-Williams needed hospital admission for her own illness. Ms Stewart-Williams father died when she was 2-3 years old and her first adoptive father brought her up until the age of 9. She spent a period in foster care between 9 and 16. Ms stewart-Williams has a younger sister, and one stepsister and two stepbrothers from her mother's side.

4.2 Ms Stewart-Williams was born and brought up in London. It is documented that she appears to have achieved all normal developmental milestones. She has trained as a nurse at Putney

Hospital and then Barnet Hospital until the age of 16. Until she was 31 years old, she worked as a community care worker in a hostel. Thereafter, she has expressed the wish to pursue her education and applied for an Open University course in Photography but has not been able to pursue that due to a lack of financial resources. She stopped working for a period after the birth of her son James. She is currently employed full-time as a Community Support Worker for Thamesreach Broadway.

5. Interview with Ms Stewart-Williams

5.1 This was conducted in a room in one of the housing wings in HMP Holloway on 15th July 2009.

5.2 She explained the offence, and said that she had gone to Caroline Hugo's place of work and was asked to leave but when she didn't the police was called and she was taken to Wandsworth police station and given a warning. She spent the night in the cells and was released home but two days later she informed Caroline Hugo by email and phone that she would be at her shop the following day and when she arrived the police were again called.

5.3 She said emphatically "I love her", and said there was no change in her feelings since she knew Carolyn had said "no" to her affection. She described how she had entertained Caroline's children and had shared meals at their home and Carolyn's son Louis had watched DVD's with her own son, James. She said that they had given her an her son lifts to school and a gifts of a video play but the last time they met socially was 3 and a half to 4 years ago. She said that Carolyn had reduced the frequency of her contact after Yvonne had sent her an email disclosing her feelings four years ago. She stated adamantly that she had never attempted to touch her and had not intention of trying to do so, but was unable to estimated the frequency of gifts and letters she had sent because she said that these were given "*unconditionally*" and it was hard to say how often she had done so.

5.4 She said after the contact with Carolyn had stopped her husband continued to help her with lifts to school and gradually she resumed some sort of contact with Carolyn. She said in the past few years there had been periodic phone calls but there had been a break in the middle although she continued to feel the same love but hadn't acted on it. She said that this was because she was engaged in a 12-step Narcotics Anonymous programme meetings and had gone through them twice. She said that the fourth step is to take an inventory of the people you'd harmed, and she had discussed her feelings for Carolyn with her sponsor, who had "given their option about this situation". She said that the 12-step recommendation is for people not to engage in relationships during the first year of the programme. After two years the advice she got from her sponsor in the 12-step Programme was that she was ready to resume relationships again as a gateway to normal living. She then started online dating with Gaydar. She said that she had been socialising with other people in the 12-step programme, and had gone out to art galleries, cinemas, etc. She said that she had become close to people and had been on dates with other women for example having tea at Fortnum & Mason, or going to a Matthew Bourne production at the ballet. However, she has remains celibate for the past 6 years, she said that although she had met some amazing women it was not the same attraction she felt to Carolyn Hugo.

She said that she continued to read Carolyn's Internet blogs for a long time ahd had been writing about her on her own blog and had sent her an email about the mental heath anti-stigma work she was soing as part of the Rethink campaign.

5.5 In terms of face -t-face contact she said that in approximately November or December of 2008 she took James to Carolyn's shop to buy gifts and she was there but they did not speak. She said that she had also seen her on a bus back in November 2007 but apart from these incidents had not really had any contact with her.

5.6 She summarised the timeline of events. September 2004 is when they had first met as their children were attending the same school, socialised together and did the school run. In approximately in November or December in 2004 she first declared her love to Caroline in email. November 12th 2005 was when she joined the 12-step programme (although this is a narcotic anonymous programme and she stopped using drugs years previously she thought it would be helpful to progress to her next step in terms of her mental health issues). November 2007 was the time she first started thinking bout starting relationships with other people and said that she had given occasional gifts, read Caroline's blog and had gone to the shop on a fairly regular basis. She said that is was in February 2009 that she had her fist personal contact with Caroline Hugo again.

5.7 I asked Yvonne if she thought that their frequency of contact was related to her mental health and she said that "life has it's ups and downs" and she had "never felt better and was happy and content, satisfied and was after anything". She reiterated that she had a "deep love for Carolyn Hugo" and at distance, and whether or not she saw her made no difference. She said that she was her "soul mate and this transcended all time". She said that she is " taking one day at a time", but said that her love was "beyond infinity because it was about spirit and not a physical attraction". She said if she did not see Carolyn this would not stop her feelings towards her. She said with some force that she had no intention of physically touching her because this would be "one step too far". She said she wasn't "leering at her or anything like that" it was something "purely emotional and spiritual". She talked about Carolyn's "adorable" children, Louis and Isadora, and viewed them as extension's of their mother.

5.8 I took some further detail about her relationship histories and she said it was in 1979 when she had her first lesbian relationship when she was working in Wandsworth as a nursing assistant. She said she has had a few "crushes" on boys and had kissed one or two and she saw men a primarily being there for friendship. She described herself as being a "straight man in a woman's body". She described her first trip to Jamaica at the age of 26 when she had a "deep, deep love", like she one she has for Carolyn Hugo to a man called Andrew, who is now married with four children. She described them as being best friends and she told him about her love, but that the fact was the majority of her friends were gay and that her sexual orientation was lesbian. She said he reciprocated her feelings, but she could nt make physical contact with him, despite sleeping in the same bed as him one night, and reported that they are still in touch and he is in fact James' godfather. She said they have attended Christenings together and she also knows his wife, and Ms. Stewart-Williams said that she rather regretted the fact that she was not straight because she would otherwise be happily married to him.

5.9 She had experienced childhood sexual abuse in her early life and described herself as being an adult survivor of this and felt that she had fully worked through the process via group therapy and in the 12-step programme. She said this was one of the reasons she connected to Andrew, as this also has been an experience he had been through. She described how her mum had always been very protective of her, but when she was "mentally incapacitated she wasn't able to keep watch" and neighbour and other people had sexually abused her about the age of 6 or 7 years old. She said it also continued when she was in a children's home until she went left foster care at the age of 15 or 16. She said this is one of the reasons she watched over James carefully as much as if he was a girl because she was well aware that sexual abuse can affect both male and female children.

5.10 When asked about her reactions towards the charge she said, "I am guilty, the evidence is there" but when asked about the impact it might have had on Carolyn Hugo she said, "I can not read other's minds. My love is selfish in that it's me giving as apposed to her taking, but I can't know what it is she thinks".

5.11 On Mental State Examination she presented as a well build Black British woman with a baseball cap on and short dreadlocked hair. She was wearing casual cloths and had good personal hygiene. Her speech was normal in rate, volume, form and tone and there were no signs of thought disorder. Her mood was subjectively "happy" and objectively euthymic. She reported sleeping between eight and sixteen hours per night and reported good energy, appetite and concentration and in fact was reading a copy of ' Anthony and Cleopatra' by Shakespeare when I commenced the interview. She denied any psychotic symptoms such as passivity phenomena, thought interference, communications from the television and there was no evidence of delusions other than her delusion of love held about Carolyn. She denied any hallucinations to me, but did admit to hearing voices when Dr Law assed her on the 10th of the month. She was cognitively intact and said she did not feel it was a relapse in her mental illness, thought this was a unrelated incident and was prepared to go through with the consequences of the legal progress.

6. Conclusion

6.1 Ms Stewart-Williams suffers from schizoaffective disorder, which is a chronic relapsing remitting mental illness. In her case relapses have been characterised by a gradual period of decline in social functioning before florid psychotic phenomena appears. She has responded extremely well to Trifluoperazine at relatively low doses and her social function between episodes is excellent. The current presenting features are disorganisation in her attendance of appointments with her son in foster care over the past couple of months and some concerns from her employer about her interactions with colleagues. The behaviour of harassment towards Caroline Hugo represents Erotomania, and appears to have been ongoing for the past four years, but the frequency and intensity have waxed and waned. It is of note that the increase in frequency of her unwanted contacts with Carolyn Hugo has occurred during the same time frame as the concerns expressed by her son's social worker and her employer.

6.2 During that period she had been on a low dose Trifluoperazine at just 1mg, and the evidence from previous relapses points to this behaviour dis-inhibition being one manifestation of a deterioration of her general mental state. Historically the appearance of other psychotic symptoms such as thought disorder and florid hallucinations and overtly disturbed behaviour have occurred later on in the course of a relapse, so the absences of these on mental state examination when assessed is relatively characteristic for her.

6.3 In terms of her prognosis it is likely that her condition will remain throughout her life and is likely to follow a similar course of relapses and remissions although the relapses can be minimised by complying with medication.

7. Future Risk to Carolyn Hugo & her Family

7.1 Although my observation is that the erotomanic behaviour has worsened along with deterioration in her general mental health, it seems clear that the ideas are maintained even when her mental health is at its optimum. What does differ is the intensity to which she acts upon these feelings. Outside a secure environment the chances of her action on these are high and although there is no historical evidence of her acting in an aggressive manner towards people for whom she has held infatuations in the past, she does have a history of aggression during previous relapse of her illness. Ms. Stewart-Williams has spoken about the Hugo children as being extensions of their mother, so the risks may well extend to them.

7.2 Research evidence (Rosenfeld, B. Violence Risk Factors in Stalking and Obsessional Harassment: A review and Preliminary Meta-Analysis. *Criminal Justice and Behaviour* 2004; 31:9) suggests that the risks of aggression towards the victim are lower for those that have a psychotic illness then those without, and that the presence of threats towards the victim is not a reliable predictor of future violence. Those involved in stalking behaviour that did not make threats beforehand also had a significant rate of violence towards the subject of their infatuation. A prior intimate relationship with the victim was a predictor of violence. Clinical experience suggests that the risk of violence is elevated at the point at which the subject finally acknowledges the non-reciprocal nature of their affection and feels rejection.

8. Recommendations

8.1 My recommendation would therefore be for the court to consider a forensic treatment section (S37/41) to enable her mental health to be appropriately managed in an inpatient setting, with both medication, psychological approaches and relapse prevention work, and enable a full psychosexual risk assessment and management plan to be made.

8.2 Her current treatment of Trifluoperazine has been increased from 1 to 4mg and she has had less than a week of the higher dose, and it takes approximately six weeks to be fully efective. Given that during previous relapses she has usually had doeses of over 10mg it would be reasonable to increase this dose further depending on her repsonse. Ther recommendation would be for her to be on life lon Trifluoperazine at a dose of at least 4mg or above as this seems to be the minimum dose that has held her in the past.

8.3 Given her response to both group psychotherapy and engagement in the 12-step progress has contributed to prolonged periods of stability, further engagement in psychotherapy would be another recommendation. Relapse prevention work should form the basis for care co-ordinator sessions.

8.4 Contact with her son James has been suspended at present, and the Children Looked After Team will need to do a reassessment of future contact arrangements when the outcome of the Court case is known.

8.5 Geographical separation may be something the court wishes to consider, given the longstanding nature of the erotomania, to reduce future risks.

I understand that in writing this report my duty is first to the court and to the best of my knowledge the information contained on it is full and accurate.

Prepared By Dr Kitty Seed Specialty Registrar to Dr Harvey Wickham Consultant Psychiatrist

Court Report for Yvonne Stewart Williams on 15th July 2009.

After reading the report, the judge decided to send me to Elleen Skellern 3 Ward, SLAM South London and Maudsley psychiatric hospital on a section 37. I arrived on Thursday 20th August 2009.

The following letter dated 29th October 2009 was written from SLAM to Thames Reach: [My employer]

Yvonne Patricia Stewart-Williams...

Apologies for the delay in a full reply to your letter dated 14/08/09 requesting information about the above. I have recently returned from long term leave and this was passed onto me.

I will endeavour to answer your specific questions in turn below:

Has Yvonne been given a custodial sentence?

No, For sentencing she was transferred to our hospital under section 37 of the Mental Health Act for treatment. No restrictions were made on her discharge from us (i.e. a section 41was not put into place). This means she can be discharged as and when in the view of her current treating team that it is appropriate to do so.

What was the offence that Yvonne has been convicted of and what is the sentence?

Yvonne was convicted of a charge of harassment without violence. As above, for sentencing she was transferred to the Maudsley Hospital, rather than back to prison (she had already been on remand in Holloway Prison, as I understand it from my records, from the 01/07/09). She was transferred to our ward on the 20/08/09.

What are the details about the nature of the offence?

Yvonne was charged with harassment without violence towards and individual, who will be referred to here as CH. She was inititally arrested on the 29/06/09 ad then again on the 01/07/09 for breaching a harassment warning against her, which had been issued on the 29/06/09. The police records state that she had known the victim since September 2004 as their children attended the same school. Over a five year period Yvonne had sent CH numerous gifts and letters, emails and text messages, as well as posting information about her feelings about CH on her internet blog. Yvonne herself has told us how she and CH had become friends over that period and she had been welcomed into CH's home and indeed had shared some childcare responsibilities such as taking their children to school together, That is to say Yvonne has described how CH reciprocated her friendship initially, however she did not reciprocate Yvonne's declared love for her, CH and her husband had met with Yvonne to explain that CH did not have any desire or intention for a romantic relationship with Yvonne but following this explanation Yvonne had not accepted that and had continued to contact CH excessively. On the 29/06/09 police records state that CH contacted them as the situation had escalated with Yvonne arriving at her shop and then refusing to leave. At that time the police issued Yvonne with a warning, however early the next morning she again contacted CH by email stating she would visit the shop again later and again reiterating her love for her and her children. She subsequently visited the shop again the next day and again refused to leave, so the police were once again called and she was arrested.

What is the confirmed medical reason for Yvonne's hospitalisation?

Yvonne has a diagnosis of schizoaffective disorder, a chronic relapsing and remitting mental illness. In her case it is of note that prior to the above events her medication had been gradually reduced in the community as she had been very well for a period of time. It would seem that, with hindsight, the level of her medication was too low to maintain her health. There were no concerns about her actually taking the medication as such. It is of note that she has a history of engaging well with her community mental health team.

As a background to the above offence, Yvonne's mental state had been thought to be deteriorating. As far as I can see from her records the first indication to services that she might not be so well was in April this yearm when she informed the community team she was feeling "dazed and fuzzy". Following this there were concerns raised in the community by the foster carers of Yvonne's son that her behaviour had become more chaotic around arranged appointments to see her son. By the 19th June the community team received contact from your service noting a decline in Yvonne's level of functioning at work and unusual problems arisingm such as late attendance, which is out of character for her. It is perhaps of note that at the time she told the community team she felt concerned that colleagues were bullying her at work in a homophobic manner and the doctor she saw at the time was puzzled by this given that Yvonne had previously spoken of her work colleagues as being very supportive.

Following her arrest and subsequent remand to Holloway Prison Yvonne was seen by her community team and her psychiatrist at the time Dr Kitty Seed prepared a full psychiatric report for the court for the purposes of Yvonne's sentencing. The conclusion of this report was that Yvonne had indeed had a relapse of her schizoaffective illness and that sentencing to a hospital for treatment would be appropriate. It was noted that in future her longstanding medication of Trifluoperazine will need to be maintained at a dose of at least 4mg or above. In addition to hospital treatment it was recommended Yvonne continue with her group psychotherapy, a programme of psychological treatment that she is well engaged with and keen to continue.

It was also stated in this report that although Yvonne's more chaotic behaviour was understood to have occurred in the context of a relapse of her illness, it was noted that Yvonne has a history of similar although less extreme behaviour when her mental state has seemingly been relatively stable in the community. That is to say Yvonne has developed inappropriate attachments to individuals who have not reciprocated her feelings, and she has not desisted in contacting them them to express those feelings despite their request to do so. For example in July 2004 she wrote several letters to a previous female consultant, requiring her care to be passed over to a male colleague. It would seem likely therefore that even when well and at her best, there remain some difficulties for Yvonne in terms of developing close attachments to people, and understanding the boundaries of those attachments, so tat she can form close relationships with people which are reciprocated, mutually satisfying and not essentially one-sided. Without disclosing further detailed personal information here in this context, it is also important to mention that in addition to Yvonne's schizoaffective disorder, there are other very good reasons in terms of traumatic early childhood experiences, which have left Yvonne with understandable difficulties in terms of close relationships. As stated previously, it is very positive that Yvonne is wishing to continue to work on these difficulties through psychotherapy.

When is Yvonne likely to be released from hospital?

Yvonne is likely to be discharged in the very near future, subject to satisfactory home leave on section from hospital.

Will Yvonne be able to return to work?

Yes. Yvonne is keen to return to work. She is clearly an intelligent woman with a broad skill base and certainly we would encourage her to do so. I think the issue here will be for her to return to work at a time and in a way negotiated with yourselves that compliments rather than hinders her recovery from her recent episode. I would certainly suggest she stay off sick from work for a matter of a few weeks after discharge in order to negotiate her return to work with yourselves in a considered, thoughtful way. Clearly she will under review from her community mental health team during this period after discharge so they too will be able to liaise with yourselves if required.

Yours sincerely

Dr Nicola Byrne
Consultant Psychiatrist
ES3

I was discharged from Elleen Skellern 3 Ward, SLAM- South London and Maudsley Psychiatric Hospital, on the 16th November 2009.

Recovery

Tuesday 26th January 2010

Dear Yvonne,

Today I met with Dr Izmeth, my community psychiatrist and Grace Isiaka, my care co-ordinator at David Pitt House. Dr Izmeth indicated that I am making a good recovery. Due to ill effects from my 12mgs Trifluoperazine [I had been on 30mgs during my inpatient stay in SLAM] Dr Izmeth agreed that it could be reduced to 10mgs daily. She asked if I was still inclined to send letters to C. This is something that I did whilst an inpatient. I told her that I wasn't sending letters, gifts, cards or writing about C on my blogs http://mum-careconcern.blogspot.com/ although I am still reading C's web blog and thinking about her regularly.

Sunday 31st January 2010

Dear Yvonne,

Today, at my local Quaker meeting for worship, I spent time speaking to Noel an elder about the reason that I was in prison. I confessed to him that I still look at C's web blog and think about her, but felt that love needed to be a two-way affair. Noel implied that there was no hope as far as this romance, for me. So this evening I opened an account with the on-line dating agency, Match.com

Wednesday 3rd February 2010

Dear Yvonne,

Today my e-book, 'Altered Perceptions,' was published. As I started to read it, I recalled that the very first sentence was about C.

Thursday 4th February 2010

Dear Yvonne,

Today I picked up a Memorandum from the South Western Magistrate Court regarding my conviction for my employers. They need it in order to do a risk assessment because I gained this criminal record whilst in their employ, and I work with vulnerable clients. The Memorandum detailed a brief description of my crime towards C as follows:

Offences

1 Harassment without violence
Between 29/06/2009 and 01/07/2009 at 15 Hildreth Street, Balham, London SW12 pursued a course of conduct which amounted to the harassment of Carolyn HUGO and which you knew or ought to have known amounted to the harassment of her in that letters, emails, text messages were sent, Aslo you attended the victims home address as part of an obsessive harassment of her. Contrary to section 2(1) and (2) of the Protection from Harassment Act 1997. Contrary to Section 2(1) and (2) of the Protection from Harassment Act 1997

No Offence Level URN recorded

Plea: Guilty - 02/07/2009

Results
Hospital Order
To be admitted to and detained at Maudsley Hospital.

Friday 5th February 2010

Dear Yvonne,

Each day, Match.com has been sending me possible matches for women seeking women dating. None have caught my eye yet. I am still thinking about C. I have decided to open a FaceBook account. During the possess I came across C's account with FaceBook and I felt tempted to add her as a friend. But I resisted.

Sunday 6th February 2010

Dear Yvonne,

Today I went to Nelson Ward, in the Landor Road Hosptal site. It is part of the SLAM NHS Trust and now houses the old Elleen Skellern 3 Women's Ward. I went to see a nurse called Katie, who asked me to tell her when my e-book, Altered Perceptions, was published. When I arrived, Katie wasn't on duty but the other nurses recognised me and after a time asked if I was still obsessed with C and if I was still contacting her and writing about her on my http://lifeafterinprisonmentpsychiatrichosp.blogspot.com/ blog. I could say no to the latter but to the former I said yes.

Monday 7th February 2010

Dear Yvonne,

At 7:00 this morning, I re-engaged with my programme and I re-read question 22 to my temporary Sponsor on the telephone. It was suggested that I distanced myself from my qualifier. I have decided to spend the day and sleep the night at my mother's home. My mother still loves me unconditionally and on release from Holloway Women's Prison into SLAM, when I spoke to my mother on the telephone. My mother said that she had been worried about me during my absence. And then she received my prison letters. I wrote regular letters from prison, mostly to my mother, son and C.

Tuesday 8th February 2010

Dear Yvonne,

Today, I updated my Shift-Speakers' Bureau biography. It now reads:

Yvonne

Yvonne is 48 and lives in south London. She has been diagnosed with schizo-affective disorder and erotomania, and is employed part time.

Yvonne say her mother admitted to a psychiatric hospital when she was just seven. Her mother's mental health problems lasted for a decade and Yvonne ended up in a children's home, where some members of staff made disparaging comments about her mother.

In 1993, Yvonne was admitted to a psychiatric hospital after friends grew concerned about her behaviour, the first of 15 admissions. In 2009 during an acute psychiatric episode she was taken to Holloway Women's Prison before being treated in hospital. Yvonne was most recently admitted to hospital in 2009.

Yvonne has recently been diagnosed with erotomania: erotomania occurs during psychotic episodes and is a type of delusion in which the affected person believes that another person, usually a stranger, is in love with him or her.

When Yvonne was treated in hospital in 2005, her only child was taken into long-term foster care. Yvonne is now allowed to have contact with her son once a week, and she sees her social worker each fortnight.

Yvonne works as a mental health floating support worker with a homeless charity. Her manager is aware of her medical history and her colleagues are also aware. In 2020, Yvonne had an e-book published, Altered Perceptions, a diary of her life during 18 months. "In this diary I reveal that for me it is not so much whether mental illness can be cured, but what one does in life in between each acute psychiatric episode. A kind of walking between the raindrops, until you get wet experience." Yvonne carries out voluntary work with the Maudsley Hospital internet technology group, and with

Stonewall, the lesbian and gay organisation.

Stigma cost her some friendships and saw her lose contact with the gay and lesbian community. She took the initiative with the latter point, arranging for a free gay community newspaper to be delivered throughout the Maudsley.

Yvonne believes professional discrimination has affected her treatment and life: initially she was forced to sleep in a four-bed dormitory with three men because she was a lesbian. She says that she was given large quantities of anti-psychotic medication rather than talk therapy because she was black, and she was initially not taken seriously at her child's school.

"Medication has at times caused me to shake, drool, feel drowsy and unable to speak properly. When I asked for my medication to be reduced so that I would be able to cope with my child-care responsibilities, my psychiatrist would not listen. Social services have no qualms with my parenting skills except when the medication ceases to take effect."

Yvonne has been told that people with mental health issues are stupid, or are bad parents.

Yvonne's mother has been a mentor to Yvonne: she visits her in hospital and has accompanied her to court.

Yvonne hopes her involvement with the Speakers' Bureau will give her an opportunity to explain to the media that one in four people experience mental health problems - but life can still go on.

Wednesday 10th February 2010

Dear Yvonne,

At the Herne Hill book shop, on my way to my Connexions, group psychotherapy at SLAM today, I purchased, MAYA by Alistair Campbell. This is the second book of Alistair's that I have bought. The first book was ALL IN THE MIND, which I bought in time for his public talk about his personal experience of mental illness and book signing at the SouthBank last year. During his questions and answers session, I asked Alistair if he would consider being an Ambassador for Mental Health. which I posted on my blog. This evening, I joined the group "UK GAY GIRLS (I know there's at least 8,999 Gay UK women on Facebook)", thanks to Elaine Mckenzie. I figured that if I am going to find a woman that I am not deluded about then if I am at least moving in gay girl circles then that is a start. And with the same sentiment in mind, I am going to consider accepting the invitation to 'FUTURE FUSION CLUB NIGHT from my old friend Nikki Lucas.

One of the consequences of the way that my Erotomania manisfested itself in 2009, has meant that I have had a eight to nine month gap between seeing my beloved son James. This has caused me much concern as he is just ten years old. Today, I rang my son James and spent an hour talking with him. This is the third time this year that I have spoken to him. I haven't seen him since the beginning of June 2009 and the first contact that I had with him since then was Christmas day, when his social worker said that he could call me. Fortunately, my mother and I take it in turns to call James each Wednesday so it is my mother's turn to call him next week. Today James told me that it was Lyn [his foster mother]'s birthday and he had spent all of his pocket money buying her flowers. A whole week's pocket money. James told me that he was saving for something and was thinking of making something for Lyn instead. When I asked James how much he gets for his pocket money, he told me £2:00 each week!

Thursday 11th February 2010

Dear Yvonne,

Today, I accepted an invitation to Stonewall's FIT. A screening of the feature length film will take place on Thursday 11th March 2009, from 7pm at the Sallis Benney Theatre in Brighton. And followed by a drinks reception and a chance to talk to Rikki Beadle-Blair, the Director of FIT. I have met Rikki once before, last year at my Unison LGBT history month [February] celebrations. posted this on my http://onthecuspofmadness.blogspot.com/ blog. I went for a routine blood test this morning at Dulwich Hospital compliments of my GP.

Friday 12th February 2010

Dear Yvonne,
Today, I joined the Rethink campaign team's, Bradley Review consultation. The Bradley Review looked at the criminal justice system and mental health. In the first stage people are asked to share their experience of getting caught up in the criminal justice system because of mental health issues, to help make recommendations for improvement.

I will be one of the volunteers who look at the recommendations the government is taking forward, and I will be helping to shape how they will be put in place. My direct experience has qualified me to be taking part in four future consultations from March 2010 - March 2011. The consultation events will happen in London.

Saturday 13th February 2010

Dear Yvonne,

This morning, I received a letter from my GP letting me know that the results of my blood test is in and that they want to see me. Although it is not urgent. I wonder what could the matter be this time? The last time it was my clolesterol levels were too high. Maybe it is my blood pressure, after all the doctor did take three readings before he was satisfied. Or maybe I have finally got diabetes type 2 mature onset, after all most members of my family have this type of diabetes. I will try to get to the surgery on Monday.

Sunday 14th February 2010

Dear Yvonne,

Today is Valentines day and I long for that special someone... I sent most people on my mobile male and female a valentine text message today. D replied very near the end of Valentines Day saying that she loved me too and was reading 'Altered Perceptions' and didn't reply to me earlier because couldn't bring herself to put the book down because she was loving it.

Monday 15th February 2010

Dear Yvonne,

Today I joined the 'see me' launches Wall of Support. It is a campaign which invites people to show some practical support for any friend, colleague or family members experiencing mental illness. The message is that no one has to do anything special - just be there and be themselves. Be the friend they always were. It entails designing my own 'see me' badge and message of support. I have written on my badge 'see me' I'm "a one in four". The wall aims to be a declaration from anyone who's committed to fighting the stigma and discrimination of mental ill-health. When I went to the GP's today, he told me that my iron level was low. He asked me if I had been feeling tired, to which I said yes. He then prescribed me two iron tablets each day.

Tuesday 16th February 2010

Dear Yvonne,

Today I spent a couple of hours at the Stonewall http://www.stonewall.org.uk/ offices doing some voluntary work. I also booked a place for the LGBT (lesbian, gay, bisexual and trans) in Justice. This will take place in Rose Court, 2 Southwark Bridge, SE1 9HS. I will be attending on Thursday 18th February 2010. The Ministry of Justice are hosting two sessions on the history of legislation against the LGBT community. They're also appealing for help in improving their understanding of the needs of the LGBT community. So I will attend and have my say on how courts and tribunals deal with their LGBT customers. I am informed that the Gender Trust is going to be giving a fifteen minute talk at this event.

Wednesday 17th February 2010

Dear Yvonne,

Today, my employers contacted me and asked me to come and see them at 1:30pm on Friday. This is a part of my return to work process. I was informed that I will start back to work on Monday 22nd February 2010. This will be the first time that I will have been working since June 2009, before my Erotomania diagnosis. I am delighted. I have missed my clients, colleagues and work so much. Today I was invited to watch a screening of FIT at the Stonewall offices with Stonewall volunteers on Thursday 4th March 2010. I accepted the invitation. I shall cancel the Brighton screening. I have also accepted a Face Book invitation to visit the National Portrait Gallery on Saturday 27th February 2010.

Thursday 18th February 2010

Dear Yvonne,

Today someone D [a woman] invited me in a text message round to her abode for coffee. On the surface, it seems perfectly innocent but me being a love addict read into it and made one and one make twenty. I don't know if this is a date, or what. I feel nervous because I like D and I met her before C. D knows all about the facts of my imprisonment and hospitalization, in fact she visited me in hospital, rang me and came and escorted me to coffee. I don't want to be thinking the wrong thing, so I have rung a few friends and discussed my concerns. They have told me to accept it at face value and just go along as I would with a straight forward friend.

Friday 19th February 2010

Dear Yvonne,

Today I had a return to work meeting at my Strutton Ground office, with my line manager's, line manager. Before I arrived I received in the post a letter from Occupational Health, dealing the kiss of death on to any desire on my part to regain my position at Thames Reach as a floating support worker. Within the letter it stated that I can not work unsupervised. This was after they had read Dr Nicola Byrnes' letter. I have a return to work date for Monday 15th March 2010. I will have an hour in the office prior to that on Friday 12th March 2010.

Monday 22nd February 2010

Dear Yvonne,

Today, I met with Grace Isiaka at David Pitt House and collected my Stelazine anti-psychotic medication and picked up my medcert signing me back to work on the 15th March 2010. I had a conversation with Grace about coffee with D, which is planned for this forthcoming Wednesday after Connections - my group psychotherapy. Grace too told me to take it easy and not to jump to conclusions about it being a date.

Wednesday 24th February 2010

Dear Yvonne,

This afternoon, I met with D. She asked me lots of questions mostly about 'Altered Perceptions' of which she said she had read in three sittings and only had ten pages left to read. D also asked me about my son and mum and then asked me what I felt about C now? I told D that I had no ill feelings towards C and that I still loved her but understood that whatever I felt and for what ever reason's, it was over. Near when I was getting ready to leave it was time for my phone contact with my son. So I introduced D to him on the phone and they spoke for a short time. Just as I was leaving, D told me not to be too good. I replied that I don't want to be so bad that I end up in prison again. To which she said no you don't.

Thursday 25th February 2010

Dear Yvonne,

Today I did my 3rd Step Ceremony and I told my sponsor that I was told not to be too good. My sponsor smiled and asked me what that meant. I didn't have an answer. But when I got home I thought about it and thought that I must not be too slow coming forward. So I decided to send D an email thanking her for our time together and invite her out to a restaurant of her choice.

Friday 26th February 2010

Dear Yvonne,

Today, while on the journey to visit my mother in Luton, my son's social worker rang me to confirm that I had received her written correspondence and will be attending my son's review on Tuesday 2nd March 2010. When I told her that it has been at least nine months since I last saw my son and asked her about further face to face contact with my son, the social worker said that that would not be possible to sort that out at the review. I was greatly upset by this news and contacted Ros Dunning, my Dunning & Co solicitor in Camberwell to ask her if she could come to the review to support me.

Saturday 27th February 2010

Dear Yvonne,

Today, although I went to view the Irving Penn photographic exhibition at the National Portrait Gallery with the FemFlirt group of women from Facebook - organised by Elaine McKenzie of the Glass bar - this morning, I feel upset and distracted. D has not replied to my email. I think that I have read the wrong signals and have been trying to romance a straight forward friend. I have spoken to a few friends about this situation and they have each tried to comfort me, but I feel bad.

Sunday 28th February 2010

Dear Yvonne,

D answered my email with an affirmative today. I am delighted and I am left wondering if this is now considered a date?

Monday 1st March 2010

Dear Yvonne,

Neil Hickman, a Dunning & Co solicitor is going to support me at the review as Ros Dunning is out of London this week. I replied to D email and told her that I look forward to hearing from her with the date for the restaurant.

Tuesday 2nd March 2010

Dear Yvonne,

This morning, I could not get out of bed and I felt as if I could have slept forever. I feel like this most days even though I am taking the iron tablets. A complete lethargy. I can't wait to get back to work. At the review it was decided that I could have supervised contacts every other week for two hours at the contact centre. It was lovely to see my son again. He had grown in height and was over the moon to see me. He gave me a photograph of himself, some truffles and a post card. Then he went away and came back and placed twenty pounds in my hand [Almost three months of his saved pocket money]. James told me that he had made me bankrupt buying him toys.

Friday 5th March 2010

Dear Yvonne,

Today I visited my mother in Luton. Whilst with her she suggested that I continued reading some of her Jehovah's Witness pamphlets and attending the meetings. I came out to me mother again and told her that she knows that I am gay and have been so for many years and that the Witnessess disapprove of that so that. My mother said nothing, but when I was leaving she gave me a big hug and a kiss on the cheek.

Saturday 6th March 2010

Dear Yvonne,

This evening, met with my dear old friend Birgit and dined at Asmara's Eritrean restaurant in Brixton. During the meal. I had much to tell Birgit after explaining that I will be returning to work on Monday 15th March 2010 and telling her about James' review I told her about D.

Sunday 7th March 2010

Dear Yvonne,

I am distracted. Thinking about D and wondering when she is going to contact me about a day for the restaurant. Today I left a voicemail on her phone telling her that I just wanted to hear her voice. D then left a voicemail on my phone saying that she is going to call me tomorrow. I can hardly wait!

Tuesday 9th March 2010

Dear Yvonne,

D did not call yesterday and I am disappointed and upset. I have sent her a text message expressing this, but wishing her a good day anyway whilst hoping to hear from her soon. D sent me a text apologising and asking me which evening this week I would like to have dinner with her in Caravaggio's in Camberwell? Thursday was my reply. D told me that that suited her too and that she would call me later. This evening D and I spoke for approximately twenty minutes. She told me that she had had a meeting with management at the Maudsley Psychiatric Hospital and they had agreed to there being a group started for LGBT (lesbian, gay, bisexual and trans) Mental health service users. I congratulated her on her success. At the end of the conversation which sorted out the time that we would meet (7:30pm) D told me that she was looking forward to seeing me. I am left wondering if she likes me too?

Wednesday 10th March 2010

Dear Yvonne,

Connections group psychotherapy session today was one for me to remember. The facilitators, Jack and Will asked me how I know that my date with D was a date? "Had I snogged her and not told anyone?" In the end I explained that I thought it was a date because D had twice visited me in hospital, given me her mobile and landline numbers and email address and rang and emailed and texted me. D had taken me out for coffee and invited me out to a public talk. Furthermore D had invited me to her place for a coffee and given me her home address and had accepted my dinner invitation. Will and Jack reluctantly agreed that this might be a date. They did remind me that I have an Erotomania diagnosis and might not be the best judge. After group I went to visit my mother in Luton. This week my mother spoke about my lesbianism. In fact I had not hear my mother use the word lesbian so often. She told me that I was her favourite child and that she loved me.

Thursday 11th March 2010

Dear Yvonne,

This evening I arrived at the restaurant half an hour early with flowers for D. I chose a table at the front and D arrived on time. She looked beautiful, she had had her hair done and she was glowing. We dined and spoke for almost two and a half hours. During which time D asked me if I had done something with my hair? and told me that she wanted to take me for a drive to one of her favourite spots when the weather gets warmer. When we finished dining and was standing outside the restaurant I gave her the flowers and she gave me a kiss on the cheek, then I left her. All the way home on the bus, I thought about that kiss!

Friday 12th March 2010

Dear Yvonne,

I didn't sleep for the whole of last night. I had drank an expresso's at Caravaggio's. I was still thinking about that kiss. I sent a text message to D and she replied telling me that she had "enjoyed dinner last night and had woke up to a beautiful vase of flowers" She hoped that I had fun at work and am welcomed back. She told me that she would contact me soon and in brackets she wrote "(Remember, be good, but not too good)". By mid day I was at work collecting my keys and particapating in a return to work meeting at my Strutton Ground office. Much has changed since my absence. But I was welcomed back.

Monday 15th March 2010

Dear Yvonne,

Today was my first day back at work after HMP Holloway Women's prison and the Maudsley psychiatric hospital. I am delighted to be back at work and I was made welcomed. I feel as If I am new to the job so my induction is welcomed. I started work at 10am and had a four hour day. I got my password to the computer and spent most of today reading policies and procedure. I am grateful to Thames Reach for it's approach I have been to hell and back and I still have my job. Whilst at work today my son's social worker rang me and asked me what time do I want to see my son. I told her at a time that works for him. She told me that she will contact Lyn and Pete (his foster carers) and get back to me. Dunning & Co Sollicitors also contacted me today to tell me that my mental health team had been in touch. and they would be pleased to sent my son's social worker the report, once they had my written permission to do so. So after I finished work today, I popped into Dunning & Co Solicitors to see Neil Hickman and he sent a fax to them. I felt tired getting out of bed this morning and only improved once I had drunk an expresso. I know that it will get better.

Wednesday 17th March 2010

Dear Yvonne,

Today at Connections (my group psychotherapy) I was asked if I was sure that my feelings about D wasn't my Erotomania manesfesting itself. They asked when I last spoke with D and told me to invite her for a walk in the park and ask her what she feels about me. I felt stressed but after the group, I sent a text to D inviting her to the Victoria and Albert museum this forthcoming Sunday. Within fifteen minutes D replied, saying that she was busy this Sunday, otherwise she would have loved to go to the V&A with me. She thanked me for asking her. Naturally I was disappointed but liked D's reply.

Thursday 18th March 2010

Dear Yvonne,

This evening after consulting a few friends about what the group had said yesterday, I rang D and told her what was said in Connections. D told me that it was not in my head. That she does like me in that way and that she had thought about it and I was the type of person that she would like to go out with. It is just that she does not want to go out with anyone at the moment. I told D that it was okay with me and that we could take it slow because I have, my son, my mum, a full time job and my political aspirations. So I don't have a lot of time on my hands. We then spoke for about twenty minutes before ending the call. I am over the moon that D feels that way about me and that it is not in my head and one sided!

Sunday 21st March 2010

Dear Yvonne,

Today I sent an email to D inviting her to view 'I love you, Phillip Morris' with me at the Peckham Multiplex this Wednesday at 4pm. I am looking forward to going to the cinema with D so that I can sit and hold her hand.

Monday 22nd March 2010

Dear Yvonne,

This afternoon, I had my CPA (Care Plan Approach) and present was me, Dr Izmeth (my psychiatrist) Grace Isiaka (my Care Coordinator) and my son's social worker. It went well and Dr Izmeth agreed to send my son's social worker a report so that my chances of having contact with my son would be increased. Haven't heard from D yet.

Wednesday 24th March 2010

Dear Yvonne,

Today I told Connections what D had said. They were pleased and said that I was very brave. I had been sending text messages to D but she stopped responding. And there was no response to my emailed invitation to the cinema. I am disappointed. I think that I have overwhelmed D and for me it feels like what I ended up in Prison for. But this time it is more painful.

Thursday 25th March 2010

Dear Yvonne,

This evening I rang D and left a message on her answer machine. I was sorry not to be able to talk to her in person, but I will look forward to her call. After this call I have decided not to send anymore texts, emails or phone calls to D until she contacts me. I feel sad.

Friday 26th March 2010

Dear Yvonne,

Today marks the end of two weeks of four hours each day at work completed. The next two weeks will be six hours each day. I visited my mother after work today, on my journey there my son's social worker rang and told me that she had received my mental health report from my solicitor but had not received one from Dr Izmeth. She then told me that she is going to re-apply for supervised contact and told me that she was hoping that this could take place next Saturday. This piece of news pleased me. On the train home from my mum's I suddenly remembered that D had told me over dinner at Caravaggio's that she was going on holiday soon. And now I am thinking that that is the reason that she is not in contact with me. I feel a bit better.

Saturday 27th March 2010

Dear Yvonne,

I am still waking up feeling very tired. Today I missed canvassing for my political party in the morning. This afternoon I was supposed to have a photo shoot with them but it started raining and had to be postponed. I was told today that if I wanted to be put on the ballet box for people to vote for me as a local Councillor then I would have to be nominated by ten residents of my Coldharbour Ward. It took me three hours to find three nominators.

Tuesday 30th March 2010

Dear Yvonne,

This morning, whilst I was at work on day two of my six hours per day fazed return to my Westminster mental health floating support team, Cleo my son's social worker rang me to say that I might be able to see my son James on a supervised contact session in a contact centre this Easter Saturday at 3pm. She told me that she would re-contact me when it was arranged. This evening a member of my political party came to my abode so that I could sign some papers, so that my name can be on the ballot box for this forthcoming election as a Councillor candidate.

Wednesday 31st March 2010

Dear Yvonne,

Today it was a hard task to wake up and go to work, but once I left my abode I felt better. This lunchtime was the first time that I would be leaving work and going to my Connections psychotherapy group and returning to work. It was good to see Will and Jack at the group and I was pleased to tell everyone there how I was getting on. Today was the last of three group sessions that was attended by Malek, a psychiatrist. Next week will be no group due to the Bank Holiday. On my way back to work from the group Cleo rang and told me that there was no contact centre available at 3pm this Saturday, for me to have a supervised contact session with my son. Cleo told me that she would get back to me. This evening I received a email from 10 Downing Street. Re: Government response to petition. saying: You signed a petition asking the Prime Minister to " address the social and cultural barriers that a diagnosis of schizophrenia imposes on an individual labelled with this disorder." The Prime Minister's Office has responded to that petition and you can view it here: http://www.number10.gov.uk/Page23049   Prime Minister's Office Petition information - http://petitions.number10.gov.uk/CASL-CAMPAIGN/ I also received a text message from a political party member telling me that we now have all ten signatures!

Thursday 1st April 2010

Dear Yvonne,

This lunchtime I went to occupational health in St Pancras hospital and saw Dr Sue Smith. Then I went to work. My senior manager emailed me today with an my appointment to see me regarding redeployment next Friday at 12.30pm with my line manager. Today was team meeting day. During the team meeting, Cleo rang and told me that she had made a decision to let the contact between me and my son James go ahead at 3.15pm on Saturday for two hours. I am delighted! Today I sent D an email. I haven't heard from D for a while. I think that she is fed up with me.

Friday 2nd April 2010

Dear Yvonne,

Today is Good Friday and I have spent most of it in bed. I have done very little today besides sent text messages and talk on the phone. I sent D a text and she replied with an multimedia text. I am pleased. I have replied to her text.

Saturday 3rd April 2010

Dear Yvonne,

Today I had supervised contact with my son. He was eagerly waiting for me at the front window of his foster parents home. On my arrival James gave me a big hug. How he has grown. He is nearly as tall as me. We had supervised contact with Iris. She drove us to Greenwich in her vehicle and we went to the museum. My son chose a pizza to eat at the cafe, looked at a few items in the museum, took a couple of photos and then it was time to return home because the two hours were finished! It was so lovely to be with James and I returned him to Pete's (James' foster carer) safe keeping. This evening I logged on to my computer and picked up my email from it and found that D had replied to the email that I sent on Thursday. I then realised that my mobile phone was not collecting my emails. Then whilst replying to D's reply, I found that D had sent me a email on the 22nd March 2010 explaining that though she liked me very much and thought of me as special, she could not be in a relationship with me just now. I'm gutted.

Sunday 4th April 2010

Dear Yvonne,

This Easter Sunday, I went to Kew Gardens for 11.30am with a friend. We stayed walking around and eating in there until 7pm and then we went to Richmond and walked along the riverfront. It was wonderful and I got home quite late but I couldn't go to bed until I had replied to D's email dated 22 March. I had thought about it all day.

Monday 5th April 2010

Dear Yvonne,

This morning I rang D. We didn't speak for long because she was on her way to a football match. However D told me that she would reply to my email. It was lovely to hear her voice. I then spent the rest of the day in bed, sleeping off and on.

Tuesday 27th April 2010

Dear Yvonne,

Today I went to David Pitt House, my community mental health team, to see the forensic team. I was with a doctor and a nurse for two hours. Dr Kitty Seed, had referred me to forensic last year after I had been arrested for the first time.

Friday 7th May 2010

Dear Yvonne,

Yesterday was polling day for the general and local election. After I finished my 9-5 shift at work, I helped my party by first being a teller at a polling station and then being a knocker up. Today I woke up to a hung parliament. I went to the town hall this afternoon to see my local councillor candidate count for Lambeth's Coldharbour. I got 458 votes.

Monday 10th May 2010

Dear Yvonne,

Today, there was an article written about my experiences of mental health stigma and discrimination in the Daily Mirror Newspaper. I also went to Rethink, in Vauxhall, to participate in the Lord Bradley Report panel for people with experience of coming in contact with the criminal justice system with a mental health problem. Today Labour's Prime minister Gordon Brown announced that he will be stepping down from the leadership of his party.

Tuesday 11th May 2010

Dear Yvonne,

Today I had an annual leave day from work and was at home to hear Prime minister Gordon Brown resign as Prime minister and my Conservative Party leader David Cameron become Prime minister with the Liberal Democrates leader Nick Clegg becoming deputy prime minister.

Monday 25th October 2010

Dear Yvonne,

It is almost a whole year since I was discharged from my last psychiatric inpatients admission. This month I attended the 'Insatiable Moon film premiere for World Mental Health Day on Monday 11th October 2010 at Cineworld in the Haymarket, London. I also celebrated my 49th birthday on the 13th October 2010. And I am looking forward to being redeployed at work from a mental health floating support worker, to an Evening Support Worker in a hostel for homeless people. To date I have received three emailed newsletters from C, and I have now unsubscribed from them.

Tuesday 26th October 2010

Dear Yvonne,

At 10am this morning, whilst at work, I received a telephone call from Luton Police to inform me that my mother has died.